PERIPLUS

POCKET
KOREAN
DICTIONARY

Korean–English
English–Korean

SECOND EDITION

Compiled by Seong-Chul Shin & Gene Baik
Revised and expanded by Jinny Kim

PERIPLUS

Published by Periplus Editions (HK) Ltd.

www.periplus.com

Copyright © 2003, 2016 Periplus Editions (HK) Ltd.

LCC Card No. 2004558651
ISBN: 978-0-7946-0774-6

Distributed by:

Asia Pacific
Berkeley Books Pte Ltd
3 Kallang Sector #04-01
Singapore 349278
Tel: (65) 6741 2178; Fax: (65) 6741 2179
inquiries@periplus.com.sg
www.periplus.com

Japan
Tuttle Publishing
Yaekari Building, 3rd Floor
5-4-12 Osaki, Shinagawa-ku
Tokyo 141-0032, Japan
Tel: (81) 3 5437 0171; Fax: (81) 3 5437 0755
sales@tuttle.co.jp
www.tuttle.co.jp

North America, Latin America & Europe
Tuttle Publishing
364 Innovation Drive
North Clarendon, VT 05759-9436 U.S.A.
Tel: 1 (802) 773-8930; Fax: 1 (802) 773-6993
info@tuttlepublishing.com
www.tuttlepublishing.com

24 23 22 21 20 19
10 9 8 7 6 5 4 3   1812MP

Printed in Singapore

Contents

Introduction

This Pocket Dictionary is an indispensable companion for visitors to Korea and for anyone in the early stages of learning Korean. It contains all the 12,000 essential words, idioms and expressions that are most commonly encountered in colloquial, everyday speech.

For the sake of clarity, only the common Korean equivalents for each English word have been given. When an English word has more than one possible meaning, with different Korean equivalents, each meaning is listed separately, with a clear explanatory gloss. The layout is clear and accessible, with none of the abbreviations and dense nests of entries typical of many small dictionaries.

Korean is spoken in both South Korea (the Republic of Korea) and North Korea (the Democratic People's Republic of Korea), as well as in parts of China, Japan, and Central Asian nations such as Kazakhstan and Uzbekistan (formerly republics of the Soviet Union), and has well over 70 million speakers in the Korean peninsula alone.

It is not clearly related to any other languages of the world, although some linguists claim that it belongs to the Altaic family, which is made up of the Turkic, Mongolian, and Manchu language groups. It also has some striking structural similarities to Japanese, but whether Korean and Japanese are genetically related remains in dispute.

The earliest form of the Korean writing system, dating from the early centuries CE, was also borrowed from Chinese, but was not widely adopted because of the structural and phonetic differences between the languages. For many centuries, Chinese was accepted as the literary language of Korea, and the native vernacular was not recorded in writing.

The current form of written Korean (known as Hangul in South Korea and as Chosongul in North Korea) was invented in the 15th century at the command of King Sejong. However, for some centuries thereafter it was eschewed by the literate in favor of expression in Chinese; only toward the end of the 19th century was literacy in Korean promoted as an instrument of national pride.

In Korean script each syllable is represented by a cluster of elements representing the constituent consonants and vowels, normally arranged from left to right and top to bottom within the cluster. In South Korea there is also still some limited use of Chinese characters mixed in with Hangul, although these differ somewhat from the forms now used in China, and their pronunciation has been adapted to Korean.

In this dictionary every Korean word and phrase is written in the Korean script, and also clearly transliterated into the Roman alphabet. There is no universally agreed way of writing Korean in the Roman alphabet, but this dictionary uses the new system approved and implemented by the South Korean government in 2000. The Korean-English section of the dictionary is arranged according to the alphabetical order of these romanized forms.

For guidance on the pronunciation, please refer to pages vi to viii. Korean is not a tonal language, but it does have an unfamiliar set of "tensed" consonants, represented in this transcription by double letters.

The Korean verbs are given in the traditional "dictionary form," unmarked for the differences in speech style between "informal polite," "formal polite" and "plain."

The Korean language is spoken in three different levels, depending on the social status, age, and relationship between speaker and listener. The honorific or formal polite level of Korean is used when speaking to elders, to people you meet for the first time, and to those in authority or of superior status. The honorific level uses special verb endings, nouns, pronouns, and adjectives when referring to these groups of people. The standard form of Korean is the most common and is spoken to people older than you or equal in status. These would include professional coworkers. The standard form of Korean is characterized by the ending "**yo**" tacked onto words. And the informal or humble form of Korean is used in casual speech, with those younger than you, or those older than you but in a close relationship, such as with a family member. You will also hear informal speech when a person is talking about himself/herself or to himself/herself. Informal speech doesn't use special endings on words.

Pronunciation

Korean words and expressions in this book are romanized using the Revised Romanization of Korean prepared and authorized by the Korean Government (refer to p. v). Along with the principles of this system, some transcription conventions are adopted as follows:

(a) Words are romanized according to sound rather than to Korean spelling. However, in the case of verbs, the transcription of tensed sounds has been minimized so that the user can identify and utilize the verb stem without much confusion (e.g., "to be/**itda**" instead of "**itta**");

(b) Where there is an expression consisting of more than one word, a space is given to mark the word boundary;

(c) Where necessary, a dot (.) is used to mark the syllable boundary so that confusion in pronunciation can be avoided;

(d) Three dots (...) are used in a grammatical phrase where a noun is required;

(e) For descriptive words, both adjectival verb forms (e.g., to be pretty/**yeppeuda**) and adjective forms (e.g., pretty/**yeppeun**) are given.

(f) In the English to Korean section of the dictionary, the abbreviations—sb, sth—represent "somebody" and "something."

The Korean Alphabet and Roman Letters

Consonants

(1) Simple consonants

ㄱ	**g, k**	ㄴ	**n**	ㄷ	**d, t**	ㄹ	**r, l**	ㅁ	**m**
ㅂ	**b, p**	ㅅ	**s**	ㅇ	**ng**	ㅈ	**j**	ㅊ	**ch**
ㅋ	**k**	ㅌ	**t**	ㅍ	**p**	ㅎ	**h**		

(2) Double consonants

ㄲ	**kk**	ㄸ	**tt**	ㅃ	**pp**	ㅆ	**ss**	ㅉ	**jj**

Vowels

(1) Simple vowels

ㅏ	**a**	ㅓ	**eo**	ㅗ	**o**	ㅜ	**u**	ㅡ	**eu**
ㅣ	**i**	ㅐ	**ae**	ㅔ	**e**	ㅚ	**oe**	ㅟ	**wi**

(2) Compound vowels

ㅑ **ya**	ㅕ **yeo**	ㅛ **yo**	ㅠ **yu**	ㅒ **yae**
ㅖ **ye**	ㅘ **wa**	ㅙ **wae**	ㅝ **wo**	ㅞ **we**
ㅢ **ui**				

Reading Romanized Korean

There is a very important distinction between the reading of the romanized Korean and the English. The Korean romanization system depicts the sound of Korean in English letters to help foreigners be able to communicate in Korean. Because English letters used in romanized Korean are "sound symbols," they have to be pronounced in one certain way only. They should not be treated as those in English words. In English words, the sound value assigned to a certain letter can vary in different words. For example, *a* in "apple," "father," "syllable" and "date" all have different sound values. Unless you have learned the English phonetic symbols, you might read romanized Korean *a* differently from the expected sound depending on what romanized Korean words you have. For example, you might read *a* as the *a* in "apple" when you see the romanized Korean word "**sam**/삼/three"; but you might read it as *a* in "syllable" when you see the *a*s in the romanized Korean word "**saram**/사람/person."

To help you avoid this type of confusion, below are some examples of English words that correspond in sound with some of the romanized Korean vowels and consonants (use these as an approximate guide only).

Vowels: eo, eu, **ae** and **oe** are single vowels in romanized Korean as shown below. Therefore careful attention should be given to these vowels: take care that you are not splitting them into two. Also, careful attention should be given to "**u**/우"—do not read it as an English "you." Some common vowels which might confuse you could be:

a	아	<u>a</u>h, f<u>a</u>ther	(shorter than these *a*s)
eo	어	b<u>i</u>rd, s<u>e</u>rve	
o	오	<u>O</u>h, p<u>o</u>re	(shorter than this *a* or *o*)
u	우	b<u>oo</u>k, sch<u>oo</u>l	(shorter that these *oo*s)
eu	으	brok<u>e</u>n, gold<u>e</u>n	
i	이	b<u>ee</u>, sh<u>ee</u>p	(shorter than these *ee*s)
ae	애	<u>a</u>pple, b<u>a</u>d	
e	에	b<u>e</u>d, <u>e</u>gg	
oe	외	w<u>ea</u>r, w<u>e</u>lcome	

Consonants: You won't have much trouble in pronouncing romanized Korean consonants except for some tensed ones which require a relatively strong muscular effort in the vocal organs without the expulsion of air. Here are some examples:

kk	ㄲ	s<u>k</u>i, s<u>k</u>y	(*k* after *s*)
tt	ㄸ	s<u>t</u>eak, s<u>t</u>ing	(*t* after *s*)
pp	ㅃ	s<u>p</u>eak, s<u>p</u>y	(*p* after *s*)
ss	ㅆ	<u>s</u>ea, <u>s</u>ir	(*s* before a vowel)
jj	ㅉ	bri<u>dg</u>e, mi<u>dg</u>et	(similar to a tutting sound in an exhaling way)

List of Abbreviations

ADJ	adjective
ADV	adverb
CONJ	conjunction
GR	greeting
EXCLAM	exclamation
INTERJ	interjection
N	noun
NUM	numeral
PREP	preposition
PHR	phrase
PP	postpositional particle
V	verb

Korean–English

A

-a/eo boda −아/어 보다 V try out –ing

-a/eo deurida −아/어 드리다 V (*humble form* of −어/아 주다)

-a/eo juda −아/어 주다 V do something for another's benefit

-a/eo juseyo −아/어 주세요 V please (request for something)

-a/eodo jota −아/어도 좋다 V may, can, be allowed to: **bammeogeonni** 밥어도 좋다 you may eat; **boado jota** 보아도 좋다 you may look

-a/eoya hada −아/어야 하다 V must, have to, ought to

abeoji 아버지 N father

achim 아침 N morning

achim iljjik 아침 일찍 ADV early in the morning

achim siksa 아침 식사 N breakfast, morning meal

achim siksahada 아침 식사하다 V to eat breakfast

adeul 아들 N son

adeukhada, adeukhan 아득하다, 아득한 ADJ far, distant, long way: **adeukhan seom** 아득한 섬 an island far in the distance

adeukhada, adeukhan 아득하다, 아득한 ADJ remote, dim, faint: **adeukhan chueok** 아득한 추억 distant memory; **adeukhan yennal** 아득한 옛날 remote past

adunhada, adunhan 아둔하다, 아둔한 ADJ stupid, dull

aebeolle 애벌레 N larva, caterpillar

aechak 애착 N attachment, affection

aecheoropda 애처롭다 ADJ pitiful

aedeuribeu 애드리브 N ad lib, improvisation

aegyo 애교 N charms, winsomeness

(ae)hobak (애)호박 N zucchini, pumpkin, squash

aejeong 애정 N affection

aekjeot 액젓 N fish sauce

aesseuda 애쓰다 V to make efforts, struggle

aetaeuda 애태우다 V to eat one's heart out

aewandongmul 애완동물 N pet (*animal*)

agassi 아가씨 N miss, young female adult

agi 아기 N baby

aheun 아흔 NUM ninety

ahop 아홉 NUM nine

ai 아이 N child, offspring

aidieo 아이디어 N idea

aillaendeu 아일랜드 N Ireland

aireoni 아이러니 N irony

aiseu keurim 아이스크림 N ice cream

ajangajang 아장아장 ADV with toddling steps

ajeossi 아저씨 N uncle, mister, male adult

ajik 아직 ADV still, even now: **ajik han siya** 아직 한 시야 It's still one o'clock

ajik 아직 ADV yet: not yet: **ajik ireul kkeunnaeji motaetda** 아직 일을 끝내지 못했다 haven't finished one's work yet

ajjilhada 아찔하다 ADJ giddy, dizzy, faintish

aju 아주 ADV very, so, pretty, quite, extremely

ajumeoni 아주머니 N aunt, ma'am (*married female*)

akdam 악담 N curse

akdang 악당 N villain

akgi 악기 N (*musical*) instrument

akkapda 아깝다 ADJ regrettable, unfortunate: **akkaun silpae** 아까운 실패 a regrettable failure

akkida 아끼다 V to cherish, value, hold (sth) dear: **akkineun haksaeng** 아끼는 학생 beloved student

akkida 아끼다 V to save, economize, conserve: **mureul akkida** 물을 아끼다 conserve water

akkida 아끼다 V to spare (*oneself*): **momeul akkida** 몸을 아끼다 be sparing of oneself

A

akkimeopsi 아낌없이 ADV unsparingly, generously: **akkim eopsi juneun namu** 아낌 없이 주는 나무 The Giving Tree

aksuhada 악수하다 V to shake hands: **daetongnyeonggwa aksuhada** 대통령과 악수하다 shake hands with the president

al 알 N egg

alda/anda 알다/안다 V to be acquainted: **sarameul jal anda** 사람을 잘 안다 be well acquainted with a person

alda 알다 V to know: **munjeui dabeul alda** 문제의 답을 알다 know the answer for a question

allak uija 안락 의자 N armchair, recliner

allida 알리다 V to inform, let someone know

allyak 알약 N pills, tablets

ama 아마 ADV perhaps, maybe, possibly, probably

amachueo 아마추어 N amateur

amgi 암기 N memorization

amgiryeok 암기력 N (one's power of) memory

amho 암호 N password, code

amnyeok 압력 N pressure

amso 암소 N cow

amudo -ji anta 아무도 -지 않다 PHR nobody is…-ing: **amudo chatji anta** 아무도 찾지 않다 Nobody is seeking

amudo ...anida 아무도 ...아니다 PHR nobody is ...: **amudo namankeumeun anida** 아무도 나만큼은 아니다 Nobody is as much as I am

amugeotdo anida 아무것도 아니다 PHR It is nothing

amulda 아물다 V to heal

amuri 아무리 ADV no matter how: **amuri eoryeowodo** 아무리 어려워도 no matter how hard it is

amuteun 아무튼 ADV anyway

an 안 ADV no, not, don't (with verbs and adjectives): **an gada** 안 가다 not go (don't go); **an hada** 안 하다 not do (don't do); **an ilgeun chaek** 안 읽은 책 a book one hasn't read

an ikda/igeun 안 익다/익은 ADJ unripe, under-cooked: **an igeun gogi** 안 익은고기 under (un)cooked meat; **an igeun ttalgi** 안 익은 딸기 unripe strawberries

an.gae 안개 N fog, mist

an.gyeong 안경 N eyeglasses, spectacles

anae 아내 N wife

anaunseo 아나운서 N announcer, anchor

anbujeonhada 안부전하다 V to say hello

an(j)da 앉다 V to sit down

andwaetda! 안됐다! PHR what a pity!, that's a shame!, I'm sorry: **andwaetda** 안됐다 feel sorry for (about)

andwaetda 안됐다 PHR didn't pass: **siheome andwaetda** 시험에 안됐다 failed one's exam; **seungjine andwaetda** 승진에 안됐다 didn't pass one's promotion test

...ane(seo) ...안에(서) ADV inside of

aneukhada, aneukhan 아늑하다, 아늑한 ADJ snug, cozy: **aneukhan gonggan** 아늑한 공간 cozy space

aneun saram 아는 사람 N acquaintance

aneunchehada 아는체하다 V to pretend to know

...aneuro ...안으로 ADV into

anganhim 안간힘 N holding back an urge

anggapeum 앙갚음 N revenge, retaliation

angida 안기다 V to be embraced

angmong 악몽 N nightmare: **angmongeul kkuda** 악몽을 꾸다 have a nightmare

...anida ...아니다 ADJ no, not (with nouns): **chaegi anida** 책이 아니다 not a book; **geu chaegi anida** 그 책이 아니다 It's not the (that) book

anieyo 아니에요 V no (in honorific form)

anio 아니오 V no (in honorific form, when answering)

anjeonhada, anjeonhan 안전하다, 안전한 ADJ secure, safe: **anjeonhan pinancheo** 안전한 피난처 a safe shelter; **anjeonhan jikjang** 안전한 직장 a secure job

anjjok 안쪽 N inside

annaehada 안내하다 V to lead, guide

annaeseo 안내서 N guidebook

annaeso 안내소 N information booth

annyeonghaseyo 안녕하세요 PHR hello, hi, how are you? (in honorific form)

annyeonghi gaseyo 안녕히 가세요 PHR goodbye to a person leaving (*in honorific form*)

annyeonghi gyeseyo 안녕히 계세요 PHR goodbye to a person staying (*in honorific form*)

apateu 아파트 N apartment, flat

apbak 압박 N pressure

...ape(seo) ...앞에(서) ADV before, in front of

apeuda 아프다 V to ache

apeuda, apeun 아프다, 아픈 ADJ ill, sick, sore, painful

apeugehada 아프게 하다 V to hurt (*cause pain*)

apeuro 앞으로 ADV forward

apeuronaagada 앞으로 나아가다 V to advance, go forward

apgarim hada 앞가림하다 N to look after oneself: **nae apgarimeun hal su iseo** 내 앞가림은 할 수 있어 I can take care of myself

araboda 알아보다 V to look into: **sisereul araboda** 시세를 알아보다 look into the market value

araboda 알아보다 V to recognize: **saramdeul araboda** 사람을 알아보다 recognize a person

arachaeda 알아채다 V to notice, realize, be aware of: **wiheomeul arachaeda** 위험을 알아채다 notice a danger

...arae ...아래 N the bottom

arae.e 아래에 ADV below, under

araecheung 아래층 N downstairs

araero 아래로 ADV down, downward

areubaiteu 아르바이트 N a part-time job

areuhentina 아르헨티나 N Argentina

areumdapda, areumdaun 아름답다, 아름다운 ADJ beautiful, pretty: **areumdaun yesul jakpum** 아름다운 예술 작품 a beautiful artwork

areungeorida 아른거리다 V to glimmer, flicker

aryeonhada 아련하다 ADJ dim, faint, vague: **aryeonhan yet chueok** 아련한 옛 추억 dim recollection; **aryeonhan dalbit** 아련한 달빛 a vague moonlight

asagada 앗아가다 V to take away, snatch away

aseuraseulhada 아슬아슬하다 ADJ risky, close, critical, dangerous

asia 아시아 N Asia

aswiwohada 아쉬워하다 V to miss, feel the lack of: **aswiun jakbyeol** 아쉬운 작별 a sorrowful farewell

atopi 아토피 N atopy

aulleo 아울러 ADV in addition, besides, at the same time

autsaideo 아웃사이더 N outsider

B

babo 바보 N fool, moron

bachida 바치다 V to dedicate, consecrate

bachida 바치다 V to give, present

bada 바다 N ocean, sea

badadeurida 받아들이다 V to accept

badageobuk 바다거북 N (*sea*)turtle

badak 바닥 N area, place: **sijang badak** 시장 바닥 the market area

badak 바닥 N field, business: **i badageun naega jal anda** 이 바닥은 내가 잘 안다 I know this business well

badak 바닥 N floor, the bottom: **mikkeureoun badak** 미끄러운 바닥 a slippery floor

badaknada 바닥나다 V to be depleted, run out: **innaesimi badaknada** 인내심이 바닥나다 running out of patience

badasseuda 받아쓰다 V to take dictation, take down

badatga 바닷가 N beach, coast, the seashore

...bae ...배 N times (*multiplying*): **daseot bae bissada** 다섯 배 비싸다 five times more expensive

bae 배 N belly, abdomen, stomach: **ttungttunghan bae** 뚱뚱한 배 a fat tummy

bae 배 N ship, boat, ferry: **gogijabi bae** 고기잡이 배 a fishing boat

bae.uda 배우다 V to learn

bae.uja 배우자 N partner, spouse

bae-uja 배우자 PHR let's learn: **hangugeoreul baeuja** 한국어를 배우자 Let's learn Korean

baebureuda 배부르다 ADJ full, stuffed

baechu 배추 N Chinese cabbage

baedalhada 배달하다 V to deliver

baegopeuda, baegopeun 배고프다, 배고픈 ADJ hungry: **baegopeun saja** 배고픈 사자 a hungry lion

B

baehoehada 배회하다 v to loiter (*about*), wander

baek 백 NUM hundred

baek 백 (가방) N bag

baekhwajeom 백화점 N department store

baem 뱀 N snake

baengman 백만 NUM million

baeseolhada 배설하다 v to excrete: **nopyemureul baeseolhada** 노폐물을 배설하다 discharge waste from one's body

baesimwon 배심원 N jury

bagaji 바가지 N gourd (*dipper*), calabash

bagajiguelda 바가지 긁다 v to nag, henpeck

bagajisseuda 바가지 쓰다 v to be overcharged, ripped off: **bagajireul sseotda** 바가지를 썼다 I've been ripped off

bageumjil 박음질 N backstitch

baguni 바구니 N basket

baiollin 바이올린 N violin: **baiollineul kyeoda** 바이올린을 켜다 play the violin

baireoseu 바이러스 N virus

baji 바지 N pants, trousers

bajjak 바짝 ADV completely, closely

bakbong 박봉 N small salary, poor pay

bakchada 박차다 v to kick, storm out

bakchigi 박치기 N head-butt

bakda 박다 v to drive, hammer: **moseul bakda** 못을 박다 hammer a nail

bakda 박다 v to hit, crash, bump: **charo garodeungeul bakda** 차로 가로 등을 박았다 crash into a street lamp

bakda 박다 v to mount, stud: **mokgeorie rubireul bakda** 목걸이에 루비를 박다 mount a ruby onto a necklace

bakda 박다 v to sew: **jaebongteullo chimatdaneul bakda** 재봉틀로 치맛 단을 박다 hem a skirt on the sewing machine

bakda, balgeun 밝다, 밝은 ADJ light, bright: **balgeun bul** 밝은 불 a bright light

bakhida 밝히다 v to disclose, reveal: **sasireul bakhida** 사실을 밝히다 reveal the fact

bakhida 밝히다 v to enunciate: **uisareul bakhida** 의사를 밝히다 define one's position

bakhida 밝히다 v to light up: **bureul bakhida** 불을 밝히다 turn up the light

bakja 박자 N beat, rhythm

bakkat(jjok) 바깥(쪽) N outside

...bakke ...밖에 ADV out

bakkuda 바꾸다 v to change, switch

baksu 박수 N applause: **baksu galchae** 박수 갈채 a storm of applause

baksuchida 박수치다 v to clap, applaud

bakwi 바퀴 N wheel

bal 발 N foot

balgabeotda 발가벗다 v to get naked

balgeurehada 발그레하다 ADJ reddish, rosy, flushed

balgwanghada 발광하다 v to radiate

balgwanghada 발광하다 v to run mad, go crazy

balgyeonhada 발견하다 v to discover

baljjeon 발전 N electricity generation

baljjeon 발전 N development, progress

baljjeonhada 발전하다 v to develop, advance, grow: **jeongchi munjero baljjeonhada** 정치 문제로 발전하다 grow into a political issue

baljjeonsikida 발전시키다 v to develop: **gisureul baljjeonsikida** 기술을 발전시 키다 develop technology

balkkarak 발가락 N toe

balmok 발목 N ankle

balmyeonghada 발명하다 v to invent

baltop 발톱 N toenail, claw, talon

balttal 발달 N development, growth

bam 밤 N night

bame 밤에 ADV at night

bamnajeopsi 밤낮없이 ADV always, day and night: **bamnajeopsi ilhada** 밤낮없이 일했다 work night and day

bamneukke 밤 늦게 ADV late at night

ban 반 N half: **banman juseyo** 반만 주세요 Please give me half

ban 반 (학급) N class: **museun banini?** 무슨 반이니? What class are you in?

banana 바나나 N banana

banbal 반발 N resistance, defiance

banbaji 반바지 N short pants

banbokhada 반복하다 v to repeat

bandae(ui) 반대 N opposite, contrary

bandaehada 반대하다 v to object, oppose, protest

bandeusi 반드시 ADV certainly, surely, without fail

bandeutada 반듯하다 ADJ straight,

square, neat: **imokgubiga bandeutada** 이목구비가 반듯하다 have well-defined (good) features

baneujilhada 바느질하다 v to sew

baneul 바늘 N needle

baneung 반응 N reaction, response

baneunghada 반응하다 v to react, respond, reply

bang 방 N room

bang.eohada 방어하다 v to defend

bangapda 반갑다 ADJ glad, happy, welcome: **mannaseo bangapseumnida** 만나서 반갑습니다 Nice to meet you

bangbeop 방법 N way, method, manner

banggeum 방금 ADV a moment ago, just now

banghae 방해 N bother, disturbance, hindrance

banghaehada 방해하다 v to bother, disturb, hinder

banghak 방학 N vacation (*school*)

banghyang 방향 N direction

bangida 반기다 v to greet, welcome

bangjihada 방지하다 v to prevent

bangmulgwan 박물관 N museum

bangmun 방문 N visit

bangmunhada 방문하다 v to pay a visit

bangmyeol 박멸 N eradication, extermination

bangnamhoe 박람회 N exhibition

bangsong 방송 N broadcast

bangsonghada 방송하다 v to broadcast

bangsu 방수 N water-resistant: **bangsu sigye** 방수 시계 water-proof watch

bangyeok 반격 N counterattack, responsive attack

banjeon 반전 N reverse, reversal

banji 반지 N ring (*jewelry*)

banjjagida 반짝이다 v to twinkle, sparkle, glitter: **byeoldeuri banjjagida** 별들이 반짝이다 the stars are twinkling

banmal 반말 N low form of speech, casual form of

bannap 반납 N return, turn-in

bannyeonghada 반영하다 v to reflect, apply: **yeoroneul bannyeonghada** 여론을 반영하다 reflect public opinion

bansa 반사 N reflection

bansahada 반사하다 v to reflect

banseong 반성 N self-examination

bap 밥 N rice (*cooked*), meal

bappeuda, bappeun 바쁘다, 바쁜 ADJ busy (*doing something*): **bappeuda** 바쁘다 be busy; **bappeun saramdeul** 바쁜 사람들 busy people

bappi 바삐 ADV busily, briskly

baraboda 바라보다 v to look at, watch: **maheuneul baraboda** 마흔을 바라본다 being on the verge of turning 40

baraboida 바라보이다 v to come into view, be in sight

barada 바라다 v to desire, hope, wish

baraeda 바래다 v to fade (*away*), discolor: **saek baraen sajin** 색 바랜 사진 a faded photo

bareuda 바르다 ADJ upright, true: **yeuiga bareuda** 예의가 바르다 well-mannered

bareuda 바르다 v to cover, plaster: **pureul bareuda** 풀을 바르다 paste (*glue*)

bareuda 바르다 v to debone: **saengseonui ppyeoreul bareuda** 생선의 뼈를 바르다 (de)bone fish

bareuda 바르다 v to spread on: **ppange jaemeul bareuda** 빵에 잼을 바르다 spread jam on bread

barageonde 바라건대 ADV hopefully

baram 바람 N wind, breeze

bareumhada 발음하다 v to pronounce

baro 바로 ADV straight, directly

baro geugeoyeyo! 바로 그거예요! PHR exactly! just so! that's it!

baro jigeum 바로 지금 ADV just now, right now

barojapda 바로잡다 v to correct, rectify: **otareul barojapda** 오타를 바로잡다 correct typos

barojapda 바로잡다 v to reform, amend, restore: **haengsireul barojapda** 행실을 바로잡다 amend one's conduct; **maeumeul barojapda** 마음을 바로잡다 reform oneself

barojapda 바로잡다 v to straighten, adjust

basakhan 바삭한 ADJ crunch, crispy: **basakbasakhan kuki** 바삭바삭한 쿠키 crunchy cookies

baseurak 바스락 ADJ, ADV faint(ly), indistinct(ly)

B

bassak 바싹 ADV completely

bassak 바싹 ADV thinly, haggardly

bassak 바싹 ADV tightly, firmly

batang 바탕 N (the) ground, nature: **batangi joeun saram** 바탕이 좋은 사람 a man of good disposition

batang 바탕 N background

batchida 받치다 V to grow desperate, have a fit of anger: **age batchida** 악에 받치다 have a fit of anger

batchida 받치다 V to hold up, support: **byeogeul gidungeuro batchida** 벽을 기둥으로 받치다 hold up the wall with a post

batchim 받침 N prop, support

batda 받다 V to suit one's taste (*palate*): **(momi) sureul an batda** (몸이) 술을 안 받다 can't handle alchohol

batda 받다 V to saturate oneself with (*sunshine or moonlight*): **haetbicheul (heumppeok) batda** 햇빛을 (흠뻑) 받다 saturate oneself with sunlight

batda 받다 V to receive: **pyeonjireul batda** 편지를 받다 receive a letter

batjul 밧줄 N rope

bawi 바위 N rock

begae 베개 N pillow

bekkida 베끼다 V to copy, transcribe

belteu 벨트 N belt

beodunggeorida 버둥거리다 V to struggle, wriggle, flounder

beogeopda 버겁다 ADJ unmanageable, too big to handle

beokchada 벅차다 ADJ beyond one's power: **i iri naegeneun neomu beokchada** 이 일이 나에게는 너무 벅차다 This is beyond my power

beokchada 벅차다 ADJ overwhelmed: **gippeumeuro gaseumi beokchada** 기쁨으로 가슴이 벅차다 overwhelmed by joy

beolchik 벌칙 N penal regulations

beolda 벌다 V to earn

beolgeobeoseun 벌거벗은 ADJ naked

beolgeobeotda 벌거벗다 V to be naked

beolgeum 벌금 N fine, penalty (*punishment*)

beolle 벌레 N insect

beollida 벌리다 V to open, stretch: **ne ibeul keuge beollyeora** 네 입을 크게 벌려라 open your mouth wide

beollida 벌리다 V to make a profit: **doni jal beollida** 돈이 잘 벌리다 make good money

beolsseo 벌써 ADV already

beomin 범인 N criminal

beomjoe 범죄 N offense, crime

beomurida 버무리다 V to mix together

beon.gae 번개 N lightning

beonho 번호 N number

beonyeokhada 번역하다 V to translate

beop 법 N laws, legislation

beoreujeokgeorida 버르적거리다 V to writhe, squirm

beoreut 버릇 N habit

beoreuteopda, beoreuteomneun 버릇없다/버릇없는 ADJ naughty, rude: **beoreuseopda** 버릇없다 be rude; **beoreunteomneun haengdong** 버릇없는 행동 an inappropriate behavior

beorida 버리다 V to throw away, throw out: **sseuregireul beorida** 쓰레기를 버리다 throw out trash

beorida 버리다 V to abandon, desert: **moksumeul beorida** 목숨을 버리다 abandon one's life

beoseot 버섯 N mushroom

beoseu 버스 N bus

beoseu jeonggeojang 버스 정거장 N bus station

beotda 벗다 V to take off (*clothes, glasses, hat, socks*): **angyeongeul beotda** 안경을 벗다 take off one's glasses

beotda 벗다 V to clear oneself of a false charge: **numyeongeul beotda** 누명을 벗다 clear oneself of a false charge

beoteo 버터 N butter

beotgyeojida 벗겨지다 V to be taken off, come off

beteunam 베트남 N Vietnam

beullauseu 블라우스 N blouse

beuraejieo 브래지어 N bra

beureikeu 브레이크 N brake

beureikeu bapda 브레이크 밟다 V to step on brakes

beurokeolli 브로컬리 N broccoli

bi 비 N rain

bibeon 비번 N day off: **bibeonida** 비번이다 be off duty

bicham 비참 N misery

bichamhada 비참하다 ADJ wretched

bidio (rekodeu) 비디오 (레코드) N video recorder, VCR

bidio (teipeu) 비디오 (테이프) N video cassette

biga oda 비가 오다 V to rain

bigeuk 비극 N tragedy

bigida 비기다 V to tie, halve a match

bigyohada 비교하다 V to compare

bihaeng 비행 N flight

bihaeng 비행 N wrongful deed: **bihaengeul jeojireuda** 비행을 저지르다 commit a misdeed

bihaeng cheongsonyeon 비행 청소년 N a juvenile delinquent

bihaenggi 비행기 N aeroplane, airplane, plane

bija 비자 N visa

bijeuniseu 비즈니스 N business, trade

bijjaru 빗자루 N broom

bilbutda 빌붙다 V to mooch off, sponge off

bilding 빌딩 N building

billida 빌리다 V to borrow: **doneul billida** 돈을 빌리다 borrow money from a person

billyeojuda 빌려주다 V to lend: **doneul billyeojuda** 돈을 빌려주다 lend money to a person

biman 비만 N obesity

bimil 비밀 N secret

bimireul jikida 비밀을 지키다 V to keep a secret

binan 비난 N criticism

binanhada 비난하다 V to blame, accuse

binbeonhada, binbeonhan 빈번하다, 빈번한 ADJ frequent

binbu 빈부 N wealth and poverty: **binbuui gyeokcha** 빈부의 격차 the gap between the rich and the poor

bingha 빙하 N glacier

bingsu 빙수 N shaved ice (with syrup)

binhyeol 빈혈 N anemia

binjeonggeorida 빈정거리다 V to be sarcastic

binmal 빈말 N empty talk, flummery

binnada 빛나다 V to shine, sparkle

binnagada 빗나가다 V to digress, wander off

binnagada 빗나가다 V to go astray

binnagada 빗나가다 V to go wide, miss: **gwanyeogeul binnagada** 과녁을 빗나가다 go wide off the mark

binnaneun 빛나는 ADJ shiny

binso 빈소 N mortuary

binteolteori 빈털터리 N penniless, coal and cake

binteumeopda/binteumeomneun 빈틈없다/빈틈없는 ADJ tight (space): **binteumeomneun gonggan** 빈틈없는 공간 a tight space

binteumeopda/binteumeomneun 빈틈없다/빈틈없는 ADJ meticulous, precise (character): **binteumeomneun kkomkkomhan seonggyeok** 빈틈없는 꼼꼼한 성격 a meticulous character

binu 비누 N soap

biokhada, biokan 비옥하다, 비옥한 ADJ fertile

birida 비리다 ADJ fishy

birok-(eu)l jirado 비록 -(으)ㄹ 지라도 ADV though, although: **birok biga ol jirado** 비록 비가 올 지라도 though it's raining, though it might rain

birok-jiman 비록 -지만 ADV even though, though: **birok nalssiga chupjiman** 비록 날씨가 춥지만 although it's cold

bisang(satae) 비상(사태) N emergency

biseo 비서 N secretary

biseuket 비스켓 N biscuit

biseuthada, biseutan 비슷하다, 비슷한 ADJ similar, alike: **gwansimsaga biseuthada** 관심사가 비슷하다 have similar interests; **biseutan saenggimsae** 비슷한 생김새 similar faces

bissada, bissan 비싸다, 비싼 ADJ expensive: **bissan deureseu** 비싼 드레스 an expensive dress

bit 빛 N light

bit 빗 N comb

bit 빚 N debt

bitbalchida 빗발치다 V to hail, rain: **bitbalchineun hangui** 빗발치는 항의 a storm of protest

bitjaengi 빚쟁이 N creditor, money lender

bitjida 빚지다 V to owe

biutda 비웃다 V to laugh at

biyeolhada, biyeolhan 비열하다, 비열한 ADJ dishonorable, shameful

biyong 비용 N cost, expense, fee

biyul 비율 N percentage, ratio

B

boda 보다 v to look at, watch, see, view

...boda (deo) ...보다 (더) ADV (more) than (*comparison*): **ujeongeun don boda deo gwihada** 우정은 돈 보다 더 귀하다 Friendship is more valuable than money

...boda ohiryeo ...보다 오히려 ADV rather than...

bodaphada 보답하다 v to repay, requite

bogeonso 보건소 N health center

bogo 보고 N report

bogohada 보고하다 v to report

bogwanhada 보관하다 v to save, keep

boheom 보험 N insurance

bohoguyeok 보호구역 N wildlife sanctuary, reserve

bohohada 보호하다 v to protect

boida 보이다 v to demonstrate, display: **yonggireul boida** 용기를 보이다 demonstrate courage

boida 보이다 v to be seen, come in sight: **pyojipani nune boida** 표지판이 눈에 보이다 a sign came into sight

bojang 보장 N guarantee

bojeung 보증 N guarantee

bojeunghada 보증하다 v to guarantee

bojo 보조 N help, aid: **jeongbu bojoreul batda** 정부 보조를 받다 receive government aid

bokda 볶다 v to pester, importune, ride: **saramdeul bokda** 사람을 볶다 importune a person

bokda 볶다 v to roast, stir-fry: **gireume gogireul bokda** 기름에 고기 를 볶다 stir-fry meat with oil

bokdo 복도 N corridor, hall

bokgeun 복근 N abdominal muscle

bokgwon 복권 N lottery

bokjaphada, bokjapan 복잡하다, 복잡한 (공간) ADJ busy, crowded: **bokjapan geori** 복잡한 거리 crowded streets

bokjaphada, bokjapan 복잡하다, 복잡한 ADJ complicated: **bokjapan sanghwang** 복잡한 상황 a complex situation

boksa 복사 N copy, photocopy

boksahada 복사하다 v to copy, photocopy

bolpen 볼펜 N ball point pen

bom 봄 N spring (*season*)

bomul 보물 N treasure

bonaeda 보내다 v to send: **pyeonjireul bonaeda** 편지를 보내다 send a letter

bonaeda 보내다 v to spend (*time*): **siganeul bonaeda** 시간을 보내다 spend time

bonbu 본부 N headquarters

bonggeup 봉급 N salary

bonghada 봉하다 v to seal

bongtu 봉투 N envelope

bonneung 본능 N instinct

boreumdal 보름달 N full moon

bosalpida 보살피다 v to take care of, look after

bosang 보상 N compensation, indemnification: **bosangeul batda** 보상을 받다 obtain a compensation

boseok 보석 N jewelry

boseu 보스 N boss

boseyo! 보세요! PHR look!

botong 보통 N average

botong(ui) 보통(의) ADJ regular, normal, average

boyeojuda 보여주다 v to show: **sinbunjeungeul boyeojuda** 신분증을 보 여주다 show an ID

boyu 보유 N possession, reserve

bu 부 N department: an administration department

bu 부 N wealth: **buui sangjing** 부의 상징 a symbol of wealth

bu.eok 부엌 N kitchen

bu.in 부인 N madam (*term of address*)

bubun 부분 N part (*not whole*)

bubunjeogeuro 부분적으로 ADV partly

buchae 부채 N fan (*for cooling*)

buchae 부채 N debt

buchida 부치다 v to fan: **buchaereul buchida** 부채를 부치다 fan oneself

buchida 부치다 v to post, mail: **soporeul buchida** 소포를 부치다 mail a package

buchugida 부추기다 v to instigate, incite

budeureopda, budeureo.un 부드럽 다, 부드러운 ADJ soft: **pibuga budeureopda** 피부가 부드럽다 have soft skin; **budeureo.un baram** 부드러운 바람 soft wind

bulssanghada 불쌍하다 ADJ pitiable

bujang 부장 N manager

bujok 부족 N tribe

bukdongjjok 북동쪽 N north-east
bukhan 북한 N North Korea
bukjjok 북쪽 N north
bukkeureopda, bukkeureoun 부끄럽다, 부끄러운 ADJ ashamed, embarrassed: **bukkeureopda** 부끄럽다 be ashamed of oneself; **bukkeureoun gwageo** 부끄러운 과거 a shameful past
bukkeureowohada 부끄러워하다 V to be ashamed, shy, bashful: **silsue daehae bukkeureowohada** 실수에 대해 부끄러워하다 be ashamed of one's mistakes; **malhagi bukkeureowohada** 말하기 부끄러워하다 be shy to speak
bukseojjok 북서쪽 N north-west
bul 불 N fire: **bureul kkeuda** 불을 끄다 put out a fire
bul 불 N light (*lamp*): **bureul kkeuda** 불을 끄다 turn off the light; **bureul kyeoda** 불을 켜다 turn on the light
bulganeunghada/-han 불가능하다/-한 ADJ impossible
bulgyo 불교 N Buddhism
bulgyosinja 불교신자 N Buddhist
bulhaeng 불행 N misfortune, unhappiness
bulhaenghada, bulhaeng 불행하다, 불행한 ADJ unhappy: **bulhaenghada** 불행하다 be unhappy; **bulhaenghan eorin sijeol** 불행한 어린 시절 an unhappy childhood
bulhaenghagedo 불행하게도 ADV unfortunately: **bulhaenghagedo** 불행하게도 as ill luck would have it
bulkkonnori 불꽃놀이 N fireworks
bullida, bullineun 불리다, 불리는 V to be called, named: **keopicherira bullineun nyeolmae** 커피체리라 불리는 열매 a fruit called coffee-cherry
bullihada 분리하다 V to separate
bulpiryohada, bulpiryohan 불필요하다, 불필요한 ADJ unnecessary: **bulpiryohan jichul** 불필요한 지출 unnecessary expenses
bulppeobida, bulppeop(ui) 불법이다, 불법(의) ADJ illegal
bulpyeong 불평 N complaint
bulpyeonghada 불평하다 V to complain
bultago itda 불타다 V to be in flames, aflame: **jibi bultago itda** 집이 불타고 있다 a house is on fire; **boksusime**

bultada 복수심에 불타다 burn with revenge; **sarangeuro bultada** 사랑으로 불타다 be aflame with love; **danpungeuro bultaneun san** 단풍으로 불타는 산 a mountain ablazing with autumn foliage
bumbineun 붐비는 ADJ crowded, busy: **gajang bumbineun sigan** 가장 붐비는 시간 the busiest hour
bumbida 붐비다 V to be congested, jammed: **saramdeullo bumbida** 사람들로 붐비다 congested with people
bumo 부모 N parents
bun 분 N minute: **sesi isipbun** 3시 20분 It's 20 (*minutes*) past three
bun 분 N person (*in honorific form*): **han bun** 한 분 one person
bunbyeollyeok itda/inneun 분별력 있다/있는 ADJ sensible
bungdae 붕대 N bandage
bunsilmul 분실물 N lost property
bunwigi 분위기 N atmosphere, ambience
burangam 불안감 N anxiety
bureo.um 부러움 N envy
bureojida 부러지다 V to break: **balmogi bureojida** 발목이 부러지다 break one's ankle
bureojin 부러진 ADJ broken: **bureojin pal** 부러진 팔 a broken arm
bureojyeo nagada 부러져나가다 V to fracture, give way, snap: **gidungi bureojyeonagatda** 기둥이 부러져나갔다 The pillars gave way
bureopda 부럽다 ADJ envious: **dangsini bureopda** 당신이 부럽다 I envy you
bureowohada 부러워하다 V to envy: **seonggongeul bureowohada** 성공을 부러워하다 envy one's success
bureuda 부르다 V to call, summon: **chingureul bureuda** 친구를 부르다 call a friend
bureujitda 부르짖다 V to cry out: **gotongeuro bureujitda** 고통으로 부르짖다 cry out (*roar*) with pain
bureuptteuda 부릅뜨다 V to glare
bureuteuda 부르트다 V to blister: **piroro ipsuri bureuteuda** 피로로 입술이 부르트다 blistered lips from fatigue
burida 부리다 V to manage, handle
burun 불운 N bad luck

B

busang 부상 N injury, wound: **gabyeoun busang** 가벼운 부상 a minor injury

busanhan 부산한 ADJ bustling, busy

busanghada 부상하다 V to emerge, rise: **ingiseutaro busanghada** 인기스타로 부상하다 emerge as a big star

buseureogi 부스러기 N crumbs, chip

busok 부속 N part, component (*of machine*)

busok 부속 N affiliate: **busok siseol** 부속 시설 affiliated facilities; **busok byeongwon** 부속 병원 a hospital in affiliation

but 붓 N brush

butakhada 부탁하다 V to ask for, request (*informally*)

butakhamnida 부탁합니다 PHR please (*request for help*)

butda 붓다 V to pour: **mureul butda** 물을 붓다 pour water

butda 붓다 V to swell, puff up: **eolguri butda** 얼굴이 붓다 have a swollen face

butda 붙다 V to stick to

...buteo ...부터 PP from (*time*): **jigeum-buteo jayuda** 지금부터 자유다 free from now

butjapda 붙잡다 V to hold, grasp

buyuhada 부유하다 V to float: **murwie buyuhada** 물위에 부유하다 float on the water

buyuhan 부유한 ADJ rich, wealthy, well off: **buyuhan jiban** 부유한 집안 a wealthy family

byeo 벼 N rice (*plant*)

byeok 벽 N wall

byeol 별 N star

byeollo 별로 ADV not really, not particularly: **oneureun byeollo bappeuji anta** 오늘은 별로 바쁘지 않다 not particularly busy today

byeong 병 N bottle: **juice byeong** 쥬스 병 a juice bottle

byeong 병 N disease, illness: **bulchiui byeong** 불치의 병 an incurable illness

byeong.won 병원 N hospital

byeonhohada 변호하다 V to plead, defend (*with words*)

byeonhosa 변호사 N lawyer

C

cha 차 N tea: **han janui cha** 한 잔의 차 a cup of tea

cha 차 N car: 신형 차 new-model car

cha.aek 차액 N difference, margin, the difference between two prices

chabunhada 차분하다 ADJ calm, relaxed, quiet

chabyeolhada 차별하다 V to distinguish, discriminate, differentiate

chada 차다 ADJ cold, chilly: **barami eoreumjanggachi chada** 바람이 얼음장같이 차다 The wind is as cold as ice

chada 차다 V (*emotion*) to be full of, filled with: **gippeumeuro gadeuk chada** 기쁨으로 가득 차다 be filled with joy

chada 차다 V (*space*) to be filled, full, crowded: **seunggaegeuro gadeuk chan beoseu** 승객으로 가득 찬 버스 a bus full of passengers

chada 차다 V to kick: **gongeul ballo chada** 공을 발로 차다 kick a ball

chada 차다 V to put on, wear: **sigye-reul chada** 시계를 차다 wear a watch

chada 차다 V to reject, refuse: **aeineul chada** 애인을 차다 dump a boy (*girl*) friend

chada 차다 V to be satisfied with, content with: **maeume chaji anneunda** 마음에 차지 않는다 prove (*be*) unsatisfactory

chadan 차단 N block, cut-off

chadanbong 차단봉 N toll bar

chado 차도 N improvement of illness: **byeongsega chadoreul boigo itda** 병세가 차도를 보이고 있다 showing improvements in an illness

chado 차도 N roadway, highway: **chadoe chaga manta** 차도에 차가 많다 roadway full of cars

chae.uda 채우다 V to fill, stuff, pack

chaegim 책임 N duty, responsibility

chaegim itda/inneun 책임 있다/있는 ADJ responsible: **chaegim itda** 책임이 있다 be responsible for; **chaegim inneun dapbyeon** 책임 있는 답변 a responsible answer

chaejeom 채점 N marking, grading

chaek 책 N book

chaekbeolle 책벌레 N bookworm

chaekjapda 책잡다 v to find fault with: **chaegeul japida** 책을 잡히다 (*be*) found fault with

chaekjapida 책잡히다 v to be called to account, found to be blameable

chaekkkochi 책꽂이 N bookshelf

chaeksang 책상 N desk

chaempi.eon 챔피언 N champion

chaemu 채무 N debt, liabilities

chaenggida 챙기다 v to care for, look after: **geongangeul kkeumjjigi chaengginda** 건강을 끔찍이 챙긴다 take great care of one's health; **eomeonireul jal chaenggyeodeuryeora** 어머니를 잘 챙겨드려라 Take good care of your mother!

chaenggida 챙기다 v to pack: **yeohaenggal jimeul chaenggida** 여행갈 짐을 챙기다 pack for a trip

chaesik 채식 N vegetable diet

chaesikjuuija 채식주의자 N vegetarian

chaeso 채소 N vegetables, greens

chaetaek 채택 N adoption, acceptance

chaetaekhada 채택하다 v to pass, adopt, approve, select

chagam 차감 N deduction, subtraction

chagamhada 차감하다 v to deduct, take away

chagapda 차갑다 ADJ cold, icy, frosty

chageunchageun 차근차근 ADV in a calm and orderly way

chago 착오 N mistake, error

chago 차고 N garage (*for parking*)

chai 차이 N difference (*in quality*)

chajaboda 찾아보다 v to look up

chaji 차지 N occupancy, occupation

chajihada 차지하다 v to hold, rank: **useungeul chajihada** 우승을 차지하다 win the championship

chajihada 차지하다 v to occupy, take up: **chaeksangi bangui baneul chajihanda** 책상이 방의 반을 차지한다 The desk takes up half of the space in the room

chajihada 차지하다 v to win, take possession of: **maeumeul chajihada** 마음을 차지하다 win (*capture*) a person's heart; **yusaneul chajihada** 유산을 차지하다 claim one's inheritance

chajil 차질 N setback, snag: **gyehoege**

chajiri saenggida 계획에 차질이 생기다 a glitch in the plan

chakgak 착각 N illusion, delusion: **chakgage ppajida** 착각에 빠지다 delude oneself

chakgakhada 착각하다 v to mistake A for B, delude oneself

chakhada 착하다 ADJ good, nice

chaksilhada 착실하다 ADJ reliable, solid, trustworthy

chalgwasang 찰과상 N abrasion, scratch

challa 찰나 N instant, moment: **baro geu challae** 바로 그 찰나에 at that very moment

challanggeorida 찰랑거리다 v to lap, splash

challanhada 찬란하다 ADJ brilliant, splendid

chama 차마 ADV can't bear to

chamda 참다 v (*emotion*) to repress, swallow, control: **hwareul chamda** 화를 참다 control one's temper; **chungdongeul chamda** 충동을 참다 suppress one's temptation

chamda 참다 v (*physiology*) to suppress, hold back, restrain

chamda 참다 v to bear, endure, stand: **gonaneul chamda** 고난을 참다 endure hardship

chamdamhada 참담하다 ADJ terrible, tragic

chameolmi 차멀미 N carsickness

chamgahada 참가하다 v to participate

chamgireum 참기름 N sesame oil

chamgo 참고 N reference, consultation

chamgohada 참고하다 v to refer to, consult

chamgoseo 참고서 N reference book, study-aid book

chamgyeon 참견 N interference, meddling

chamgyeonhada 참견하다 v to meddle in, butt in

chamhada 참하다 ADJ good, nice and pretty

chamhoehada 참회하다 v to repent, confess

chamhokhada 참혹하다 ADJ gruesome, horrendous

chamkkae 참깨 N sesame seeds

chamnamu 참나무 N oak (*tree*)

C

chamoe 참외 N melon

chamseokhada 참석하다 v to attend: **hoeuie chamseokhada** 회의에 참석하다 attend a meeting

chamtteut 참뜻 N true meaning

chamyeohada 참여하다 v to join in, participate in: **seongeo undonge chamnyeohada** 선거 운동에 참여하다 join in an election campaign

chanam 차남 N second son

chanbaram 찬바람 N cold wind: **chanbarami ssaengssaeng bulda** 찬바람이 쌩쌩 불다 The cold wind wailed

chanchanhi 찬찬히 ADV thoroughly, carefully

changbaekhada 창백하다 ADJ pale, pallid

changchanghada 창창하다 ADJ bright, promising: **changchanghan amnal** 창창한 앞날 a promising future

changgu 창구 N window, counter (for paying, buying tickets)

changjak 창작 N creation (writing, composition)

changjohada 창조하다 v to create: **mueseo yureul changjohada** 무에서 유를 창조하다 make something out of nothing

changmun 창문 N window (in house, building)

changnyukhada 착륙하다 v to land (plane)

changpihada! 창피하다! PHR I'm so ashamed!

changpihada/changpihan 창피하다/ 창피한 ADJ be embarrassed: **changpihada** 창피하다 be embarrassed; **changpihan jilmun** 창피한 질문 an embarrassing question

chanjang 찬장 N cupboard

chanmul 찬물 N cold water: **chanmuldo wiaraega itda** 찬물도 위아래가 있다 elder before younger, there is a proper order for everything

chansa 찬사 N praise, eulogization, high compliment

chansareul bonaeda 찬사를 보내다 v to pay one's tribute of praise, ladle out praise, pay a high compliment

chanseong 찬성 v to agree

chanseu 찬스 N a chance, opportunity

chansongga 찬송가 N hymn, psalm

chanyeo 차녀 N second daughter

chapssal 찹쌀 N glutinous rice

charari 차라리 ADV rather, rather than: **charari jukgo sipda** 차라리 죽고 싶다 I'd rather die

charida 차리다 v to fix, prepare, set up: **bapsangeul charida** 밥상을 차리다 set the table

charyang 차량 N vehicle

charye 차례 N order, turn: **charyereul gidarida** 차례를 기다리다 wait for one's turn

charye 차례 N ancestor memorial rites: **charyereul jinaeda** 차례를 지내다 have a memorial service for one's ancestors

charyeoipda 차려입다 v to dress up

chaseok 차석 N no. 2, second in rank

chaseon 차선 N lane (traffic)

chaseon 차선 N the second best (plan): **choeseoni animyeon chaseoneul taekhara** 최선이 아니면 차선을 택하라 Go for the second best if you can't have the best

chatda 찾다 v to find, seek, look for, search for

chawon 차원 N dimension, level

chejung 체중 N weight

chejung.i julda 체중이 줄다 v to lose weight

chejung.i neulda 체중이 늘다 v to gain weight

chekeuhada 체크하다 v to check, verify

chekeumunui(ui) 체크무늬(의) N checked (pattern)

cheobakda 처박다 v to ram, shove, stuff

cheobang(jeon) 처방(전) N prescription

cheobeol 처벌 N punishment

cheoeum 처음 N first, first time, beginning

cheojida 처지다 v to be inferior to

cheojida 처지다 v to droop, sag: **cheojin eokkae** 처진 어깨 dropped shoulders

cheojida 처지다 v to fall behind: **gyeongjueseo dwiro cheojyeotda** 경주에서 뒤로 처졌다 fell behind in the race

cheokchu 척추 N spine

cheol 철 N iron
cheolbuji 철부지 N indiscreet person
cheolchik 철칙 N ironclad rule, principle
cheoljjahada 철자하다 V to spell
cheoljjeohada, cheoljjeohan 철저하다, 철저한 ADJ complete, thorough: **modeun ire cheoljjeohada** 모든 일에 철저하다 thorough in everything; **cheoljjeohan geomsa** 철저한 검사 a thorough inspection
cheolmul 철물 N hardware
cheolsae 철새 N migratory bird
cheolssa 철사 N wire
cheolsu 철수 N withdrawal, pullout
cheolsuhada 철수하다 V to evacuate, withdraw
cheoltto 철도 N railroad, railway
cheomeokda 처먹다 V to pig out, snarf down: **babeul cheomeokda** 밥을 처먹었다 shovel rice into one's mouth
cheon 천 NUM thousand: **cheon gaeui sagwa** 천 개의 사과 a thousand apples
cheon 천 N cloth, fabric: **cheoneul jjada** 천을 짜다 weave a fabric
cheon.guk 천국 N heaven
cheonam 처남 N brother-in-law (*wife's brother*)
cheoncheonhi 천천히 ADV slowly
cheondung 천둥 N thunder
cheongbaji 청바지 N blue jean
cheongdong 청동 N bronze
cheonggaeguri 청개구리 N a refractory child
cheonggaeguri 청개구리 N tree frog
cheonggak 청각 N sense of hearing
cheongguseo 청구서 N invoice, bill
cheonggyeol 청결 N cleanliness
cheongnyeon 청년 N youth, young people
cheongseungmatda 청승맞다 ADJ plaintive, ominously sorrowful
cheongsogi 청소기 N vacuum cleaner: **cheongsogireul dollida** 청소기를 돌리다 operate a vacuum cleaner
cheongsohada 청소하다 V to clean
cheongsonyeon 청소년 N adolescent, teenager
cheongsunhada 청순하다 ADJ pure hearted
cheonjae 천재 N genius
cheonjang 천장 N ceiling

cheonjinnanmanhada 천진난만하다 ADJ naive, innocent
cheonjugyo 천주교 N Catholicism
cheonmunhak 천문학 N astronomy
cheonninsang 첫인상 N first impression
cheonnyeondeokseureopda 천연덕스럽다 ADJ brazen, thick-skinned, shameless
cheonsa 천사 N angel
cheonsik 천식 N asthma
cheonyeo 처녀 N virgin
...cheoreom ...처럼 PP like, as: **cheonsacheoreom** 천사처럼 like an angel
...cheoreom boida ...처럼 보이다 V to look like: **cheonsacheoreom boida** 천사처럼 보이다 look like an angel
cheoreopda 철없다 ADJ immature, infantile: **ajik cheori eopda** 아직 철이 없다 still immature
cheorihada 처리하다 V to sort out, deal with
cheorihaenaeda 처리해내다 V to manage, succeed: **eoryeoun ireul cheorihaenaeda** 어려운 일을 처리해 내다 manage to bring sth to a success
cheoryanghada 처량하다 ADJ desolate, sorrowful
cheosinhada 처신하다 V to behave
cheot beonjjae 첫 번째 N first
cheseu 체스 N chess
cheung 층 N floor: **icheung** 이층 second floor
cheung 층 N layer: **ojon cheung** 오존 층 ozone layer
cheung jjari 층 짜리 N story (*of a building*): **sipcheung jjari geonmul** 10층 짜리 건물 a 10-story building
chida 치다 V to hit, strike
chijeu 치즈 N cheese
chikkwa(uisa) 치과(의사) N dentist
chil 칠 N paint, coat: **peinteu chil** 페인트 칠 a coat of paint
chil 칠 NUM seven: **je chirui** 제 칠의 the 7th
chilhada 칠하다 V to paint (*house, furniture*)
chilsip 칠십 NUM seventy
chima 치마 N skirt
chimdae 침대 N bed
chimdaesiteu 침대시트 N bedsheet
chimgu 침구 N bedding, bedclothes

C

chimsil 침실 N bedroom

chincheok 친척 N relatives, family

chingchan 칭찬 N praise

chingchanhada 칭찬하다 V to praise

chin.gu 친구 N friend

chingho 칭호 N title, designation

chinhada, chinhan 친하다, 친한 ADJ intimate, close together: **nuguwa chinhada** 누구와 친하다 be close to someone; **chinhan chingu** 친한 친구 a close friend

chinjeolhada, chinjeolhan 친절하다, 친절한 ADJ kind, friendly: **moduege chinjeolhada** 모두에게 친절하다 be kind to everyone; **chinjeolhan saram** 친절한 사람 a friendly person

chirwol 칠월 N July

chiryo 치료 N treatment, cure, remedy (*medical*)

chiryohada 치료하다 V to treat, care, cure (*medically*)

chissol 칫솔 N toothbrush

chisu 치수 N measurement, size

chiyak 치약 N toothpaste

chodae 초대 N invitation

chodaehada 초대하다 V to invite (*formally*)

choegeun(e) 최근(에) N lately

choeseoneul dahada 최선을 다하다 V to do one's best,

choeso 최소 N least (*smallest amount*)

chojohaehada, cojohaehaneun 초조해하다 다/-하는 ADJ nervous

chokollet 초콜렛 N chocolate

chong 총 N gun

chu.eok 추억 N memories

chucheonhada 추천하다 V to recommend

chucheukhada 추측하다 V to guess

chuga(ui) 추가의 ADJ extra

chukchukhada/-han 축축하다, 축축한 ADJ damp: **badagi chukchukhada** 바닥이 축축하다 the floor is wet (*damp*); **chukchukhan ot** 축축한 옷 damp clothes

chukgu 축구 N soccer

chukhahada 축하하다 V to celebrate

chukhahaeyo! 축하해요! PHR congratulations!

chukje 축제 N festival

chukso 축소 N reduction

chulbal 출발 N departure

chulcheo 출처 N origin, source

chulgu 출구 N exit, way out

chulpanhada 출판하다 V to publish

chulseokhada 출석하다 V present (*here*)

chum 춤 N dance

chumchuda 춤추다 V to dance

chungbunhada, chungbunhan 충분하다, 충분한 ADJ enough: **i jeongdomyeon chungbunhada** 이 정도면 충분하다 This is enough; **chungbunhan jeunggeo** 충분한 증거 enough evidence

chungdol 충돌 N collision

chungdolhada 충돌하다 V to collide

chunggo 충고 N advice

chunggohada 충고하다 V to advise

chupda, chuun 춥다, 추운 ADJ cold: **chupda** 춥다 feel cold (*or* it is cold); **chuun jiyeok** 추운 지역 a cold area

chwijik 취직 N employment

chwimi 취미 N hobby

chwisohada 취소하다 V to cancel

chyeobusuda 쳐부수다 V to defeat

D

da.eum 다음 N following

da.eumju 다음 주 N next week

da.eumui 다음의 ADJ next (*in line, sequence*)

da haetda 다 했다 PHR to have done something: **sukjereul da haetda** 숙제를 다 했다 have done one's homework

da tada 다 타다 PHR burned down, out: **jibi da tabeoryeotda** 집이 다 타버렸다 The house was burned down

dabunhi 다분히 ADV much, quite

dachaeropda 다채롭다 ADJ colorful, diversified

dachida 다치다 V to be hurt

dachida 닫히다 V to close, shut

dachin 닫힌 ADJ closed: **dachin mun** 닫힌 문 a closed door

dachin 다친 ADJ hurt, injured: **dachin saram** 다친 사람 an injured person

dadari 다달이 ADV month to (*by*) month, monthly: **jipsereul dadari naeda** 집세를 다달이 내다 pay rent monthly

dadeumda 다듬다 V to polish, revise:

munjangeul dadeumda 문장을
다듬다 revise one's writing
dadeumda 다듬다 v to prune, clean:
namutgajireul dadeumda 나뭇가지를
다듬다 prune a tree; **baechureul
dadeumda** 배추를 다듬다 clean a
cabbage (*for kimchi*)
dadeumda 다듬다 v to trim, groom:
meorireul dadeumda 머리를 다듬다
get a trim (*hair*)
dadok 다독 n extensive reading
dadokgeorida 다독거리다 v to pat,
comfort, console
dae.uhada 대우하다 v to treat (*behave
towards*)
daebu 대부 n loan
daebubun 대부분 n most (*the most of*)
daechehada 대체하다 v to replace:
Areul Bro daechehada A를 B로 대체
하다 replace A with B
daechero 대체로 ADV generally, mostly:
daechero malgeun nalssi 대체로 맑은
날씨 mostly clear weather
daedanhada, daedanhan 대단하다,
대단한 ADJ great, impressive,
magnificent
daedap 대답 n answer, response
(*spoken*)
daedaphada 대답하다 v to answer,
respond, reply (*spoken*)
daegakseon 대각선 n diagonal
daegakseoneuro 대각선으로 ADV
diagonally
daegakseonui 대각선의 ADJ diagonal
daegang 대강 ADV roughly,
approximately
daehak 대학 n university
daehaksaeng 대학생 n college student
daehanminguk 대한민국 n Korea
daehwa 대화 n conversation
daejeophada 대접하다 v to treat
(*something special*)
daemeoriin 대머리인 ADJ bald
daeryuk 대륙 n continent
daesa 대사 n ambassador
daesagwan 대사관 n embassy
...daesine ...대신에 PP instead of: **jeotgarak daesine pokeureul sayong-
hada** 젓가락 대신에 포크를 사용하다
use forks instead of chopsticks
daetongnyeong 대통령 n president

daeyang 대양 n ocean
daeyeongjeguk 대영제국 n United
Kingdom
dagalsaek 다갈색 n dark brown
dagaoda 다가오다 v to come closer,
approach
dagaseoda 다가서다 v to draw near:
gakkai dagaseoda 가까이 다가서다
approach closely
dageuchida 다그치다 v to press, urge,
push: **dageuchida** 다그치다 press
(*chase*) for answers
dageupada 다급하다 ADJ pressing,
urgent
dagukjeok 다국적 n multinational
dagwa 다과 n refreshments
dahaenghi 다행히 ADV fortunately
dahyeoljillui 다혈질의 ADJ hot-
blooded, short-tempered
daiamondeu 다이아몬드 n diamond
daieoteu 다이어트 n diet
dajeongdagamhan 다정다감한 ADJ
kind and sensitive
dajeonghada 다정하다 ADJ
affectionate, friendly
dajim 다짐 n resolution
dajimbatda 다짐받다 v to get an
assurance from sb
dajimhada 다짐하다 v to pledge, assure
dajjagojja 다짜고짜 ADV without
notice, without reason
dak 닭 n chicken
dakchida 닥치다 v to befall, come near
dakchida 닥치다 v to shut up
(*impolite*): **ip dakchyeo!** 입 닥쳐!
Shut your mouth!
dakda 닦다 v to polish: **gudureul
dakda** 구두를 닦다 polish one's shoes
dakda 닦다 v to wipe: **teibeureul
dakda** 테이블을 닦다 wipe the table;
nunmureul dakda 눈물을 닦다 wipe
one's tears
dakgogi 닭고기 n chicken meat
dal 달 n month
dal 달 n moon: **boreumdal** 보름달 a
full moon
dalda, dan 달다, 단 ADJ sweet
dalkomhada 달콤하다 ADJ sweet
dallaeda 달래다 v to soothe, pacify:
uneun agireul dallaeda 우는 아기를
달래다 pacify a crying baby
dallajida 달라지다 v to alter, change,

shift, vary: **sanghwangi dallajyeotda** 상황이 달라졌다 The situation has changed

dallida 달리다 V to run

dallyeok 달력 N calendar

dalpaengi 달팽이 N snail

dalseonghada 달성하다 V to attain, achieve, accomplish: **mokpyoreul dalseonghada** 목표를 달성하다 achieve one's goal

dam 담 N fence, wall

daman 다만 ADV merely, simply: **naneun daman geuga haengbok-hagil baral ppunida** 나는 다만 그가 행복하길 바랄 뿐이다 I only wish his happiness

dambae 담배 N cigarette

dambae pida 담배 피다 V to smoke (*tobacco*)

damda 닮다 V to resemble

damdanggwan 담당관 N action officer

damnyo 담요 N blanket

damokjeok 다목적 N multipurpose

dan 단 N hem: **chimaui dan** 치마의 단 hem of a skirt

dan 단 N bundle, bunch, sheaf (*counting unit*): **sigeumchi se dan** 시금치 세 단 three bunches of spinach

dan 단 ADV but, only, merely

dan.gye 단계 N step

dana 단아 N elegance, grace

danahada 단아하다 ADJ elegant, graceful

dananhada 다난하다 ADJ eventful, full of difficulties

danbaekjil 단백질 N protein

danche 단체 N organization, group, team

danchu 단추 N button

danchuk 단축 N shortening, reduction

danchukhada 단축하다 V to curtail, shorten, reduce

dandanhada, dandanhan 단단하다, 단단한 ADJ hard, solid, firm

dandokui 단독의 ADJ exclusive, solo, independent

daneo 단어 N word

dangam 단감 N sweet persimmon

dangcheomdoeda 당첨되다 V to win a prize (*lottery*)

dangdolhada 당돌하다 ADJ daring, bold, plucky

dangdolhada 당돌하다 ADJ rude,

abrupt, forward

dangeori 단거리 N short distance

danggeun 당근 N carrot

danggida 당기다 V to pull

danghwanghada/-haehada 당황하다/-해하다 V to be embarrassed, taken aback, flustered

dangol 단골 N regular (*customer*): **dangol sonnim** 단골 손님 a regular customer; **dangol sikdang** 단골 식당 a favorite restaurant

dangyeol 단결 N unity, union

danhohada 단호하다 ADJ firm, stern

danida 다니다 V to attend, work for: **hakgyo danida** 학교에 다니다 attend school; **joeun jikjange danida** 좋은 직장에 다니다 work for a reputable company

danida 다니다 V to frequent, go: **byeongwone danida** 병원에 다니다 go to a hospital (*regularly*)

danida 다니다 V to hang out with, go around with: **dongari chingudeulgwa eoullyeo danida** 동아리 친구들과 어울려 다니다 hang out with club friends

danida 다니다 V to transit, pass: **i noseoneuro beoseuga daninda** 이 노선으로 버스가 다닌다 The bus passes through this route

danjeonghada, danjeonghan 단정하다, 단정한 ADJ neat, tidy: **danjeonghan nyongmo** 단정한 용모 a decent appearance

danji 단지 ADV just, only, merely

danjjak 단짝 N best friend

danmuji 단무지 N pickled radish

dannyeok 단역 N a minor role

dannyeonko 단연코 ADV definitely, by far: **dannyeonko geureon ireun eopseul geotsida** 단연코 그런 일은 없을 것이다 It will definitely not happen; **dannyeonko igot eumsigi gajang mannitda** 단연코 이곳 음식이 가장 맛있다 By far, this place has the best food

danpung 단풍 N fall foliage

danpungnamu 단풍나무 N maple (*tree*)

danpyeon 단편 N short piece

danpyeonsoseol 단편소설 N short sketch, short novel

danpyeonyeonghwa 단편영화 N short

film

dansik 단식 N fast, fasting: **geuneun samil dongan dansikhaetda** 그는 3일 동안 단식했다 he fasted for 3 days

dansik 단식 N single game, singles: **namja dansik gyeonggi** 남자 단식 경기 mens singles (*games*)

dansikhada 단식하다 V to fast

dansokhada 단속하다 V to crack down, bust: **daedaejeogin mayak dansogi iseotda** 대대적인 마약 단속이 있었다 There was a big drug bust

dansokhada 단속하다 V to guard, control: **mundansok dandanhi haera** 문단속 단단히 해라 Make sure to lock the door!

dansu 단수 N suspension of water supply

dansu 단수 N the singular

dansume 단숨에 ADV in one breath, in one sitting

dansunhada, dansunhan 단순하다, 단순한 ADJ plain (*not fancy*), simple, naïve: **sanghwangeun dansunhada** 상황은 단순하다 the situation is simple; **dansunhan saram** 단순한 사람 a simple-minded person

danwi 단위 N unit, measure

danyeogada 다녀가다 V to drop in, come by, stop by: **chinguga uri jibe danyeogatda** 친구가 우리 집에 다녀갔다 My friend stopped by and then left

danyeooda 다녀오다 V to go and return: **nampyeoni chuljangeul danyeowatda** 남편이 출장을 나녀왔다 My husband went on a trip and returned

dapjang 답장 N answer, response (*written*)

dapjanghada 답장하다 V to answer, respond, reply (*written*)

darabeorin 닳아버린 ADJ worn out (*clothes*)

daraekki 다래끼 N a sty, hordeolum

darak 다락 N attic, loft

daramjwi 다람쥐 N squirrel

daranada 달아나다 V to fly, flee, run away

daranaeda 달아내다 V to weigh out

darangeo 다랑어 N bluefin tuna

dareuda, dareun 다르다, 다른 ADJ

different: keugiga dareuda 크기가 다르다 different in size; **dareun jongnyu** 다른 종류 a different kind

dareumeopda 다름없다 ADJ be the same

dareun 다른 ADJ another, other (*different*): **geunyeo oee tto dareun se yeoja** 그녀 외에 또 다른 세 여자 three other women beside her

dari 다리 N bridge: **darireul geonneoda** 다리를 건너다 cross over a bridge

dari 다리 N leg: **darireul ppida** 다리를 삐다 sprain one's legs

darida 다리다 V to iron (*clothing*)

darin 달인 N expert, master

daruda 다루다 V to treat, deal with, handle

daseot 다섯 NUM five

dasi 다시 ADV again

daso 다소 N somewhat, a bit: **daso bulkwaehada** 다소 불쾌하다 feel a bit unpleasant

daseurida 다스리다 V to discipline, punish: **joeineul maero daseurida** 죄인을 매로 다스리다 discipline a law-breaker with punishment

daseurida 다스리다 V to govern, rule: **narareul daseurida** 나라를 다스리다 govern a nation

daseurida 다스리다 V to subdue, control: **hwareul daseurida** 화를 다스리다 control one's anger

dasogosi 다소곳이 ADV modestly, shyly

dasogotada 다소곳하다 ADJ modest, courteous

dasugyeol 다수결 N majority vote: **dasugyeore ttareuda** 다수결에 따르다 accept the majority decision

datda 닫다 V to close, shut

datuda 다투다 V to quarrel

datum 다툼 N duel, quarrel, fight

dayang 다양 N diversity, variety

dayanghada 다양하다 ADJ various, diverse

de.uda 데우다 V to heat: **jjigaereul deuda** 찌개를 데우다 heat up the soup

deo 더 ADV more (*comparative*)

deo jeokda/jeogeun 더 적다/적은 ADJ less (*smaller amount*)

deo jota/jo.eun 더 좋다/좋은 ADJ better: **gyeouri deo jota** 겨울이 더

좋다 like winter better; **deo joeun seontaek** 더 좋은 선택 a better choice

deo maneun 더 많은 ADJ more of (*quantity*)

deo nappeuda/nappeun 더 나쁘다/나쁜 ADJ worse

deohada 더하다 V to add

deolda 덜다 V to lessen, lighten, ease

deolda 덜다 V to subtract, deduct from, take off

deombida 덤비다 V to come at, jump at, spring at

deonjida 던지다 V to throw

deopda 덮다 V to cover, close

deopda, deo.un 덥다, 더운 ADJ hot (*temperature*)

deoreopda, deoreo.un 더럽다, 더러운 ADJ dirty

deukjeom 득점 N score

deul 들 N (*plural particle*): **neollyeojin otdeul** 널려진 옷들 scattered clothes

deul 들 N field: **deure naga ilhada** 들에 나가 일하다 work in the fields

deulleuda 들르다 V to stop by, pay a visit

deumulda, deumun 드물다, 드문 ADJ rare, scarce

deung 등 N back (*part of body*)

deung 등 N lamp

deunggeup 등급 N degree, level

deunggi upyeon 등기 우편 N registered post

deungnokhada 등록하다 V to register

deureo.oda 들어오다 V to come in

deureogada 들어가다 V to enter

(deureo)ollida (들어)올리다 V to lift, raise

deureseu 드레스 N dress, frock

deutda 듣다 V to hear, listen

dibidi 디비디 N DVD

dijain 디자인 N pattern, design

dijeoteu 디저트 N dessert, sweets

diseukaunteu 디스카운트 N discount

diseuket 디스켓 N diskette

do 도 N degrees (*temperature*): **yeongha samdo** 영하 3도 3 degrees below zero

do 도 N degrees (*level, standard*): **do-reul neomda** 도를 넘다 cross the line

do 도 N right way (*religious*): **doreul dakda** 도를 닦다 cultivate oneself morally or religiously

...do ...도 PP also, too: **geugeotdo jota**

그것도 좋다 That is good, too

...do ...do-ji anta ...도 ...도 -지 않다 V neither...nor: **keujido jakjido anta** 크지도 작지도 않다 neither big nor small

...do ...do anida ...도 ...도 ...아니다 V neither...nor: **dondo myeongyedo anida** 돈도 명예도 아니다 neither money nor power

...do ttohan ...도 또한 ADV as well: **nado ttohan geureoke neukkinda** 나도 또한 그렇게 느낀다 I feel the same way

...do ttohan -ji anta ...도 또한 -지 않다 V nor

...do ttohan ...anida ...도 또한 ...아니다 V nor

dobak 도박 N gamble

dochak 도착 N arrival

dochakhada 도착하다 V to reach, arrive, get

dodohada 도도하다 ADJ haughty, proud, arrogant

doduk 도둑 N thief

doeda 되다 V to become

dogi itda/inneun 독이 있다/있는 ADJ poisonous

dogu 도구 N tool, utensil, instrument

dogyo 도교 N Taoism

dojeon 도전 N challenge

dok(yak) 독(약) N poison

dokan sul 독한 술 N hard liquor

dokbang 독방 N single room, solitary cell

dokbeoseot 독버섯 N poisonous mushroom

dokbojeogin 독보적인 ADJ unrivaled, unequaled, matchless

dokgam 독감 N flu: **dokgam jusa** 독감 주사 a flu shot

dokhada 독하다 ADJ malicious, spiteful, vicious: **geu yeojaneun dokhada** 그 여자는 독하다 She is vicious

dokhada 독하다 ADJ potent, pungent, strong: **dokhan nyak** 독한 약 strong medicine; **hyangi dokhada** 향이 독하다 potent smell

dokhada 독하다 ADJ unyielding, unflinching

dokhak 독학 N self-education

dokhakhada 독학하다 V to study by oneself

dokhugam 독후감 N book report

doksik 독식 N monopoly
doksikhada 독식하다 V to monopolize
doksin 독신 N single (*not married*)
dol 돌 N stone
dolboda 돌보다 V to look after, take care of: **aireul dolboda** 아이를 돌보다 take care of a child
dolda 돌다 V to turn around
dolgorae 돌고래 N dolphin
dollida 돌리다 V to steer, spin
dollyeoboda 돌려보다 V to pass on, switch, turn
dollyeobonaeda 돌려보내다 V to send back, return
dollyeojuda 돌려주다 V to return, give back
domanggada 도망가다 V to run away
don 돈 N money
donbangseoge anda 돈방석에 앉다 V to be rolling in the dough, sit on a pile of money
...dong.an ...동안 during, for
dong.eopja 동업자 N partner (*in business*)
dong.i 동의 N agreement
dong.ihada 동의하다 V to agree
dongari 동아리 N club, group: **gateun dongari membeo** 같은 동아리 멤버 club member
donggong 동공 N pupil
donggul 동굴 N cave
dongjak 동작 N movement, motion
dongjeon 동전 N coin
dongjjok 동쪽 N east
dongmul 동물 N animal
dongmurwon 동물원 N zoo
dongnipan 독립한 ADJ free, independent
dongniphada 독립하다 V to become independent: **gyeongjejeogeuro dongnipada** 경제적으로 독립하다 achieve financial independence
dongnipui 독립의 ADJ independent
dongnyo 동료 N co-worker, colleague
dongsaeng 동생 N younger brother or sister
dongsang 동상 N statue
dopda 돕다 V to assist, help
doragada 돌아가다 V to go back, return: **jibeuro doragada** 집으로 돌아가다 go back home
doraoda 돌아오다 V to come back, return: **goguge doraoda** 고국에 돌아

오다 return to one's native country
doro 도로 N road
doseogwan 도서관 N library
dosi 도시 N city
dosiui 도시의 ADJ urban
dotguda 돋구다 V to stimulate, excite, incite: **immaseul dotguda** 입맛을 돋구다 work up an appetite; **heungeul dotguda** 흥을 돋구다 add to the amusement; **hwareul dotguda** 화를 돋구다 rub someone the wrong way
dotori 도토리 N acorn: **dotori ki jaegi** 도토리 키 재기 A miss is as good as a mile; **gaebabe dotori** 개밥에 도토리 fifth wheel
doum 도움 N assistance, help
dowajuseyo! 도와주세요! PHR help!
du bae 두 배 N double
du beonjjaeui 두 번째의 ADJ second: **dubeonjjaero keun** 두번째로 큰 second-largest
dubu 두부 N bean curd, tofu
dudeurida 두드리다 V to knock, tap
dugo gada 두고 가다 V to leave behind and go
dugo oda 두고 오다 V to leave behind and come
duk 둑 N bank (*of river*)
dukkeopda, dukkeo.un 두껍다, 두꺼운 ADJ thick (*of things*)
dul 둘 NUM two
dul da 둘 다 ADV both
dunggeulda, dunggeun 둥글다, 둥근 ADJ round (*shape*)
dungji 둥지 N nest
dwaeji 돼지 N pig
dwaejigogi 돼지고기 N pork
dwi 뒤 N back, rear, tail
dwie 뒤에 ADV behind (*space*)
dwie 뒤에 ADV after (*time*)
dwijibeojida 뒤집어지다 V to cave over
dwijibeojin 뒤집어진 ADJ overturned, upside down
dwijipda 뒤집다 V to turn over, flip over
dwiro 뒤로 ADV backward
dwiro gada 뒤로 가다 V to reverse, back up
dwittaragada 뒤따라가다 V to follow behind

E

...e ...에 PP in (*time, years*)

...e ...에 PP in, at, on (*location*)

...e ...에 PP on (*of dates*)

...e ...에 PP to (*destination*)

...e daehae ...에 대해 about (*regarding, concerning*)

...e daehae malhada ...에 대해 말하다 v to talk about

...e daehae mureoboda ...에 대해 물어보다 v to ask about

...e daehae nonjaenghada ...에 대해 논쟁하다 v to argue over

...e dallyeo.itda ...에 달려있다 v to depend on

...e gichohan ...에 기초한 ADJ based on

...e gwanhayeo ...에 관하여 v regarding, concerning

...e iksukhada ...에 익숙하다 ADJ to know, be acquainted with

...e oreuda ...에 오르다 v to climb up (*hills, mountains*)

...e sokada ...에 속하다 v to belong to

...e uihae ...에 의해 ADV by

...e uihamyeon ...에 의하면 ADV according to

...ege ...에게 PP to, toward: **neoege** 너에게 to you, **chinguege** 친구에게 to a friend

eeokeon 에어컨 N air conditioner

ellibeiteo 엘리베이터 N elevator

elliteu 엘리트 N elite

eneoji 에너지 N energy

enganhada 엔간하다 ADJ quite, enough, if possible: **enganhaeseoneun mareul deutji anneunda** 엔간해서는 말을 듣지 않는다 quite stubborn; **enganhi jom haera** 엔간히 좀 해라 Enough is enough; **enganhamyeon chamseokhagi baranda** 엔간 하면 참석하기 바란다 Please attend if at all possible

enjin 엔진 N engine

enuri 에누리 N chaffer, discount

eo.ullida 어울리다 v to socialize with, associate with, get along with: **nuguwado jal eoullida** 누구와도 잘 어울리다 get along with anyone

eo.ullineun 어울리는 ADJ fitting, suitable: **jal eoullineun bubu** 잘 어울리는

부부 (커플) a well-matched couple; **eoullineun haengdong** 어울리는 행동 proper behavior; **teibeulgwa eoullineun uija** 테이블과 어울리는 의자 a chair with matching table

-eo/a boda -어/아 보다 v try out -ing

-eo/a deurida -어/아 드리다 v (*humble form of* -어/아 주다)

-eo/a juda -어/아 주다 v to do something for another's benefit

-eo/a juseyo -어/아 주세요 PHR please (*request for something*)

-eo/ado jota -어/아도 좋다 ADJ may, can, be allowed to

-eo/aya hada -어/아야 하다 v must, have to, ought to

eoanibeongbeonghada 어안이벙벙 하다 ADJ dumbfounded

eobu 어부 N fisherman

eochapi 어차피 ADV anyway

eocheogunieopda 어처구니없다 ADJ preposterous, ridiculous

eodeomatda 얻어맞다 v to be beaten

eodeomeokda 얻어먹다 v to get treated to, be called names

eodideunji 어디든지 ADV anywhere, everywhere: **jeonguk eodideunji baedal ganeunghamnida** 전국 어디 든지 배달 가능합니다 we deliver anywhere in the country

eodie 어디에 ADV where

eodiedo ...eopda 어디에도 없다 PHR it is nowhere...

eodin.ga 어딘가 ADV somewhere

eodiro gaseyo? 어디로 가세요? PHR where are you going to?

eodukhada 어둑하다 ADJ dusky, dim

eodupda, eoduun 어둡다, 어두운 ADJ dark, gloomy, bleak, dim: **bakki eodupda** 밖이 어둡다 It's dark outside; **eoduun saekkkal** 어두운 색깔 dark colors; **pyojeongi eodupda** 표정 이 어둡다 have a gloomy face; **eoduun mirae** 어두운 미래 a bleak future; **eoduun bulbit** 어두운 불빛 a dim light

eodupda, eoduun 어둡다, 어두운 ADJ weak, bad (*hearing, eye-sight*): **gwiga eodupda** 귀가 어둡다 be hard of hearing; **nuni eodupda** 눈이 어둡다 be weak-sighted

eodupda, eoduun 어둡다, 어두운 ADJ poor sense of direction, bad with

directions: **gil luni eodupda** 길 눈이
어둡다 be bad with directions

eodupda, eoduun 어둡다, 어두운 ADJ
familiar with, not to be (*information*):
jirie eodupda 지리에 어둡다 not
familiar with the area; **sesang
muljeonge eodupda** 세상 물정에
어둡다 be ignorant of the world

eodupda, eoduun 어둡다, 어두운 ADJ
blinded (*by greed*): **yoksim (gwollyeok)
e nuni eodupda** 욕심 (권력)에 눈이 어
둡다 be blinded by greed (*power*)

eoduwojida 어두워지다 ADJ to
become dark

eoeop 어업 N fishery

eogeumni 어금니 N molar (*tooth*)

eogida 어기다 v to violate

eogida 어기다 v to break (*promise,
rules*): **yaksogeul eogida** 약속을 어기
다 break one's promise (*word*)

eogida 어기다 v not to be punctual:
siganeul eogida 시간을 어기다 not to
be punctual, not to be on time

eogulhada 억울하다 ADJ to be under
unfair/false accusation: **eogulhan
numyeongeul sseuda** 억울한 누명을
쓰다 be unjustly accused

eohak 어학 N linguistics

eohang 어항 N fish tank

eoi 어이 INTERJ hey! you! (*impolite*)

eoi 어이 N how, why

eoieopda 어이없다 ADJ absurd

eoje 어제 N yesterday

eojeongjjeonghada 어정쩡하다 ADJ
noncommittal

eojireopda 어지럽다 ADJ dizzy, giddy

eojireuda 어지르다 v to make a mess

eojjeolsueopda 어쩔수없다 ADJ unavoidable

eojjeonji 어쩐지 ADV no wonder: **eojjeonji gibuni joa boideora** 어쩐지 기
분이 좋아 보이더라 No wonder you
look happy

eojjeonji 어쩐지 ADV somehow:
eojjeonji seulpeuda 어쩐지 슬프다
I feel sad somehow

eojungganhada 어중간하다 ADJ halfway

eokcheuk 억측 N speculation

eokhida 얽히다 v to get intertwined

eokjehada 억제하다 v to hold back,
restrain

eokjeonseung 역전승 N come-from-
behind victory: **eokjeonseungeul
geodueotda** 역전승을 거두었다 win a
come-from-behind victory

eokjeonseung 역전승 N come-from-
behind victory

eokjiro 억지로 ADV forcibly, unwillingly: **eokjiro ireul hada** 억지로 일을
하다 work unwillingly

eokjiseureopda 억지스럽다 ADJ
affected, practiced, unnatural

eokjiseureopda 억지스럽다 ADJ obstinate, insistent

eokjiuseum 억지웃음 N forced laugh

eokkae 어깨 N shoulder

eokkaedongmu 어깨동무 N put arms
around each other's shoulders, side
by side

eokseda 억세다 ADJ tough, coarse

eolbeomurida 얼버무리다 v to speak
ambiguously, equivocate

eolchu 얼추 ADV nearly: **eolchu biseutada** 얼추 비슷하다 nearly the same

eolda 얼다 v to be frozen: **bari eolda**
발이 얼다 have frozen feet

eollida 얼리다 v to freeze: **mureul
eollida** 물을 얼리다 freeze water

eolgul 얼굴 N face

eolgani 얼간이 N dork, jerk

eolleun 얼른 ADV quickly, right away

eollon 언론 N press, journalism

eolloin 언론인 N journalist

eolluk 얼룩 N stain

eolmana 얼마나 ADV how much, how
many

eolmana maniyo? 얼마나 많아요?
PHR how many? how much?

eolmana oraeyo? 얼마나 오래요?
PHR how long?

eolmayeyo? 얼마예요? PHR how
much is it?

eolppajida 얼빠지다 v to be stunned,
dazed

eomaeomahada 어마어마하다 ADJ
tremendous

eomcheongnada 엄청나다 ADJ exorbitant

eomeona, sesang.e! 어머나 INTERJ
my goodness!

eomeoni 어머니 N mother

eomgyeokhada, eomgyeokan
엄격하다/엄격한 ADJ strict

E

eomhada 엄하다 ADJ severe, strict
eomho 엄호 N cover, protection
eomji 엄지 N thumb
eommilhage 엄밀하게 ADV strictly, exactly
eomnyeonhi 엄연히 ADV undoubtedly, clearly
eomsal 엄살 N exaggeration of pain
eomsalburida 엄살부리다 V to exaggerate pain, make a fuss: **eomsareul burida** 엄살을 부리다 make a fuss about trifles
eomuk 어묵 N fish paste
eomulgeorida 어물거리다 V to equivocate, prevaricate
eon 언 ADJ frozen
eonchida 얹히다 V to be placed on, be laid on
eonchida 얹히다 V to have indigestion: **jeonyeok meogeun geotsi eonchida** 저녁 먹은 것이 얹히다 dinner is still sitting in the tummy
eonchyeosalda 얹혀살다 V to live off
eonda 얹다 V to place, put on, lay
eondeok 언덕 N hill
eoneo 언어 N language
eoneu 어느 CONJ which
eoneu geoyo? 어느 거요? PHR which one?
eoneu jjokdo -ji anta 어느 쪽도 -지 않다 ADJ neither
eoneu jjokdo ..anida 어느 쪽도....아니다 ADJ neither
eongamsaengsim 언감생심 N how dare...? cannot dare
eoneudeot 어느덧 ADV before one knows
eongdeong.i 엉덩이 N bottom, buttocks
eongdeongbanga 엉덩방아 N pratfall
eongeup 언급 N reference, mention
eonggeojuchumhada 엉거주춤하다 V to half-sit half-rise
eonggeojuchumhada 엉거주춤하다 V to waver, hesitate
eonggeopgyeore 엉겁결에 ADV in a moment of bewilderment
eonggeumeonggeum 엉금엉금 ADV crawling, go on all fours
eongkeumhada 엉큼하다 ADJ wily, sly, sneaky
eongkida 엉키다 V to tangle, get tangled
eongmaeda 얽매다 V to bind, tie

eongmaeida 얽매이다 V to be bound
eongmang 엉망 N mess, wreck
eongmang.ida, eongmang.in 엉망이다, 엉망인 ADJ messy, chaotic
eongnullida 억눌리다 V to be oppressed, repressed
eongnureuda 억누르다 V to refrain, suppress
eongnyu 억류 N detention, interment
eongseonghada 엉성하다 ADJ poor, careless: **eongseonghan geukbon** 엉성한 극본 poorly written script
eongteori 엉터리 N nonsense, sham
eonhaeng 언행 N speech and behavior: **eonhaeng ilchi** 언행 일치 acting up to one's words; **gyeongbakhan eonhaeng** 경박한 언행 frivolous behavior
eonjaeng 언쟁 N argument, quarrel
eonje 언제 PRON when
eonjeojuda 얹어주다 V to give extra: **hanareul deo eonjeojuda** 하나를 더 얹어주다 give one extra
eonjjanta 언짢다 ADJ upset, displeased
eonnagada 엇나가다 V to go astray
eonni 언니 N older sister (female's)
eonnyak 언약 N verbal promise
eonseong 언성 N voice, tone: **eonseongeul nopida** 언성을 높이다 raise voices
eontteut 언뜻 ADV in an instant
eonulhada 어눌하다 ADJ inarticulate
eopbo 업보 N karma
eopda 업다 V to give (a person) a piggyback
eopda 엎다 V to overthrow: **hyeon jeongbureul eopda** 현 정부를 엎다 overthrow the present government
eopda 엎다 V to turn over: **bapsangeul eopda** 밥상을 엎다 overturn a table in anger
...eopda, ...eomneun ...없다, ...없는 ADJ non-existent, nothing, none
eopdeurida 엎드리다 V to lie face down, prostrate
eopjeok 업적 N achievements
eopjong 업종 N type of industry: **museun eopjonge jongsahasinayo?** 무슨 업종에 종사하시나요? What type of business are you in?
eopseojida 없어지다 V to disappear
eopseojin 없어진 ADJ to be lost, missing

...eopsi ...없이 ADV without

eopsinnyeogida 업신여기다 V to look down upon

eoreobutda 얼어붙다 V to freeze

eoreolhada 얼얼하다 ADJ burning, stinging

eoreum 얼음 N ice

eoreumpan 얼음판 N icy ground: **(sal) eoreumpan wireul geotda** (살)얼음판 위를 걷다 walking on thin ice

eoreun 어른 N adult

eoreunseureopda 어른스럽다 ADJ mature: **naie bihaeseo eoreunseureopda** 나이에 비해서 어른스럽다 mature for one's age

eorida, eorin 어리다, 어린 ADJ young

eoridungjeolhada/-haehada 어리둥 절하다/-해하다 V be puzzled

eorigwang 어리광 V to play the baby to

eorimeopda 어림없다 ADJ far from it!, absurd!, not a chance!

eorini 어린이 N child (*young person*)

eoriseokda, eoriseogeun 어리석다, 어리석은 ADJ stupid, silly, foolish

eorumanjida 어루만지다 V to stroke, pat

eoryeopda, eoryeo.un 어렵다, 어려 운 ADJ difficult, hard

eoryeompussi 어렴풋이 ADV dimly, vaguely

eoryeoum 어려움 N hardship

eoryeowohada 어려워하다 V to feel uncomfortable with

eosaekhada 어색하다 ADJ awkward

eoseo 어서 ADV quickly

eoseo oseyo! 어서 오세요! PHR welcome!

eoseolpeuda 어설프다 ADJ clumsy, fumbling, sloppy

eoseoyo! 어서요! INTERJ come on!, let's go! hurry!

eoseulleonggeorida 어슬렁거리다 V to prowl, saunter, loiter

eosurukhada 어수룩하다 ADJ credulous, naïve

eosuseonhada 어수선하다 ADJ disordered, untidy

-eot/at- -었/았- (*past tense suffix*)

eotbiseutada 엇비슷하다 ADJ similar, leg and leg

eotda 얻다 V to get, receive, obtain

eotgallida 엇갈리다 V to have disagreement: **mokgyeokjaui jinsuri eot-**

gallida 목격자의 진술이 엇갈리다 testimony of the witnesses is not matching

eotgallida 엇갈리다 V to have mixed feelings: **huibiga eotgallida** 희비가 엇갈리다 mixed feelings of joy and sadness

eotgallida 엇갈리다 V to miss each other: **giri eotgallida** 길이 엇갈리다 missed each other on the way

eotgeujeokke 엊그저께 N a couple of days ago

eotteoke 어떻게 ADJ how

eotteon 어떤 ADV what kind of?, which?

eotteon 어떤 ADV some

eotteon geot 어떤 것 ADJ, N something

eotteon saram 어떤 사람 ADJ, N somebody, someone

eoyeotada 어엿하다 ADJ (*to become*) respectable, decent, honorable

ereo 에러 N error

esei 에세이 N essay

...eseo ...에서 PP from (*starting point*)

...eseo ...에서 PP in, at, on (*location of action*)

...eseo ...에서 PP of, from

eseukeolleiteo 에스컬레이터 N escalator

etiket 에티켓 N etiquette

eukbakjireuda 윽박지르다 V to bully, browbeat

eukkaeda 으깨다 V to crush, smash

-(eu)l jul alda -(으)ㄹ 줄 알다 V to know how to

-(eu)l jul moreuda -(으)ㄹ 줄 모르다 V not know how to

-(eu)l su itda -(으)ㄹ 수 있다 ADJ can, be able to, be capable of

-(eu)l sudo itda -(으)ㄹ 수도 있다 ADJ could, might: **biga ol sudo itda** 비가 올 수도 있다 It could (*might*) rain

-(eu)l ttae -(으)ㄹ 때 N when, at the time

-(eu)l ttaekkaji -(으)ㄹ 때까지 PP until

-(eu)l ttaemada -(으)ㄹ 때마다 PP every time, whenever

-(eu)l/(eu)n/neun+(*object*) -(으)ㄹ/ (으)ㄴ/는+(사물) PP the object which

-(eu)l/(eu)n/neun+(*person*) -(으)ㄹ/ (으)ㄴ/는+(사람) PP the person who

...eul/reul ...을/를 PP (*object particle*)

E

...eul/reul geochyeoseo ...을/를 거쳐 서 v via

...eul/reul je.oehago ...을/를 제외하 고 v except

...eul/reul tonghayeo ...을/를 통하여 v through, past

...eul/reul tonghayeo ...을/를 통하여 v way, by way of

...eul/reul uisikhada ...을/를 의식하 다 v to be conscious of

...eul/reul wihan ...을/를 위한 ADJ for

eumak 음악 N music

eumban 음반 N record, a disc

eumchi 음치 N tone-deaf

eumhaehada 음해하다 v to malign, slander

eumji 음지 N shaded ground

eumju 음주 N drinking: **eumjuunjeo-neul hamyeon an doenda** 음주운전 을 하면 안 된다 Never drink and drive

eumnyo 음료 N drink, refreshment

eumnyosu 음료수 N soft drink

eumpyo 음표 N (*musical*) note

eumseong mesiji 음성 메시지 N voice mail

eumsik 음식 N food

eumsikjeom 음식점 N restaurant

eun 은 N silver

-(eu)n jeogi itda -(으)ㄴ 적이 있다 ADJ ever, to have done

...eun/neun ...은/는 PP as for, speaking of (*topic marker*)

-(eu)n/neun che hada -(으)ㄴ/는 체 하다 v to pretend

-(eu)n/neun/(eu)l+(*object*) -(으)ㄴ/는/ (으)ㄹ+ (사물) PP the object which

-(eu)n/neun/(eu)l+(*person*) -(으)ㄴ/ 는/(으)ㄹ+ (사람) PP the person who

eunbal 은발 N silver hair

eunchong 은총 N grace, (*divine*) blessing

euneo 은어 N slang

euneo 은어 N sweetfish

euneunhada 은은하다 ADJ delicate, soft, subdued

eungdap 응답 N answer, reply

eungdapada 응답하다 v to give an answer

eungeori 응어리 N lump: **banjuk eun-geori** 반죽 응어리 lumps in dough

eungeori 응어리 N resentment, bitterness (*deeply rooted*): **gaseume eun-**

georiga jida 가슴에 응어리가 지다 harbor ill feelings

eunggeup 응급 N emergency

eunggeupchiryo 응급치료 N first aid, emergency treatment

eunghada 응하다 v to comply with

eungjinghada 응징하다 v to chastise

eungseokburida 응석부리다 v to behave like a spoiled child

eungsihada 응시하다 v to apply for an examination

eungsihada 응시하다 v to fixate, gaze

eungwon 응원 N cheer

eungwondan 응원단 N cheerleading squad

eungwonhada 응원하다 v to cheer, root for, support

eunhaeng 은행 N bank (*finance*)

eunhye 은혜 N kindness, favor, grace: **bumonimui eunhye** 부모님의 은혜 debt to one's parents' love

eunin 은인 N a benefactor: **saeng-myeongui eunin** 생명의 은인 savior of one's life

eunmilhada 은밀하다 ADJ covert, furtive

eunnyeonjunge 은연중에 ADV tacitly, implicitly

eunpyehada 은폐하다 v to conceal, cover up

eunsaek 은색 N silver (*color*)

eunsincheo 은신처 N hideout

euntoe 은퇴 N retirement

-(eu)reo -(으)러 PP in order to

eureumjang 으름장 N threat, intimidation

eureureonggeorida 으르렁거리다 v to fight, quarrel

eureureonggeorida 으르렁거리다 v to snarl, growl, roar

eurieurihada 으리으리하다 ADJ magnificent, grand

...(eu)ro ...(으)로 PP toward, to (*direction*)

...(eu)ro ...(으)로 PP with (*by means of*)

...(eu)ro boida ...(으)로 보이다 v to look, seem, appear

...(eu)ro hyanghada ...(으)로 향하다 v to head for, toward

eurye 의례 ADJ ritual, phatic, formality: **gungmin eurye** 국민 의례 The Pledge of Allegiance

-(eu)ryeogo hada -(으)려고 하다 v to intend, mean

euseudaeda 으스대다 v to swagger, show off, boast

euseuseuhada 으스스하다 ADJ ghostly, spooky

-(eu)seyo -(으)세요 (*honorific polite ending*): **anjuseyo** 앉으세요 Have a seat (*please*)

eusseukgeorida 으쓱거리다 v to strut, shrug

eutteum 으뜸 N the best, the top: **eutteum ganeun hakgyo** 으뜸 가는 학교 the best of schools

ewossada 에워싸다 v to surround, enclose

G

ga.eul 가을 N autumn, fall

...ga/i ...가/이 PP (*subject marker*)

-ga/i eopda/eomneun -가/이 없다/없는 ADJ lacking, missing

ga bonjeogi itda 가 본적이 있다 v to have been to somewhere

gabal 가발 N wig

gabang 가방 N bag

gaboda 가보다 v to go around, visit

gabyeopda, gabyeo.un 가볍다, 가벼운 ADJ light (*not heavy/severe*)

gachi 가치 N value, good

gachida 갇히다 v to be locked in

gachi gada 같이 가다 v to accompany

gachi itda 가치 있다 ADJ to be worth

gachulhada 가출하다 v to run away from home

gada 가다 v to go

gadadeumda 가다듬다 v to clear one's throat, catch one's breath: **moksorireul gadadeumda** 목소리를 가다 듬다 clear one's throat; **hoheubeul gadadeumda** 호흡을 가다듬다 catch one's breath

gadadeumda 가다듬다 v to fix, adjust (*clothes*): **ot maemusaereul gadadeumda** 옷 매무새를 가다듬다 straighten one's dress

gadadeumda 가다듬다 v to pull oneself together: **jeongsineul gadadeumda** 정신을 가다듬다 calm oneself down

gadeuk chada 가득 차다 v to be full

gadeuk chan 가득 찬 ADJ filled, full

gadak 가닥 N strand, yarn, string: **sil han gadak** 실 한 가닥 a piece of string

gadeukhada 가득하다 ADJ brimful

gaduda 가두다 v to cage in, shut in, lock in

...gae ...개 N item, piece (*counting unit*): **chokollet du gae** 초콜렛 두 개 two pieces of chocolate

gae 개 N dog

gaein 개인 N individual

gaein(ui) 개인의 ADJ individual, personal, private: **gaeinui jaesan** 개인의 재산 a personal asset; **gaeinui jayu** 개인의 자유 the freedom of the individual; **gaein gyeongyeong** 개인 경영 a private enterprise

gaeksil 객실 N room, cabin (*hotel/boat*)

gage 가게 N shop, store

gageum(nyu) 가금(류) N poultry

gagu 가구 N furniture

gagyebu 가계부 N household account book

gagyeok 가격 N price, value (*cost*)

gagyeyak 가계약 N provisional contract

gaideu 가이드 N guide, lead

gaiphada 가입하다 v to join, go along

gajang 가장 ADV most (*superlative*)

gajang 가장 N head of household, breadwinner: **sonyeon sonyeo gajang** 소년 소녀 가장 a child-headed household

gajang 가장 N disguise: **jeokguneuro gajanghada** 적군으로 가장하다 disguise oneself as an enemy

gajang nappeuda/nappeun 가장 나쁘다/나쁜 ADJ worst

gajangjari 가장자리 N border, edge

gajeonghada 가정하다 v to suppose

gajeonjepum 가전제품 N electric home appliances

gajeungseureopda 가증스럽다 ADJ despicable, detestable

gaji 가지 N branch (*of tree*): **gajireul kkeokda** 가지를 꺾다 break a branch

gaji 가지 N eggplant, aubergine

gaji 가지 N kind (of), sort (of), variety (of): **yeoreogajiui chaek** 여러가지의 책 various kinds of books

gajida 가지다 v to have, take, hold

gajigo nolda 가지고 놀다 v to play around

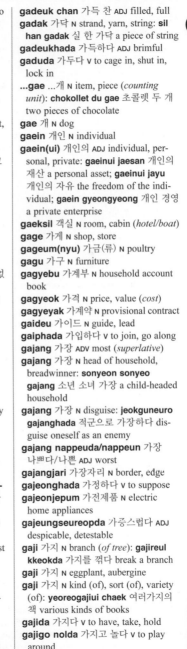

G

gajireonhi 가지런히 ADV uniformly, neatly: **gajireonhi noyeoinneun sinbal** 가지런히 놓여있는 신발 neatly placed shoes

gajjaida, gajja(ui) 가짜이다, 가짜(의) ADJ fake, false (*imitation*)

gajok 가족 N family

gajuk 가죽 N leather

gajyeo.oda 가져오다 V to bring, fetch, carry

gajyeogada 가져가다 V to carry

gajyeogada 가져가다 V to take, remove

gakbyeolhada 각별하다 ADJ particular, especial: **gakbyeolhan sai** 각별한 사이 a(n) (*extra*) special relationship

gakbyeolhi 각별히 ADV particularly

gakdo 각도 N angle

gakgakui 각각의 ADJ each, every, separate

...gakkai(e) ...가까이(에) ADV around, nearby

gakkaseuro 가까스로 ADV barely, narrowly: **ireul gakkaseuro kkeunnaeda** 일을 가까스로 끝내다 barely finished work

gakkaun geori 가까운 거리 ADJ, N a stone throw, short distance

gakkawojida 가까워지다 V to approach, near, closer (*time*): **gyeolmare gakkawojida** 결말에 가까워지다 draw to an end

gakkawojida 가까워지다 V to approach, near, closer (*distance*): **mokjeokjie gakkawojida** 목적지에 가까워지다 get near to the destination

gakkawojida 가까워지다 V to become intimate with, friends with, close with: **seoro gakkawojida** 서로 가까워지다 become intimate with each other

gakkeum 가끔 ADV sometimes, from time to time, occasionally

gakkuda 가꾸다 V to cultivate, grow, raise: **kkocheul gakkuda** 꽃을 가꾸다 grow flowers

gakkuda 가꾸다 V to improve one's appearance: **mommaereul gakkuda** 몸매를 가꾸다 get oneself into shape

gakkuda 가꾸다 V to tend, decorate: **jip baneul jal gakkuda** 집 안을 잘 가꾸다 decorate one's house

galbi 갈비 N rib: **yangnyeom galbi** 양념 갈비 marinated rib

galgu 갈구 N thirst, craving

galguhada 갈구하다 V to long for, thirst for

galgyeosseuda 갈겨쓰다 V to scribble

gallanota 갈라놓다 V to divide, split, pull apart

gallaseoda 갈라서다 V to break up, divorce: **gyeolhonhan ji ilnyeon mane gallaseotda** 결혼한 지 1년 만에 갈라섰다 divorced after a year of marriage

gallimgil 갈림길 N forked road, crossroad: **saengsaui gallimgire seoda** 생사의 갈림길에 서다 hover between life and death

galmaegi 갈매기 N (*sea*) gull

galsaek 갈색 N brown

galsaekui 갈색의 ADJ brown

gamanduda 가만두다 V to leave alone: **geureul gamanduji anketda** 그를 가만두지 않겠다 I won't leave him alone. I'll give it to him

gamang 가망 N hope, probability: **wankwaedoel gamangi eopda** 완쾌될 가망이 없다 no hope for full recovery

gamanhi 가만히 ADV still, calmly: **gamanhi anjaitda** 가만히 앉아있다 sit still

gamanitda 가만있다 V to remain still

gamdanghada 감당하다 V to cope with, handle

gamdonghada 감동하다 V to be touched by, be moved

gamgagi eopda/eomneun 감각이 없다/없는 ADJ numb

gamgeum 감금 N imprisonment

gamgeumhada 감금하다 V to imprison

gamgi 감기 N cold, flu

gamgyullyu 감귤류 N citrus

gamja 감자 N potato

gamjeong 감정 N emotion

gamjeong 감정 N appraisal, valuation

gamok 감옥 N jail, prison

gamsahada 감사하다 V to thank

gamsahamnida! 감사합니다! PHR thank you!

gamtanhada 감탄하다 V to admire

gamujapjapada 가무잡잡하다 ADJ tanned: **gamujapjapan pibu** 가무잡잡한 피부 tanned skin

gamum 가뭄 N drought

gamun 가문 N one's family (*clan*)

gamuseureumhada 가무스름하다 ADJ darkish

gamyeomsikida 감염시키다 V to infect

gamyeon 가면 N mask

gamyeong 가명 N false name, assumed name

gan 간 N liver: **gane gibyeoldo an gada** 간에 기별도 안 가다 barely begin to satisfy one's hunger

gan 간 N salt seasoning: **gani matda** 간이 맞다 be well-seasoned

gananhada, gananhan 가난하다, 가난한 ADJ poor

ganboda 간보다 V to taste (*to see if it's properly seasoned*)

gancheop 간첩 N spy

gandanhada, gandanhan 간단하다, 간단한 ADJ brief, short, simple

ganeudarata, ganeudaran 가느다랗다, 가느다란 ADJ slender

ganeum 가늠 N guesstimate

ganeumhada 가늠하다 V to guesstimate, judge

ganeun gire 가는 길에 ADV on the way

ganeunghada, ganeunghan 가능하다, 가능한 ADJ possible

ganeungseong 가능성 N possibility

ganeungwimeokda 가는귀먹다 V (*amblyacousia*) to be hard of hearing

gang 강 N river

gang.ui 강의 N lecture, classes (*at university*)

gang.yohada 강요하다 V to force, compel

gangcheol 강철 N steel

gangdo, doduk 강도, 도둑 N burglar

gangmak 각막 N cornea

gangmok 각목 N lumber

gangnangkong 강낭콩 N kidney beans

gangsa 강사 N lecturer (*at university*)

gangu 간구 N earnest request

ganguhada 간구하다 V to beg, entreat

gangwa 간과 N failure to notice

gangwahada 간과하다 V to disregard, overlook: **jageun silsudo gangwahaji aneul geotsida** 작은 실수도 간과하지 않을 것이다 won't overlook even a small mistake

ganho 간호 N nursing, care

ganhohada 간호하다 V to nurse, care for

ganhok 간혹 N occasionally

ganhosa 간호사 N nurse

ganjang 간장 N soy sauce

ganjeolhada 간절하다 ADJ earnest, eager

ganjeolhi 간절히 ADV desperately, eagerly

ganjikhada 간직하다 V to cherish, preserve

ganjireom 간지럼 N tickle: **ganjireom-eul tada** 간지럼을 타다 be ticklish

ganjireopda 간지럽다 ADJ feeling ticklish

gannyeom 간염 N hepatitis

ganpan 간판 N signboard

gansinhi 간신히 ADV barely, hardly: **ireul gansinhi kkeunmachida** 일을 간신히 끝마치다 barely finished one's work

ganyalpeuda 가냘프다 ADJ feeble, slender

gap 값 N cost, price

gapareuda 가파르다 ADJ steep, sharp: **gapareun jeolbyeok** 가파른 절벽 a steep cliff

gapjagi 갑자기 ADV suddenly

gappunhada 가뿐하다 ADJ easy, light

garaanda 가라앉다 V to feel down: **gibuni garaanda** 기분이 가라앉다 feeling down

garaanda 가라앉다 V to sink, go under: **baega garaanjatda** 배가 가라앉았다 the boat has sunk

garaanda 가라앉다 V to subside, calm down: **pokpungi garaanjatda** 폭풍이 가라앉았다 the storm has died down

garae 가래 N phlegm, sputum: **moge garaega kkeulta** 목에 가래가 끓다 have phlegm in one's throat

garaipda 갈아입다 V to change, switch (*clothes*)

garangbi 가랑비 N drizzle, mist: **garangbie ot jeonneun jul moreunda** 가랑비에 옷 젖는 줄 모른다 Many drops make a flood

garatada 갈아타다 V to transfer: **beoseueseo jihacheollo garatada** 버스에서 지하철로 갈아타다 transfer to subway train from a bus

gareuchida 가르치다 V to teach

gareuda 가르다 V to split, divide

gareumaareultada 가르마를 타다 V to part one's hair

G

garida 가리다 v to hide, conceal: **hyungteoreul garida** 흉터를 가리다 cover a scar

garikida 가리키다 v to point to (at): **mokjeokjireul garikida** 목적지를 가리키다 point at a destination

garo 가로 N width, breadth

garochaeda 가로채다 v to snatch, steal, intercept: **gongeul garochaeda** 공을 가로채다 intercept a ball

garochaeida 가로채이다 v to get seized, be snatched

garodeung 가로등 N street light

garojireuda 가로지르다 v to cross, cut across: **gireul garojilleogada** 길을 가로질러가다 cut across the street

garomakda 가로막다 v to interrupt, obstruct, block

garomakhida 가로막히다 v to be obstructed, be blocked

garosu 가로수 N roadside tree

garu 가루 N powder

garyeonaeda 가려내다 v to sort out, assort, classify: **gajjareul garyeonaeda** 가짜를 가려내다 sort out an imitation

garyeonhada 가련하다 ADJ piteous

garyeopda 가렵다 ADJ itchy, itching

gaseum 가슴 N chest (breast)

gasik 가식 N affectation, pretense

gasollin 가솔린 N gasoline

gasoropda 가소롭다 ADJ laughable

gasu 가수 N singer

gatda, gateun 같다, 같은 ADJ equal, identical, same, alike

gatteunhada 가뜬하다 ADJ light, casual

gatteunhi 가뜬히 ADV lightly

gaunde 가운데 N middle, center

gawi 가위 N scissors

ge 게 N crab

-ge -게 PP (adverbial suffix)

-ge boida -게 보이다 v to look, seem, appear

-ge hada -게 하다 v to let, allow

ge.eureuda, ge.eureun 게으르다, 게으른 ADJ lazy

gedaga 게다가 ADV besides, in addition

geim 게임 N game

geo.i 거의 ADV almost, nearly

geo.i -ji anta 거의 -지 않다 ADV hardly, rarely, seldom

geo.i eopda/eomneun 거의 없다/없는 ADJ few, little, almost none

geo.in 거인 N giant

geo.ul 거울 N mirror

geobuk 거북 N turtle (land)

geochilda, geochin 거칠다, 거친 ADJ rough, wild

geodaehada, geodaehan 거대하다, 거대한 ADJ huge

geogi 거기 PRON there

geojeol 거절 N refusal

geojeolhada 거절하다 v to decline, refuse, reject

geojinmalhada 거짓말하다 v to lie, tell a falsehood

geojisida, geojit(ui) 거짓이다, 거짓(의) ADJ false (not true)

geokjeonghada 걱정하다 v to worry

geokkuroui 거꾸로의 ADJ reversed, backwards

geolda 걸다 ADJ foul-mouthed, be rough in speech: **ibi geolda** 입이 걸다 have a nasty tongue

geolda 걸다 v to hang: **byeoge geurimeul geolda** 벽에 그림을 걸다 hang a picture on the wall

geolda 걸다 v to make a wager: **jaesaneul geolda** 재산을 걸다 stake one's fortune on something

geolda 걸다 v to initiate, strike up a conversation: **mareul geolda** 말을 걸다 initiate a conversation

geolsang 걸상 N stool, chair

geommeokda 겁먹다 v to be scared, frightened

geommeogeun 겁먹은 ADJ frightened: **geommeogeun ai** 겁먹은 아이 a frightened child

geomsahada 검사하다 v to test

geomtohada 검토하다 v to examine

geon.ganghada, geon.ganghan 건강하다, 건강한 ADJ healthy: **sinchejeogeuro geonganghada** 신체적으로 건강하다 be in good physical health; **geongang sikpum** 건강 식품 health foods

geonbae! 건배! INTERJ cheers!

geonchuk 건축 N architecture

geonjohada, geonjohan 건조하다, 건조한 ADJ dry (humidity): **geonjohan gwail** 건조한 과일 dried fruit

geonneoda 건너다 v to cross, go over:

gireul geonneoda 길을 건너다 cross the street

geonneopyeone 건너편에 ADV across from

geonneoseo 건너서 PP across

georaehada 거래하다 V to trade, exchange

georeoseo 걸어서 ADV on foot: **georeoseo gada** 걸어서 가다 go on foot; **georeoseo hakgyoe gada** 걸어서 학교에 가다 walk to school

geori 거리 N distance

geori 거리 N street

georonhada 거론하다 V to bring up (topic), mention

geotda 걷다 V to walk: **gireul geotda** 길을 걷다 walk along the street

geowi 거위 N goose

-get- -겠- may, would (conjecture)

geu 그 PRON he, him

geu.ui 그의 ADJ his

geu (geot) 그(것) PRON that (near listener)

geu dong.an 그 동안 N meanwhile

geu hu 그 후 N afterwards, then

geu isang 그 이상 N further, additional

geu yeoja 그 여자 PRON she

geu yeoja-ui 그 여자의 ADJ her

geu yeoja.ui (geot) 그 여자의 (것) N her (hers)

geubakke 그밖에 ADV else, anything else

geudeul 그들 PRON they, them

geudeurui (geot) 그들의 (것) N their (theirs)

geujeokke 그저께 N day before yesterday

geukdoro 극도로 ADV extremely

geukjang 극장 N theater (drama)

geuljja 글자 N character (written)

geum 금 N gold

geumaek 금액 N amount

geumanduda 그만두다 V to stop, cease, quit

geumanduseyo! 그만두세요! PHR stop it!

geumhada 금하다 V to forbid

geumi gada 금이 가다 V to crack, split, fracture: **ppyeoe geumi gada** 뼈에 금이 가다 have a fracture on a bone

geumi gan 금이 간 ADJ cracked: **geumi gan kkotbyeong** 금이 간 꽃병 a cracked vase

geumjidoeda 금지되다 V to be forbidden, prohibited, restricted: **beobeuro geumjidoeda** 법으로 금지되다 be prohibited by law

geumjidoen 금지된 ADJ forbidden

geumsok 금속 N metal

geumul 그물 N net

geumyoil 금요일 N Friday

geun.geo 근거 N basis: **geungeo eomneun** 근거 없는 baseless, groundless

geuncheoe 근처에 ADV around here, nearby

geuneul 그늘 N shade

geunmyeonhan 근면한 ADJ hardworking, industrious

geunyuk 근육 N muscle

geuraedo 그래도 ADV nevertheless

geuraeseo 그래서 ADV so, therefore, thus

geureochi aneumyeon 그렇지 않으면 ADV or else, otherwise

geureochiman 그렇지만 ADV but, however (conjunction)

geureoji maseyo! 그러지 마세요! PHR don't do that!

geureoke haseyo 그렇게 하세요 PHR please do so (go ahead)

geureomeuro 그러므로 ADV therefore

geureomyeon 그러면 ADV then

geureomyo! 그럼요! INTERJ indeed!

geureon 그런 ADV such

geureona 그러나 ADV however, but

geureonde 그런데 ADV by the way

geurida 그리다 V to draw, paint (a painting)

geurigo 그리고 ADV and

geurim 그림 N picture, drawing, painting

geurimja 그림자 N shadow

geuriwohada 그리워하다 V to miss (loved one)

geurup 그룹 N group

geuttae 그때 N then

-gi -기 N (nominalizer)

-gi jeone -기 전에 ADV before -ing

-gi sijakhada -기 시작하다 V begin to

-gi ttaemune -기 때문에 ADV because, since

-gi wihaeseo -기 위해서 ADV in order that, so that

gi.eok 기억 N memories

gi.eokhada 기억하다 V to remember

G

gibonjeogida, gibonjeogin 기본적이다, 기본적인 ADJ basic

gibun 기분 N mood

gibun jota/jo.eun 기분 좋다/좋은 ADJ pleasant

gibuni sanghada 기분이 상하다 v to be offended, displeased

gibun sanghagehada 기분 상하게 하다 v to offend

gibuni sanghan 기분이 상한 ADJ upset, unhappy

gicha 기차 N train

gicharo 기차로 ADV by rail

gichim 기침 N cough

gichimhada 기침하다 v to cough

gicho 기초 N base, foundation, bottom

gidaehada 기대하다 v to expect

gidarida 기다리다 v to wait for

gidohada 기도하다 v to pray

gidokgyo 기독교 N Christianity

gidokgyosinja 기독교신자 N Christian

gidomun 기도문 N prayer: **jugidomun** 주기도문 The Lord's Prayer

gidung 기둥 N post, column

gigan 기간 N period (*of time*)

gigeum 기금 N funds, funding

gigeun 기근 N famine

gigye 기계 N machine

gigyeryu 기계류 N machinery

gihoe 기회 N chance, opportunity

gihu 기후 N climate

gija 기자 N reporter

gilda, gin 길다, 긴 ADJ long (*length*)

gildeuryeojida 길들여지다 v to be accustomed to, to be trained

gildeuryeojin 길들여진 ADJ tame

gin.geuphada, gin.geupan 긴급하다, 긴급한 ADJ urgent

ginjang.eul pulda 긴장을 풀다 v to relax

ginjanghada 긴장하다 v to become tense

ginjanghan 긴장한 ADJ tense

ginyeommul 기념물 N monument

ginyeompum 기념품 N souvenir

gipda, gipeun 깊다, 깊은 ADJ deep: **gipeun umul** 깊은 우물 a deep well

gipda, gipeun 깊다, 깊은 ADJ remote: **gipeun san sok** 깊은 산 속 a remote mountain

gipda, gipeun 깊다, 깊은 ADJ pro-

found: **gipeun tteut** 깊은 뜻 a deep (*profound*) meaning

gipda, gipeun 깊다, 깊은 ADJ considerate: **sogi gipeun saram** 속이 깊은 사람 a thoughtful person, a man of prudence

gippal 깃발 N flag

gippeuda, gippeohada 기쁘다, 기뻐하다 v to be pleased

gippeum 기쁨 N joy

gippeun 기쁜 ADJ glad

gireul ilta 길을 잃다 v to get lost (*can't find way*)

gireum 기름 N oil

giri 길이 N length

-giro hada -기로 하다 v to agree to do something

-giro hada -기로 하다 v to decide to, set

gisa 기사 N article (*in newspaper*): **gisareul sseuda** 기사를 쓰다 write an article

gisa 기사 N engineer: **jeongi gisa** 전기 기사 an electrical engineer

gisa 기사 N knight: **gabot nibeun gisa** 갑옷 입은 기사 a knight in armor

...go hada ....고 하다 v that (*introducing a quotation*)

-go itda -고 있다 v be -ing

-go naseo -고 ADV after -ing

-go sipda -고 싶다 ADJ want to

goa 고아 N orphan

goche 고체 N solid

gochida 고치다 v to correct: **danjeomeul gochida** 단점을 고치다 correct one's shortcomings

gochida 고치다 v to fix, repair, mend: **keompyuteoreul gochida** 컴퓨터를 고치다 fix a computer

gochu 고추 N chilli pepper

gochujang 고추장 N chilli paste

godae(ui) 고대(의) ADJ ancient

gogi 고기 N meat

gogi japda 고기 잡다 v to fish

gogi wanja 고기 완자 N meatball

gohwan 고환 N testicles

gojangnada 고장나다 v to break down (*car, machine*)

gojangnan 고장난 ADJ out of order, broken

gojip sen 고집 센 ADJ stubborn, determined

G

goksik 곡식 N grain

golchi apeun 골치 아픈 ADJ troublesome, annoying, causing a headache

golmokgil 골목길 N alley, lane

golpeu 골프 N golf

golttongpum 골동품 N antiques

gomapda, gomaun 고맙다, 고마운 ADJ grateful

gomapdago jeonhada 고맙다고 전하다 PHR to say thank you

gompang.i 곰팡이 N fungus

gomu 고무 N rubber

gong 공 N ball

gong 공 NUM zero

gong.won 공원 N gardens, park

gong.ye 공예 N crafts

gong.yega 공예가 N craftsman

gongbuhada 공부하다 V to study, learn

gongchaek 공책 N notebook

gonggan 공간 N room, space

gonggeuphada 공급하다 V to provide

gonggi 공기 N air

gonggong(ui) 공공(의) ADJ public

gonggyeok 공격 N attack (*in war*), assault

gonghang 공항 N airport

gongjang 공장 N factory

gongjeonghada/-han 공정하다/-한 ADJ just, fair

gongmul 곡물 N grain, cereal

gongmuwon 공무원 N officials (*government*)

gongsanghada 공상하다 V to daydream

gongsik(ui) 공식(의) ADJ official, formal

gongsonhada, gongsonhan 공손하다, 공손한 ADJ polite

gongteo 공터 N field, empty space

-gonhaetda -곤했다 V used to do something: **urineun noraereul bureugon haetda** 우리는 노래를 부르곤 했다 we used to sing

goreuda 고르다 V to select

gosohada 고소하다 V to accuse, file a lawsuit: **sagijoero gosohada** 사기죄로 고소하다 accuse sb of fraud

gosohada 고소하다 V to gloat over (*somebody's misfortune*)

gosohada 고소하다 PHR that serves you right!

gosohada 고소하다 ADJ savory aroma, tasty flavor: **kkae bongneun naemsaega gosohada** 깨 볶는 냄새가 고소하다 The smell of roasting sesame seeds is aromatic

gosokdoro 고속도로 N highway

got 곧 ADV at once, immediately, soon

got hoebokhaseyo! 곧 회복하세요! PHR get well soon!

gotong 고통 N suffering

goyang.i 고양이 N cat

goyohada, goyohan 고요하다, 고요한 ADJ silent, still, quiet, calm

goyonghada 고용하다 V to employ, hire: **jigwoneul goyonghada** 직원을 고용하다 hire an employee

goyongju 고용주 N employer

gu 구 NUM nine: **gubunui il** 구분의 일 one ninth

gu 구 N district, borough: **jibang gu** 지방 구 provincial town, **yongsangu** 용산구 Yongsan-gu district

gu 구 N phrase

gugyeonghada 구경하다 V to watch (*show, movie*)

gujohada 구조하다 V to rescue

guk 국 N broth, soup

gukga 국가 N nation, country

gukga(ui) 국가(의) ADJ national

gukhoe 국회 N parliament

gukja 국자 N dipper, ladle

gukjejeogida, gukje(jeogin) 국제적이다, 국제(적인) ADJ international

gukjeok 국적 N nationality

guksu 국수 N noodles

gul 굴 N oyster

gumeong 구멍 N hole

gundae 군대 N troops

gung 궁 N palace: **deoksugung** 덕수궁 Deoksu Palace

gunin 군인 N soldier

gunsa(ui) 군사(의) ADJ military

gupda 굽다 V to bake, roast, grill: **kukireul gupda** 쿠키를 굽다 bake cookies

guri 구리 N copper

guwol 구월 N September

gwa 과 N chapter, lesson: **sibigwa** 12과 chapter 12

gwa 과 N department

...gwa/wa ...과/와 CONJ, PP and

gwabu 과부 N widow

G

gwaenchanayo! 괜찮아요! PHR don't mention it!, you're welcome! It's alright!

gwaenchanta 괜찮다 ADV okay

gwahak 과학 N science

gwail 과일 N fruit

gwaja 과자 N confectionery, biscuit, cookie, cracker

gwallichaegimja 관리책임자 N manager (*person in charge*)

gwallyeondoeda/-doen 관련되다/-된 V to involve

gwan.gwanggaek 관광객 N tourist

gwan.gye 관계 N relationship

gwangjang 광장 N square, town square

gwanse 관세 N duty (*import tax*)

gwanseup 관습 N custom, tradition

gwansimi itda/inneun 관심이 있다/ 있는 V to be interested in

gwi 귀 N ear

gwibin 귀빈 N guest of honor

gwiga meogeun 귀가 먹은 ADJ deaf

gwiga meokda 귀가 먹다 V to become deaf

gwigeori 귀걸이 N earrings

gwihage yeogida 귀하게 여기다 V to value

gwijunghada, gwijunghan 귀중하다, 귀중한 ADJ precious

gwisin 귀신 N ghost

gwiyeopda, gwiyeo.un 귀엽다, 귀여 운 ADJ cute

gwolli 권리 N rights

gwonhan 권한 N authority (*power*): **gwonhani itda** 권한이 있다 have the right to (*do*); **gwonhaneul buyeohada** 권한을 부여하다 give sb the authority to (*do*)

gyedan 계단 N stairs, steps

gyegeup 계급 N rank, class

gyegok 계곡 N valley

gyehoek 계획 N plan

gyehoekhada 계획하다 V to plan

gyejeol 계절 N season

gyeo.u 겨우 ADV barely

gyeo.ul 겨울 N winter

gyeokda 겪다 V to suffer, undergo

gyeolbaekhada, gyeolbaekan 결백 하다, 결백한 ADJ innocent

gyeolgwa 결과 N effect, result

gyeolgwaroseo 결과로서 ADV resulting from, as a result

gyeolham 결함 N defect: **sinchejeok gyeolham** 신체적 결함 a physical defect; **seonggyeokjeok gyeolham** 성격적 결함 flaws in character

gyeolhonhada 결혼하다 V to marry, get married

gyeolhonhada/-han 결혼하다/-한 V to get married

gyeolhonsik 결혼식 N wedding ceremony

gyeoljjeong 결정 N decision

gyeoljjeonghada 결정하다 V to decide

gyeolko -ji anta 결코 -지 않다 ADJ never

gyeolko ...anida 결코 ...아니다 ADJ never

gyeolseokan 결석한 ADJ absent (*from school*)

gyeolseokhada 결석하다 V to miss, cut (*a class*)

gyeonbon 견본 N sample

gyeong.u 경우 N case

gyeongchal 경찰 N police

gyeongchalgwan 경찰관 N police officer

gyeongchalseo 경찰서 N police station

gyeongchi 경치 N scenery, view

gyeonggijang 경기장 N stadium, sports arena

gyeonggireulhada 경기를 하다 V to play (*a game*)

gyeonggo 경고 N warning

gyeonggohada 경고하다 V to warn

gyeonggye 경계 N boundary, border (*between countries*)

gyeongheom 경험 N experience

gyeongheomhada 경험하다 V to experience

gyeonghohada 경호하다 V to watch over, guard

gyeongjaeng 경쟁 N competition

gyeongjaenghada 경쟁하다 V to compete

gyeongjaengsangdae 경쟁상대 N rival

gyeongje 경제 N economy

gyeongjejeogida/-jeogin 경제적이다/ -적인 ADJ economical: **gyeongjejeogin seungyongcha** 경제적인 승용차 an economical vehicle

gyeongmaehada 경매하다 V to auction

gyeongmaero pallida 경매로 팔리다 V to be auctioned off

gyeongnyeohada 격려하다 v to encourage

gyeongnyeok 경력 N career, work experience

gyeongsa 경사 N slope

gyeongsa 경사 N happy occasion: **jibane gyeongsaga natda** 집안에 경사가 났다 The family has an occasion to celebrate

gyeran 계란 N egg

gyesan.gi 계산기 N calculator

gyesanhada 계산하다 v to calculate

gyesanseo 계산서 N bill

gyesokhada 계속하다 v to continue

gyocha(ro) 교차(로) N intersection

gyohoe 교회 N church

gyohwanhada 교환하다 v to exchange (*money, opinions*)

gyosu 교수 N professor, lecturer

gyotong 교통 N traffic

gyoyuk 교육 N education

gyoyukhada 교육하다 v to educate

gyuchik 규칙 N rules

H

habansin 하반신 N lower (*half of the*) body

hada 하다 v to do, perform an action: **gongbuhada** 공부하다 to study; **ilhada** 일하다 to work

hadeudiseukeu 하드디스크 N hard disk

hae 해 N harm: **haereul kkichida** 해를 끼치다 do harm

hae 해 N the sun: **haega jigi jeon** 해가 지기 전 before sunset

hae.oe(ui) 해외(의) ADJ overseas: **haeoe sijang** 해외 시장 overseas market; **haeoe yeohaeng** 해외 여행 overseas travel

hae.oe.e(seo) 해외에(서) ADV abroad: **haeoeeseo geunmuhada** 해외에서 근무하다 work abroad

haebaragi 해바라기 N sunflower

haeboda 해보다 v to try: **ireul haeboda** 일을 해보다 try a job

haebyeon 해변 N the seashore

haebyeong 해병 N marine

haedoji 해돋이 N sunrise

haedong 해동 N thaw

haegohada 해고하다 v to fire, dismiss, terminate (*job*): **jongeobwoneul haegohada** 종업원을 해고하다 dismiss an employee

haegyeolhada 해결하다 v to resolve, solve: **munjereul haegyeolhada** 문제를 해결하다 solve a problem

haehyeop 해협 N strait: **daehan haehyeop** 대한 해협 the Korea Strait

haemul 해물 N seafood: **haemul japtang** 해물 잡탕 seafood medley; **haemul yori** 해물 요리 seafood plate

haendeupon 핸드폰 N cell phone, mobile phone: **haendeuponeuro yeollakhae boseyo** 핸드폰으로 연락해 보세 요 try calling her (*his*) cell phone

haeng.uneul bimnida! 행운을 빕니 다! PHR good luck!

haengbangbulmyeongdeon 행방불 명된 ADJ go missing (*person*): **haengbangbulmyeongdoen sonyeo** 행방불명된 소녀 a missing girl

haengbok 행복 N happiness

haengbokhada, haengbokan 행복 하다, 행복한 ADJ happy: **deo eopsi haengbokhada** 더 없이 행복하다 be as happy as can be; **haengbokhan gyeolhon** 행복한 결혼 a happy marriage

haengdong 행동 N action: **danche haengdong** 단체 행동 group action

haenghada 행하다 v to act, do, conduct: **seoneul haenghada** 선을 행하다 practice virtue; **uisigeul haenghada** 의식을 행하다 conduct a ceremony

haengin 행인 N pedestrian

haengsa 행사 N event: **yeonjung haengsa** 연중 행사 annual functions

haengseong 행성 N planet

haengwi 행위 N act, deed

haeppit 햇빛 N sunlight: **haetbicheul boji motada** 햇빛을 보지 못하다 keep indoors

haeropda, haero.un 해롭다, 해로운 ADJ harmful: **nune haeropda** 눈에 해 롭다 bad for one's eyes; **haeroun hwangyeong** 해로운 환경 a harmful environment

haesuyok 해수욕 v to swim in the sea: **haesuyogeul jeulgida** 해수욕을 즐기 다 have a dip in the ocean

haetsal 햇살 N sunbeams

H

hageup 하급 N lower class

hagoupsaeng 하급생 N underclassman

...hago ...하고 PREP with (*along*): **chinguhago yeohaengeul gada** 친구하고 여행을 갔다 go on a trip with a friend

hagwon 학원 N private school, (*educational*) institute

hain 하인 N servant: **hain burideut hada** 하인 부리듯 하다 treat sb like a servant

hakbeol 학벌 N academic clique

hakgyo 학교 N school: **godeunghakgyo** 고등학교 (*senior*) high school

haksaeng 학생 N student

halmeoni 할머니 N grandmother

haltta 핥다 V to lick: **jeopsireul halda** 접시를 핥다 lick a plate

hama 하마 N hippopotamus

hamateomyeon 하마터면 ADV almost, nearly: **hamateomyeon keunillal ppeon haetda** 하마터면 큰일날 뻔 했다 something bad almost happened

hambangnun 함박눈 N big snowflakes

hamchuk 함축 N implication

hamkke 함께 ADV together

hamnijeogida/-jeogin 합리적이다/ -적인 ADJ reasonable, rational: **hamnijeogin seontaek** 합리적인 선택 a rational choice

hamnyu 합류 N integration

hamnyuhada 합류하다 V to integrate, join

hamulmyeo 하물며 ADV even less, much less

han ssang 한 쌍 N a pair of: **han ssangui yeonin** 한 쌍의 연인 a pair of lovers

han.gugeo 한국어 N Korean (*language*)

han.guk saram 한국 사람 N Korean (*nationality*)

hana 하나 NUM one: **dul jung hana** 둘 중 하나 one of the two

hana deo 하나 더 ADV one more, another

hanbamjjung 한밤중 N midnight: **hanbamjjungkkaji** 한밤중까지 far into the night

hanbok 한복 N hanbok, Korean dress

haneul 하늘 N sky: **pureun haneul** 푸른 하늘 blue sky

haneulgeorida 하늘거리다 V to sway, swing

haneunim 하나님 N God: **hananimui**

eunhye 하나님의 은혜 the grace of God

hang.uihada 항의하다 V to protest, complain

hangaropda 한가롭다 ADJ be free, have nothing to do

hangbok 항복 N surrender

hanggong 항공 N aviation, flying

hanggong.upyeon 항공우편 N airmail

hanggonggi 항공기 N airplane, plane

hanggongsa 항공사 N airline companies

hanggu 항구 N harbor, port

hanghaehada 항해하다 V to sail

hangmun 항문 N anus

hangnyeok 학력 N academic background

hangsang 항상 ADV always

hanguk 한국 N Korea: **hanguk jeonjaeng** 한국 전쟁 Korean War

hangye 한계 N limit

hanji 한지 N (*traditional*) Korean paper

hanji 한지 N cold area, cold region

hannyak 한약 N oriental (*herb*) medicine

hansimhada 한심하다 ADJ pathetic

...hante ...한테 PP to, at, for, by (*a person*): **chinguhante hwareul naeda** 친구한테 화를 내다 be angry at a friend; **gaehante doreul deonjida** 개한테 돌을 던지다 throw a stone at a dog

...hanteseo ...한테서 PP from, of, through: **chinguhanteseo on pyeonji** 친구한테서 온 편지 a letter from a friend: **jigwonhanteseo sosigeul deutda** 직원한테서 소식을 듣다 hear news from an employee

hanyeo 하녀 N maid, maidservant

hapbeopjeogida, hapbeopjeogin 합법적이다, 합법적인 ADJ legal, legitimate: **hapbeopjeok jeongbu** 합법적 정부 a legitimate government

hapchi 합치 N agreement, coincidence

hapchida 합치다 V to combine, unite: **himeul hapchida** 힘을 합치다 join forces

hapdang 합당 N merger of political parties

hapgye 합계 N total: **hapgyereul naeda** 합계를 내다 do the sum (*of*)

hapgyeokhada 합격하다 V to pass

(*exam*): **usuhan seongjeogeuro hapgyeokhada** 우수한 성적으로 합격하다 pass with flying colors

hapil 하필 ADV of all things, of all occasions (*in the world*)

hapseong(ui) 합성(의) ADJ composite, synthetic: **hapseong sajin** 합성 사진 composite photograph; **hapseong seomnyu** 합성 섬유 synthetic textiles

hapum 하품 N yawn

harabeoji 할아버지 N grandfather

haru 하루 N a day, one day

haru.ui 하루의 ADJ daily

hasoyeonhada 하소연하다 V to moan, pour out: **nunmullo hasoyeoneul hada** 눈물로 하소연을 하다 moan in tears

hasukjip 하숙집 N boarding house

hayata, hayan 하얗다, 하얀 ADJ white

heeojida 헤어지다 V to part from, separate

heeom 헤엄 N swimming: **ttang jipgo heeomchigi** 땅 짚고 헤엄치기 a piece of cake

heeonada 헤어나다 V to get out of, get over, get through, free from: **bingoneseo heeonada** 빈곤에서 헤어나다 get out from poverty

hejipda 헤집다 V to dig up, turn up

hengguda 헹구다 V to wash, rinse

heobeokji 허벅지 N thigh

heoga 허가 N licence, permit

heogi 허기 N hunger

heogijida 허기지다 ADJ starved, famished

heogong 허공 N the air, void

heogu 허구 N fiction, fabrication

heolgeopda 헐겁다 ADJ loose, baggy

heoltteutda 헐뜯다 V to slander, speak ill of sb: **neul nameul heoltteunneunda** 늘 남을 헐뜯는다 always speak ill of someone

heomnan 험난 N hardship, adversity

heomnanhada 험난하다 ADJ difficult, hard

heonggeop 헝겊 N a piece of cloth

heorakhada 허락하다 V to allow, permit

heosulhada 허술하다 ADJ lax, slack

heotalhada 허탈하다 V to be dejected, dispirited

heotsomun 헛소문 N groundless rumor: **heotsomuneul peotteurida** 헛

소문을 퍼뜨리다 spread a false rumor

heoyong 허용 N permission, tolerance

hepeuda 헤프다 ADJ easy (*woman's character*): **geunyeoneun haengsiri hepeuda** 그녀는 행실이 헤프다 she's easy

hepeuda 헤프다 ADJ wasteful: **sseumsseumiga hepeuda** 씀씀이가 헤프다 spend money wastefully

heuk 흙 N earth, soil

heundeulda 흔들다 V to shake, swing, wave

heundeulheundeulhada/-han 흔들흔들하다/-한 ADJ loose, wobbly: **heundeulheundeulhan uija** 흔들흔들한 의자 a wobbly chair

heungjeonghada 흥정하다 V to bargain, haggle: **gagyeogeul heungjeonghada** 가격을 흥정하다 bargain with sb over the price (of)

heunhada, heunhan 흔하다, 흔한 ADJ common, familiar: **i jiyeogui gyotongjeongcheneun heunhada** 이 지역의 교통정체는 흔하다 a traffic jam is common in this area; **heunhan jangmyeon** 흔한 장면 a familiar scene

heurida, heurin 흐리다, 흐린 ADJ cloudy, overcast, dull: **muri heurida** 물이 흐리다 the water is cloudy; **nuni heurida** 눈이 흐리다 have dim eyes; **haneuri heurida** 하늘이 흐리다 the sky is overcast

him 힘 N force, power, strength

himitda, himinneun 힘있다, 힘있는 ADJ powerful: **himinneun saram** 힘있는 사람 an influential person

himjjul 힘줄 N tendon

himseda, himsen 힘세다, 힘센 ADJ strong

hisaeng 희생 N sacrifice

hisaenghada 희생하다 V to sacrifice

hoebokdoeda 회복되다 V to be (*get*) better, cured, recovered: **geongangeul hoebokhada** 건강을 회복하다 regain one's health

hoebokhada, hoebokan 회복하다, 회복한 ADJ recovered

heon.geum 헌금 N offering

hoengpo 횡포 N tyranny: **hoengporeul burida** 횡포를 부리다 tyrannize, domineer, bully

hoesa 회사 N company, firm

H

hoesaek(ui) 회색(의) ADJ gray

hoesik 회식 N dining together (*workplace*)

hoewon 회원 N member: **myeongye-hoewon** 명예회원 honorary member; **pyeongsaenghoewon** 평생회원 life member

hoju 호주 N Australia

hoju saram 호주 사람 N Australian (*nationality*)

hojumeoni 호주머니 N pocket

hol 홀 N hall

hollansikida 혼란시키다 V to confuse

hollansikineun 혼란시키는 ADJ confusing

hondonghada 혼동하다 V to mistake A for B, garble: **gonggwasareul hondonghada** 공과사를 혼동하다 mix up public and private affairs

hongkong 홍콩 N Hong Kong

hongsi 홍시 N soft persimmon

hongsu 홍수 N flood

honja(seo) 혼자(서) ADV alone

honjadoen 혼자된 ADJ became alone, widowed

honjaitda 혼자 있다 PHR alone, I'm alone

honmihada 혼미하다 N stupefaction, bewilderment

horabi 홀아비 N widower

horang.i 호랑이 N tiger

horangnabi 호랑나비 N swallowtail (*butterfly*)

Hormon 호르몬 N hormone

hosa 호사 N extravagance, luxury: **hosareul nurida** 호사를 누리다 live a luxurious life

hosaseureopda 호사스럽다 ADJ ostentatious

hosu 호수 N lake

hotel 호텔 N hotel

huchu 후추 N pepper, black

huhoehada 후회하다 V to regret

hullyeon 훈련 N training, drill

hullyunghada 훌륭하다 ADJ excellent, magnificent

humchida 훔치다 V to steal

hwa 화 N anger

hwabun 화분 N pot

hwachanghada/-han 화창하다/-한 ADJ sunny, clear, bright (*weather*): **nalssiga hwachanghada** 날씨가 화창

하다 It's sunny and clear

hwahak 화학 N chemistry

hwahap 화합 N harmony, concord

hwajangsil 화장실 N toilet, restroom

hwakdaehada 확대하다 V to enlarge: **sajineul hwakdaehada** 사진을 확대하다 enlarge a photo

hwakdaehada 확대하다 V to expand: **susaui beomwireul hwakdaehada** 수사의 범위를 확대하다 expand the scope of an investigation; **goyongeul hwakdaehada** 고용을 확대하다 expand employement

hwakdaehada 확대하다 V to magnify, blow up: **hyeonmigyeongeuro hwakdaehada** 현미경으로 확대하다 magnify an object with a microscope

hwakgohada/-han 확고하다/-한 ADJ determined, stubborn, firm: **gyeolsimhi hwakgohada** 결심히 확고하다 stand firm in one's resolution

hwakjanghada 확장하다 V to expand, grow larger: **dororoeul hwakjanghada** 도로를 확장하다 widen a street; **seryeogeul hwakjanghada** 세력을 확장하다 expand one's influence

hwaksilhada, hwaksilhan 확실하다, 확실한 ADJ certain, sure: **chulcheoga hwaksilhada** 출처가 확실하다 be from a reliable source; **hwaksilhan bangbeop** 확실한 방법 a sure method

hwalttong 활동 N activity: **guhohwaldong** 구호활동 relief activities

hwan.gyeong 환경 N the environment

hwanan 화난 ADJ angry, cross: **hwanan gisaek** 화난 기색 a look of anger

hwanada 화나다 V to be infuriated, aggavated

hwanbul 환불 N refund

hwangak 환각 N illusion

hwanghon 황혼 N dusk, twilight years

hwangi 환기 N ventilation

hwanho 환호 N cheer, ovation

hwanja 환자 N patient (*medical*)

hwanjeonhada 환전하다 V to change, exchange (*money*)

hwannyul 환율 N rate of exchange (*for foreign currency*)

hwanyeonghada 환영하다 V to welcome

hwasal 화살 N arrow

hwasan 화산 N volcano

hwasang 화상 N burn (*injury*)

hwayoil 화요일 N Tuesday

hwiballyu 휘발유 N gasoline, petrol

hwidureuda 휘두르다 V to brandish, swing

hyanggiropda 향기롭다 ADJ fragrant, aromatic

hyang 향 N incense, fragrance, aroma: **hyangeul piuda** 향을 피우다 burn incense; **hyangi ganghada** 향이 강하다 have a strong scent

hyangnak 향락 N enjoyment, pleasure

hyangnyo 향료 N spices

hyangsillyo 향신료 N spices and condiments

hyangsu 향수 N perfume

hyangsuppyeong 향수병 N homesickness

hyeo 혀 N tongue

hyeolgi 혈기 N vigor, vitality: **hyeolgi-wangseonghada** 혈기왕성하다 be passionate, be vigorous

hyeolgwan 혈관 N blood vessel

hyeomui 혐의 N suspicion, charge

hyeon.geum 현금 N cash, money

hyeon.geumeuro bakkuda 현금으로 바꾸다 V to cash a check

hyeondae(ui) 현대(의) ADJ modern

hyeong 형 N older brother (*male's*)

hyeongbu 형부 N brother-in-law (*elder sister's husband*)

hyeonggwangdeung 형광등 N fluorescent light

hyeongpyeoneopda 형편없다 ADJ terrible, dreadful

hyeonjang 현장 N scene of action

hyoongje 형제 N brother, sibling

hyeongseonghada 형성하다 V to shape, form

hyeonsil 현실 N actuality, reality

hyeongsu 형수 N sister-in-law (*wife of one's elder brother*)

hyeonjae 현재 N the present, now

hyeonmyeonghada, hyeonmyeong-han 현명하다, 현명한 ADJ wise: **hyeonmyeonghan pandan** 현명한 판단 sound judgment

hyeopbak 협박 N threat, blackmail

hyeopdong 협동 N cooperation, collaboration

hyeoraek 혈액 N blood

hyeorap 혈압 N blood pressure

hyeonsanghada 현상하다 V to develop (*film*): **pileum (sajin)eul hyeonsanghada** 필름 (사진)을 현상하다 develop a film (*pictures*)

hyetaek 혜택 N benefit, boon

hyodohada 효도하다 V to be filial to parents

hyu.ga 휴가 N holiday, vacation

hyu.il 휴일 N holiday (*a day off*)

I

i 이 PRON this, these: **i saram** 이 사람 this person

i 이 N tooth, teeth: **ireul dakda** 이를 닦 다 brush one's teeth

i 이 NUM two: **i deohagi ineun sa** 이 더하기 이는 사 two plus two equals four

i meil 이 메일 N email: **imeireul hwaginhada** 이메일을 확인하다 check one's email

i meil bonaeda 이 메일 보내다 V to email

...i/ga ...이/가 PP (*subject marker*)

...i/ga eopda/eomneun ...이/가 없다/ 없는 ADJ lacking, non-existing

ibajihada 이바지하다 V to contribute to

ibalhada 이발하다 V to have a haircut (*male hair*)

ibalsa 이발사 N barber

ibalso 이발소 N barbershop

ibeo boda 입어 보다 V to try on (*clothes*): **saeoseul ibeoboda** 새옷을 입어보다 try on new clothes

ibiinhugwa 이비인후과 N otolaryngology, ENT

ibul 이불 N blanket: **ibureul deopda** 이불을 덮다 cover with a blanket

ibyeol 이별 N parting, farewell

ibyeon 이변 N mishap, accident

ichyeojida, ichyeojin 잊혀지다, 잊혀 진 V to be forgotten

ichyeojin 잊혀진 ADJ forgotten: **ityeo-jin gieok** 잊혀진 기억 a forgotten memory

idaero 이대로 ADV as it is

ideumhae 이듬해 N the following year

ieojida 이어지다 V be connected: **i gireun gosokdorowa ieojinda** 이 길은 고속도로와 이어진다 The road is connected to the highway

ieojida 이어지다 v to be continued: **gwageoui jeontongi hyeonjaekkaji ieojida** 과거의 전통이 현재까지 이어지다 Past traditions continue to this day

ieopon 이어폰 N earphone

ieukgo 이윽고 ADV soon, finally: **ieukgo bami doeeotda** 이윽고 밤이 되었다 Finally, the night falls

...ieyo/yeyo ...이에요/예요 PP be (*copula, polite ending*): **geugeoseun keompyuteoyeyo** 그것은 컴퓨터예요 That is a computer; **geugeoseun gabangiyeyo** 그것은 가방이에요 It's a bag

igeot 이것 PRON this: **igeoseun naegeotsida** 이것은 내것이다 This is mine

igeotdeul 이것들 N these: **igeotdeureun sseulmoeopda** 이것들은 쓸모 없다 These are useless

igeullu 이글루 N igloo

igida 이기다 v to beat, win, defeat: **geimeseo igida** 게임에서 이기다 win a game

igil 익일 N the next day

igollada 이골나다 v to be inured to, sick of: **ireon iriramyeon igori natda** 이런 일이라면 이골이 났다 I'm inured to this kind of work; **ramyeoniramyeon igori nanda** 라면이라면 이골이 난다 I'm sick of eating ramen

igudongseong 이구동성 N unanimous voice: **igudongseongeuro oechida** 이구동성으로 외치다 cry in chorus

igwa 이과 N natural sciences

igwol 이월 N the next month

igyeonaeda 이겨내다 v to overcome: **jasineul igyeonaeda** 자신을 이겨내다 control (*conquer*) oneself; **byeongeul igyeonaeda** 병을 이겨내다 get over one's illness

ihaehada 이해하다 v to understand: **jal ihaehada** 잘 이해하다 understand well; **jalmot ihaehada** 잘못 이해하다 misunderstand

ihaeryeok 이해력 N comprehension: **cheongchwi ihaeryeok** 청취 이해력 listening comprehension

ihaesim 이해심 N understanding: **geuneun ihaesimi maneun saramida** 그는 이해심이 많은 사람이다 He is very understanding

ihonhada 이혼하다 v to divorce: **habui ihonhada** 합의 이혼하다 divorce by mutual agreement

ihonhan 이혼한 ADJ divorced

...ihu ...이후 N since, after: **geu nal ihu** 그 날 이후 since that day; **daseotsi ihu** 5시 이후 after 5 o'clock

iik 이익 N profit

ija 이자 N interest (*money*): **ijareul gapda** 이자를 갚다 pay back interest

ijeon(ui) 이전의 ADJ previous, former: **ijeonui gyeongheom** 이전의 경험 previous experience

ijikhada 이직하다 v to change jobs

ijipteu 이집트 N Egypt

ikda 읽다 v to read: **chaegeul rikda** 책을 읽다 read a book

ikda 익다 v to grow, ripen: **byeoga ikda (igeoganda)** 벼가 익다 (익어간다) the rice is ripening

ikda 익다 v to be boiled, cooked: **gogiga deol igeotda** 고기가 덜 익었다 the meat is not cooked yet

ikda 익다 ADJ skilled, experienced: **sone ikda** 손에 익다 be skilled in; **mome ikda** 몸에 익다 be accustomed to

ikda 익다 ADJ accustomed to, familiar with: **nachi ikda** 낯이 익다 be familiar with (*a person or a sight*)

ikhi 익히 ADV know well: **geunyeoui ireumeul rikhi algo itda** 그녀의 이름을 익히 알고 있다 Her name is well-known

ikhida 익히다 v to become acquainted, familiar with: **eolgureul ikhida** 얼굴을 익히다 be familiarized with (*faces*)

ikhida 익히다 v to become proficient, master: **gisureul ikhida** 기술을 익히다 master the technique of

ikhida 익히다 v to cook, boil: **eumsigeul ikhida** 음식을 익히다 boil (*cook*) food

ikhida 익히다 v to ripen: **jal igeun podoju** 잘 익은 포도주 round (*aged*) wine

ikkeulda 이끌다 v to shepherd, lead: **gundaereul ikkeulda** 군대를 이끌다 lead an army, **bareun gillo ikkeulda** 바른 길로 이끌다 guide a person to the right path

ikkeullida 이끌리다 v to be driven,

carried away: **gamjeonge ikkeullida** 감정에 이끌리다 to be attracted to, be driven by emotions

ikkeullida 이끌리다 v to be led, guided: **eomeoni sone ikkeullyeo hakgyo gatda** 어머니 손에 이끌려 학교에 갔다 led to school by mom's hand

ikki 이끼 N moss, liverwort

iksahada 익사하다 v to drown

iksalseureopda 익살스럽다 ADJ comical

iksukhada 익숙하다 ADJ to be acquainted, accustomed to

il 일 N job, work, occupation

ilbanjeogeuro 일반적으로 ADV generally

ilbanjeogida/-jeogin 일반적이다/ -적인 ADJ general, all-purpose

ilbanmi 일반미 N sticky rice

ilbon 일본 N Japan

ilbon saram 일본 사람 N Japanese (nationality)

ilboneo 일본어 N Japanese (language)

ilchul 일출 N sunrise

ilgan 일간 N daily: **ilgan sinmun** 일간 신문 daily newspaper

ilgi 일기 N diary, daybook

ilgop 일곱 NUM seven

ilhada 일하다 v to work: **yeolsimhi ilhada** 열심히 일하다 work hard

ilheun 일흔 NUM seventy

ilji 일지 N diary, journal

imo 이모 N aunt

imobu 이모부 N uncle (husband of maternal aunt)

imokgubi 이목구비 N facial features, looks: **imokgubiga tturyeohada** 이목구비가 뚜렷하다 have well-defined features

ilmol 일몰 N sunset

ilttan 일단 ADV first, for now

ima 이마 N forehead

imdaehada 임대하다 v to rent

immyeong 임명 N appointment

imsi(ui) 임시(의) ADJ temporary: **imsiui il** 임시의 일 an odd job

imsinhada 임신하다 v to be pregnant: **cheosaireul imsinhada** 첫아이를 임 신하다 be pregnant with one's first baby

in.gan 인간 N human

in.gongjeogida, in.gongjeogin 인공 적이다, 인공적인 ADJ artificial, man-made: **ingongjeogin areumdaum** 인 공적인 아름다움 artificial beauties

...inbun ...인분 N portion, serving: **bulgogi iinbun** 불고기 2인분 a double order (portion) of bulgogi

inae 이내 ADV at once, promptly

inae 이내 ADV in, by: **samsipbun inaero gagetseumnida** 30분 이내로 가겠습니다 Be there in 30 minutes

Indo 인도 N India: **indo yeohaeng** 인도 여행 a trip to India

indo 인도 N sidewalk: **chaga indokkaji deureowatda** 차가 인도까지 들어왔다 The vehicle drove into the sidewalk

indohada 인도하다 v to deliver, transfer

indohada 인도하다 v to extradite

indohada 인도하다 v to guide, lead

indonesia 인도네시아 N Indonesia

ingicheok 인기척 N indication of a person being around

ingkeu 잉크 N ink

ingmyeong 익명 N anonymity

ingonghoheup 인공호흡 N CPR

ingongwiseong 인공위성 N satellite

in.gu 인구 N population

ingwon 인권 N human rights

injeonghada 인정하다 v to admit, confess: **jalmoseul injeonghada** 잘못을 인정하다 admit one's fault

inkki itda/inneun 인기 있다/있는 ADJ popular

innaehada 인내하다 v to endure

innaesimitda/-inneun 인내심 있다/ -있는 ADJ patient (calm)

inpeulleisyeon 인플레이션 N inflation

insaeng 인생 N life

insahada 인사하다 v to greet: **kkakdeunni insahada** 깍듯이 인사하다 greet politely

insamal 인사말 N greetings: **insamareul geonneda** 인사말을 건네다 say hi (to)

insang.eul juda 인상을 주다 v to make an impression: **gangnyeolhan insangeul juda** 강렬한 인상을 주다 make a strong impression

insangjeogida, insangjeogin 인상적 이다, 인상적인 ADJ impressive: **insangjeogin jangmyeon** 인상적인 장 면 an impressive (memorable) scene

insik 인식 N awareness, realization

insikhada 인식하다 V to realize, recognize: **wiheomeul insikhada** 위험을 인식하다 recognize danger

inswaehada 인쇄하다 V to print

inteonet 인터넷 N Internet

ip 입 N mouth: **ibi ssada** 입이 싸다 have a big mouth

ip 잎 N leaf: **ipi jin namu** 잎이 진 나무 a bare (leafless) tree

ipda 입다 V to wear, put on (clothes): **jakeseul ipda** 자켓을 입다 put on a jacket

ipda 입다 V to incur, suffer: **keun sonhae (pihae)reul ipda** 큰 손해 (피해)를 입다 suffer a great damage

ipda 입다 V to be injured: **sagoro sangcheoreul ipda** 사고로 상처를 입다 be hurt in an accident

ipda 입다 V to be indebted to, favored with: **eunhyereul ipda** 은혜를 입다 be indebted to, receive great kindness

ipgu 입구 N entrance, way in

ipjangkkwon 입장권 N ticket (for entertainment)

ipsul 입술 N lips: **dotomhan ipsul** 도톰한 입술 full lips

irang 이랑 PP with (more casual than 하고): **samchonirang sanchaegeul hada** 삼촌이랑 산책을 하다 go for a walk with uncle

ireobeorida 잃어버리다 V to lose, mislay: **gabangeul ireobeorida** 가방을 잃어버리다 lose a bag

ireobeorin 잃어버린 ADJ lost (missing)

ireonada 일어나다 V to get up (from bed): **achime ireonada** 아침에 일어나다 get up in the morning

ireonada 일어나다 V to happen, occur: **gijeogi ireonada** 기적이 일어나다 a miracle happens; **jeonjaengi ireonada** 전쟁이 일어나다 a war breaks out

ireoseoda 일어서다 V to stand up: **jarieseo ireoseoda** 자리에서 일어서다 rise from one's seat

ireuda 이르다 V to arrive at, get to: **mokjeokjie ireuda** 목적지에 이르다 reach one's destination

ireuda 이르다 V to tell, say, …: **haji mallago dandanhi ireuda** 하지 말라고 단단히 이르다 make sure to tell sb not to do (something)

ireuda 이르다 V to tell on, tattle on: **jalmoseul ireuda** 잘못을 이르다 tattle on sb to sb

ireuda 이르다 V to reach: **gyeollone ireuda** 결론에 이르다 reach a conclusion

ireul temyeon 이를 테면 ADV as one might say

ireum 이름 N name, given name

ireumpyo 이름표 N name tag

ireun 이른 ADJ early: **ireun achim** 이른 아침 early morning

ireunba 이른바 ADV what is called, so called

iri(ro) 이리(로) ADV here, to this way: **iriro oseyo** 이리로 오세요 Please come this way; **iriro wa** 이리로 와 Come here

iropda 이롭다 ADJ profitable, favorable, beneficial

iruda 이루다 V to accomplish, achieve: **sowoneul iruda** 소원을 이루다 have one's wish fulfilled; **mokjeogeul riruda** 목적을 이루다 achieve one's goal

iruda 이루다 V to make, form: **gajeongeul iruda** 가정을 이루다 start a family

irueojida 이루어지다 V to be accomplished, come true: **kkumi irueojida** 꿈이 이루어지다 a dream comes true

irueojida 이루어지다 V to consist of, be made up of

irueojida 이루어지다 V to be reached, be made

irwol 일월 N January

iryoil 일요일 N Sunday

isahada 이사하다 V to move

isanghada, isanghan 이상하다, 이상한 ADJ strange

iseulbi 이슬비 N drizzle

iseullamgyo 이슬람교 N Islam

iseullamgyodo 이슬람교도 N Muslim

isikhada 이식하다 V to transplant: **sinjang isik** 신장 이식 kidney transplant

isiljikgohada 이실직고하다 V to tell the truth

isip 이십 NUM twenty

isyu 이슈 N issue

issusigae 이쑤시개 N toothpick

itda 있다 V be, to exist: **nalji mothaneun saedo itda** 날지 못하는 새도 있다 There are birds that can't fly

itda 있다 v to have, own: **uri jibeneun jeongwoni itda** 우리 집에는 정원이 있다 We have a garden in our house; **doni itda** 돈이 있다 to have money

itda 있다 v to be situated, located: **geu gangeun dosi namjjoge itda** 그 강은 도시 남쪽에 있다 The river is located south of the city

itda 잊다 v to forget: **gwageoreul itda** 과거를 잊다 forget the past

iteul 이틀 N two days

iteunnal 이튿날 N the next day

itorok 이토록 ADV this much, like this

iui 이의 N objection: **iuireul jegihada** 이의를 제기하다 raise an objection

iut(saram) 이웃(사람) N neighbor

iwol 이월 N February

iyagi 이야기 N story (*tale*): **yennal iyagi** 옛날 이야기 an old story, a bedtime story, a fairy tale

iyu 이유 N reason

iyun 이윤 N profit, returns: **keun iyuneul naeda** 큰 이윤을 내다 make big profits

J

ja 자 N ruler

jaa 자아 N ego, self

jaanaeda 자아내다 v to evoke, arouse: **dongjeongsimeul jaanaeda** 동정심을 자아내다 evoke one's sympathy

jabadanggida 잡아당기다 v to pull, draw

jabaek 자백 N confession

jabagada 잡아가다 v to take, haul off

jabal(jeok) 자발(적) N voluntary

jabameokda 잡아먹다 v to butcher and eat, devour

jabatteda 잡아떼다 v to play innocent: **yonguijaneun beomhaengeul jabattetda** 용의자는 범행을 잡아뗐다 The suspect denied the crime

jabi 자비 N mercy: **jabireul bepulda** 자비를 베풀다 show mercy to

jabon 자본 N capital

jabusim 자부심 N pride, self-respect: **jabusimi ganghada** 자부심이 강하다 have much pride in oneself

jachigwon 자치권 N right of autonomy

jachwi 자취 N cooking for oneself (*living alone*)

jachwi 자취 N traces, signs, marks: **jachwireul gamchugo sarajida** 자취를 감추고 사라지다 disappear without a trace

jada 자다 v to sleep, go to bed: **iljjik jada** 일찍 자다 go to bed early; **natjameul jada** 낮잠을 자다 take a nap

jadong eungdapgi 자동 응답기 N answering machine

jadongcha 자동차 N automobile, car, motor vehicle

jadonggui 자동의 ADJ automatic

jadu 자두 N plum

jaebaehada 재배하다 v to grow, cultivate: **nongjangmureul jaebaehada** 농작물을 재배하다 grow crops

jaebeol 재벌 N conglomerate, chaebol

jaebongteul 재봉틀 N sewing machine

jaechaegi 재채기 N sneeze: **jaechaegireul chamda** 재채기를 참다 hold a sneeze

jaechaegihada 재채기하다 v to sneeze

jaechi 재치 N wit, tact

jaechok 재촉 N pressing, urging

jaechokhada 재촉하다 v to urge, push, rush, hurry: **georeumeul jaechokhada** 걸음을 재촉하다 quicken one's step (*pace*); **daedabeul jaechokhada** 대답을 재촉하다 press for an answer

jaeda 재다 v to measure: **mommugereul jaeda** 몸무게를 재다 weigh oneself

jaeju 재주 N ability, talent: **gumbengido gureuneun jaejuga itda** 굼벵이도 구르는 재주가 있다 Everybody has some talent

jaem 잼 N jam

jaemi 재미 N pleasure, amusement

jaemiitda, jaemiinneun 재미있다, 재미있는 ADJ funny, interesting: **jeongmal jaemiitda!** 정말 재미있다! What fun!; **jaemiinneun saram** 재미있는 사람 a man with a sense of humor

jaemiitge bonaeda 재미있게 보내다 v to have fun

jaenan 재난 N disaster

jaengban 쟁반 N tray

jaengjaenghada 쟁쟁하다 ADJ prominent, distinguished

jaepan 재판 N trial

J

jaeryo 재료 N material, ingredient: **cheonnyeonjaeryo** 천연재료 natural materials

jaesaeng 재생 N reproduction: **jaesaengpum** 재생품 recycled product

jaesaeng 재생하다 V to play (*video, audio*): **bidioreul jaesaenghada** 비디오를 재생하다 play video

jaesan 재산 N property, wealth: **gonggongjaesan** 공공재산 public property

jagal 자갈 N gravel, pebble

jageop 작업 N work, operation

jageuk 자극 N stimulation

jagi 자기 N self

jago itda 자고 있다 ADJ asleep

jaguk 자국 N mark, stain

jagung 자궁 N uterus

jagyeok 자격 N qualification: **jagyeogeul gatchuda** 자격을 갖추다 hold qualification

jagyeok 자격 N right: **yoguhal jagyeogi itda** 요구할 자격이 있다 have a right to demand

jagyong 작용 N function, effect

jagyonghada 작용하다 V to effect, work

jahwasang 자화상 N self-portrait

jajangga 자장가 N lullaby

jaje 자제 N self-control

jajeon 자전 N rotation

jajeon.geo 자전거 N bicycle, bike

jajeong 자정 N midnight

jajinhada 자진하다 V to volunteer

jajireojida 자지러지다 V to be petrified

jajireojida 자지러지다 V to scream in tears

jajireojida 자지러지다 V to shriek with laughter

jajonsim 자존심 N pride

jaju 자주 ADV often

jajusaek(ui) 자주색 N purple

jakbyeol 작별 N farewell, parting: **jakbyeoreul gohada** 작별을 고하다 say farewell

jakda, jageun 작다, 작은 ADJ little, small, tiny, short (*height*)

jakdonghada 작동하다 V to work, operate, run

jaket 자켓 N coat, jacket

jakga 작가 N writer

jakgok 작곡 N composition (*music*)

jakgokhada 작곡하다 V to compose (*music*)

jakjeon 작전 N strategy

jakku 자꾸 ADV repeatedly, often

jakpum 작품 N (*piece of*) work

jakseonghada 작성하다 V to fill out, prepare

jal 잘 ADV well

jal doegireul baranda 잘 되기를 바란다 PHR wish you the best

jal garago jeonhada 잘 가라고 전하다 V to say goodbye

jal haesseoyo! 잘 했어요! INTERJ well done! good job!

jal igeun 잘 익은 ADJ well-done, well-cooked, well-ripe

jal ikda/igeun 잘 익다/익은 ADJ well-cooked, well-done

jallida 잘리다 V to be cut (*off*), be chopped

jalmot 잘못 N fault, mistake, error

jalsaenggida, jalsaenggin 잘생기다, 잘생긴 ADJ handsome, good-looking

jaman 자만 N conceit, pride

jamae 자매 N sister

jambok 잠복 N stakeout

jambokhada 잠복하다 V to remain dormant: **geu baireoseuneun hwaldonghagi jeon botong samgaewol dongan chenaee jambokhanda** 그 바이러스는 활동하기 전 보통 3개월 동안 체내에 잠복한다 The virus lies dormant for 3 months until it becomes active

jamdeulda 잠들다 V to fall asleep, sink into a slumber

jamgeuda 잠그다 V to lock: **muneul jamgeuda** 문을 잠그다 lock the door

jamgeuda 잠그다 V to fasten, button up: **danchureul jamgeuda** 단추를 잠그다 button up

jamgeuda 잠그다 V to turn off: **baelbeureul jamgeuda** 밸브를 잠그다 turn off the valve

jamgida 잠기다 V to be locked, fastened: **muni jamgida** 문이 잠기다 The door is locked

jamgida 잠기다 V to grow hoarse: **mogi jamgida** 목이 잠기다 get hoarse

jamgida, jamgin 잠기다, 잠긴 V to be submerged, flooded: **mure jamgida** 물에 잠기다 sink under water

jamjada 잠자다 V to be smoothed down, lie down

jamjaeryeok 잠재력 N potentiality

jamjari 잠자리 N bed, bedstead: **jam-jarie deulda** 잠자리에 들다 go to bed

jamjari 잠자리 N dragonfly: **nara-ganeun jamjari** 날아가는 잠자리 a flying dragonfly

jamkkan 잠깐 ADV for a moment, a while

jamkkanmanyo! 잠깐만요! INTERJ just a moment!, wait please!

jamkkodae 잠꼬대 N rubbish, non-sense, silly talk: **jamkkodae gateun sori haji mara** 잠꼬대 같은 소리 하지 마라 Stop talking nonsense

jamkkodae 잠꼬대 N sleep talking

jamot 잠옷 N pajamas

jamsi 잠시 ADV for a short time, for a moment

jamsu 잠수 N submergence

jamulsoe 자물쇠 N lock

janchi 잔치 N festival

jandon 잔돈 N change (*money, coin*)

jang 장 N sheet (*of paper*)

jang 장 N cabinet

jang.ae 장애 N handicap

jang.in 장인 N father-in-law

jangdam 장담 N guarantee, big talk: **hoeonjangdam** 호언장담 big talk, loud boast

janggap 장갑 N gloves

janggeori 장거리 N long distance

janghakgeum 장학금 N scholarship

jangma 장마 N rainy season, monsoon

jangmi 장미 N rose

jangmo 장모 N mother-in-law

jangmun 작문 N composition, writings

jangnae 장래 N future, tomorrow

jangnan 장난 N mischief, fun

jangnanchida 장난치다 V to romp about

jangnankkam 장난감 N toy

jangnyeon 작년 N last year

jangnyesik 장례식 N funeral

jangsigi doen 장식이 된 ADJ decorative, fancy

jangsik(mul) 장식(물) N ornament

jangso 장소 N place

janhok 잔혹 N cruelty, brutality

janinhada, janinhan 잔인하다, 잔인한 ADJ cruel

janjanhada 잔잔하다 ADJ still, tranquil

janyeo 자녀 N sons and daughters

japcho 잡초 N weeds

japda 잡다 V to capture, catch: **gongeul japda** 공을 잡다 catch a ball

japida 잡히다 V to be caught, captured

japida 잡히다 V to be grabbed

japji 잡지 N magazine

japojagihada 자포자기하다 V to give up on oneself

jappajida 자빠지다 V to fall down, tumble: **dwiro jappajyeodo koga kkaejinda** 뒤로 자빠져도 코가 깨진다 The bread always falls buttered side down

jarada 자라다 V to grow: **mureongmu-reok jarada** 무럭무럭 자라다 grow up quickly and healthy

jarang 자랑 N boast, show off

jarangseureopda/-reon 자랑스럽다/-런 ADJ proud, boastful

jareogada 자러가다 V to go to bed

jareuda 자르다 V to cut

jari 자리 N seat, room, space, position, location, site

jarip 자립 N self-reliance

jaryeok 자력 N magnetism

jaryeok 자력 N one's own efforts

jasal 자살 N suicide

jaseok 자석 N magnet: **seoro jaseok-cheoreom kkeullida** 서로 자석처럼 끌리다 fascinated by each other

jaseon 자선 N charity

jasin 자신 N confidence

jasin itda 자신 있다 ADJ to be confident

jasinui 자신의 ADJ own, personal

jason 자손 N descendant, offspring

(ja)su (자)수 N embroidery

jataek 자택 N one's house

jaukhada 자욱하다 ADJ dense, thick: **jaukhan angae** 자욱한 안개 a thick fog

jawon 자원 N resources

jayeon 자연 N nature

jayeon(ui) 자연의 ADJ natural

jayu 자유 N freedom, liberty

jayugwon 자유권 N right of freedom

jayul 자율 N autonomy

jayuropda, jayuroun 자유롭다, 자유로운 ADJ free of restraints

je 제 N I, my (*humble form*): **jega hagetseumnida** 제가 하겠습니다 I will do it; **je yeoja chingu imnida** 제 여자 친구 입니다 She is my girlfriend

J

je sigane 제 시간에 ADV on time: **je sigane dochakhada** 제 시간에 도착하다 arrive on time

je.an N suggestion

je.anhada 제안하다 V to suggest

je.uihada 제의하다 V to offer, suggest

jechulhada 제출하다 V to present, submit

jegeohada 제거하다 V to get rid of, eliminate, remove

jehan 제한 N limit, restriction

jehanhada 제한하다 V to limit, restrict

jeil 제일 ADV most (*superlative*), number 1: **jeil jungyohan geot** 제일 중요한 것 most important thing

jeil jota/jo.eun 제일 좋다/좋은 ADJ best

jejohada 제조하다 V to manufacture, produce, make

jemok 제목 N title (*of book, film*): **yeonghwa jemok** 영화 제목 title of a movie

jeo 저 PRON I, me (*humble form*): **jeoneun yeol sal imnida** 저는 열 살입니다 I am ten years old

jeo 저 PRON that, those: **jeo saram** 저 사람 that person

jeo.ul 저울 N scales

jeo geot 저 것 PRON that

jeo geotdeul 저 것들 N those

jeochuk 저축 N saving

jeogeodo 적어도 ADV at least

jeogeung(ryeok) 적응(력) N adaptation, accommodation

jeogi 저기 N over there

jeogiap 저기압 N bad mood, under the weather: **oneul jeogiabida** 오늘 저기압이다 feeling low today

jeogiap 저기압 N low (*atmospheric*) pressure

jeojangdoeda 저장되다 V to be preserved, stored

jeojanghada 저장하다 V to store, save, reserve

jeojeollo 저절로 ADV by itself, naturally

jeok 적 N enemy

jeokda 적다 V to note down, write down

jeokda, jeogeun 적다, 적은 ADJ little (*not much*)

jeokdanghada, jeokdanghan 적당하다, 적당한 ADJ appropriate, right, proper, suitable: **jeokdanghan jigeop** 적당한 직업 a suitable calling; **jeokdanghan saram** 적당한 사람 someone suitable; **jeokdanghan ttae** 적당한 때 right time

jeoksida 적시다 V to soak, wet, humidify: **sugeoneul jeoksida** 수건을 적시다 wet a towel

jeoksida 적시다 V to get teary: **nunsiureul jeoksida** 눈시울을 적시다 be moved to tears

jeol 절 N temple

jeolban 절반 N half

jeoldae 절대 N absoluteness

jeollyak 전략 N tactic, strategy: **jeollyageul jjada** 전략을 짜다 establish a strategy

jeolmeum 젊음 N youth, youthfulness

jeolmeuni 젊은이 N youth (*young person*)

jeom 점 N point, dot

jeomchajeogeuro 점차적으로 ADV gradually

jeomjanta, jeomjaneun 점잖다, 점잖은 ADJ gentle, respectable: **jeomjaneun saram** 점잖은 사람 a fine gentleman

jeommuneuui 점무늬의 ADJ spotted (*pattern*)

jeompeuhada 점프하다 V to jump

jeomsim siksa 점심 식사 N lunch, midday meal

jeomsim siksahada 점심 식사하다 V to eat lunch

jeomulda 저물다 V to grow dark

jeomwon 점원 N sales assistant, shopkeeper

jeonche 전체 N entirety, whole

jeonche(ui) 전체의 ADJ entire, whole, all of

jeoncheol 전철 N subway train

...jeone ...전에 ADV previously, formerly

jeone 전에 ADV before, ago, earlier

jeong.i 정의 N justice

jeong.o 정오 N noon, midday

jeong.won 정원 N garden, yard

jeongbiso 정비소 N repairs shop, service center

jeongbo 정보 N information

jeongbu 정부 N government

jeongchihak 정치학 N political science

44

J

jeongdang 정당 N party (*political*)

jeongdanghan 정당한 ADJ just, fair, legal

jeongdo 정도 N degree, limit: **jeongdoui munje** 정도의 문제 a matter of degrees

jeongdo 정도 N right path, right method: **jeongdoeseo beoseonada** 정도에서 벗어나다 stray from the right path

jeongdo 정도 N to a certain extent, to some degree: **eoneu jeongdo** 어느 정도 to some extent

jeongdondoeda 정돈되다 V to be orderly, organized

jeongdondoen 정돈된 ADJ neat, tidy

jeongdonhada 정돈하다 V to tidy up, straighten up, put in order, set right

jeonggeul 정글 N jungle

jeonghada 정하다 V to fix, decide, determine

jeonghada 정하다 V to appoint, nominate

jeonghwakhada, jeonghwakan 정확하다, 정확한 ADJ exact, accurate

jeonghwakhi 정확히 ADV exactly, precisely

jeon.gi 전기 N electricity

jeon.gi(ui) 전기의 ADJ electric

jeongjang 정장 N suit, formal dress

jeongjikhada, jeongjikan 정직하다, 정직한 ADJ honest, honorable, truthful

jeongmal 정말 ADV really, truly

jeongmaryo? 정말요? INTERJ really?

jeongmyeon 정면 N front, façade

jeongnihada 정리하다 V to arrange, organize, clean up

jeongnyeol 정열 N passion

jeongnyujang 정류장 N stop, station (*bus, train*)

jeongsagakhyeong 정사각형 N square (*shape*)

jeongsang 정상 N peak, summit

jeongsangjeogida/jeongsangjeogin 정상적이다/정상적인 ADJ normal

jeonguk 전국 N the whole country

jeongwaja 전과자 N ex-convict

jeonhwa batda 전화 받다 V to answer the phone

jeonhwabeonho 전화번호 N telephone number

jeonhwagi 전화기 N telephone

jeonhwahada 전화하다 V to ring, call, dial (*on the telephone*)

jeonhyeongjeogida/-jeogin 전형적이다/-적인 ADJ typical

jeonhyeongjeogida/-jeogin 전형적이다/-적인 ADJ archetypal

jeonja 전자 N electron

jeonja 전자 N the former: **jeonjawa huja** 전자와 후자 the former and the latter

jeonja jepum 전자 제품 N electronics, electronic products

jeonja(ui) 전자의 ADJ electronic, electromagnetic

jeonjaeng 전쟁 N war, battle

jeonjaenghada 전쟁하다 V to make war

jeonjaupyeon 전자우편 N e-mail

jeonmun.ga 전문가 N expert

jeonnyeom 전념 N concentration of mind

jeonnyeomhada 전념하다 V to concentrate, dedicate

jeonnyul 전율 N shudder, shiver

jeonpa 전파 N electromagnetic wave

jeonpahada 전파하다 V to spread, propagate

jeonsaeng 전생 N previous life

jeonseol 전설 N legend

jeonsi 전시 N display

jeonsihoe 전시회 N exhibition

jeonsin 전신 N the whole body

jeontongjeokin 전통적인 ADJ traditional, conventional, old-fashioned, old school: **jeontongjeogin gachigwan** 전통적인 가치관 traditional values

jeontu 전투 N battle

jeonyeok 저녁 N evening

jeonyeok siksa 저녁 식사 N dinner, evening meal

jeonyeok siksahada 저녁 식사하다 V to eat dinner

jeopda 접다 V to fold

jeopgeunhada 접근하다 V to approach, draw near

jeopsi 접시 N dish, platter

jeopsibatchim 접시받침 N dish cloth, saucer

jeoreon 저런 INTERJ oh dear!

jeoryak 절약 N frugality, saving

jeotda 젖다 V to get wet, drenched

jeotjeun 젖은 ADJ wet

jeotgarak 젓가락 N chopsticks

J

jeseucheo 제스처 N gesture

jeulgeopda, jeulgeoun 즐겁다, 즐거운 ADJ enjoyable, happy, pleasant

jeulgeopge bonaeda 즐겁게 보내다 V to enjoy oneself

jeulgida 즐기다 V to enjoy

jeung.o 증오 N hatred

jeungga 증가 N increase

jeunggahada 증가하다 V to increase, rise

jeunggeo 증거 N proof

jeunggi 증기 N steam

jeungmyeonghada 증명하다 V to prove

jeungmyeongseo 증명서 N certificate

-ji anta -지 않다 ADJ no, not (*with verbs and adjectives*)

-ji maseyo -지 마세요 V Please don't: **malhaji maseyo** 말하지 마세요 Please do not speak (*please be quiet*)

-ji motada -지 못하다 V cannot

jibang 지방 N fat, grease

jibang 지방 N region

jibe doraoda 집에 돌아오다 V to return home

jibe gada 집에 가다 V to go home

jibul 지불 N payment

jibuldoeda 지불되다 V to be paid

jibuldoen 지불된 ADJ paid

jibulhada 지불하다 V to pay

jibung 지붕 N roof

jiburaek 지불액 N payment

jichulgeum 지출금 N expenses

jida 지다 V to lose, be defeated

jido 지도 N map: **segyejido** 세계지도 a map of the world

jidohada 지도하다 V to supervise, guide: **hakseubeul jidohada** 학습을 지도하다 coach one's study

jidoja 지도자 N leader

jigap 지갑 N wallet

jigeop 직업 N job, occupation, profession

jigeum dangjang 지금 당장 N right now

jigu 지구 N Earth, the world

jigwon 직원 N employee

jijeokhada 지적하다 V to point out

jijeom 지점 N branch

jijihada 지지하다 V to support

jijin 지진 N earthquake

jikida 지키다 V to guard, keep

jiksagakhyeong 직사각형 N rectangle

jilmun 질문 N question

jiltu 질투 N jealousy

jiltuhada 질투하다 V to feel jealous, envy

jim 짐 N baggage, package, load: **jimeul jida** 짐을 지다 bear a load

jinada 지나다 V to pass, go by, go through: **jajeongi jinada** 자정이 지나다 past midnight

jinan 지난 ADJ former

jinan bam 지난 밤 N last night

jinan ju 지난 주 N last week

jinchalhada 진찰하다 V to examine, check up

jingmul 직물 N fabric, textile

(jingmureul) jjada (직물을) 짜다 V to weave

jingmyeonhada 직면하다 V to face

jinhada, jinhan 진하다, 진한 ADJ thick, strong: **pineun mulboda jinhada** 피는 물보다 진하다 Blood is thicker than water

jinjjaui 진짜의 ADJ genuine, real, authentic

jinju 진주 N pearl

jinyeol 진열 N display

jinyeolhada 진열하다 V to display

jip 집 N home, house

jipjunghada 집중하다 V to concentrate

jipye 지폐 N bill (*currency*), bank note

jipyeongseon 지평선 N horizon

jiri(hak) 지리(학) N geography

jiruhada, jiruhaehada 지루하다, 지루해하다 ADJ bored

jiruhada, jiruhan 지루하다, 지루한 ADJ boring, dull: **jiruhan yeonghwa** 지루한 영화 a boring movie

jisihada 지시하다 V to instruct, direct

jisik 지식 N knowledge

jisokhada 지속하다 V to last, continue, endure

jitda 짓다 V to build, make, construct: **jibeul jitda** 집을 짓다 build a house

jitda 짓다 V to cook: **babeul jitda** 밥을 짓다 cook rice

jitda 짓다 V to conclude, close: **gyeolloneul jitda** 결론을 짓다 draw a conclusion

jitda 짓다 V to shed tears: **nunmureul jitda** 눈물을 짓다 dabbing tears from one's eyes

J

jiwi 지위 N rank, status, position

jiyeok 지역 N area, region

jiyeon 지연 N delay

jiyeondoeda 지연되다 V to be delayed

jiyeondoen 지연된 ADJ delayed, postponed

jjada, jjan 짜다, 짠 ADJ salty: **sogeumeun jjada** 소금은 짜다 salt is salty

jjada, jjan 짜다, 짠 ADJ stingy, tightfisted: **jjan saram** 짠 사람 a stingy person

jjada, jjan 짜다, 짠 V to squeeze out tears: **nunmureul jjada** 눈물을 짜다 squeeze out tears

jjada, jjan 짜다, 짠 V to squeeze (*press*) oil: **gireumeul jjada** 기름을 짜다 extract oil from

jjada, jjan 짜다, 짠 V to brainstorm: **aidieoreul jjada** 아이디어를 짜다 brainstorm ideas

jjagi 짜기 N weaving

jjajeung.i nada 짜증이 나다 V to get annoyed, irritated

jjida 찌다 V to steam: **gogumareul jjida** 고구마를 찌다 steam sweet potatoes

jjida 찌다 V to get fat: **sari jjida** 살이 찌다 get fat

jjigae 찌개 N soup (*spicy stew*)

jjin 찐 ADJ steamed

jjinggeurida 찡그리다 V to frown

jjitda 찢다 V to tear, rip

jjochanaeda 쫓아내다 V to chase away, chase out

jjogaeda 조개다 V to break apart

jjok 쪽 N side

jjotda 쫓다 V to chase, run after

jjuk ttaragada 쭉 따라가다 V to follow along

joahada 좋아하다 V to like, care for, be fond of, be pleased by

joajida 좋아지다 V to get better, improve

jobu 조부 N grandfather

jobumo 조부모 N grandparents

...jochado ...조차도 PP even (also)

joechaekgameul neukkida 죄책감을 느끼다 V to feel guilty

jogak 조각 N carving, sculpture

jogak 조각 N piece, portion, section, cut, slice

jogakhada 조각하다 V to carve, sculpt

jogeum 조금 N a little bit

johwa 조화 N harmony, balance

johwa 조화 N condolence flower

johwa 조화 N artificial flower

johwa 조화 N mysterious phenomenon

johwadoeda 조화되다 V to be in harmony with, blend in

johwadoen 조화된 ADJ harmonious

joka 조카 N nephew

jokattal 조카딸 N niece

jokkeon 조건 N condition, terms

jokki 조끼 N vest

jollida 졸리다 V to feel sleepy, tired

jollin 졸린 ADJ sleepy, drowsy

jomo 조모 N grandmother

jon.gyeong 존경 N respect

jon.gyeonghada 존경하다 V to respect

jong.eobwon 종업원 N waiter, waitress, worker

jong.i 종이 N paper

jonggyo 종교 N religion

jongnyu 종류 N kind, type, sort

jonjaehada 존재하다 V to exist

jopda, jobeun 좁다, 좁은 ADJ narrow

joribeop 조리법 N recipe

joriphada 조립하다 V to assemble, put together

josahada 조사하다 V to investigate, research

josang 조상 N ancestor

josimhada 조심하다 V to be careful

josimhaseyo! 조심하세요! INTERJ be careful!, look out!

jota, jo.eun 좋다, 좋은 ADJ good, fine, nice

joyonghada, joyonghan 조용하다, 조용한 ADJ quiet

ju 주 N week

jubu 주부 N housewife

juchahada 주차하다 V to park (*car*)

juda 주다 V to give

jugan 주간 N weekly

jugeum 죽음 N death

jugeun 죽은 ADJ dead

jugeup 주급 N wages

jugida 죽이다 V to kill, murder

ju.in 주인 N host

jujanghada 주장하다 V to insist

juje 주제 N topic

jujeohada 주저하다 V to hesitate

jujeonja 주전자 N jug, pitcher

jukda 죽다 V to die

jul 줄 N queue, line, rope, string

J

julda 줄다 v to decrease, reduce
julmunui 줄무늬 N stripe
julmunuiui 줄무늬의 ADJ striped patterned
julseoda 줄서다 v to line up, queue
jumal 주말 N weekend
jumin 주민 N resident, inhabitant
jumokhada 주목하다 v to pay attention
jumun 주문 N order (*placed for food, goods*)
jumunhada 주문하다 v to place an order
junbi 준비 N preparation
junbidoeda 준비되다 v to be prepared, ready
junbidoen 준비된 ADJ prepared, ready
junbihada 준비하다 v to prepare, arrange, get ready
junbisikida 준비시키다 v to prepare, make ready
jung.ang 중앙 N center, middle
jung.ang(ui) 중앙의 ADJ central
jung.yohada, jung.yohan 중요하다, 중요한 ADJ important
jung.yoseong 중요성 N importance
jungdaehada, jungdaehan 중대하다, 중대한 ADJ serious, important
junggan 중간 N middle, center
junggugeo 중국어 N Chinese (*language*)
jungguk 중국 N China
jungguk saram 중국 사람 N Chinese (*nationality*)
jungsim 중심 N center, middle
jungsimji 중심지 N pivot, capital, center
jungsimui 중심의 ADJ centric
jupda 줍다 v to pick up, lift, find
jurida 줄이다 v to decrease, reduce, cut down, downsize, narrow down
juro 주로 ADV mostly, mainly
jusa 주사 N injection
jusa 주사 N an act out of drunkenness
jusahada 주사하다 v to inject
juso 주소 N address
juwibaegyeong 주위배경 N surroundings
...juwie ...주위에 ADV around, surrounding
juyohan 주요한 ADJ main, major, primary
juyuso 주유소 N gas station

jwi 쥐 N rat
jyuseu 쥬스 N juice

K

kadeu(nori) 카드(놀이) N cards, game
kaedi 캐디 N caddie (*golf*)
kaedillak 캐디락 N Cadillac
kaemkodeo 캠코더 N camcorder
kaempein 캠페인 N campaign
kaempeoseu 캠퍼스 N campus
kaemping 캠핑 N camping
kaemutda 캐묻다 v to interrogate
kaenada 캐나다 N Canada
kaenaeda 캐내다 v to dig up, dig out: bimireul kaenaeda 비밀을 캐내다 dig out secrets
kaendi 캔디 N candy
kaenggeoru 캥거루 N kangaroo
kaereol 캐럴 N (*Christmas*) carol
kaereomel 캐러멜 N caramel
kaereot 캐럿 N carat
kaerikeocheo 캐리커처 N caricature
kaerikteo 캐릭터 N character
kajino 카지노 N casino
kakao 카카오 N cacao
kakisaek 카키색 N khaki (*color*)
kakteil 칵테일 N cocktail
kal 칼 N knife
kalguksu 칼국수 N cup noodles
kaljaguk 칼자국 N cut from a sword
kaljil 칼질 N cutting
kaljilhada 칼질하다 v to cut, chop
kallal 칼날 N blade of a knife
kallori 칼로리 N calorie
kalmatda 칼맞다 v to get stabbed
kalsyum 칼슘 N calcium
kambodia 캄보디아 N Cambodia
kamelleon 카멜레온 N chameleon
kameo 카메오 N cameo
kamera 카메라 N camera
kameramaen 카메라맨 N cameraman
kamkamhada 캄캄하다 ADJ dismal, hopeless: nunapi kamkamhada 눈앞이 캄캄하다 I feel hopeless
kamkamhada 캄캄하다 ADJ pitch-dark, dark: bakki kamkamhada 밖이 캄캄하다 It's dark outside
kan 칸 N blank: bin kaneul chaeuseyo 빈 칸을 채우세요 Please fill in the blanks
kan 칸 N Cannes

kan 칸 N room

kan 칸 N room (*counting unit*): **bangi myeot kanieyo?** 방이 몇 칸이에요? How many rooms?

kaneisyeon 카네이션 N carnation

kanibal 카니발 N carnival

kanmagi 칸막이 N partition, divider

kanu 카누 N canoe

kape 카페 N a café, a coffee house

kapein 카페인 N caffeine

kapeteu 카페트 N carpet

kapulje 카풀제 N car pool system

kare 카레 N curry

kariseuma 카리스마 N charisma

kaseteu 카세트 N cassette

kaseutella 카스텔라 N sponge cake

katallogeu 카탈로그 N catalog

kategori 카테고리 N category

katusa 카투사 N KATUSA, Korean Augmentation of the US army

kauboi 카우보이 N cowboy

kaunseulleo 카운슬러 N counselor

kaunteu 카운터 N counter (*for paying, buying tickets*)

keibeul 케이블 N cable

keikeu 케이크 N cake

kenggida 켕기다 V to feel uneasy (*out of guilty conscience*)

keodarata 커다랗다 ADJ huge, great

keojida 커지다 V to grow larger

keolkeolhada 컬컬하다 ADJ feeling thirsty: **mogi keolkeolhada** 목이 컬컬하다 feel thirsty

keollipeullawo 컬리플라워 N cauliflower

keommaeng 컴맹 N computer illiterate

keompyuteo 컴퓨터 N computer

keomyunikeisyeon 커뮤니케이션 N communication

keomyuniti 커뮤니티 N community

keonyeong 커녕 PP anything but, far from

keop 컵 N cup

keopi 커피 N coffee

keorieo 커리어 N career

keorikyulleom 커리큘럼 N curriculum

keoteun 커튼 N curtain

keuda, keun 크다, 큰 ADJ big, large

keugi 크기 N size

keullaesik 클래식 N classic

keulleop 클럽 N club (*night*)

keumjikhada 큼직하다 ADJ quite big

keunkodachida 큰코다치다 V to pay dearly

keuraekeo 크래커 N cracker, salty biscuit

keuriseumaseu 크리스마스 N Christmas

ki 키 (열쇠) N key

ki keuda/keun 키 크다/큰 ADJ tall

kibodeu 키보드 N keyboard (*of computer*)

kikkikgeorida 킥킥거리다 V to giggle, chuckle

killogeuraem 킬로그램 N kilogram

killomiteu 킬로미터 N kilometer

kiseu 키스 N kiss

kiseuhada 키스하다 V to kiss

kiuda 키우다 V to allow illness to get worse: **byeongeul kiuda** 병을 키우다 let the illness progress

kiuda 키우다 V to bring up, nurse a child: **aireul kiuda** 아이를 키우다 nurture a child

kiuda 키우다 V to build up: **geunnyugui himeul kiuda** 근육의 힘을 키우다 build up muscles

kiuda 키우다 V to train: **injaereul kiuda** 인재를 키우다 train a hidden competent person

kiuda 키우다 V to turn up: **bollyumeul kiuda** 볼륨을 키우다 turn up the volume

kiwi 키위 N kiwi fruit

kkadaropda, kkadaroun 까다롭다, 까다로운 ADJ fussy, picky, difficult (*character*): **kkadaroun sikseong** 까다로운 식성 be particular about food; **kkadaroun saram** 까다로운 사람 a man hard to please

kkadaropda, kkadaroun 까다롭다, 까다로운 ADJ complicated: **kkadaroun munje** 까다로운 문제 a complicated matter

kkae.eo itda 깨어 있다 ADJ awake

kkae.eo nada 깨어나다 V to awake, wake up

kkae.uda 깨우다 V to wake someone up

kkaejida 깨지다 V to break

kkaejin 깨진 ADJ broken, shattered

kkaekkeuthada, kkaekkeutan 깨끗하다, 깨끗한 ADJ clean

kkaetteurida 깨뜨리다 V to break, crush, destroy

K

...kkaji ...까지 PP until, by

kkalgae 깔개 N mat

kkaman kong 까만 콩 N black beans

kkamata, kkaman 까맣다, 까만 ADJ black

kkangtong 깡통 N can, tin

...kke ...께 PP to (*a person*) (*honorific of* 에게, 한테)

kkeojida 꺼지다 V to go out, be extinguished, be blown out

kkeojida 꺼지다 V one's eyes become hollow

kkeopjireul beotgida 껍질을 벗기다 V to peel

...kkeseo ...께서 PREP (*honorific subject particle*): **seonsaengnimkkeseo malsseumhasyeotda** 선생님께서 말씀하셨다 the teacher spoke

kkeuda 끄다 V off: to switch off, turn off

kkeun 끈 N string

kkeunjeok.kkeunjeokhada/-han 끈적끈적하다/-한 ADJ sticky

kkeunnada 끝나다 V to be over, finished, done, complete, gone

kkeunnaeda 끝내다 V to complete, end, finish, close

kkeunnan 끝난 ADJ finished

kkeurida 끓이다 V to boil, heat, simmer: **mureul kkeurida** 물을 끓이다 boil water

kkeurida 끓이다 V to worry, seethe: **hwaro sogeul kkeurida** 화로 속을 끓이다 seethe with anger

kkeurin 끓인 ADJ boiled

kkeut 끝 N tip, end, finish, edge

kkochaeng.i 꼬챙이 N skewer

kkok matda 꼭 맞다 V to fit perfectly

kkokdaegi 꼭대기 N top, apex, summit

kkori 꼬리 N tail

kkot 꽃 N flower

kkotbyeong 꽃병 N vase

kkul 꿀 N honey

kkum 꿈 N dream

kkumida 꾸미다 V to decorate

kkumkkuda 꿈꾸다 V to dream

kkyeo.anda 껴안다 V to embrace

ko 코 N nose

ko golda 코 골다 V to snore

koalla 코알라 N koala

kokkiri 코끼리 N elephant

kokkumeong 콧구멍 N nostril

kokoneot 코코넛 N coconut

kolla 콜라 N cola

kollokgeorida 콜록거리다 V to keep hacking, coughing

koneo 코너 N corner

kong 콩 N bean

kongnamul 콩나물 N bean sprouts

konnorae 콧노래 N humming

konsenteu 콘센트 N (*electric*) outlet

konseoteu 콘서트 N concert

kontenteurenjeu 콘텐트렌즈 N contact lens

konteseuteu 콘테스트 N contest

koppulso 코뿔소 N rhino

koreoseu 코러스 N chorus

koseumoseu 코스모스 N cosmos

kossuyeom 콧수염 N mustache

koteu 코트 N coat, overcoat

kouseum 코웃음 N sniff, sneer: **kouseumeul chida** 코웃음을 치다 laugh scornfully

kuki 쿠키 N cookie, sweet biscuit

kupon 쿠폰 N coupon

kwaegam 쾌감 N exhilaration

kwaerak 쾌락 N pleasure, enjoyment

kwaeyu 쾌유 N recovery from illness: **kwaeyureul bilda** 쾌유를 빌다 wish a person a full recovery

kwijeu 퀴즈 N quiz

kwikwihada 퀴퀴하다 ADJ musty, fusty

kyeoda 켜다 V to switch on, turn on: **radioreul kyeoda** 라디오를 켜다 turn on the radio

kyeoda 켜다 V to play string instruments: **baiollineul kyeoda** 바이올린을 켜다 play the violin

kyeoda 켜다 V to stretch oneself: **gijigaereul kyeoda** 기지개를 켜다 stretch oneself

kyeojyeo itda 켜져 있다 ADJ on (*turned on, left on*)

M

ma.eul 마을 N village, town

ma.eum 마음 N heart

ma.eum pyeon hada 마음 편 하다 V to feel at ease, feel at home

ma.eumeul bakkuda 마음을 바꾸다 V to change one's mind

mabeop 마법 N magic

machal 마찰 N friction, rubbing

machan.gajiro 마찬가지로 ADV likewise, alike

machim 마침 ADV just in time

machimnae 마침내 ADV finally

machimpyo 마침표 N period (*end of a sentence*)

machwi 마취 N anesthesia, narcotism

madang 마당 N yard, garden

mae 매 ADJ every, each: **mae dal** 매 달 every month, each month

mae 매 N hawk

mae 매 N paper counting unit: **jongi baengmae** 종이 100 매 100 sheets of paper

mae 매 N rod, spanking: **maereul matda** 매를 맞다 be beaten

maebeon 매번 N every time

maeda 매다 V to tie

maeil 매일 N every day

maejang 매장 N shop, store

maeje 매제 N brother-in-law (*younger sister's husband*)

maejeom 매점 N cafeteria, canteen

maejeonghada 매정하다 ADJ hardhearted

maejindoen 매진된 ADJ sold out

maekju 맥주 N beer

maekkeunhada 매끈하다 ADJ smooth, silky

maekkeureopda/-reo.un 매끄럽다/ -러운 ADJ smooth, silky

maekomhada 매콤하다 ADJ hot, spicy

maemolchada 매몰차다 ADJ cold, harsh

maengse 맹세 N oath, vow, pledge

macpda, mae.un 맵다, 매운 ADJ hot, spicy

maepyo 매표 N ticketing

maeryeokjeogida, maeryeokjeogin 매력적이다, 매력적인 ADJ attractive

maeryeokjeogin 매력적인 ADJ charming, attractive

maeteuriseu 매트리스 N mattress

maeumdaero 마음대로 ADV as one pleases, at one's (*own*) discretion: **ne maeumdaero mueonnideun gollara** 네 마음대로 무엇이든 골라라 Choose whatever you want

maeumkkeot 마음껏 ADV to one's heart's content: **geuneun maeumkkeot sorireul jilleotda** 그는 마음껏 소리를 질렀다 He shouted to his heart's content

magae 마개 N stopper, cork, plug

magyeonhan 막연한 ADJ vague, obscure

maheun 마흔 NUM forty

maikeu 마이크 N microphone

maineoseu 마이너스 N minus

majak 마작 N mahjong

majeun pyeon 맞은 편 N opposite side

majeun pyeonui 맞은 편의 ADJ on the opposite side of

majimakui 마지막의 ADJ final, last

majuchida 마주치다 V to meet: **siseoneul majuchida** 시선을 마주치 다 make eye contact

majuchida 마주치다 V to run into, bump into: **yet chingureul uyeonhi majuchida** 옛 친구를 우연히 마주치 다 bump into an old friend

makda, malgeun 맑다, 맑은 ADJ clear, pure, clean: **malgeun mul** 맑은 물 clear water; **malgeun nun** 맑은 눈 clear eye; **malgeun jeongsin** 맑은 정 신 sober mind; **malgeun guk** 맑은 국 watery soup

makdaegi 막대기 N stick, pole

makgan 막간 N intermission: **makganui hyusik** 막간의 휴식 break during an intermission

makhida 막히다 V to be clogged, blocked, plugged: **singkeuga makhida** 싱크가 막히다 the sink is clogged

makhida 막히다 V to be congested with heavy traffic: **giri makhida** 길이 막히다 the road is congested

makhida 막히다 V to be at a loss for words with anger

makhida 막히다 V to be breathtaking, suffocating: **sumi makhige yeppeuda** 숨이 막히게 예쁘다 breathtakingly beautiful; **deowiro sumi makhida** 더위로 숨이 막히다 be suffocated with heat

makhida/makin 막히다/막힌 ADJ narrow-minded, inflexible, stubborn: **apdwiga makhin saram** 앞뒤가 막힌 사람 a stubborn person

makjunghan 막중한 ADJ heavy, vital, critical

mal 말 N horse

mal 말 N language

malbeoreut 말버릇 N one's manner of speaking

M

maldatum N 말다툼 quarrel

malhada 말하다 V to say, speak, talk, tell

malleisia 말레이시아 N Malaysia

mallida 말리다 V to dry

mallida 말리다 V to break up a fight: **ssaumeul mallida** 싸움을 말리다 stop a fight

mallijangseong 만리장성 N the Great Wall of China

mallyuhanuen 만류하는 ADJ dissuasive

malsseong 말썽 N trouble: **malsseong-kkureogi** 말썽꾸러기 trouble-maker

mamuri 마무리 N finish, completion: **ireul mamuri jitda** 일을 마무리 짓다 complete a work

man 만 ADV only

man 만 N bay

man 만 NUM ten thousand

manchwihad 만취한 V to be plastered

mandeulda 만들다 V to make, produce

mandu 만두 N dumpling

maneul 마늘 N garlic

maneun 많은 ADJ lots of

mang 망 N net

mang 망 N lookout: **mangeul boda** 망을 보다 keep a lookout

mangchi 망치 N hammer

manggajida 망가지다 V to be out of order, broken

manggak 망각 N forgetfulness: **man-ggagui gang** 망각의 강 Lethe

manggo 망고 N mango

mangnae 막내 N the youngest

mangnyeonhwe 망년회 N year-end party

mangsang 망상 N delusion, fantasy

mangsin 망신 N shame, disgrace

mangsinseureopda 망신스럽다 ADJ dishonorable, shameful

mangukgi 만국기 N flags of all nations

manhwa 만화 N cartoon

manhoe 만회 N recovery, retrieval

mani 많이 ADV a lot, many, much

manjida 만지다 V to touch

manjokhada 만족하다 ADJ to be content with, satisfied with

manjokhada, manjokaehada 만족하다, 만족해하다 V to be satisfied

manjoksikida 만족시키다 V to satisfy

mankkikhada 만끽하다 V to enjoy to the fullest: **jayureul mankkikhada** 자유를 만끽하다 enjoy one's freedom to the fullest

manmanhada 만만하다 ADJ be full of ambition

manmanhada 만만하다 ADJ be full of self-confidence

manmanhageboda 만만하게 보다 V to make light of a person: **nareul manmanhi boji maseyo** 나를 만만히 보지 마세요 I wasn't born yesterday

manmul 만물 N all things, all creation

mannada 만나다 V to meet

manneung 만능 N omnipotence, being almighty

mannyeon 만년 N forever (*always*): **mannyeon gwajang** 만년 과장 a forever section chief

mannyeon 만년 N myriad years (*ten thousand years*)

mannyeon 만년 N one's later years

mannyeonhada 만연하다 ADJ rampant, prevalent

mansak 만삭 N last month of pregnancy

manta, maneun 많다, 많은 ADJ many, much

maraton 마라톤 N marathon

mareuda, mareun 마르다, 마른 V to dry

mareuda 마르다 V to lose weight, become thin, become slim

mareun 마른 ADJ dry: **mareun anju** 마른 안주 dried snack, bar snack

mareun 마른 ADJ skinny, thin, slim: **bijjeok mareun** 비쩍 마른 (*too*) skinny

maria 마리아 N the Virgin Mary

maru 마루 N floor

maryeok 마력 N horsepower

maryeon 마련 N arrangement

maryeonhada 마련하다 V to arrange, prepare: **bangbeobeul maryeonhada** 방법을 마련하다 arrange a solution

masajihada 마사지하다 V to massage

masi nada 맛이 나다 V to smack of (*flavor, taste*)

masida 마시다 V to drink

masitda, masinneun 맛있다, 맛있는 ADJ delicious, tasty

mask 마스크 N (*face*) mask

mat 맛 N taste

matboda 맛보다 V to taste (*sample*)

matchuda 맞추다 V to set, assemble

matda, manneun 맞다, 맞는 ADJ correct, right, suitable

matda, manneun 맞다, 맞는 ADJ timely: **ttaee manneun jochi** 때에 맞는 조치 a timely measure

matda, manneun 맞다, 맞는 ADJ lawful

matda, manneun 맞다, 맞는 V to greet, welcome, receive: **sonnimeul matda** 손님을 맞다 welcome (*greet*) a guest

matda, manneun 맞다, 맞는 V to be hit, struck, beaten, slapped

matgida 맡기다 V to leave, put, check (*in*), deposit: **gwijungpumeul matgida** 귀중품을 맡기다 place valuables in (*person's*) custody

matgida 맡기다 V to assign, entrust: **chaegimeul matgida** 책임을 맡기다 give responsibility to

mauseu 마우스 N mouse (*computer*)

mayak 마약 N narcotics, drug

meolmi 멀미 N (*motion*) sickness

memareun 메마른 ADJ barren, infertile: **memareun ttang** 메마른 땅 a barren land

memareun 메마른 ADJ prosaic: **gamjeongi memareun saram** 감정이 메마른 사람 a prosaic person

memo 메모 N note, message, memo

menyu 메뉴 N menu

meogida 먹이다 V to feed

meokda 먹다 V to eat

meolda, meon 멀다, 먼 ADJ far

meomchuda 멈추다 V to stop, halt

meomureuda 머무르다 V to stay, remain

meong 멍 N bruise

meonjeo 먼저 ADV first, earlier, beforehand

meonji 먼지 N dust

meori 머리 N head

meori(karak) 머리(카락) N hair

meotjida, meotjin 멋지다, 멋진 ADJ wonderful, nice, cool

meriyaseu 메리야스 N undershirt

meseukkeopda 메스껍다 ADJ to be nauseous, sick

mesiji 메시지 N message

mianhadago jeonhada 미안하다고 전하다 V to say sorry

mianhamnida! 미안합니다! PHR I am sorry! excuse me! (*apology*)

michida, michin 미치다, 미친 ADJ mad, crazy, insane

mideum 믿음 N belief, faith

mideumjikhada 믿음직하다 ADJ reliable, dependable

miguk 미국 N America, United States

miguk saram 미국 사람 N American

mikkeureopda 미끄럽다 ADJ slippery

milda 밀다 V to push

milkkaru 밀가루 N flour

miljeophada 밀접하다 V to be interrelated, intimate

millyeonada 밀려나다 V to be pushed out: **sijang jarieseo millyeonada** 시장 자리에서 밀려나다 be kicked out of the Mayor's seat

millyeooda 밀려오다 V to wash over, surge: **huhoega millyeooda** 후회가 밀려오다 be overwhelmed by regrets

milsuhada 밀수하다 V to smuggle

minibeoseu 미니버스 N minibus

minjok 민족 N ethnic group

minjuju.i 민주주의 N democracy

minmitada 밋밋하다 ADJ flat, plain

minpye 민폐 N public nuisance, private nuisance

minyeo 미녀 N beauty

mipda 밉다 ADJ ugly, homely, detestable

mirae 미래 N future: in future

miri 미리 ADV beforehand, in advance

miso 미소 N smile

misojitda 미소짓다 V to smile

mitcheon 밑천 N seed money: **mitcheoni deureonada** 밑천이 드러나다 run out of funds

mitda 믿다 V to believe, trust

mitjida 밑지다 V to lose, suffer a loss

miwohada 미워하다 V to hate

miyong 미용 N beauty culture, cosmetic treatment

mobeom 모범 N model, example

modeun 모든 ADJ all, every, whole, entire

modeun geot 모든 것 N everything

modeun got 모든 곳 N everywhere

modeun jongnyu.ui 모든 종류의 ADJ every kind of

modeun saram 모든 사람 N everybody, everyone

mo.euda 모으다 V to assemble, gather: **jaryoreul moeuda** 자료를 모으다 gather data; **du soneul moeuda** 두 손을 모으다 put two hands together (*for prayer*)

M

modu 모두 N all, altogether, in total

mogi 모기 N mosquito

moida 모이다 V to gather, flock: **jeon-gugeseo moida** 전국에서 모이다 gather from all over the country

mogyoil 요요일 N Thursday

mogyok 목욕 N bath

mogyokgaun 목욕가운 N bathrobe

mogyokhada 목욕하다 V to bathe, take a bath

mogyoksil 목욕실 N bathroom

mohohada, mohohan 모호하다, 모호한 ADJ vague

moim 모임 N meeting: **jeonggi moim** 정기 모임 a regular meeting

moja 모자 N cap, hat

mojaikeu 모자이크 N mosaic

mok 목 N neck

mok(gumeong) 목(구멍) N throat

mokdori 목도리 N scarf, muffler

mokgeori 목걸이 N necklace: **jinju mokgeori** 진주 목걸이 a pearl necklace

mokgyeokhada 목격하다 V to witness

mokgyeokja 목격자 N witness

mokjeok 목적 N purpose: **mokjeok uisik** 목적 의식 a sense of purpose

mokjeokji 목적지 N destination

mokpyo 목표 N goal

moksa 목사 N pastor, minister

moksori 목소리 N voice

moksum 목숨 N life, breath of life

molduhada 몰두하다 V to be absorbed, be immersed

mollaboda 몰라보다 V to fail to recognize

mollae 몰래 ADV stealthily, surreptitiously

mollida 몰리다 V to be accused of: **beomineuro mollida** 범인으로 몰리다 be branded as a suspect

mollida 몰리다 V to be cornered, be pushed

mollida 몰리다 V to flock, be swamped with: **inpaga mollida** 인파가 몰리다 be swamped with people

mollyeodanida 몰려다니다 V to go around in groups

mom 몸 N body

momgajim 몸가짐 N demeanour

mommae 몸매 N (body) figure, shape

mongmareun 목마른 ADJ thirsty

moniteo 모니터 N monitor (of computer)

monmattanghada 못마땅하다 ADJ disagreeable, not to liking

morae 모래 N sand: **moraeseong** 모래성 a sand castle

moranaeda 몰아내다 V to drive out, expel

more 모레 N day after tomorrow

morip 몰입 N immersion, devotion

mosida 모시다 V to serve: **bumoreul mosida** 부모를 모시다 have one's parents with

mot 못 ADV can't, not: **noraereul mot handa** 노래를 못 한다 can't sing

mot 못 N nail (spike)

moteo 모터 N motor, engine

motsaenggida, motsaenggin 못생기다, 못생긴 ADJ ugly

moyang 모양 N form, shape

moyok 모욕 N insult

moyokhada 모욕하다 V to insult

mudeom 무덤 N grave

mudeopda, mudeo.un 무덥다, 무더운 ADJ sweltering, muggy

mudida 무디다 ADJ dense, dull, slow: **mudin saram** 무딘 사람 a dense person

mudida 무디다 ADJ dull, blunt: **mudin kallal** 무딘 칼날 a dull blade

mueosideunji 무엇이든지 ADV anything, whatever

mueot 무엇 N what

muge 무게 N weight

mugeopda, mugeo.un 무겁다, 무거운 ADJ heavy

mugereul dalda 무게를 달다 V to weigh

mugi 무기 N weapon

mugwansim 무관심 N indifference

muhan 무한 N infinity, limitless

muhyo 무효 N invalidity, nullity

mujakjeong 무작정 ADV blindly, thoughtlessly

mujoe 무죄 N innocence: **mujoe seongo** 무죄 선고 acquittal

mukda 묵다 V to stay, lodge: **hotere mukda** 호텔에 묵다 stay at a hotel

mukda, mukeun 묵다, 묵은 ADJ old, outdated, old-fashioned: **mugeun gimchi** 묵은 김치 old (well-fermented) kimchi; **mugeun saenggak** 묵은 생각 a timeworn idea; **mugeun gwanseup** 묵은 관습 old customs

mukda, mulgeun 묽다, 묽은 ADJ thin, watery: **mulgeun soseu** 묽은 소스 thin sauce

mul 물 N water

mulche 물체 N object, thing

mulda 물다 V to bite

muldeulda 물들다 V to dye, get dyed

mulgeon 물건 N thing

mulgyeolchida 물결치다 V to wave

muljil 물질 N matter, substance

mulkkogi 물고기 N fish

mullida 물리다 V to get bitten: **mogie mullida** 모기에 물리다 bitten by a mosquito

mullida 물리다 V to get tired of: **satange mullida** 사탕에 물리다 get sick and tired of candy

mullida 물리다 V to put off, postpone

mullida 물리다 V to take back, return: **doneul mulleojuda** 돈을 물러주다 pay a refund

mullon 물론 ADV of course

mulso 물소 N buffalo (*water buffalo*)

mumigeonjohada/-han 무미건조하다/-한 ADJ bland

mun 문 N door, gate

mun.guryu 문구류 N stationery

munanhi 무난히 ADV with ease, easily

munhak 문학 N literature

munhwa 문화 N culture

munjang 문장 N sentence

munje 문제 N problem, question, trouble, matter

munjireuda 문지르다 V to scrub: **salsal munjireuda** 살살 문지르다 scrub lightly

munpeopp 문법 N grammar

munseo 문서 N document, letter

munuiui 무늬의 ADJ patterned: **kkonmunuiui** 꽃무늬의 floral patterned

mureoboda 물어보다 V to enquire, ask

mureup 무릎 N knee

muri 무리 N group, bunch

murihan 무리한 ADJ too much: **murihan yogu** 무리한 요구 an unreasonable demand

muryehada, muryehan 무례하다, 무례한 ADJ impolite, rude

muryeo 무려 ADV as many as, to the prodigious number of

muryo(ui) 무료의 ADJ free of charge

museo.um 무서움 N fear

museopda, museo.un 무섭다, 무서운 ADJ scary, frightening

museopda, museowohada 무섭다, 무서워하다 ADJ afraid, scared

museun irieyo? 무슨 일이에요? PHR what happened? what's going on?

musihada 무시하다 V to ignore: **saramdeul musihada** 사람을 무시하다 look down upon a person

musikhada, musikan 무식하다, 무식한 ADJ ignorant

mutda 묻다 V to bury

muyeok 무역 N trade, commerce

mwo hasigeyo? 뭐 하시게요? PHR what for?

mworago hasyeosseoyo? 뭐라고 하셨어요? PHR pardon me? what did you say?

mworagoyo? 뭐라고요? INTERJ what?

myeon 면 N cotton

myeondohada 면도하다 V to shave

myeoneuri 며느리 N daughter-in-law

myeong.ye 명예 N honor: **myeongye-hweson** 명예훼손 defamation of one's character

myeongbaekhada, myeongbaekan 명백하다, 명백한 ADJ obvious

myeongbaekhi 명백히 ADV apparently, obviously

myeongdan 명단 N list

myeonghwakhada, myeonghwakan 명확하다, 명확한 ADJ definite

myeongjeol 명절 N holiday (*festival*): **myeongjeoreul soeda** 명절을 쇠다 observe a holiday

myeongnyeong 명령 N command, order

myeongnyeonghada 명령하다 V to order, command

myeonhada 면하다 V to avoid, get away

myeonheojjeung 면허증 N licence, permit

myeonjeop 면접 N interview: **gaebyeol myeonjeop** 개별 면접 an individual interview

myeot 몇 N some, several, a few: **myeot saram** 몇 사람 a few people

myeot 몇 N how many? how old? what time?

myeot sarieyo? 몇 살이에요? PHR how old?

M

myeot siyo? 몇 시요? PHR what time?
myosahada 묘사하다 v to describe

N

na 나 PRON I, me: **naneun haksaeng-imnida** 나는 학생입니다 I am a student.; **nareul ppobajuseyo** 나를 뽑아주세요 Please pick me
na.ui 나의 (것) N my, mine: **naui bang** 나의 방 my room; **naui geotsida** 나의 것이다 it's mine
nabang 나방 N moth
nabi 나비 N butterfly
nache 나체 N nude
nadaeda 나대다 v to act frivolous, behave carelessly
nadeuri 나들이 N outing, excursion, picnic
nae 내 N I, my: **naega jeil jalhaeyo** 내가 제일 잘해요 I am the best; **nae dongsaengi deo keoyo** 내 동생이 더 커요 My brother is bigger
nae 내 것 N mine
nae.il 내일 N tomorrow
naedeonjida 내던지다 v to throw out, give up
naegi 내기 N bet, wager: **naegireul hada, naegireul geolda** 내기를 하다, 내기를 걸다 place a bet
naejo 내조 N the wife's help
naembi 냄비 N pan, pot
naemilda 내밀다 v to push out, stick out: **hwahaeui soneul laemilda** 화해의 손을 내밀다 stick out hands for reconciliation
naemsae 냄새 N odor, smell
naemsaematda 냄새맡다 v to smell
naemsaenada 냄새나다 v to stink, smell
naemsaenada 냄새나다 ADJ suspicious, smell fishy
naengbangdoen 냉방된 ADJ air-conditioned
naengjanggo 냉장고 N refrigerator
naengjanghada 냉장하다 v to keep cool, refrigerate
naengjanghan 냉장한 ADJ chilled, refrigerated
naengkeum 냉큼 ADV quickly, immediately
naengnanbang 냉난방 N air conditioning and heating

naenyeon 내년 N next year
naeppumda 내뿜다 v to breathe out, spurt out: **bureul naeppumneun yong** 불을 내뿜는 용 a fire-breathing dragon
naerida 내리다 v to take down, unload: **teureogeseo jimeul naerida** 트럭에서 짐을 내리다 unload a truck
naerida 내리다 v to get off, disembark: **chaeseo naerida** 차에서 내리다 get out of the car
naerida 내리다 v to bring down, lower, cut down: **gagyeogeul naerida** 가격을 내리다 lower a price
naeryeonota 내려놓다 v to set down, take down
naeseon 내선 N extension (*telephone*)
nagada 나가다 v to go out, exit, leave, go forth
nagada 나가다 v to go off, power out
nagada 나가다 v to cost, be worth, weigh
nageune 나그네 N drifter, wanderer
nagin 낙인 N brand, stigma: **nagini jjikhida** 낙인이 찍히다 be branded as
nagyeop 낙엽 N fallen leaves
nai 나이 N age
nai manta/maneun 나이 많다/많은 ADJ old age
naillon 나일론 N nylon
najung.e 나중에 ADV later
najung.e bopsida! 나중에 봅시다! PHR see you later!
nakbang 낙방 N failure in an examination
nakcheon 낙천 N optimism: **nakcheonjeok** 낙천적 be optimistic
nakdamhada 낙담하다 v to be discouraged, be bummed out
nakji 낙지 N small octopus
nakje 낙제 N fail, flunk
nakjehada 낙제하다 v to fail, flunk
nakseo 낙서 N scribble, graffiti
naksi 낚시 N fishing
nal 날 N day: **siheom nal** 시험 날 an exam day; **seollal** 설날 New Year's day
nal (geosui) 날 (것의) ADJ raw, uncooked: **nal saengseon** 날 생선 raw fish
nalda 날다 v to fly
nalgae 날개 N wing
naljja 날짜 N date, day

nalkaropda, nalkaroun 날카롭다, 날카로운 ADJ sharp, keen: **nalkaroun kal** 날카로운 칼 a sharp knife; **nalka-roun tongchallyeok** 날카로운 통찰력 keen insight

nallida 날리다 V to fly: **jongibihaeng-gireul nallida** 종이비행기를 날리다 fly a paper airplane

nalssaeda 날쌔다 ADJ quick, agile

nalssi 날씨 N weather

nalssinhada, nalssinhan 날씬하다, 날씬한 ADJ slim, slender, lean

nalttwida 날뛰다 V to leap (up), jump

nalttwida 날뛰다 V to rave with fury: **hwaga naseo michyeo nalttwida** 화가 나서 미쳐 날뛰다 go ballistic, hit the ceiling

namda, nameun 남다, 남은 ADJ left, remaining: **nameun eumsik** 남은 음식 leftover (food)

namdaemun 남대문 N the South Gate, namdaemun

namdareuda 남다르다 ADJ peculiar, eccentric, odd

namdareuda 남다르다 ADJ unique, extraordinary, uncommon: **paesyeon-gamgagi namdareuda** 패션감각이 남다르다 unique (excellent) sense of fashion

namdongjjok 남동쪽 N south-east

nameoji 나머지 N rest, remainder, leftover

namgeuk 남극 N the South Pole

namgida 남기다 V to leave, save, set aside

namhan 남한 N South Korea

namja 남자 N man

namja chin.gu 남자 친구 N boyfriend

(namja) seonggi (남자) 성기 N penis

namjjok 남쪽 N south

nammae 남매 N brother and sister

namnyeo 남녀 N man and woman

nampyeon 남편 N husband

namseojjok 남서쪽 N south-west

namseong 남성 N male

namu 나무 N tree, wood

namurada 나무라다 V to scold, blame: **haksaengeul namurada** 학생을 나무라다 scold a student

namuro doen 나무로 된 ADJ wooden

namutgaji 나뭇가지 N branches (of tree)

nancheohada, nancheohan 난처하다, 난처한 ADJ akward, difficult, embarrassing

nandong 난동 N rampage: **nandon-geul burida** 난동을 부리다 make a disturbance

nangan 난간 N handrail, railing

nangman 낭만 N romance

nanhaehan 난해한 ADJ abstruse, com-plicated

nanip 난입 N trespass(ing), intrusion

nanjaengi 난쟁이 N dwarf, pigmy

nanjangpan 난장판 N chaos, bedlam: **nanjangpani doeda** 난장판이 되다 fall into utter confusion

nantu 난투 N fistfight: **nantugeugeul beorida** 난투극을 벌이다 tussle with someone

nanu.eojida 나누어지다 V to be divided into, divided by

nanu.eojin 나누어진 ADJ divided, dipartite

nanu.eojuda 나누어주다 V to hand out, distribute, pass out

nanuda 나누다 V to divide, share, seg-ment, dissect: **ttokgachi nanuda** 똑같이 나누다 divide equally

nanutsem 나눗셈 N division (math)

napal 나팔 N trumpet, bugle

napchi 납치 N hijack, kidnapping

napjak 납작 ADV flat

nappeuda, nappeun 나쁘다, 나쁜 ADJ bad, wrong, poor, ill-natured, unpleas-ant: **nappeun nalssi** 나쁜 날씨 bad weather; **pumjiri nappeun sangpum** 품질이 나쁜 상품 poor quality prod-uct; **maeumssiga nappeun** 마음씨가 나쁜 ill-natured; **gibuni nappeun** 기분이 나쁜 unpleasant

napulgeorida 나풀거리다 V to flutter softly

nara 나라 N country (nation)

naragada 날아가다 V to fly away, take wings: **naraganeun bihaenggi** 날아가는 비행기 a flying airplane

nareunhada 나른하다 ADJ languid, drowsy: **nareunhan moksori** 나른한 목소리 a drowsy voice

nasa 나사 N screw

naseoda 나서다 V to appear, turn up: **jibeul saryeoneun sarami naseotda** 집을 사려는 사람이 나섰다 a potential buyer of the house showed up

naseoda 나서다 v to interfere in: **namui ire naseoji mara** 남의 일에 나서지 마라 Don't stick your nose into others' business

naseoda 나서다 v to set off

naseoda 나서다 v to take action: **jeongbuga josae naseotda** 정부가 조사에 나섰다 The government set out an investigation

nat 낮 N day, daytime

nat gae 낱개 N piece, item, unit: **nat-gae pojang** 낱개 포장 individual packaging

nata 낳다 v to give birth

natda, najeun 낮다, 낮은 ADJ low

natseon saram 낯선 사람 N stranger

ne 네 INTERJ yes

nektai 넥타이 N necktie, tie

neo 너 N you (informal)

neogeureopda, neogeureoun 너그럽다, 너그러운 ADJ generous: **neogeureoun taedo** 너그러운 태도 generous attitude

neohui(deul) 너희(들) N you (informal, plural): **neohuineun han timida** 너희는 한 팀이다 You are all in one team

neolda 널다 v to hang, spread (out): **ppallaereul neolda** 빨래를 널다 hang laundry to dry

neomboda 넘보다 v to covet

neomboda 넘보다 v to hope

neomeojida 넘어지다 v to fall, trip, tumble

neomgyeojuda 넘겨주다 v to hand over, pass on

neomu 너무 ADV too, so, overly

neomu mani 너무 많이 ADV too much

neonsenseu 넌센스 N nonsense

neopda, neolbeun 넓다, 넓은 ADJ wide, spacious, broad, big, large

net 넷 NUM four

neteu 네트 N net

neteuwokeu 네트워크 N network

neujeodo 늦어도 ADJ at the latest

neukda 늙다 v to grow old

neukdae 늑대 N wolf

neukkida 느끼다 v to feel

neukkim 느낌 N feeling

neullida 늘리다 v to increase: **jae-saneul neullida** 재산을 늘리다 increase one's fortune

-neun -는 PP (present-tense noun-modifying suffix)

-neun/(eu)n che hada -는/(으)ㄴ 체 하다 v to pretend

-neun dong.an -는 동안 N while

-neun jung -는 중 N middle: in the middle of doing something

-neun/(eu)n/(eu)l+(object) -는/(으)ㄴ/(으)ㄹ+ (사물) PP the object which

-neun/(eu)n/(eu)l+(person) -는/(으)ㄴ/(으)ㄹ+ (사람) PP the person who

...neun/eun ...는/은 PP as for, speaking of (topic marker)

-neunde iksukhada -는데 익숙하다 ADJ used to, accustomed to

-neunde/(eu)nde -는데/(으)ㄴ데 PP (background information)

neungcheong 능청 N sway, sly

neungnyeok 능력 N ability

neungnyul 능률 N efficiency

neungsukhada, neungsukan 능숙하다, 능숙한 ADJ skillful, experienced

neup 늪 N marsh, swamp

neureonada 늘어나다 v to extend, stretch: **gomujuri jal neureonada** 고무줄이 잘 늘어나다 the rubber stretches easily

neurida, neurin 느리다, 느린 ADJ slow: **georeumi neurida** 걸음이 느리다 be a slow walker

neutda, neujeun 늦다, 늦은 ADJ late: **neujeun jeomsim** 늦은 점심 late lunch

neutdeowi 늦더위 N late summer heat

neutdungi 늦둥이 N late child (of old parents): **sasibe neutdungireul boda** 40에 늦둥이를 보다 have a late child at age 40

nikotin 니코틴 N nicotine

nim 님 N (honorific suffix for addressing)

nochida 놓치다 v to miss, lose

nochul 노출 N exposure, disclosure

nodong 노동 N labor

noe 뇌 N brain

noeul 노을 N sunset glow

nogeum 녹음 N tape recording

nogida 녹이다 v to captivate, enslave, bewitch: **aeganjangeul nogida** 애간장을 녹이다 captivate (men's) heart

nogida 녹이다 v to dissolve, melt down: **momeul nogida** 몸을 녹이다

warm oneself up, **seoltangeul nogida**
설탕을 녹이다 dissolve sugar

nogonhada 노곤하다 ADJ languid,
exhausted

noida 놓이다 V to be installed: **dariga
noida** 다리가 놓이다 a bridge is
being built

noida 놓이다 V to be placed in: **wiheomhan sanghwange noida** 위험한 상황에
놓이다 be put in a dangerous situation

noin 노인 N elderly

nokda 녹다 V to melt, thaw

nokhwahada 녹화하다 V to videotape

nolda 놀다 V to play

nollada, nollawohada 놀라다, 놀라
워하다 V to be surprised, astonished

nollapda, nollaun 놀랍다, 놀라운 ADJ
surprising

nolli 논리 N logic

nollim 놀림 N banter

non 논 N rice fields

nonbat 논밭 N farmland, fields and
paddies

nongdam 농담 N joke

nongeop 농업 N agriculture, farming

nonggigu 농기구 N agricultural implements

nonggu 농구 N basketball

nongjang 농장 N farm

nongsusan 농수산 N agriculture and
fisheries

nonjaeng 논쟁 N argument

nonjaenghada 논쟁하다 V to argue

nonje 논제 N subject of discussion

nonjeom 논점 N (*disputed/moot*) point,
topic

nonmun 논문 N treatise, thesis

nonsul 논술 N statement, enunciation

nopda, nopeun 높다, 높은 ADJ high

nopi 높이 N height, level

nopimmal 높임말 N honorific (*expres-
sion/word*)

nopittwigi 높이뛰기 N high leap

norae 노래 N song

noraehada 노래하다 V to sing

norata, noran 노랗다, 노란 ADJ yellow

noriteo 놀이터 N playground

noryeok 노력 N effort

noryeokhada 노력하다 V to make an
effort

nosimchosa 노심초사 N exertion of
the mind

nota 놓다 V to place, put, place, release:
yeomnyeoreul nota 염려를 놓다 put
one's mind at ease; **chaegeul chaeksange nota** 책을 책상에 놓다 place a
book on a desk

noye 노예 N slave

noyeom 노염 N anger, rage

nubida 누비다 V to crisscross: **jeon-
gugeul nubida** 전국을 누비다 all
over the map

nubida 누비다 V to quilt: **ibureul
nubida** 이불을 누비다 quilt a blanket

nuga 누가 N, PP who: **nuga oneunga?**
누가 오는가? Who is coming?

nugu 누구 N who: **nugureul mannanna?** 누구를 만났나? Whom did
you meet?

nugudeunji 누구든지 ADV anybody,
anyone

nullida 눌리다 V to be kept down:
jubyeon gangdaeguge nullida 주변
강대국에 눌리다 be repressed by surrounding powerful countries

nullida 눌리다 V to be overwhelmed:
hwanan gisee nullida 화난 기세에
눌리다 intimidated by one's temper

nullida 눌리다 V to be squashed:
napjakhage nullin ppang 납작하게
눌린 빵 a loaf of bread squashed flat

nun 눈 N eye: **nuneul gamda** 눈을
감다 close one's eyes

nun 눈 N snow

nuna 누나 N older sister (*male's*)

nunbyeong 눈병 N eye disease,
oculopathy: **nunbyeongi nada** 눈병이
나다 have eye trouble

nunchori 눈초리 N giving a look:
seongnan nunchori 성난 눈초리 an
angry look; **gyeongmyeorui nunchori**
경멸의 눈초리 a scornful look;
uisimui nunchori 의심의 눈초리 a
look of suspicion; **monmattanghan
nunchori** 못마땅한 눈초리 a look of
dissatisfaction

nuni oda 눈이 오다 V to snow

nunkkeopul 눈꺼풀 N eyelid:
pigoneuro mugeoun nunkkeopul
피곤으로 무거운 눈꺼풀 heavy eyelids
from fatigue

nunmeolda 눈멀다 V to become blind

nunmeon 눈먼 ADJ blind

nunmul 눈물 N tears

N

nunsaram 눈사람 N snowman

nunsseolmi 눈썰미 N quick eye for learning things: **nunsseolmiga itda** 눈썰미가 있다 be quick in visual learning

nunsseop 눈썹 N eyebrow

nunuseum 눈웃음 N smile with one's eyes

nupda 눕다 V to lie down

nupida 눕히다 V to lay

nureuda 누르다 V to press

nyujillaendeu 뉴질랜드 N New Zealand

nyuseu 뉴스 N news

O

o 오 NUM five

obeun 오븐 N oven

obutada 오붓하다 ADJ cozy, comfy

oda 오다 V to come: **isaoda** 이사오다 move in; **gakkai oda** 가까이 오다 draw closer

odap 오답 N incorrect answer

odobangjeong 오도방정 N giddiness, frivolity

odongtonghada 오동통하다 ADJ chubby

odumak 오두막 N hut, shack

oebak 외박 N stay-out , sleep-out

oechida 외치다 V to shout, yell

oegugin 외국인 N foreigner

oeguk(ui) 외국의 ADJ foreign

oegyogwan 외교관 N diplomat

oemo 외모 N appearance, looks

oemyeonhada 외면하다 V to turn away, look away

oenjjok 왼쪽 N left-hand side

oeropda, oeroun 외롭다, 외로운 ADJ lonely

oeroum 외로움 N loneliness: **geunyeoneun oeroumeul gyeondiji mothanda** 그녀는 외로움을 견디지 못한다 She can't stand loneliness

oesik 외식 N eating out, dining out

oetori 외톨이 N single (*solitary, lonely*) person

oettan 외딴 ADJ isolated, deserted

oetu 외투 N overcoat: **oetureul ipda** 외투를 입다 put on an overcoat

ogakhyeong 오각형 N pentagon

ogam 오감 N five senses

ogeori 오거리 N five-way crossing

ogeuradeulda 오그라들다 V to shrivel (up): **ogeuradeun dari** 오그라든 다리 shrivelled up legs

ogi 오기 N competitive spirit, refusal to yield

ohae 오해 N misunderstanding

ohu 오후 N afternoon

oi 오이 N cucumber

oin 오인 N misconception

ojeon 오전 N morning: **ojeon yeodeolsi** 오전 8시 8 in the morning

ojik 오직 ADV merely, simply, solely

ojing.eo 오징어 N squid

ojirap 오지랖 N being meddlesome, nosy: **ojirapi neolda** 오지랖이 넓다 be nosy

oksari 옥살이 N prison life

oksusu 옥수수 N sweet corn

olbareuda 올바르다 ADJ right, rightful

olchaengi 올챙이 N tadpole, polliwog

olgami 올가미 N noose, snare

olke 올케 N sister-in-law (*brother's wife*)

ollagada 올라가다 V to go up, climb, lift: **samcheunge ollagada** 3층에 올라가다 go up to the 3rd floor

ollain 온라인 N online

ollida 올리다 V to raise, lift, increase: **imgeumeul ollida** 임금을 올리다 raise wages

olppaemi 올빼미 N owl

olta, oreun 옳다, 옳은 ADJ right, correct

omda 옮다 V to be infected, catch something from sb: **chinguege gamgiga omda** 친구에게 감기가 옮다 catch a cold from a friend

omgida 옮기다 V to move, shift: **buseoreul omgida** 부서를 옮기다 move to a different department

omgida 옮기다 V to transmit, spread: **byeongeul omgida** 병을 옮기다 transmit illnesses (*diseases*); **ireul omgida** 이를 옮기다 spread lice

omgida 옮기다 V to put into action: **saenggageul haengdonge omgida** 생각을 행동에 옮기다 put one's ideas into action

omul 오물 N rubbish, filth

oncheon 온천 N hot spring

ondegandeeopda 온데간데없다 ADJ vanish into thin air

P

ondo 온도 N temperature
oneul 오늘 N today
oneulppam 오늘밤 N tonight
oneun gire 오는 길에 ADV on the way
ongat 온갖 ADJ all, every: ongat yeokgyeong 온갖 역경 every kind of
adversities
ongi 온기 N warmth, heat: namainneun
ongi 남아있는 온기 lingering warmth
ongjolhada 옹졸하다 ADJ narrow-
minded: ongjolhan saram 옹졸한 사
람 a narrow-minded man, a petty man
onhwahada 온화하다 ADJ warm, calm,
mild, quiet
onjeonhada 온전하다 ADJ intact,
sound, whole
onjongil 온종일 N, ADV all day
onnyuhada 온유하다 ADJ gentle, mild
onsil 온실 N greenhouse: onsil sogui
hwacho gachi salda 온실 속의 화초
같이 살다 live a sheltered/shepherded
life
onsu 온수 N warm (hot) water
onsunhada 온순하다 ADJ meek,
docile
ontong 온통 N everything
onui 오누이 N brother and sister
oppa 오빠 N older brother (female's)
orae, oraen 오래, 오랜 ADV longtime
oraedoeda, oraedoen 오래되다,
오래된 ADJ old (of things)
oragohada 오라고하다 V to invite, tell
to come
orak 오락 N pleasure, amusement,
entertainment
orenji 오렌지 N orange, citrus
orenjisaekui 오렌지새익 ADJ orange
(color)
oreuda 오르다 V to rise, ascend
oreunaerida 오르내리다 V to go up
and down
oreunjjok 오른쪽 N right-hand side
ori 오리 N duck
oroji 오로지 ADV solely, only
oryu 오류 N error
osim 오심 N wrong refereeing, bad call
osip 오십 NUM fifty
osipgyeon 오십견 N frozen shoulder
ossakhada 오싹하다 ADJ bloodcurdling, hair-raising
ot 옷 N clothes, clothing, garment
ot beotda 옷 벗다 V to get undressed

ot ipda 옷 입다 V to get dressed
otcharim 옷차림 N dress, attire, outfit:
danjeonghan otcharim 단정한 옷차림
tidy outfit, proper attire
otgam 옷감 N cloth
otgeori 옷걸이 N (coat) hanger
otgit 옷깃 N neckband, collar: otgiseul
seuda 옷깃을 세우다 pull up one's
collar
otobai 오토바이 N motorcycle
owol 오월 N May
oyeom 오염 N pollution

P

pa.eophada 파업하다 V to go on strike
paak 파악 N grasp, understanding
pachulso 파출소 N police substation
pachungnyu 파충류 N reptiles
Pacific Ocean 태평양 N the Pacific
(ocean): taepyeongyangcheoreom
neolbeun maeum 태평양처럼 넓은
마음 a heart that is as big as the
Pacific Ocean
pada 파다 V to dig: ttangeul pada 땅을
파다 dig in the ground
pado 파도 N surf, wave (in sea)
paeda 패다 V to beat, hit: heumssin
dudeulgyeo paeda 흠씬 두들겨 패다
beat sb to a pulp
paeda 패다 V to break, chop: jangjageul
paeda 장작을 패다 chop firewood
paekseu 팩스 N fax (machine): paekseu iseuseyo? 팩스 있으세요? Do
you have a fax machine?
paekseu 팩스 N fax (message): paekseu badeusyeoseoyo? 팩스 받으셨어
요? Did you get a fax?
paekseu bonaeda 팩스 보내다 V to
fax: paekseu bonaeda 팩스를 보내다
send a fax
paen 팬 N fan (admirer)
paengi 팽이 N top
paengpaenghada 팽팽하다 ADJ firm,
wrinkleless (skin): paengpaenghan
pibu 팽팽한 피부 firm skin
paengpaenghada 팽팽하다 ADJ taut,
tight: paengpaenghan batjul 팽팽한
밧줄 a tightrope
paenti 팬티 N briefs, panties,
underpants
pagodeulda 파고들다 V to dig into:

P

munjereul gipi pagodeulda 문제를 깊이 파고들다 dig into inside details of an issue

pagodeulda 파고들다 v penetrate into: oeroumi ppyeotsokkkaji pagodeunda 외로움이 뼛속까지 파고든다 Loneliness is piercing my heart

pagodeulda 파고들다 v to snuggle into: agiga eomma pumeul pagodeureotda 아기가 엄마 품을 파고들었다 The baby snuggled into mom's arms

pagoedoeda, pagoedoen 파괴되다, 파괴된 v to be destroyed, demolished

pagoe 파괴 N destruction

pagoehada 파괴하다 v to destroy

pagyeon 파견 N dispatch

painaepeul 파인애플 N pineapple

pajama 파자마 N pajamas

pajang 파장 N wavelength, impact

pal 팔 N arm: pareul deulda 팔을 들다 raise one's arm

pal 팔 NUM eight: pal gopagi ineun sibyuk 팔 곱하기 이는 16 eight times two equals sixteen

palda 팔다 v to sell: ssage palda 싸게 팔다 sell sth cheap

palgeori 팔걸이 N armrest

palja 팔자 N destiny, fate: saram palja sigan munje 사람 팔자 시간 문제 A cat may look at a king

palja 팔자 N out-toed gait

paljjang 팔짱 N folded arms, crossed arms

paljji 팔찌 N bracelet

palkkumchi 팔꿈치 N elbow

pallanggeorida 팔랑거리다 ADJ flutter, flap

pallida 팔리다 v to be sold: heolgapse pallida 헐값에 팔리다 be sold at a giveaway price

palsip 팔십 NUM eighty: palsip pal 팔십 팔 eighty-eight

pamuchida 파묻히다 v to be buried in

pamun 파문 N ripple, water ring: pamuneul ireukida 파문을 일으키다 create a stir

pamutda 파묻다 v to bury, entomb

pangyeol 판결 N (*judicial*) decision, judgment: pangyeoreul naerida 판결을 내리다 reach a verdict

panjajip 판자집 N shack

panji 판지 N cardboard

panmae jung 판매 중 N for sale

panmaedae 판매대 N stall, stand (*market*)

panmyeongnada 판명나다 v to become clear, be ascertained

panpanhada 판판하다 ADJ level, even

panorama 파노라마 N panorama

parang 파랑 N blue (*color*)

parata, paran 파랗다, 파란 ADJ blue

pari 파리 N fly (*insect*)

parwol 팔월 N August

paryeomchihan 파렴치한 ADJ conscienceless, shameless

pat 팥 N red bean

pati 파티 N party (*event*)

pedal 페달 N pedal

peiji 페이지 N page

peinteu 페인트 N paint: peinteu han tong 페인트 한 통 a can of paint

peipeo 페이퍼 N paper

pen 펜 N pen

pensing 펜싱 N fencing

peoljjeokttuida 펄쩍 뛰다 v to go berserk with (*anger, joy*): hwaga naseo peoljjeok ttwida 화가 나서 펄쩍 뛰다 go berserk with anger

peomeokda 퍼먹다 v to gobble

peompeu 펌프 N pump

peongpeojimhada 펑퍼짐하다 ADJ wide and flabby: peongpeojimhan ko 펑퍼짐한 코 a flat nose

peosenteu 퍼센트 N percent

peotteurida 퍼뜨리다 v to spread, diffuse

peullaseutik 플라스틱 N plastic

peulleogeu 플러그 N plug (*electric*)

peulleoseu 플러스 N plus

peulluteu 플루트 N flute

peurogeuraem 프로그램 N program

pi 피 N blood

pibu 피부 N skin

pigonhada, pigonhan 피곤하다, 피곤한 ADJ tired, worn out: jeongsinjeogeuro pigonhada 정신적으로 피곤하다 mentally tired

pigoyong.in 피고용인 N employee

pilgi 필기 N taking notes, note

pilleum 필름 N film (*for camera*): pilleumeul gamda 필름을 감다 rewind the film

pillipin 필리핀 N Philippines

pilsu.ida, pilsu(ui) 필수이다, 필수(의)

62

ADJ compulsory, mandatory, indispensable

pinggye 핑계 N excuse, pretext: **pinggyereul daeda** 핑계를 대다 make excuses

pingkeusaek 핑크색 N pink

pinjanhada 핀잔하다 V to scold, rebuke: **pinjaneul juda** 핀잔을 주다 tell sb off

pipbak 핍박 N persecution

pirohada, pirohan 피로하다, 피로한 ADJ weary, fatigued

piryeon 필연 N inevitability, necessity

piryo 필요 N necessity, need

piryohada 필요하다 V to need

piryohada, piryohan 필요하다, 필요한한 V to be in need of

pisin 피신 N escape, refuge

pitjul 핏줄 N vein, blood vessel

poak 포악 N violence

pochak 포착 N capture, catch: **gihoereul pochakhada** 기회를 포착하다 catch a chance

podo 포도 N grapes

podoju 포도주 N wine

pogeon 폭언 N violent language, verbal abuse: **pogeoneul hada** 폭언을 하다 use violent language

pogeunhada 포근하다 ADJ snug

pogi 포기 N abandonment, surrender: **ajik pogihagien ireuda** 아직 포기하기엔 이르다 too early to give up

pogi 포기 N head (*cabbage*): **baechu han pogireul sada** 배추 한 포기를 사다 buy a head of cabbage

pogu 폭우 N torrential rain

pohamdoen, pohamhaeseo 포함된, 포함해서 ADJ included, including: **nareul pohamhaeseo** 나를 포함해서 including myself

pohamhada 포함하다 V to involve, include, incorporate

pohyo 포효 N bellow, howling

pojang 포장 N packing, pack (*up*)

pok 폭 N width, range: **pogi il miteo** 폭이 1 미터 1 meter in width

pokbal 폭발 N explosion

pokeu 포크 N fork

pokgyeok 폭격 N bombing, bombardment

pokhaeng 폭행 N assault, attack, rape

pokju 폭주 N reckless driving

pokpo 폭포 N waterfall

pokpung 폭풍 N storm

pokseol 폭설 N heavy snow

pokso 폭소 N burst of laughter

pongni 폭리 N excessive profits: **budanghage pongnireul chwihada** 부당하게 폭리를 취하다 make excessive profits

pongno 폭로 N exposure, disclosure

pongnohada 폭로하다 V to reveal, expose: **bujeongeul pongnohada** 부정을 폭로하다 expose injustice

poong 포옹 N embrace, hug

posang 포상 N prize

poseuteo 포스터 N poster

powi 포위 N encirclement, envelopment: **jeokdeurege powidanghada** 적들에게 포위당하다 surrounded by enemies

ppalda 빨다 V to suck

ppalgata, ppalgan 빨갛다, 빨간 ADJ red

ppalli 빨리 ADV quickly

ppalliyo! 빨리요! INTERJ hurry up!

ppang 빵 N bread

ppareuda, ppareun 빠르다, 빠른 ADJ quick, fast, rapid

ppeotppeothada/-han 뻣뻣하다/-한 ADJ stiff, rigid, unfriendly, starchy: **ppeotppeotan eokkae** 뻣뻣한 어깨 stiff shoulders; **ppeotppeotan saram** 뻣뻣한 사람 a rigid person, an inflexible person

ppuri 뿌리 N root (*of plant*)

ppyam 뺨 N cheek: **ppyameul matda** 뺨을 맞다 be slapped

ppyeo 뼈 N bone

puksinhada 푹신하다 ADJ soft, cushiony

pul 풀 N grass

pulbat 풀밭 N lawn, meadow

pullida 풀리다 V to abate: **chuwiga pullida** 추위가 풀리다 The cold weather has abated

pullida 풀리다 V to be allayed: **hwaga pullida** 화가 풀리다 anger melts away

pullida 풀리다 V to be removed, be untied: **sinbalkkeuni pullida** 신발끈이 풀리다 shoelaces came undone

pumgyeok 품격 N dignity, class

pumhaeng.i jota/jo.eun 품행이 좋다/좋은 ADJ well-behaved, (*character*) with good moral

pungseon 풍선 N balloon

P

pungsok 풍속 N wind velocity

pungyo 풍요 N richness, abundance

pureonota 풀어놓다 V to untie, unpack, undo

pureuda, pureun 푸르다, 푸른 ADJ green

pye 폐 N lungs

pyehwallyang 폐활량 N lung capacity

pyeoda 펴다 V to spread, open, unfold, stretch: **saega nalgaereul pyeoda** 새가 날개를 펴다 birds spread wings; **kkumeul pyeoda** 꿈을 펴다 unfold one's dream

pyeolchida 펼치다 V to unfold, stretch, open, spread

pyeollihada, pyeollihan 편리하다, 편리한 ADJ convenient, handy: **chwigeupagi pyeollihan** 취급하기 편리한 easy to manipulate

pyeonaeda 펴내다 V to publish: **chae-geul pyeonaeda** 책을 펴내다 publish a book

pyeonanhada/-han 편안하다/-한 ADJ comfortable: **maeumi pyeonanhada** 마음이 편안하다 feel at ease

pyeondo 편도 N one way

pyeondopyo 편도표 N one-way ticket

pyeondutong 편두통 N migraine

pyeongbeomhada/-han 평범하다/ -한 ADJ ordinary, plain, common

pyeongdeung 평등 N equality: **pyeong-deunghage daehada** 평등하게 대하다 treat (persons) equally

pyeonggyun 평균 N average (numbers)

pyeonghaeng 평행 N parallel, paral-lelism

pyeonghwa 평화 N peace

pyeonghwaropda, pyeonghwaroun 평화롭다, 평화로운 ADJ peaceful

pyeongjun 평준 N level, equality

pyeongkkahada 평가하다 V to appraise, evaluate, size up, estimate

pyeongmin 평민 N commoner

pyeongmyeon 평면 N plane

pyeongok 편곡 N arrangement (music)

pyeongsangsi 평상시 N ordinary times, the usual

pyeongpyeonghada/-han 평평하다/ -한 ADJ even, flat, smooth, level: **pyeongpyeonghan ttang** 평평한 땅 level ground; **pyeongpyeonghan ko** 평평한 코 a flat nose

pyeongsaeng 평생 N lifetime

pyeongso 평소 N everyday

pyeongyeon 편견 N prejudice, bias

pyeonhada 편하다 ADJ easy, comfortable

pyeonip 편입 N transfer (college)

pyeonji 편지 N letter

pyeonji yeollakhada 편지 연락하다 V to correspond, write letters

pyeonjip 편집 N compilation, edit

pyeonseong 편성 N formation

pyeonsik 편식 N unbalanced diet, deviated food habit

pyo 표 N ticket: **pyoreul sada** 표를 사다 buy a ticket

pyo 표 N diagram, graph, chart: **pyoreul geurida** 표를 그리다 draw a graph

pyobaek 표백 N bleaching

pyochang 표창 N (official) commen-dation

pyodok 표독 N ferocity, brutality

pyogi 표기 N declaration, spelling

pyohyeonhada 표현하다 V to express, state

pyoje 표제 N heading, title

pyojeong 표정 N (facial) expression

pyomyeon 표면 N surface: **dal pyom-yeon** 달 표면 the surface of the moon

pyopi 표피 N epidermis

pyoryu 표류 N drift, drifting

pyosi 표시 N sign, mark

R

-rdeut tada -ㄹ듯 하다 V to be about

-rgeot gatda -ㄹ것 같다 ADJ to look, seem, be likely: **biga ol geot gatda** 비가 올 것 같다 It looks like it's going to rain

-rkka hada -ㄹ까 하다 V to be going: **jibe galkka handa** 집에 갈까 한다 I may be going home

-rmoyangida -ㄹ모양이다 ADJ look like

-rneunjido moreuda -ㄹ는지도 모르 다 V may (might) be: **ama geureolleunjido moreunda** 아마 그럴 는지도 모른다 That may be possible

-rsueopda -ㄹ수없다 ADJ cannot, be unable to: **ireul je sigane kkeunnael su eopda** 일을 제 시간에 끝낼 수 없 다 The work cannot be done on time

-rsuitda -ㄹ수있다 ADJ can, be able

-ryeogo deulda -려고 들다 v be about to, going to

ramp 램프 N lamp

rabel 라벨 N label

rabendeo 라벤더 N lavender

radio 라디오 N radio

raep 랩 N rap: **noraehamyeo raebeul hada** 노래하며 랩을 하다 raps while singing

raep 랩 N wrap: **nameun eumsigeul laebe ssada** 남은 음식을 랩에 싸다 wrap leftover food with plastic wrap

raepeuting 래프팅 N rafting

raibeol 라이벌 N rival

raillak 라일락 N lilac

raisenseu 라이센스 N license

raiteo 라이터 N lighter

raiteu 라이트 N lightweight (*boxer*)

ramyeon 라면 N instant noodle, ramen

raunji 라운지 N lounge

regyulleo 레귤러 N regular

reijeo 레이저 N laser

reinkoteu 레인코트 N raincoat

reiseu 레이스 N lace, lacework, trim with lace: **reiseuga dallin chima** 레이스가 달린 치마 a lace-trimmed skirt

reiseu 레이스 N race: **jadongcha reiseu** 자동차 레이스 a car race

remon 레몬 N lemon, citrus

remoneideu 레모네이드 N lemonade

renjeu 렌즈 N lens

renteoka 렌터카 N rental car

reokbi 럭비 N rugby

reonchi 런치 N lunch

reondeon 런던 N London

reosia 러시아 N Russia

repocheu 레포츠 N leisure-sports

reseulling 레슬링 N wrestling

reseun 레슨 N lesson

reseutorang 레스토랑 N restaurant

...reul/eul ...를/을 PP (*object particle*): **gabangeul sada** 가방을 사다 buy a bag; **chingureul mannada** 친구를 만나다 meet a friend

...reul/eul geochyeoseo ...를/을 거쳐서 ADV via: **yureobeul geochyeoseo doraoda** 유럽을 거쳐서 돌아오다 return via Europe

...reul/eul je.oehago ...를/을 제외하고 v except ...: **han gyeongureul jeoehago** 한 경우를 제외하고 except in the event of...

...reul/eul tonghayeo ...를/을 통하여 ADV through, past, by way of: **gogeumeul tonghayeo** 고금을 통하여 through all ages

...reul/eul uisikhada ...를/을 의식하다 v to be conscious of

...reul/eul wihan ...를/을 위한 ADJ for

reunesangseu 르네상스 N the Renaissance

ribaundeu 리바운드 N rebound

ribeiteu 리베이트 N rebate, kickback

ribon 리본 N ribbon

ribyu 리뷰 N review

rideuhada 리드하다 v to lead, take the lead

rideum 리듬 N rhythm

rideumikeolhada 리드미컬하다 ADJ rhythmical

rieoka 리어카 N wheel-car, handcart

rieollijeum 리얼리즘 N realism

riheoseol 리허설 N rehearsal

rijoteu 리조트 N resort

rikol 리콜 N recall

rillei 릴레이 N relay

rimokeon 리모컨 N remote control

rimujin 리무진 N limousine

ringgeo 링거 IV

ringkeu 링크 N (*skating*) rink: **aiseuringkeu** 아이스링크 ice-rink

ringkeu 링크 N link: **beullogeureul lingkeuhada** 블로그를 링크하다 link blog

rinseu 린스 N rinse

ripilhada 리필하다 v to refill: **eumnyosureul lipilhaetda** 음료수를 리필했다 refill drinks

ripoteo 리포터 N reporter

ripseutik 립스틱 N lipstick

ripsingkeu 립싱크 N lip-sync

risaikeulling 리사이클링 N recycling

risepsyeon 리셉션 N reception

riseukeu 리스크 N risk

riseuteu 리스트 N list

rodeo 로데오 N rodeo

rolleo koseuteo 롤러 코스터 N (*roller*) coaster

rolleo skate 롤러 스케이트 N roller skates

roma 로마 N Rome: **romaeseoneun nomaui beobeul ttaraya handa** 로마에서는 로마의 법을 따라야 한다 When in Rome, do as Romans do

R

romaenseu 로맨스 N romance: **hyuga-jieseoui romaenseu** 휴가지에서의 로맨서 a holiday romance

romaentikhada 로맨틱하다 ADJ romantic: **geuneun maeu romaentikhada** 그는 매우 로맨틱하다 He's very romantic

romang 로망 N romance (*French*)

roseuaenjelleseu 로스앤젤레스 N Los Angeles

rosyeon 로션 N lotion

rubi 루비 N ruby

rullet 룰렛 N roulette

rum 룸 N room

ruteu 루트 N route: **guip nuteureul josahada** 구입 루트를 조사하다 investigate a purchase route

S

sa 사 NUM four

sa.eop 사업 N business

sa.eopga 사업가 N businessperson

sa bunui il 4 분의 1 NUM quarter

saakhada, saakan 사악하다, 사악한 ADJ wicked, evil, malicious

sabal 사발 N bowl

sabi 사비 N one's own expense: **sabi-reul sseuda** 사비를 쓰다 spend personal money

sabiphada 삽입하다 V to insert

sabyeol 사별 N separation by death

sachae 사채 N private loan

sachal 사찰 N temple

sachiseureopda, sachiseureo.un 사치스럽다, 평화로운 ADJ luxurious, extravagant

sada 사다 V to buy

sadam 사담 N talk privately, have a private talk: **sadameul nanuda** 사담을 나누다 have a private talk

sadari 사다리 N ladder

sadeurida 사들이다 V to stock in on, buy (*in*)

sadon 사돈 N in-laws

sae 새 N bird: **sae tte** 새 떼 a flock of birds

sae 새 N new: **sae cha** 새 차 a new car

sae.u 새우 N shrimp, prawn

saebyeok 새벽 N dawn

saeda 새다 V to leak

saegida 새기다 V to engrave: **maeume**

saegida 마음에 새기다 lay it up in one's heart

saegyeodeutda 새겨듣다 V to listen attentively to: **nae mareul saegyeo-deureora** 내 말을 새겨들어라 Bear in mind what I tell you

saegyeonpil 색연필 N color pencil

saehae bok mani badeuseyo! 새해 복 많이 받으세요! PHR happy new year!

saekkal 색깔 N color

saekki 새끼 N kid

saekki 새끼 N straw rope

saekomdalkomhada/-han 새콤달콤하다/-한 ADJ sweet and sour

saeksi 색시 N maiden, girl, wife, bride

saelleori 샐러리 N celery

saemsotda 샘솟다 V to gush out, well up: **nunmuri saemsosatda** 눈물이 샘솟았다 burst into tears

saendal 샌달 N sandals

saeng.il 생일 N birthday

saeng.il chukhahamnida! 생일 축하합니다! PHR happy birthday!

saengdong 생동 N lively motion, vividness

saenggak 생각 N idea, thoughts, mind

saenggakhada 생각하다 V to think, consider, contemplate, reckon, suppose

saenggang 생강 N ginger

saenggye 생계 N living, livelihood

saengjwi 생쥐 N mouse (*animal*)

saengmaeng 색맹 N color blindness

saengmyeong 생명 N life

saengni 생리 N period (*menstrual*)

saengnihada 생리하다 V to menstruate

saengnyak 생략 N omission, ellipsis

saengnyeonworil 생년월일 N one's date of birth (*birth date, month, year*): **saengnyeonworireul jeogeuseyo** 생년월일을 적으세요. Please write down your date of birth

saengsanhada 생산하다 V to produce

saengseon 생선 N fish

saengso 생소 N inexperience

saeropda, saeroun 새롭다, 새로운 ADJ new, fresh

saeuda 새우다 V to stay up all night: **bameul saeuda** 밤을 새우다 stay up all night

sagam 사감 N housemaster

sagi 사기 N fighting spirit, morale: **sagireul bukdotda** 사기를 북돋다 boost morale

sagi 사기 N fraud: **sagireul chida** 사기를 치다 cheat, swindle

sagikkun 사기꾼 N swindler, crook, con man

sago 사고 N accident

sagwa 사과 N apple: **sagwa han sangja** 사과 한 상자 a box of apples

sagwahada 사과하다 V to apologize: **jeongjunghi sagwahada** 정중히 사과 하다 make a polite apology

sagye 사계 N four seasons

sagyeok 사격 N shooting

sagyeong 사경 N deadly situation

sagyojeogda/-jeogin 사교적이다/-적 인 ADJ sociable, gregarious, outgoing

sahoe 사회 N society, community

sahoejeogin 사회적인 ADJ social

sahu 사후 N after one's death

sahu 사후 N after the fact: **sahucheori** 사후처리 after treatment

sahyeong 사형 N death penalty: **sahyeong seongo** 사형 선고 a death sentence

sai 사이 N gap, space

sai 사이 N interval

sai 사이 N relations: **chingu sai** 친구 사이 relations between friends; **bubu sai** 부부 사이 relations between husband and wife

saida 사이다 N cider

...saie ...사이에 ADV between: **neowa na saie** 너와 나 사이에 between you and me

saijeu 사이즈 N size

sain 사인 N signature, autograph

sainhada 사인하다 V to sign

sairen 사이렌 N siren

saja 사자 N lion

sajang 사장 N president, boss, CEO

sajeol 사절 N refusal, denial

sajeolhada 사절하다 V to refuse, deny

sajeon 사전 N dictionary

sajin 사진 N photograph

sajin jjikda 사진 찍다 V to photograph, take a picture

sajingi 사진기 N camera

sajjeogida, sajjeogin 사적이다, 사적 인 ADJ private, personal: **sajjeogin eommu** 사적인 업무 personal affairs

sajoe 사죄 N forgiveness of sin

sakbal 삭발 N tonsure

sakhida 삭히다 V to ferment, ripen: **sikhyereul sakhida** 식혜를 삭히다 ferment rice juice

sakkeon 사건 N incident, affair, event

sakkeon 사건 N case (*criminal*)

sal 살 N age, years: **se sal** 세 살 three years old

sal 살 N flesh, fat: **sari mani jjyeo-boinda** 살이 많이쪄보인다 you look fat

salda 살다 V to live, be alive

salgyun 살균 N sterilization

sallida 살리다 V to revive, bring back

sallim 살림 N housekeeping

salmeun 삶은 ADJ boiled

sam 삼 NUM three

samak 사막 N desert (*arid land*)

samang 사망 N decease, death

samda 삶다 V to boil, cook

samgakhyeong 삼각형 N triangle

samkida 삼키다 V to swallow

samo 사모 N longing, yearning

samsip 삼십 NUM thirty

samu 사무 N clerical work, office work

samul 사물 N object

samusil 사무실 N office

samwol 삼월 N March

samyeong 사명 N mission, calling

san 산 N mountain

sanae 사내 N man

sanai 사나이 N male, man

sanapda, sanaun 사납다, 사나운 ADJ fierce, wild, nasty: **sanaun gae** 사나 운 개 a fierce dog; **sanaun bada** 사나 운 바다 a rough sea

sanbul 산불 N forest fire

sanchaekhada 산책하다 V to take a walk

sandeomi 산더미 N heap, pile

saneop 산업 N industry

sang 상 N prize: **sangeul juda** 상을 주다 give sb a prize

sang 상 N table: **sangeul chiuda** 상을 치우다 clear the table

sang.a 상아 N ivory

sang.eo 상어 N shark

sang.ihada 상의하다 V to consult, discuss

sangcheo 상처 N wound, injury

sangchu 상추 N lettuce

S

sangdaebang 상대방 N opponent, the other party

sangdan 상단 N the top, the upper end

sangdanghi 상당히 ADV quite, fairly, considerably

sanggeum 상금 N prize money

sanggisikida 상기시키다 V to remind

sanggwaneopda 상관없다 PHR I have nothing to do with it, I don't care, it doesn't matter

sanghada 상하다 V to be spoilt, stale, rotten: **uyuga sanghada** 우유가 상하다 the milk has gone bad

sanghada 상하다 V to grow haggard: **piroro eolguri sanghada** 피로로 얼굴이 상하다 look haggard from fatigue

sanghada 상하다 V to get offended, hurt: **maeumi sanghada** 마음이 상하다 be distressed, take offense at

sanghwang 상황 N situation, conditions: **gyeongje sanghwang** 경제 상황 economic climate

sangin 상인 N merchant

sangja 상자 N box, chest, crate, case

sangnyanghada 상냥하다 ADJ gentle, affectionate

sangoljjagi 산골짜기 N ravine, gorge

sangpum 상품 N goods, products

sangsanghada 상상하다 V to imagine

sangsil 상실 N loss, forfeiture

sangsok 상속 N succession, inheritance

sangtae 상태 N condition, state: **geongang sangtae** 건강 상태 one's physical condition

sangui 상의 N shirts

sanho 산호 N coral

sanso 산소 N grave, tomb

sanso 산소 N oxygen

sansu 산수 N arithmetic, calculation

sanyang 사냥 N hunting, hunt

sanyangkkun 사냥꾼 N hunter

sarainneun 살아있는 ADJ alive

sarajida 사라지다 V to vanish, disappear

saram 사람 N person, human

saramdeul 사람들 N people

saranamda 살아남다 V to survive

sarang 사랑 N love

saranghada 사랑하다 V to love

sarangni 사랑니 N wisdom tooth

sarangseureopda, sarangseureo. un 사랑스럽다, 사랑스러운 ADJ lovely, adorable, endearing

sareoreum 살얼음 N thin coat of ice

sari 사리 N noodles

sari 사리 N self-interest

sari 사리 N small crystals found among cremated remains of monks and regarded as sacred relics

sarip 사립 N private establishment

sarojapda 사로잡다 V to catch alive, capture: **maeumeul sarojapda** 마음을 사로잡다 capture one's heart

sarojapida 사로잡히다 V to be a slave to, be captured: **jeogui pororo sarojapida** 적의 포로로 사로잡히다 be captured alive by the enemy

sarye 사례 N reward, compensation

saryeo 사려 N consideration: **geuneun maeu saryeo gipda** 그는 매우 사려 깊다 He's very considerate

saryo 사료 N consideration, considered judgment

saryo 사료 N feedstuff: **dwaejiege saryoreul juda** 돼지에게 사료를 주다 feed a pig

sasaek 사색 N deadly pale look: **eolgulbichi sasaegi doeda** 얼굴빛이 사색이 되다 turn to a deadly pale look

sasaek 사색 N meditation, contemplation: **sasaege jamgida** 사색에 잠기다 be absorbed in meditation

saseo 사서 N librarian

saseol 사설 N establish privately

saseon 사선 N deadline

saseon 사선 N diagonal line

saseum 사슴 N deer

sasil 사실 N fact

sasil ida, sasilui 사실이다, 사실의 ADJ true

sasim 사심 N ulterior motive

sasip 사십 NUM forty

sasohada, sasohan 사소하다, 사소한 ADJ trivial, minor: **sasohan il** 사소한 일 a mere trifle

sasu 사수 N marksman, shooter

satang 사탕 N candy, sweets

satangsusu 사탕수수 N sugarcane

satoe 사퇴 N resignation

saturi 사투리 N dialect

sawi 사위 N son-in-law

sawol 사월 N April

sawon 사원 N (*Buddhist*) temple, church: **sawoneul geonilda** 사원을 거닐다 walk in the temple

sawon 사원 N member, employee: **hoesaui sawon** 회사의 사원 an employee of a company

sayonghada 사용하다 V to use

sayu 사유 N reason, cause

se 세 N years, age: **sibose sonyeon** 15 세 소년 a 15 year-old boy

se.gye 세계 N world

se.gyun 세균 N germ, virus

se beonjjae 세 번째 NUM third

segi 세기 N century

seil 세일 N sale (*discounted prices*)

seje 세제 N detergent

sejuda 세주다 V to rent out

sekseu 섹스 N sex, intercourse

seo(beori)da 서(버리)다 V to stall (*car*), die

seobiseu 서비스 N service

seoda 서다 V to stand

seojeom 서점 N bookstore

seojjok 서쪽 west

seokda 섞다 V to mix, blend: **mulga-meul seokda** 물감을 섞다 mix paints

seokkida, seokkin 섞이다, 섞인 V to be mixed, blended, mingled

seolchihada 설치하다 V to install

seolgeojihada 설거지하다 V to wash the dishes

seolgyo 설교 N preaching, sermon

seolliphada 설립하다 V to establish, set up

seolmyeonghada 설명하다 V to explain

seoltang 설탕 N sugar

seom 섬 N island

seomyeong 서명 N autograph, signature

seon 선 N line (*mark*): **jikseon** 직선 a straight line

seon 선 N goodness, virtue: **seoneul haenghada** 선을 행하다 do good

seon 선 N arranged blind date: **seoneul boda** 선을 보다 see each other with a view to marriage

seon.geo 선거 N election

seon.geum 선금 N advance money, deposit

seon.go 선고 N sentence (*judgment*)

seoneulhada, seoneulhan 서늘하다, 서늘한 ADJ cool, chilly

seong 성 N surname

seong 성 N sex

seongbyeol 성별 N gender

seonggong 성공 N success

seonggonghada 성공하다 V to succeed

seongkkyeok 성격 N character, personality

seongjanghada 성장하다 V to grow (*up*), develop

seongnyang 성냥 N matches

seongseureopda, seongseureo.un 성스럽다, 성스러운 ADJ sacred, holy

seonhohada 선호하다 V to prefer

seonmul 선물 N present, gift

seonmulhada 선물하다 V to present

seonmyeonghada 선명하다 ADJ clear, vivid

seonsaengnim 선생님 N teacher

seonsaengnim 선생님 N sir

seontaek 선택 N choice

seontaekjeogida, seontaekjeogin 선택적이다, 선택적인 ADJ optional, selective, sectional

seontaekhada 선택하다 V to choose, pick, select

seorap 서랍 N drawer

seoreun 서른 NUM thirty

seorigeun 설익은 ADJ under-done, unripe, under-cooked

seoryu gabang 서류 가방 N briefcase

seoseumeopda 서슴없다 V unhesitating, be not hesitant: **seoseumeopsi malhada** 서슴없이 말하다 talk without hesitation

seotureuda 서투르다 V to be poor, unskilled

seoyang saram 서양 사람 N westerner

set 셋 NUM three

setakso 세탁소 N laundry, dry cleaner

seteu 세트 N set

sc.uda 세우다 V to establish, set up, elect, stand, found: **gongjangeul seuda** 공장을 세우다 build a factory

se.uda 세우다 V to turn up one's collar: **otgiseul seuda** 옷깃을 세우다

se.uda 세우다 V to be on the watch for, pay sharp attention to: **gwireul seuda** 귀를 세우다 prick one's ears and listen

se.uda 세우다 V to stop, pull over: **chareul seuda** 차를 세우다 pull over a car

se.uda 세우다 V to plan, form, map out: **gyehoegeul seuda** 계획을 세우다 lay out a plan

S

seukejul 스케줄 N schedule

seukeurin 스크린 N screen (*of computer*)

seukoteullaendeu 스코틀랜드 N Scotland

seullip 슬립 N slip (*petticoat, underskirt*)

seullipeo 슬리퍼 N slippers

seulpeuda, seulpeun 슬프다, 슬픈 ADJ sad

seulpeum 슬픔 N sorrow

seumul 스물 NUM twenty

seung 우승 N victory

seunggaek 승객 N passenger

seungganggi 승강기 N lift, elevator

seupeonji 스펀지 N sponge

seupeurei 스프레이 N spray

seupocheu 스포츠 N sports

seuseuro 스스로 ADV for oneself, by oneself

seutaempeu 스탬프 N stamp (*ink*)

seutail 스타일 N style

seutobeu 스토브 N stove, cooker

seuwichi 스위치 N switch

si 시 N time, hour: **se si** 세 시 3 o'clock

si 시 N town: **incheonsi** 인천시 Incheon Town

si 시 N poem, poetry: **sireul nangsong-hada** 시를 낭송하다 recite a poem

siabeoji 시아버지 N father-in-law (*husband's father*)

sibeok 십억 NUM billion

sibi 십이 NUM twelve

sibil 십일 NUM eleven

sibirwol 십일월 N November

sibiwol 십이월 N December

sibo 십오 NUM fifteen

sicheong 시청 N city hall

sida, sin 시다, 신 ADJ sour

sido 시도 N attempt

sidohada 시도하다 V to attempt

sieomeoni 시어머니 N mother-in-law (*husband's mother*)

siga 시가 N cigar

sigan 시간 N hour: **ne sigan** 네 시간 four hours

sigan 시간 N time: **sigani jal gada** 시간이 잘 가다 time flies

siganeul jal jikida/jikineun 시간을 잘 지키다/지키는 V to be punctual

siganpyo 시간표 N timetable

sigeumchi 시금치 N spinach

sigol 시골 N country (*rural area*)

sigye 시계 N clock, watch

sihap 시합 N match, game

siheom 시험 N exam, test

(siheom) boda (시험) 보다 V to take a test

sijak 시작 N beginning, start

sijakhada 시작하다 V to begin, start

sijang 시장 N market

sijang 시장 N mayor

sijjeom 시점 N time point

sijjeom 시점 N point of view

sikcho 식초 N vinegar

sikdang 식당 N restaurant

sikhida 식히다 V to cool off, cool down

sikkeureopda, sikkeureoun 시끄럽다, 시끄러운 ADJ noisy, loud, trouble-some: **sikkeureoun eumak** 시끄러운 음악 loud music; **sikkeureoun geori** 시끄러운 거리 a noisy street; **sikkeu-reoun munje** 시끄러운 문제 a trouble-some situation

siksa 식사 N meal

siksa junbihada 식사 준비하다 V to prepare, fix, make (*a meal*)

sil 실 N thread: **baneure sireul kkweda** 바늘에 실을 꿰다 thread a needle

siljikhada, siljikan 실직하다, 실직한 V to become unemployed

siljje(ui) 실제 N reality

siljjero 실제로 ADV actually, really, in fact

silkeu 실크 N silk

sillaebok 실내복 N dressing gown

sillang 신랑 N bridegroom

sillyehamnida! 실례합니다! PHR excuse me!

silmanghada, silmanghan 실망하다, 실망한한 V to be disappointed

silpae 실패 N failure: **guryokjeogin silpae** 굴욕적인 실패 a humiliating failure

silpaehada 실패하다 V to fail: **gye-hoegi silpaehada** 계획이 실패하다 fail in one's attempt

silssu 실수 N mistake

simda 심다 V to plant

simgakhada, simgakan 심각하다, 심각한 ADJ serious

simhada, simhan 심하다, 심한 ADJ severe, heavy, harsh

simin 시민 N citizen

70

simjang 심장 N heart

simman 십만 NUM hundred thousand

simnyuk 십육 NUM sixteen

simsimhada, simsimhan 심심하다, 심심한 ADJ bored

sin 신 N god

sin.gyeong sseuda 신경 쓰다 V to mind, bother, notice

sin.gyeong sseuji maseyo! 신경 쓰지 마세요! PHR never mind! don't worry about it!

sinae jungsimji 시내 중심지 N downtown

sinaegwan.gwang 시내 관광 N sightseeing

sinbal 신발 N shoes

sinbu 신부 N bride: **sillang sinbu** 신랑 신부 a newly-married couple, husband and wife

sinbu 신부 N priest

sincheonghada 신청하다 V to apply, request: **sueobeul sincheonghada** 수업을 신청하다 apply for a class

sincheongseo 신청서 N application form

singgapol 싱가폴 N Singapore

singmul 식물 N plant, vegetable

singmurwon 식물원 N botanic gardens

sinhwa 신화 N myth

sini nada, sini nan 신이 나다, 신이 난 ADJ excited, gleeful

sinjang 신장 N kidney

sinjunghada, sinjunghan 신중하다, 신중한 ADJ cautious, prudent

sinmun 신문 N newspaper

sinnada, sinnaneun 신나다, 신나는 ADJ excited, cheerful

sinseonghada, sinseonghan 신성하다, 신성한 ADJ holy, sacred

sinseonhada, sinseonhan 신선하다, 신선한 ADJ fresh

sinu.i 시누이 N sister-in-law (*husband's younger sister*)

sip 십 NUM ten

sip.pal 십팔 NUM eighteen

sipchil 십칠 NUM seventeen

sipdae 십대 N teenager

sipgu 십구 NUM nineteen

sipsa 십사 NUM fourteen

sipsam 십삼 NUM thirteen

sireohada 싫어하다 V to dislike

sitda 싣다 V to load: **teureoge**

mulgeoneul sitda 트럭에 물건을 싣다 load a truck

sitda 싣다 V to carry, put in

sitda 싣다 V to support, back up

siteu 시트 N sheet (*for bed*)

siwol 시월 N October

so.eum 소음 N noise

so.nyeon 소년 N boy

sobyeonboda 소변보다 V to urinate

soegogi 쇠고기 N beef

soetoehada 쇠퇴하다 V to decline, decay

sogaehada 소개하다 V to introduce

sogeum 소금 N salt

sogida 속이다 V to deceive, cheat: **gwageoreul sogida** 과거를 속이다 lie about one's past

sogot 속옷 N underwear

sohwabullyang 소화불량 N indigestion

soilkkeori 소일거리 N pastime, timekiller

sokdo 속도 N speed

soketeu 소케트 N socket (*electric*)

sol 솔 N brush: **chitsol** 칫솔 a toothbrush

sol 솔 N sol (*music scale*)

sol 솔 N pinetree

soljilhada 솔질하다 V to brush

somaechigi 소매치기 N pickpocket

somaechigihada 소매치기하다 V to pickpocket

somun 소문 N rumor: **somuni nada** 소문이 나다 a rumor gets started

so.nyeo 소녀 N girl

son 손 N hand

sonagi 소나기 N shower (*of rain*)

sonhae 손해 N damage, loss

sonhaeboda 손해보다 V to suffer a loss

sonja 손자 N grandson, grandchild

sonjabi 손잡이 N handle

sonjeondeung 손전등 N flashlight, torch

sonkkarak 손가락 N finger

sonmok 손목 N wrist

(sonmok)sigye (손목)시계 N watch (*wristwatch*)

sonnim 손님 N guest

sonnyeo 손녀 N granddaughter, grandchild

sonsangsikida 손상시키다 V to damage, harm, begrime

sonsugeon 손수건 N handkerchief

S

sonsure 손수레 N handcart, wheelbarrow

sontop 손톱 N nail (*finger*)

sonwi(ui) 손(위) N elder: **sonwisaram** 손위사람 one's senior

sopa 소파 N sofa, couch

sopo 소포 N parcel

sori 소리 N sound, noise

soriga keuda/keun 소리가 크다/큰 ADJ loud

soseol 소설 N novel: **jangpyeonsoseol** 장편소설 a full-length novel

soseu 소스 N sauce

soyuhada 소유하다 V to possess, own

soyumul 소유물 N possessions, belongings

ssada 싸다 V to pack, wrap

ssada, ssan 싸다, 싼 ADJ cheap, inexpensive

ssal 쌀 N rice (*uncooked grains*)

ssauda 싸우다 V to fight (*physically*)

sseokda, sseogeun 썩다, 썩은 ADJ rotten

sseuda 쓰다 V to spend (*money*): **doneul hamburo sseuda** 돈을 함부로 쓰다 spend money recklessly

sseuda 쓰다 V to write (*a letter*), compose (*a poem*), note down: **chaegeul sseuda** 책을 쓰다 write a book

sseuda, sseun 쓰다, 쓴 ADJ bitter

sseulda 쓸다 V to sweep

sseulmo eopda/eomneun 쓸모 없다/없는 ADJ useless

sseulmo itda/inneun 쓸모 있다/있는 ADJ useful

sseuregi 쓰레기 N garbage

ssi 씨 N seed

ssidi 씨디 N CD

ssidi-rom 씨디-롬 N CD-ROM

ssipda 씹다 V to chew

ssitda 씻다 V to wash

ssoda 쏘다 V to shoot

su.eop 수업 N lesson, class

su.ip 수입 N income

su.iphada 수입하다 V to import

su.ippum 수입품 N imported goods

subak 수박 N watermelon

suchi 수치 N shame, disgrace, humiliation: **suchireul danghada** 수치를 당하다 be humiliated

suchi 수치 N numerical figure, value: **jeongsang suchireul yujihada** 정상 수치를 유지하다 stay within the normal range

suchul(pum) 수출(품) N export (*goods*)

suchulhada 수출하다 V to export

sugeon 수건 N towel

sugeumhada 수금하다 V to collect payments

sugong.ye 수공예 N handicraft

suhaenghada 수행하다 V to perform, conduct: **jingmureul suhaenghada** 직무를 수행하다 do one's duties

suhaenghada 수행하다 V to fulfill, accomplish

sujja 숫자 N figure, number

sujun 수준 N level, standard: **gyeongje sujun** 경제 수준 an economical standard

sukgohada 숙고하다 V to consider, ponder, think over

sukkarak 숟가락 N spoon

sukso 숙소 N lodging

sul 술 N alcohol, liquor

sul chwihada 술 취하다 V to be drunk

suljjip 술집 N bar, pub

sumda 숨다 V to hide, go in hiding

sumgida 숨기다 V to hide, conceal

sumgyeojida, sumgyeojin 숨겨지다, 숨겨진 V to be hidden

sun.gan 순간 N moment, instant: **gyeoljeongjeogin sungan** 결정적인 순간 a crucial moment

sungbaehada 숭배하다 V to worship

sungnyeo 숙녀 N lady

sunhada, sunhan 순하다, 순한 ADJ mild, gentle, tame, meek: **sunhan dambae** 순한 담배 mild cigarettes

sunjonghada 순종하다 V to obey

sunjonghaneun 순종하는 ADJ obedient

sunjoropda, sunjoroun 순조롭다/순조로운 ADJ smooth, favoring: **sunjoroun chulbal** 순조로운 출발 a smooth start

suno.eun 수놓은 ADJ embroidered: **kkocheul sunoeun ot** 꽃을 수놓은 옷 a dress embroidered with flowers

sunseo 순서 N order, sequence, turn: **sunseoga bakkwida** 순서가 바뀌다 be out of order

sunsuhada, sunsuhan 순수하다, 순수한 ADJ pure

sunwi 순위 N ranking, placing

sup 숲 N forest

supeomaket 수퍼마켓 N supermarket

supyeongseon 수평선 N horizon

supyo 수표 N cheque, check

susang 수상 N prime minister

susibui 수십의 ADJ tens of, dozens of

susuhada, susuhan 수수하다, 수수
한 ADJ modest, simple, unostentatious:
susuhan otcharim 수수한 옷차림
dressed-down

susuryo 수수료 N fee

suyeongbok 수영복 N swimsuit

suyeonghada 수영하다 V to swim

suyeongjang 수영장 N swimming pool

suyoil 수요일 N Wednesday

swida 쉬다 V to rest, relax: iljuil gan
swida 일주일 간 쉬다 take a week off

swin 쉰 NUM fifty

swipda, swiun 쉽다, 쉬운 ADJ simple,
easy

syampu 샴푸 N shampoo

syawo 샤워 N shower (for washing)

syawohada 샤워하다 V to take a
shower

syeocheu 셔츠 N shirt

syo 쇼 N show (entertainment)

syopeuro 쇼프로 N show program

syopinghada 쇼핑하다 V to shop, go
shopping

T

tada 타다 V to burn, blaze: jal tada 잘
타다 burn well

tada 타다 V to get on, board, ride
(transport). chareul tada 차를 타다
get in(to) a car

tae.eonada 태어나다 V to be born

tae.uda 태우다 V to burn, emblaze:
babeul taeuda 밥을 태우다 burn the
rice

taea 태아 N embryo

taedo 태도 N attitude: geomanhan
taedo 거만한 태도 a haughty air

taegwondo 태권도 N taekwondo

taeguk 태국 N Thailand

taegyo 태교 N prenatal education

taeksi 택시 N taxi

taepung 태풍 N typhoon

taepyeonghada 태평하다 ADJ peaceful

taewojuda 태워주다 V to give a ride

taeyang 태양 N sun

tagonada 타고나다 V to be born with:
tagonan jaeneung 타고난 재능 an
inborn talent

taguk 타국 N foreign country

tagwol 탁월 N excellence, superiority

tagwolhada 탁월하다 ADJ excellent:
tagwolhan seontaegida 탁월한 선택
이다 Excellent choice!

tahyeop 타협 N compromise

tahyeopada 타협하다 V to make a
compromise

taipinghada 타이핑하다 V to type

taireuda 타이르다 V to admonish

takgu 탁구 N table tennis, ping-pong

takhada 탁하다 ADJ muddy, turbid

tal 탈 N mask: tareul sseuda 탈을 쓰다
wear a mask

tal 탈 N sickness, illness: tari nada 탈
이 나다 get ill

tal 탈 N problem: tareul ireukida 탈을
일으키다 cause problems

talchul 탈출 N escape

talchulhada 탈출하다 V to escape
from

tallak 탈락 N omission

tallakhada 탈락하다 V to be omitted

tallyeoginneun 탄력있는 ADJ elastic,
springy

tallyeok 탄력 N elasticity

taltoehada 탈퇴하다 V to secede from:
jojigeseo taltoehada 조직에서 탈퇴하
다 detach oneself from an organization

tamgu 탐구 N research, study

tamguhada 탐구하다 V to research

tamjeong 탐정 N detective

tamnada 탐나다 V to be desirable

tamseureopda 탐스럽다 ADJ appetizing, scrumptious: tamseureoun sagwa
탐스러운 사과 a scrumptious apple

tanno 탄로 N discovery, revelation:
eummoga tanlonada 음모가 탄로나다
a conspiracy has been revealed

tansaeng 탄생 N birth, nativity

tansuhwamul 탄수화물 N carbohydrate

tantanhada 탄탄하다 ADJ solid

tanwonhada 탄원하다 V to plead

taoreuda 타오르다 V to burn (flare,
blaze, flame) up: taoreuneun hwaet-
bul 타오르는 횃불 a flaming torch

tap 탑 N tower

tapseung 탑승 N boarding

tapseunghada 탑승하다 V to get into, board

tarak 타락 N depravity, corruption

tarakhada 타락하다 V to degrade, become depraved: **tarakhan jeongchiga** 타락한 정치가 a corrupt politician

tasal 타살 N homicide, murder

tatada 탓하다 V to put blame upon: **nameul tatada** 남을 탓하다 blame others

tawonhyeong(ui) 타원형 N oval (*shape*)

teibeul 테이블 N table

teibeul ppo 테이블 보 N tablecloth

teipeu 테이프 N tape (*scotch, adhesive*)

tellebijeon 텔레비전 N television

teniseu 테니스 N tennis

teok 턱 N chin, jaw

teokbaji 턱받이 N bib, pinafore

teokppyeo 턱뼈 N jawbone

teoksido 턱시도 N tuxedo

teoksuyeom 턱수염 N beard

teol 털 N hair, fur

teolda 털다 V to burglarize: **bin jibeul teolda** 빈 집을 털다 rob an empty house

teolda 털다 V to dust off: **meonjireul teolda** 먼지를 털다 clear dust away

teolda 털다 V to empty out: **doneul teoreo seonmureul sada** 돈을 털어 선물을 사다 spend all of one's money on a gift

teolda 털다 V to let go, leave behind: **geunsim geokjeongeul teolda** 근심 걱정을 털다 leave one's worry behind, **jarireul teolgo ireonada** 자리를 털고 일어나다 get well from one's illness

teolgari 털갈이 N moult

teomineol 터미널 N terminal

teomunieopda 터무니없다 ADJ absurd, baseless

teong bida/bin 텅 비다/빈 V to be emptied out

teong bida/bin 텅 비다/빈 V to become penniless: **jumeoniga teong bida** 주머니가 텅 비다 become penniless

teong bin 텅 빈 ADJ empty, hollow, vacant

teonota 터놓다 V to open one's heart up: **maeumeul teonota** 마음을 터놓다 confide in

teoreomeokda 털어먹다 V to spend the last penny

teoreomeokda 털어먹다 V to squander

teoreonota 털어놓다 V to confide in: **chinguege bimireul teoreonota** 친구에게 비밀을 털어놓다 confide in friends

teseuteuhada 테스트하다 V to test

teuda 트다 V to break open

teuda 트다 V to build, open

teuda 트다 V to chap

teuda 트다 V to sprout, bud

teukbyeolhada/-han 특별하다/-한 ADJ special

teukbyeolhi 특별히 ADV specially

teukgeubyeolcha 특급열차 N express train

teukgwon 특권 N privilege

teukheo 특허 N patent

teukhi 특히 ADV particularly, especially

teukjing(jeogin) 특징(적인) N characteristic

teukjingjeogin 특징적인 ADJ distinguishing

teulli 틀니 N denture

teullida, teullin 틀리다, 틀린 ADJ wrong, mistaken, false

teullimeopseoyo! 틀림없어요! PHR certainly!

teumsae 틈새 N crack, rift: **teumsaesijang** 틈새시장 niche market

teumteumi 틈틈이 ADV between times

teunteunhada 튼튼하다 ADJ strong, solid, healthy

teureojida 틀어지다 V to become estranged: **saiga teureojida** 사이가 틀어지다 become estranged from

teureojida 틀어지다 V to fall through: **gyehoegi teureojida** 계획이 틀어지다 the plan has fallen through

teureojida 틀어지다 V to be twisted, warped: **haetbiche panjaga teureojida** 햇빛에 판자가 틀어지다 the board was warped in the sun

teureok 트럭 N truck

teureomakda 틀어막다 V to stop, fill, plug

tibi 티비 N TV

tigyeoktaegyeokhada 티격태격하다 V to bicker, squabble

tim 팀 N team

tip 팁 N tip (*gratuity*)

tisyeocheu 티셔츠 N t-shirt

tochakui 토착의 ADJ indigenous, native

toehakhada 퇴학하다 v to be expelled from school

toejikhada 퇴직하다 v to retire

toejja 퇴짜 N rejection, refusal

tohada 토하다 v to vomit: **pireul tohada** 피를 토하다 vomit blood; **yeolbyeoneul tohada** 열변을 토하다 make a fiery speech

tokki 토끼 N rabbit

tokkida 토끼다 v to run away, flee

toktokhi 톡톡히 ADV harshly, severely: **joetgapseul toktokhi chireuda** 죗값을 톡톡히 치르다 pay severely for one's sin

tomato 토마토 N tomato

tong.yeoksa 통역사 N interpreter

tongchi 통치 N rule, reign

tongchihada 통치하다 v to rule over

tongdak 통닭 N chicken roasted whole

tonggwahada 통과하다 v to pass, go past

tonghaeng 통행 N pass, transit

tonghaenghada 통행하다 v to pass through

tonghakhada 통학하다 v to commute to school

tonghwa 통화 N currency

tonghwajung.ida 통화중이다 PHR the (*telephone*) line is busy!

tongjang 통장 N bankbook

tongji 통지 N notice

tongjjeung 통증 N ache, pain

tongjorim 통조림 N canned food

tongkwae 통쾌 N thrill

tongkwaehada 통쾌하다 ADJ awfully pleasant

tongno 통로 N passage, passageway

tongpung 통풍 N ventilation

tongtonghada 통통하다 ADJ chubby, plump

tongyeok 통역 N interpretation

tongyeokhada 통역하다 v to interpret, translate

top 톱 N saw

torajida 토라지다 v to become sulky

toseong 토성 N Saturn

toyoil 토요일 N Saturday

...ttaemune ...때문에 N, PP because of...: **neo ttaemune** 너 때문에 because of you

ttaerida 때리다 v to beat, strike: **meorireul ttaerida** 머리를 때리다 strike one's head

ttal 딸 N daughter

ttam 땀 N sweat

ttam heullida 땀 흘리다 v to sweat, perspire

ttang 땅 N ground, earth, land

ttangkong 땅콩 N peanut

ttareuda 따르다 v to follow, go after, obey

ttatteutam 따뜻함 N warmth

ttatteuthada, ttatteutan 따뜻하다, 따뜻한 ADJ warm

tteolda 떨다 v to shake, shiver: **darireul tteolda** 다리를 떨다 shake one's legs

tteonada 떠나다 v to leave, depart

tteoreojida 떨어지다 v to fall, drop: **jajeongeoeseo tteoreojida** 자전거에서 떨어지다 fall off a bike

tteoreojida 떨어지다 v to be run out: **doni tteoreojida** 돈이 떨어지다 run out of money

tteoreojyeoseo 떨어져서 ADV apart

tteoreotteurida 떨어뜨리다 v to drop

tto bopsida! 또 봅시다! PHR see you later!

ttohan 또한 ADV too (*also*)

ttokbareuda, ttokbareun 똑바르다, 똑바른 ADJ straight, correct, right: **ttokbareun jase** 똑바른 자세 a correct posture; **ttokbareun haengdong** 똑바른 행동 right conduct

ttokbaro 똑바로 ADV straight ahead

ttokttokhada, ttokttokan 똑똑하다, 똑똑한 ADJ smart, clever

ttoneun 또는 ADV or

ttong 똥 N poop, crap

ttukkeong 뚜껑 N lid

ttulta 뚫다 v to pierce, penetrate

ttungttunghada/-han 뚱뚱하다/-한 ADJ fat, plump, stout

tubakhada 투박하다 ADJ rough, crude, coarse

tungmyeongseureopda 퉁명스럽다 ADJ blunt, gruff, abrupt

tupyohada 투표하다 v to vote

tusu 투수 N pitcher

twi.eonaoda 튀어나오다 v to stick out, bulge, protrude, pop out

twigida 튀기다 v to fry : **gireume twigida** 기름에 튀기다 deep-fry

twigida 튀기다 v to bounce: **gongeul twigida** 공을 튀기다 bounce a ball

T

twigida 튀기다 v to splash, spit: **mureul twigida** 물을 튀기다 splash water
twigim 튀김 N fried food
twigin 튀긴 ADJ fried

U

uahada, uahan 우아하다, 우아한 ADJ elegant: **taedoga uahada** 태도가 우아하다 be graceful in manner; **uahan jatae** 우아한 자태 an elegant figure
ubak 우박 N hail
ucheguk 우체국 N post office
udong 우동 N udon
udukeoni 우두커니 ADV vacantly, blankly: **udukeoni baraboda** 우두커니 바라보다 stare blankly at
udumeori 우두머리 N chief, boss, head
udunhada 우둔하다 ADJ dull-witted
ugeulgeorida 우글거리다 v to swarm, be crowded
ugida 우기다 v to insist, persist
...ui ...의 PP (*possessive particle*): **naui chaek** 나의 책 my book; **eomeoniui ilgijang** 어머니의 일기장 mother's diary
...ui bakkate ...의 바깥에 ADV outside of...
uicheojeung 의처증 N Othello syndrome
uidae 의대 N medical school
uido 의도 N intention: **sogiryeoneun uido** 속이려는 의도 an intent to cheat
uigisochimhada 의기소침하다 ADJ be dispirited
uigiyangyanghada 의기양양하다 ADJ triumphant
uigyeon 의견 N opinion
uihakui 의학의 ADJ medical
uihok 의혹 N suspicion, doubt
uihyang 의향 N intention: **mannal uihyang** 만날 의향 an intention to meet
uihyeongje 의형제 N sworn brothers
uija 의자 N chair
uijihada 의지하다 v to lean, rely on: **chingureul uijihada** 친구를 의지하다 rely on a friend
uijok 의족 N artificial leg
uijonhada 의존하다 v to depend on: **yage uijonhada** 약에 의존하다 depend on medication
uimi 의미 N meaning: **neolbeun uimie-**

seo 넓은 의미에서 in a broad sense
uimihada 의미하다 v to mean, signify: **ppalgan bureun jeongjireul uimihanda** 빨간 불은 '정지'를 의미한다 Red light means 'stop'
uimisimjanghada 의미심장하다 ADJ very meaningful: **uimisimjanghan pyojeong** 의미심장한 표정 a serious meaningful look
uimu 의무 N duty, obligation: **segeumeul naeneun uimu** 세금을 내는 의무 a duty to pay tax
uimugam 의무감 N sense of duty: **uimugameul neukkida** 의무감을 느끼다 feel obligated
uimuneul jegihada 의문을 제기하다 v to pose a question
uinon 의논 N discussion
uinonhada 의논하다 v to discuss
uioeui 의외의 N unexpectedly
uiri 의리 N fidelity, loyalty: **uirireul jikida** 의리를 지키다 be loyal to
uiriga itda 의리가 있다 ADJ be faithful: **uiriga inneun saram** 의리가 있는 사람 a man of fidelity
uiropda 의롭다 ADJ righteous, rightful
uiryoboheom 의료보험 N medical insurance
uisa 의사 N doctor
uisikju 의식주 N food, clothing and shelter
uisimhada 의심하다 v to doubt, suspect
uisimseureopda 의심스럽다 ADJ doubtful
uiyok 의욕 N will, desire, drive
ujeong 우정 N friendship
ujjulhada 우쭐하다 v to be pompous, be inflated
uju 우주 N universe, cosmos
ujungchunghada 우중충하다 ADJ dismal, somber, dark
ukhada 욱하다 v to rouse up, burst forth
uksingeorida 욱신거리다 v to throb with pain
ul 울 N wool
ulbo 울보 N crybaby
ulda 울다 v to cry, weep
ulhwa 울화 N resentment
ullida 울리다 v to ring (*bell*): **jongeul ullida ongeul ullida** 종을 울리다 ring a bell
ullida 울리다 v to make sb cry: **sara-**

meul ullida 사람을 올리다 bring tears to one's eyes

ultari 울타리 N fence

umjigiji anta/anneun 움직이지 않다/않는 V to keep still: **yuhoge umjigiji anta** 유혹에 움직이지 않다 do not yield to temptation

umjigiji anneun 움직이지 않는 ADJ immovable, motionless, stationary: **umjigiji anneun mulche** 움직이지 않는 물체 an immovable object

umul 우물 N well (*for water*): **umul mureul gitda** 우물 물을 긷다 draw water from a well

un 운 N luck: **saeop bun** 사업 운 luck for (*in*) business; **siheom un** 시험 운 luck with (*on*) exam

un jota/jo.eun 운 좋다/좋은 ADJ lucky, fortunate

ungkeurida 웅크리다 V to crouch, huddle oneself up

uni eopda/eomneun 운이 없다/없는 ADJ unfortunate, out of luck

unjeonhada 운전하다 V to drive (*a car*)

unmyeong 운명 N destiny, fate

unmyeonghada 운명하다 V to pass away, die: **geuui harabeojiga oneul unmyeonghasyeotda** 그의 할아버지가 오늘 운명하셨다 His grandfather passed away today

upyeonmul 우편물 N mail, post

upyo 우표 N stamp (*postage*)

uramhada 우람하다 ADJ bulky, brawny, beefy: **uramhan chegyeok** 우람한 체격 a bulky frame

ureonada 우러나다 V to soak out, come off

ureonaoda 우러나오다 V to well up: **jinsimeseo ureonaoda** 진심에서 우러나오다 come from the heart

ureongchada 우렁차다 ADJ sonorous

uri 우리 N we, us: **urikkiri** 우리끼리 just us, between us, we alone

uri(ui) 우리의 ADJ our

usan 우산 N umbrella

usang 우상 N idol: **usangeul mandeulda** 우상을 만들다 cast an idol

useon 우선 N first, first of all

useongwon 우선권 N priority

useungja 우승자 N winner

useupda 우습다 ADJ laughable, ridiculous

usuhada, usuhan 우수하다, 우수한 ADJ excellent

utda 웃다 V to laugh

utgineun 웃기는 ADJ humorous, funny, hilarious: **utgineun nongdam** 웃기는 농담 a funny joke

uulhada 우울하다 ADJ depressed, gloomy, blue

uyeonhi 우연히 ADV by accident: **uyeonhi mannada** 우연히 만나다 meet by chance

uyu 우유 N milk

uyubudanhada 우유부단하다 ADJ irresolute, indecisive

W

...wa/gwa ...와/과 PP and

...wa/gwa bigyohaeseo ...와/과 비교해서 V to compare to, compare with: **jangnyeongwa bigyohaeseo** 작년과 비교해서 compared to last year; **geunyeowa bigyohaeseo** 그녀와 비교해서 as compared with her

waegokhada 왜곡하다 V to distort, twist

waesohada 왜소하다 ADJ undersized

waeyo? 왜요? PHR why?

wakseu 왁스 N wax

walgadak 왈가닥 N an unruly girl

wallyohada 완료하다 V to complete, finish

wanbyeokhada, wanbyeokan 완벽하다, 완벽한 ADJ perfect: **wanbyeokhan jisik** 완벽한 지식 perfect (*thorough*) knowledge

wandukong 완두콩 N peas, green beans

wang 왕 N king

wangbokpyo 왕복표 N return ticket

wangguk 왕국 N kingdom

wanggwan 왕관 N crown

wangja 왕자 N prince

wangtta 왕따 V to be blanked, outcast: **wangttareul danghada** 왕따를 당하다 be treated as an outcast

wangu 완구 N toy

wanjeonhada, wanjeonhan 완전하다, 완전한 ADJ whole, complete: **wanjeonhan munjang** 완전한 문장 a complete sentence

wanjeonhi 완전히 ADV completely: **wanjeonhi dareun** 완전히 다른

W

completely different; **wanjeonhi seupdeukhada** 완전히 습득하다 achieve a complete mastery

wankwaehada 완쾌하다 V to recover completely

wannap 완납 N paid in full

wanpaehada 완패하다 V to get a walloping

wanseonghada 완성하다 V to complete: **gyehoegeul wanseonghada** 계획을 완성하다 a complete plan

wenmanhada 웬만하다 ADJ good, fair, pretty

wenmankeum 웬만큼 ADV to some degree, enough, pretty: **nongdamdo wenmankeumhaera** 농담도 웬만큼해라 enough of your jokes!; **golpeureul wenmankeum chinda** 골프를 웬만큼 친다 play some golf

wepsaiteu 웹사이트 N website

wiam 위암 N gastric cancer, cancer of the stomach: **wiame geollida** 위암에 걸리다 have stomach cancer

wibae 위배 N breach

wiban 위반 N violation

wicheung 위층 N upstairs

wichihada 위치하다 V to be located, be situated

...wie ...위에 ADV above, upstairs

...wie ...위에 ADV on, at

...wie ...위에 ADV up, upward

wigi 위기 N crisis

...wihae goandoeda ...위해 고안되다 V intended for

wiheom 위험 N danger: **wiheomjiyeok** 위험지역 danger zone

wiheomhada, wiheomhan 위험하다, 위험한 ADJ dangerous: **modeun widaehan aidieoneun wiheomhada** 모든 위대한 아이디어는 위험하다 All great ideas are dangerous

wihyeophada 위협하다 V to threaten: **geongangeul wihyeopada** 건강을 위협하다 threaten one's health

wijang 위장 N camouflage, disguise: **wijanghada** 위장하다 disguise oneself as

wijang 위장 N stomach

wijaryo 위자료 N alimony, compensation: **wijaryoreul cheongguhada** 위자료를 청구하다 claim compensation, demand alimony

wijeung 위증 N perjury, false witness

wijo 위조 N forgery, fabrication

wijohada 위조하다 V to forge, counterfeit

wiro 위로 N consolation, comfort: **wiroui mareul hada** 위로의 말을 하다 offer words of consolation to

wirohada 위로하다 V to comfort, console

wisaeng 위생 N sanitation

wiseon 위선 N hypocrisy

wiseonjeogin 위선적인 ADJ hypocritical

witaeropda 위태롭다 ADJ critical, dodgy

witak 위탁 N consignment, trust

wolgeup 월급 N monthly salary: **wolgeubeul juda** 월급을 주다 pay monthly salary

wolgyeong 월경 N menstruation

wollae 원래 N, ADV originally, primarily

wolli 원리 N principle, theory

wolmal 월말 N end of the month

wolse 월세 N monthly rent

won 원 N circle: **woneul geurida** 원을 그리다 draw a circle

won 원 N wish, hope: **wondaero** 원대로 as one wished

won 원 N won (*Korean monetary unit*): **baegwon** 100원 one hundred won

won 원 INTERJ oh, dear!: **won sesange** 원 세상에 oh my goodness

wonban 원반 N disk

wonbon 원본 N original

woncheon 원천 N root, origin, source: **himui woncheon** 힘의 원천 a source of strength

wonchik 원칙 N principle

wondumak 원두막 N lookout shed

wonhada 원하다 V to want: **uisaga doegireul wonhada** 의사가 되기를 원하다 want to be a doctor

wonin 원인 N cause: **sagoui wonin** 사고의 원인 the cause of the accident

wonjajae 원자재 N raw material

wonjang 원장 N chief

wonjapoktan 원자폭탄 N atomic bomb

wonjaryeok 원자력 N atomic energy

wonjeom 원점 N the starting point: **wonjeomeuro doragada** 원점으로 돌아가다 back to square one

wonjumin 원주민 N native

wonmang 원망 N bitter feeling, grudge

wonmangseureopda 원망스럽다 ADJ reproachful, hateful

wonmanhada 원만하다 ADJ integral, complete

wonsanji 원산지 N country of origin

wonseo 원서 N application: **wonseo-reul jechulhada** 원서를 제출하다 submit an application

wonseong 원성 N complaint, murmur: **wonseongeul sada** 원성을 사다 incur the resentment of

wonsi 원시 N far-sighteded

wonsi 원시 N primitive, primeval

wonsu 원수 N enemy: **nae abeojiui wonsu** 내 아버지의 원수 enemy of my father

wonsu 원수 N sovereign, ruler: **gukga wonsu** 국가의 원수 the head of a nation

wonsung.i 원숭이 N ape, monkey

wontonghada 원통하다 ADJ bitter, resentful

woryoil 월요일 N Monday

Y

yachae 야채 N greens, vegetables: **yachae bokkeumbap** 야채 볶음밥 vegetable stir-fried rice

yadan 야단 N uproar, clamor

yagan 야간 ADJ nightly: **yagyan gyeongbi** 야간 경비 a night guard

yagollida 약올리다 V to provoke, irritate

yagu 야구 N baseball

yak 약 ADV approximately, around: **yak samsimmyeong** 약 30명 around 30 people

yak 약 N drug, medicine: **gamgi yak** 감기 약 cold medicine

yakgan 약간 ADV a bit, somewhat

yakgan(ui) 약간(의) ADV some

yakguk 약국 N drugstore, pharmacy

yakhada, yakan 약하다, 약한 ADJ weak, mild: **simjangi yakhada** 심장이 약하다 have a weak heart; **suhage yakhada** 수학에 약하다 be weak at math; **yakhan siryeok** 약한 시력 have bad sight

yakhonhada 약혼하다 V to get engaged

yakhonja 약혼자 N fiancé

yakhonnyeo 약혼녀 N fiancée

yaksok 약속 N appointment, promise

yaksokhada 약속하다 V to promise

yalmipda 얄밉다 ADJ hateful, detestable

yamjeonhada 얌전하다 ADJ coyly, well-behaved,

yang 양 N sheep: **gil ireun yang** 길 잃은 양 a stray sheep

yang 양 PRON both: **yangjjok kkeu-cheul da jareuda** 양쪽 끝을 다 자르다 cut both ends

yang 양 N miss: **gim yang!** 김 양! Ms. Kim!

yang.yukhada 양육하다 V to raise, nurture: **janyeoreul yangyukhada** 자녀를 양육하다 raise one's children

yangbaechu 양배추 N cabbage

yangchijil 양치질 N tooth brushing

yangcho 양초 N candle

yangdari 양다리 V to play it both ways, play a double game, sit on the fence

yangdong.i 양동이 N bucket

yanggogi 양고기 N lamb, mutton

yanghae 양해 N understanding, consent: **yanghaereul guhada** 양해를 구하다 ask for understanding

yangjataegil 양자택일 N choose between two, either-or

yangjjok 양쪽 N both

yangmal 양말 N socks

yangmo 양모 N wool

yangnyeom 양념 N spices

yangpa 양파 N onion

yangsim 양심 N conscience: **yangsime gachaegeul neukkida** 양심에 가책을 느끼다 compunctious

yasaeng 야생 N wild

yatboda 얕보다 V to make light of, look down on

yatda, yateun 얕다, 얕은 ADJ shallow: **yateun mul** 얕은 물 shallow water; **yateun kkoe** 얕은 꾀 transparent subterfuge

ye 예 N example: **yereul deureo** 예를 들어 for example

ye 예 INTERJ yes

yebae 예배 N worship: **yebaereul deu-rida** 예배를 드리다 have a worship service

yebang 예방 N prevention

yebang jeopjong 예방 접종 N vaccination

Y

yebanghada 예방하다 v to prevent

yegeumhada 예금하다 v to make a deposit into savings

yego 예고 N notice: **yego eopsi** 예고 없이 without notice

yego 예고 N preview (*movie*): **yegopyeoni neomu gilda** 예고편이 너무 길다 The preview is too long

ye.ibareuda, ye.ibareun 예의바르다, 예의바른 ADJ well-mannered, courteous, polite

yei 예의 N manners

yejeol 예절 N manners, etiquette: **siktagyejeol** 식탁예절 table manners; **yejeoreul moreuda** 예절을 모르다 have no sense of propriety

yekeondae 예컨대 ADV for instance, for example

yeminhada 예민하다 ADJ edgy, sensitive: **geukdoro yeminhada** 극도로 예민하다 extremely sensitive

yeneung 예능 N artistic talent, entertainments

yennal 옛날 N the old days

yeobaek 여백 N blank, margin

yeoboseyo! 여보세요! INTERJ hello! (*on phone*)

yeochahamyeon 여차하면 ADV if need be

yeodeol 여덟 NUM eight: **yeodeol si** 여덟 시 eight o'clock

yeodeun 여든 NUM eighty

yeodeureum 여드름 N pimple, zit: **yeodeureumeul jjada** 여드름을 짜다 pop a pimple

yeodongsaeng 여동생 N younger sister

yeoe 예외 N exception: **modeun ireneun yeoega itda** 모든 일에는 예외가 있다 There is an exception to all rules

yeogi 여기 N here

yeogida 여기다 v to regard, consider, treat: **chinjasikcheoreom yeogida** 친자식처럼 여기다 treat a child (*person*) as one's own

yeogwan 여관 N inn, motel

yeohaeng 여행 N trip, journey

yeohaeng jal danyeo.oseyo! 여행 잘 다녀오세요! PHR bon voyage!

yeohaenggabang 여행가방 N luggage, suitcase

yeohaenghada 여행하다 v to travel

yeohaengja 여행자 N traveler

yeoja 여자 N woman

(yeoja) seonggi (여자) 성기 N vagina

yeojachin.gu 여자 친구 N girlfriend

yeoji 여지 N room, margin: **seontaegui yeojiga eopda** 선택의 여지가 없다 have no choice

yeojjuda 여쭈다 v to ask, greet (*honorific form*)

yeok 역 N station

yeokda 엮다 v to weave, plait

yeokgyeong 역경 N adversity

yeokgyeopda, yeokgyeo.un 역겹다, 역겨운 ADJ disgusting

yeokhada 역하다 ADJ sickening, disgusting

yeokhal 역할 N role

yeokhyogwa 역효과 N counter-effect: **yeokhyogwaga nada** 역효과가 나다 cause a backfire

yeokjeong 역정 N wrath, rage

yeokkwon 여권 N passport

yeoksa 역사 N history

yeoksajeok 역사적 N historical

yeokseup 역습 N counterattack

yeoksi 역시 ADV also, as well

yeol 열 N fever: **yeori nada** 열이 나다 have a fever

yeol 열 NUM ten: **songarak yeol gae** 손가락 열 개 ten fingers

yeolbyeon 열변 N declamation

yeolbyeong 열병 N fever, febrile disease

yeolcha 열차 N train

yeolda 엷다 ADJ thin, light: **yeolbeun saek** 엷은 색 light colors

yeolda 열다 v to open: **muneul yeolda** 문을 열다 open the door

yeoldaseot 열다섯 NUM fifteen

yeoldeung 열등 N inferiority

yeoldeunghada 열등하다 ADJ inferior, of poor quality

yeoldo 열도 N archipelago

yeolgeohada 열거하다 v to enumerate

yeolgi 열기 N heat, excitement

yeolgigu 열기구 N hot air balloon

yeolgwang 열광 N enthusiasm

yeolgwanghada 열광하다 v to be enthusiastic, go wild

yeolhana 열하나 NUM eleven

yeolheul 열흘 N ten days

yeoljeon 열전 N fierce fight

yeoljeong 열정 N passion, adoration

Y

yeoljung 열중 N absorption, enthusiasm

yeoljunghada 열중하다 V be enthusiastic

yeollada 열나다 V to become feverish

yeollak 연락 N contact, call

yeollakhada 연락하다 V to contact, get in touch with

yeollam 열람 N perusal, reading

yeollamhada 열람하다 V to read, peruse

yeollida 열리다 V to open: **muni (hwak) yeollida** 문이 (확) 열리다 a door (*flies*) open

yeollu 연루 N implication, involvement

yeollyeolhada 열렬하다 ADJ ardent, passionate

yeollyeong 연령 N age, years

yeollyo 연료 N fuel

yeollyun 연륜 N years of experience

yeolmae 열매 N fruit

yeolmanghada 열망하다 V to aspire, desire: **gasuga doegireul yeolmanghada** 가수가 되기를 열망하다 desire to become a singer

yeolnet 열넷 NUM fourteen

yeolsabyeong 열사병 N heatstroke

yeolset 열셋 NUM thirteen

yeolsimhi 열심히 ADV zealously

yeolsoe 열쇠 N key (*to room*)

yeolttul 열둘 NUM twelve

yeolyeodeol 열여덟 NUM eighteen

yeolyeoseot 열여섯 NUM sixteen

yeomchi 염치 N shameless, brazen

yeomdu 염두 N mind, thought: **saenggageul yeomdue duda** 생각을 염두에 두다 keep a thought in mind

yeomjeung 염증 N inflammation

yeomjeungnada 염증나다 V to be sick and tired of: **naneun i ire yeomjeungi nanda** 나는 이 일에 염증이 난다 I am tired of this job

yeomnokche 엽록체 N chloroplast

yeomnokso 엽록소 N chlorophyll

yeomnyeo 염려 N anxiety, concern

yeomsaek 염색 N dyeing: **meorireul borasaegeuro yeomsaekhada** 머리를 보라색으로 염색하다 dye the hair purple

yeomsan 염산 N hydrochloric acid

yeomso 염소 N goat

yeomtamhada 염탐하다 V to spy on: **dareun timeul yeomtamhada** 다른 팀을 염탐하다 spy on an opposing team

yeomwon 염원 N aspiration

yeomwonhada 염원하다 V to wish

yeon 년 N year: **icheon sibi nyeon** 이천 십이 년 year 2012

yeon.gan 연간 N annual: **yeongan suip** 연간 수입 annual earnings

yeon.gi 연기 N smoke: **dambae yeongi** 담배 연기 cigarette smoke

yeon.gi 연기 N performance, acting: **insaeng choegoui yeongireul boida** 인생 최고의 연기를 보이다 give the best performance of one's career

yeon.gidoeda 연기되다 V to be postponed: **mugihan yeongidoeda** 무기한 연기되다 be postponed indefinitely

yeon.gihada 연기하다 V to delay, postpone, put off: **gyeolhoneul yeongihada** 결혼을 연기하다 delay one's wedding

yeon.gu 연구 N research

yeon.guhada 연구하다 V to research

yeon.gyeolhada 연결하다 V to connect

yeonae 연애 N date (*going out*)

yeonbi 연비 N continued ratio

yeonbi 연비 N fuel efficiency: **jadongcha yeonbiga jota** 자동차 연비가 좋다 have good fuel efficiency

yeonbong 연봉 N annual income

yeonbora 연보라 N light purple

yeonbunhong 연분홍 N light pink

yeonchakhada 연착하다 V to be belated, delayed: **yeonchakdoen gicha** 연착된 기차 a delayed train

yeonchedongmul 연체동물 N mollusks

yeoncho 연초 N beginning of the year

yeonchul 연출 N direction, production

yeonchulhada 연출하다 V to direct, produce

yeondusaek 연두색 N yellow green

yeoneo 연어 N salmon

yeong 영 NUM zero: **o dae yeong** 5:0 오 대 영 five to nothing

yeong.eo 영어 N English

yeong.wonhi 영원히 ADV forever

yeongakhada 영악하다 ADJ shrewd, clever

yeongeop 영업 N business, sales: **yeongeobeul sijakhada** 영업을 시작하다 opens for business

yeongeopu 연거푸 ADV consecutively

yeongeuk 연극 N play

Y

yeonggam 영감 N inspiration: **yeong-gameul batda** 영감을 받다 be inspired

yeonggu 영구 N permanence

yeonggujeogida, yeonggujeogin 영구적이다, 영구적인 ADJ permanent

yeongguk 영국 N England

yeonggukui 영국의 ADJ British

yeonggwang 영광 N honor, glory

yeonggwangseureopda 영광스럽다 ADJ glorious, honorable

yeonghwa 영화 N film, movie

yeonghwagwan 영화관 N movie theater

yeonghyang 영향 N influence

yeonghyang.eul juda 영향을 주다 V to affect, influence

yeongjugwon 영주권 N permanent residency

yeongnageopda 영락없다 ADJ surely, certainly

yeongnihada, yeongnihan 영리하다, 영리한 ADJ clever, bright: **yeongnihan gangaji** 영리한 강아지 a clever puppy

yeongnyeokhada 역력하다 ADJ clear, plain, obvious: **yeongnyeokhae boida** 역력해 보이다 It looks obvious that ~

yeongnyu 역류 N backflow

yeongo 연고 N ointment: **yeongoreul bareuda** 연고를 바르다 apply ointment

yeongo 연고 N relation, connection: **hangugeneun amu yeongoga eopda** 한국에는 아무 연고가 없다 have no connections in Korea

yeongsang 영상 N above zero temperature: **yeongsangui nalssi** 영상의 날씨 weather above zero temperature

yeongsang 영상 N picture, image

yeongsujeung 영수증 N receipt

yeongto 영토 N territory, dominion

yeongung 영웅 N hero, heroine

yeongusil 연구실 N laboratory

yeonguso 연구소 N research institute

yeongwon 영원 N eternity, perpetuity

yeongyang 영양 N antelope

yeongyang 영양 N nutrition: **gyunhyeonginneun yeongyang** 균형있는 영양 well-balanced nutrition

yeongyangga 영양가 N nutritive value

yeongyangsiljo 영양실조 N malnutrition

yeongyeok 영역 N territory, turf:

yeongyeogeul pyosihada 영역을 표시하다 mark one's territory

yeongyocha 연교차 N (*weather*) annual range

yeongha 영하 N below zero temperature

yeonghon 영혼 N soul, spirit

Yeonhaeju 연해주 N the Maritime Province of Siberia

yeonhaenghada 연행하다 V to haul (*a person*) in

yeonhoe 연회 N banquet

yeonhyu 연휴 N long holidays

yeonin 연인 N lover

yeonjang 연장 N extension

yeonjang 연장 N tool, instrument

yeonjanghada 연장하다 V to extend

yeonjangja 연장자 N elder

yeonju 연주 N (*musical*) performance, recital

yeonmaeng 연맹 N league, federation, union

yeonmot 연못 N pond

yeonmyeong 연명 N prolongation of life

yeonnyakhada 연약하다 ADJ delicate, feeble, fragile

yeonnyeonhada 연연하다 V to cling to, stick to

yeonpil 연필 N pencil

yeonsan 연산 N calculation

yeonsang 연상 N association

yeonsang 연상 N older: **yeonsangui yeojachingu** 연상의 여자친구 an older girlfriend

yeonse 연세 N age (*honorific form*)

yeonseol 연설 N speech

yeonseolhada 연설하다 V to make a speech

yeonseup 연습 N practice

yeonseuphada 연습하다 V to practice

yeonsi 연시 N beginning of the year: **yeonmaryeonsi** 연말연시 the end and the beginning of the year

yeonsi 연시 N soft persimmon

yeonso 연소 N burning, combustion

yeonso 연소 N youth, juvenile: **choeyeonsoja** 최연소자 the youngest person

yeonsok 연속 N continuity

yeonswae 연쇄 N chain, links

yeonyein 연예인 N entertainer, celebrity

yeonyeom 여념 V to be absorbed, be deeply occupied

yeopa 여파 N after effect

...yeope ...옆에 ADV next to, beside:
baro yeope 바로 옆에 right next to

yeopguri 옆구리 N side, flank

yeopseo 엽서 N postcard

yeorae 열애 N passionate love

yeorahop 열아홉 NUM nineteen

yeoreobun 여러분 N folks, everybody
(*audience*)

yeoreum 여름 N summer

yeoreumbanghak 여름방학 N summer break

yeorida 여리다 ADJ soft, tender, tender-hearted

yeorilgop 열일곱 NUM seventeen

yeoron 여론 N public opinion

yeoronjosa 여론조사 N poll

yeorui 열의 N zeal, enthusiasm

yeosaeng 여생 N one's remnant existent

yeoseong 여성 N female, woman:
mihon yeoseong 미혼 여성 a single woman; **gihon yeoseong** 기혼 여성 a married woman

yeoseot 여섯 NUM six (*Korean numeral*)

yeosim 여심 N woman's heart:
noraero yeosimeul sarojapda 노래로 여심을 사로잡다 captivate women's heart with songs

yeosin 여신 N goddess: **sarangui yeosin** 사랑의 여신 the goddess of love; **jayuui yeosinsang** 자유의 여신상 the Statue of Liberty

yeot 엿 N taffy

yeotae 여태 ADV up until now

yeotboda 엿보다 V to peek, watch for (*an opportunity*): **mollae yeotboda** 몰래 엿보다 sneak peek; **gihoereul yeotboda** 기회를 엿보다 wait for a chance

yeotdeutda 엿듣다 V to eavesdrop

yeou 여우 N fox

yeouida 여의다 V to be bereaved

yeoun 여운 N lingering imagery

yeowang 여왕 N queen

yeowida 여위다 V to become thin, lean

yeoya 여야 N the Ruling party and the Opposition party

yeoyu 여유 N composure

yeoyu 여유 N surplus

yeppeuda, yeppeun 예쁘다, 예쁜 ADJ beautiful, pretty

yesang 예상 N expectation

yeseup 예습 N preparation of lessons

(ye)sik (예)식 N ceremony: **gyeolhon yesik** 결혼 예식 wedding ceremony

Yesu Geuriseudo 예수 그리스도 N Jesus Christ

yesul 예술 N art

yesulga 예술가 N artist

yesun 예순 NUM sixty: **yesuni neomda** 예순이 넘다 be over sixty

yeyak 예약 N reservation

yeyakhada 예약하다 V to reserve

...yeyo/ieyo ...예요/이에요 be (*copula, polite ending*)

yocheonghada 요청하다 V to request, ask

yogeum 요금 N fare, rate, tariff: **gibon yogeum** 기본 요금 base rate; **gonggong yogeum** 공공 요금 public utility charges

yogoe 요괴 N monster, goblin

yoguhada 요구하다 V to claim, demand

yoil 요일 N day of the week: **daeum geumnyoil** 다음 금요일 next Friday

yoin 요인 N primary factor, cause

yojeom 요점 N gist, main point

yojeong 요정 N fairy

yojeum 요즘 N presently, nowadays

yok 욕 N swear, curse

yokeondae 요컨대 ADV to sum up, in sum

yongam 용암 N lava

yongdon 용돈 N pocket money, pin money: **simbureumeul hago yongdoneul batda** 심부름을 하고 용돈을 받다 receive pin money after doing chores

yonggamhada/-han 용감하다/-한 ADJ brave, daring

yonghada 용하다 ADJ admirable, commendable: **nega geu ireul haenaedani cham yonghada** 네가 그 일을 해 내다니 참 용하다 It is admirable that you made it

yonghada 용하다 ADJ skillful, dexterous

yongmang 욕망 N desire

yongmu 용무 N business, task (*to do*)

yongpum 용품 N supplies, article

yongseohada 용서하다 V to forgive

yongsucheol 용수철 N spring (*metal*)

yongsseuda 용쓰다 v to strain, bear down: **yongeul sseuda** 용을 쓰다 strain oneself to, struggle

yoranhada 요란하다 ADJ uproarious, noisy, loud

yori 요리 N cooking, cuisine, dish

yoriga doeda/doen 요리가 되다/된 ADJ cooked

yorihada 요리하다 v to cook

yorisa 요리사 N cook, chef

yosae 요새 N fortress

yoso 요소 N element

yosul 요술 N magic, witchcraft

youngseo 용서 N forgiveness, mercy

yoyak 요약 N summary

yu.ilhan 유일한 ADJ sole, only: **yuilhan chingu** 유일한 친구 only friend

yubyeollada 유별나다 ADJ odd, eccentric

yuchanghada, yuchanghan 유창하다, 유창한 ADJ fluent: **yeongeoga yuchanghada** 영어가 유창하다 speak English fluently

yuchihada 유치하다 ADJ childish, infantile: **naie bihae yuchihada** 나이에 비해 유치하다 infantile for one's age

yuchihada 유치하다 v to attract, invite: **oegugin gwangwanggaegeul yuchihada** 외국인 관광객을 유치하다 attract foreign tourists

yuchiwon 유치원 N preschool, kindergarten

yudalli 유달리 ADV unusually, especially

yudo 유도 N induction: **yudobunman** 유도분만 induced labor

yudo 유도 N Judo: **yudoseonsu** 유도선수 a Judo player

yudohada 유도하다 v to induce

yudok 유독 N solely, particularly

yudosinmun 유도신문 N leading question

yueon 유언 N will, dying wish: **yueoneul namgida** 유언을 남기다 leave a will

yuga 육아 N childcare, baby care

yugamseureopda/-seureo.un 유감스럽다/-스러운 ADJ to regret, be sorry, be regretful

yugamseureopgedo 유감스럽게도 ADV regrettably

yugan 육안 N the naked eye: **neomu jagaseo yuganeuroneun sikbyeori**

eoryeopda 너무 작아서 육안으로는 식별이 어렵다 too small to tell with the naked eye

yugyo 유교 N Confucianism

yuhada 유하다 ADJ soft, mild, genial

yuhaehada 유해하다 ADJ harmfulness

yuhaeng 유행 N fashion, vogue, trend: **yuhaengeul ttareuda** 유행을 따르다 follow the trend

yuhaengga 유행가 N popular song

yuhaengseongui 유행성의 ADJ epidemic

yuhakhada 유학하다 v to study abroad: **eoryeoseul ttae yuhageul gada** 어렸을 때 유학을 가다 go to study abroad at an early age

yuhaksaeng 유학생 N international student

yuhanhada 유한하다 ADJ limited finite

yuheung 유흥 N adult entertainment

yuhok 유혹 N temptation, lure

yuhyeong 유형 N materiality: **yuhyeong munhwajae** 유형 문화재 tangible cultural asset

yuhyogigan 유효기간 N expiration date

yuhyohada, yuhyohan 유효하다, 유효한 ADJ valid

yujoe.ida, yujoe.in 유죄이다, 유죄인 ADJ guilty (of crime)

yujeonja 유전자 N gene, DNA

yujepum 유제품 N dairy products

yuk 육 NUM six (Arabic numeral)

yukbakhada 육박하다 v to close in upon: **baek kiroe yukbakhaneun mommuge** 100 kg 에 육박하는 몸무게 weight approaching nearly 100 kg

yukche 육체 N body, flesh

yukgaejang 육개장 N spicy beef soup

yukgam 육감 N the sixth sense, hunch

yukgun 육군 N army

yukgyo 육교 N overpass, overpass bridge: **yukgyoreul geonneoda** 육교 를 건너다 cross the overpass

yukjeup 육즙 N meat juice

yukji 육지 N land, shore

yukjunghada 육중하다 ADJ bulky, heavy, massive

yukseong 육성 N human voice

yukseonghada 육성하다 v to promote: **jiyeok saneobeul yukseonghada** 지역 산업을 육성하다 promote a local business

yuksip 육십 NUM sixty

yukwaehada 유쾌하다 ADJ delightful, cheerful, merry

yuldong 율동 N rhythmic movement, dance

yulli 윤리 N ethics, morals

yullihak 윤리학 N ethics, moral philosophy

yulmu 율무 N Job's tears

yumeo 유머 N humor: **yumeoga neomchida** 유머가 넘치다 have a great sense of humor

yumeoreoseuhada 유머러스하다 ADJ humorous

yumocha 유모차 N stroller

yumul 유물 N relic, antiquity

yumyeonghada, yumyeonghan 유명하다, 유명한 ADJ famous: **gyeongchiro yumyeonghada** 경치로 유명하다 be famous for the scenery; **yumyeonghan gasu** 유명한 가수 a famous singer

yunghap 융합 N fusion, blending

yungmyeonche 육면체 N hexahedron

yungtongseongi inneun 융통성이 있는 ADJ flexible: **yungtongseongi inneun saram** 융통성이 있는 사람 a flexible person

yunnada 윤나다 ADJ glossy, shiny

yunnaeda 윤내다 V to polish, furbish, shine

yunnori 윷놀이 N game of yut

yuntaekhada 윤택하다 ADJ abundant, ample

yupohada 유포하다 V to circulate, bruit, spread: **jojakdoen sasireul yupohada** 조작된 사실을 유포하다 circulate a fabricated rumor

yupum 유품 N relics, article left by the deceased

yuraehada 유래하다 V to originate, come from

yureop 유럽 N Europe

yuri 유리 N glass (*material*)

yuryeokhada 유력하다 ADJ powerful, influential: **yuryeokhan huboja** 유력한 후보자 a strong candidate

yuryeong 유령 N ghost

yuryo 유료 N fee-charging

yusan 유산 N inheritance

yusanhada 유산하다 V to miscarry (*a baby*): **aireul yusanhada** 아이를 유산하다 have a miscarriage

yusikhada 유식하다 ADJ learned, educated

yuteonhada 유턴하다 V to take a U-turn

yutong 유통 N distribution

yuwol 유월 N June

yuyeonhada 유연하다 ADJ soft, pliable

English–Korean

A

a bit, somewhat ADV yakgan 약간

a couple of days ago N eotgeujeokke 엊그저께

a day, one day N haru 하루

a little bit N jogeum 조금

a lot, many, much ADV mani 많이

a moment ago, just now ADV banggeum 방금

a stone throw, short distance ADJ gakkaun geori 가까운 거리

abandon, desert, to V beorida 버리다: *abandon one's life* moksumeul beorida 목숨을 버리다

abandonment, surrender N pogi 포기

abate, to V pullida 풀리다: *The cold weather has abated* chuwiga pullida 추위가 풀리다

abdominal muscle N bokgeun 복근

ability N neungnyeok 능력

ability, talent N jaeju 재주: *Everybody has some talent* gumbengido gureuneun jaejuga itda 굼벵이도 구르는 재주가 있다

abortion N naktae 낙태

about *(regarding, concerning)* ADV ...e daehae ...에 대해

above zero temperature N yeongsang 영상: *weather above zero temperature* yeongsangui nalssi 영상의 날씨

above, upstairs ADV ...wie ...위에

abrasion, scratch N chalgwasang 찰과상

abroad ADV hae.oe.e(seo) 해외에(서): *work abroad* haeoeeseo geunmuhada 해외에서 근무하다

absence N 1 buje 부재 2 gyeolseok 결석 3 gyeolpip 결핍

absent *(from school)* ADJ gyeolseokan 결석한

absoluteness N jeoldae 절대

absorption, enthusiasm N yeoljung 열중

abstract ADJ chusangjeogin 추상적인

abstruse, complicated ADJ nanhaehan 난해한

absurd ADJ eoieopda 어이없다

absurd, baseless ADJ teomunieopda 터무니없다

abundant, ample ADJ yuntaekhada 윤택하다

academic background N hangnyeok 학력

academic clique N hakbeol 학벌

accelerate V gasokhwadoeda 가속화되다: *Exposure to the sun can accelerate the ageing process* haetbiche nochuldoemyeon nohwa jinhaengi gasokhwa doel su itda 햇빛에 노출되면 노화 진행이 가속화 될 수 있다

accent N 1 gangse 강세 2 eotu 어투

accept, to V badadeurida 받아들이다

accident N sago 사고

accommodate, to V sukbaksikida 숙박시키다, suyonghada 수용하다

accompany, to V gachi gada 같이 가다

accomplish, achieve, to V iruda 이루다: *achieve one's goal* mokjeogeul iruda 목적을 이루다

according to ADV ...e uihamyeon ...에 의하면

accuse, file a lawsuit, to V gosohada 고소하다: *accuse sb of fraud* sagijocro gosohada 사기죄로 고소하다

accustomed to, familiar with ADJ ikda 익다: *be familiar with (a person or a sight)* nachi ikda 낯이 익다

accustomed to, trained, to be V gildeuryeojida 길들여지다

ache, pain N tongjjeung 통증

ache, to V apeuda 아프다

achieve, to V dalseonghada 달성하다, seongchwihada 성취하다: *There's no easy way to achieve one's aim* jasinui mokjeogeul dalseonghaneun deneun swiun bangbeobi eopda 자신의 목적을 달성하는 데는 쉬운 방법이 없다

achievements N eopjeok 업적

A

acid N san 산: *The acid reacts with a base to form a salt* saneun nyeomgiwa baneunghayeo sogeumeul mandeunda 산은 염기와 반응하여 소금을 만든다

acknowledge, to V injeonghada 인정하다: *He didn't acknowledge himself defeated* geuneun jasinui paebaereul injeonghaji anatda그는 자신의 패배를 인정하지 않았다

acorn N dotori 도토리

acquaintance N aneun saram 아는 사람

acquainted, accustomed to, to be V iksukhada 익숙하다

acquainted, to be V alda/anda 알다/안다: *be well acquainted with a person* sarameul jal randa 사람을 잘 안다

acquire, to V seupdeukhada 습득하다, hoekdeukhada 획득하다

acquisition N seupdeuk 습득, hoekdeuk 획득

across PREP geonneoseo 건너서

across from ADV geonneopyeone 건너 편에

act frivolous, behave carelessly, to V nadaeda 나대다

act, deed N haengwi 행위

act, do, conduct, to V haenghada 행하다: *conduct a ceremony* uisigeul haenghada 의식을 행하다

act out of drunkenness, an N jusa 주사

action N haengdong 행동: *group action* danche haengdong 단체 행동

action officer N damdanggwan 담당관

activity N hwalttong 활동: *relief activities* guhohwaldong 구호활동

actor N baeu 배우

actuality, reality N hyeonsil 현실

actually, really, in fact ADV siljjero 실제로

ad lib, improvisation N aedeuribeu 애드리브

adaptation, accommodation N jeogeung(ryeok) 적응(력)

add, to V deohada 더하다

address N juso 주소

adjust, to V jojeolhada 조절하다: *adjust the price of the product* jepum gagyeogeul jojeolhada 제품 가격을 조절하다

adjustment N jojeol 조절

admirable, commendable ADJ yonghada 용하다: *It is admirable that you made it* nega geu ireul haenaedani cham yonghada 네가 그 일을 해내다니 참 용하다

admire, to V gamtanhada 감탄하다

admit, confess, to V injeonghada 인정하다: *admit one's fault* jalmoseul injeonghada 잘못을 인정하다

admonish, to V taireuda 타이르다

adolescent, teenager N cheongsonyeon 청소년

adoption, acceptance N chaetaek 채택

adult N eoreun 어른

adult entertainment N yuheung 유흥

advance, go forward, to V apeuro naagada 앞으로 나아가다

advance money, deposit N seon. geum 선금

adversity N yeokgyeong 역경

advice N chunggo 충고

advise, to V chunggohada 충고하다

adviser N joeonja 조언자

advocate N onghoja 옹호자, jijija 지지자

advocate, to V onghohada 옹호하다: *I don't advocate that in any way* naneun eojjaetdeun geugeoseul onghohaji anneunda 나는 어쨌든 그것을 옹호하지 않는다

aeroplane, airplane, plane N bihaenggi 비행기

affect, influence, to V yeonghyang. eul juda 영향을 주다

affectation, pretense N gasik 가식

affected, practiced, unnatural ADJ eokjiseureopda 억지스럽다

affection N aejeong 애정

affectionate, friendly ADJ dajeonghada 다정하다

affiliate N busok 부속: *affiliated facilities* busok siseol 부속 시설; *a hospital in affiliation* busok byeongwon 부속 병원

afford, to V ...hal yeoyuga itda ...할 여유가 있다

afraid, scared ADJ museopda 무섭다, museowohada 무서워하다

African ADJ apeurikaui 아프리카의; N apeurikain 아프리카인

after *(time)* ADV dwie 뒤에
after-effect N yeopa 여파
after one's death ADV sahu 사후
after the fact ADV sahu 사후
afternoon N ohu 오후
afterwards, then ADV geu hu 그 후
again ADV dasi 다시
age N nai 나이
age *(honorific form)* N yeonse 연세
age, years N **1** sal 살: *three years old* se sal 세 살 **2** yeollyeong 연령
aggressive ADJ gonggyeokjeogin 공격적인
agree, to V chanseong 찬성, donguihada 동의하다
agreement N dongui 동의
agreement, coincidence N hapui 합치
agricultural implements N nonggigu 농기구
agriculture and fisheries N nongsusan 농수산
agriculture, farming N nongeop 농업
air N gonggi 공기
air, void N heogong 허공
air conditioner N eeokeon 에어컨
airline companies N hanggongsa 항공사
airmail N hanggong.upyeon 항공우편
airplane, plane N hanggonggi 항공기
airport N gonghang 공항
album N aelbeom 앨범, sajincheob 사진첩
alcohol, liquor N sul 술
alimony, compensation N wijaryo 위자료: *claim compensation, demand alimony* wijaryoreul cheongguhada 위자료를 청구하다
alive ADJ sarainneun 살아있는
all day N, ADV onjongil 온종일
all things, all creation N manmul 만물
all, altogether, in total N modu 모두
all, every ADJ ongat 온갖: *every kind of adversities* ongat jyeokgyeong 온갖 역경
all, every, whole, entire ADJ modeun 모든
alley, lane N golmokgil 골목길
allow, permit, to V heorakhada 허락하다
almost, nearly ADV geoui 거의,

hamateomyeon 하마터면: *something bad almost happened* hamateomyeon keunillal ppeon haetda 하마터면 큰일 날 뻔 했다
alone ADV honja(seo) 혼자(서)
alone, I'm alone PHR honjaitda 혼자 있다
already ADV beolsseo 벌써
also, as well ADV yeoksi 역시
also, too ADV ...do ...도: *That is good, too* geugeotdo jota 그것도 좋다
alter, change, shift, vary, to V dallajida 달라지다
always ADV hangsang 항상
always, day and night ADV bamnajeopsi 밤낮없이: *work night and day* bamnajeopsi ilhada 그는 밤낮없이 일했다
amateur N amachueo 아마추어
amazing ADJ nollaun 놀라운
ambassador N daesa 대사
America, United States N miguk 미국: *American* miguk saram 미국 사람
American I ADJ migugui 미국의 II N migugin 미국인
amount N geumaek 금액
ancestor N josang 조상
ancestor memorial rites N charye 차례
ancient ADJ godae(ui) 고대(의)
and CONJ geurigo 그리고, ...gwa/wa ...과/와
anemia N binhyeol 빈혈
anesthesia, narcotism N machwi 마취
angel N cheonsa 천사
anger, rage N hwa 화, noyeom 노염
angle N gakdo 각도
angry, cross ADJ hwanan 화난: *a look of anger* hwanan gisaek 화난 기색
animal N dongmul 동물
ankle N balmok 발목
announcer, anchor N anaunseo 아나운서
annoyed, irritated, to get V jjajeung.i nada 짜증이 나다
annual N yeon.gan 연간: *annual earnings* yeongan suip 연간 수입
annual income N yeonbong 연봉
anonymity N ingmyeong 익명
another, other *(different)* ADJ dareun 다른

A

answer the phone, to ADJ jeonhwa batda 전화 받다

answer, reply N eungdap 응답

answer, respond, reply, to V *(spoken)* daedaphada 대답하다, *(written)* dapjanghada 답장하다

answer, response N *(spoken)* daedap 대답, *(written)* dapjang 답장

answering machine N jadong eungdapgi 자동 응답기

antelope N yeongyang 영양

antiques N golttongpum 골동품

anus N hangmun 항문

anxiety n burangam 불안감

anxiety, concern N yeomnyeo 염려

anybody, anyone ADJ nugudeunji 누구든지

anything but, far from PHR keonyeong 커녕

anything, whatever ADV mueosideunji 무엇이든지

anyway ADV amuteun 아무튼, eochapi 어차피

anywhere, everywhere ADV eodideunji 어디든지: *we deliver anywhere in the country* jeonguk eodideunji baedal ganeunghamnida 전국 어디든지 배달 가능합니다

apart ADV tteoreojyeoseo 떨어져서

apartment, flat N apateu 아파트

ape, monkey N wonsung.i 원숭이

apologize, to V sagwahada 사과하다: *make a polite apology* jeongjunghi sagwahada 정중히 사과하다

apparently, obviously ADV myeongbaekhi 명백히

appear, turn up, to V naseoda 나서다

appearance, looks N oemo 외모

appetizing, scrumptious ADJ tamseureopda 탐스럽다: *a scrumptious apple* tamseureoun sagwa 탐스러운 사과

applause N baksu 박수: *a storm of applause* baksu galchae 박수 갈채

apple N sagwa 사과: *a box of apples* sagwa han sangja 사과 한 상자

application N wonseo 원서: *submit an application* wonseoreul jechulhada 원서를 제출하다

application form N sincheongseo 신청서

apply, request, to V sincheonghada 신청하다: *apply for a class* sueobeul sincheonghada 수업을 신청하다

apply for an examination, to V eungsihada 응시하다

appoint, nominate, to V jeonghada 정하다

appointment N immyeong 임명

appointment, promise N yaksok 약속

appraisal, valuation N gamjeong 감정

appraise, evaluate, size up, estimate, to V pyeongkkahada 평가하다

approach, draw near, to V jeopgeunhada 접근하다

approach, near, be closer *(distance)*, **to** V gakkawojida 가까워지다: *get near to the destination* mokjeokjie gakkawojida 목적지에 가까워지다

approach, near, be closer *(time)*, **to** V gakkawojida 가까워지다

appropriate, right, proper, suitable ADJ jeokdanghada, jeokdanghan 적당하다, 적당한: *a suitable calling* jeokdanghan jigeop 적당한 직업; *someone suitable* jeokdanghan saram 적당한 사람; *right time* jeokdanghan ttae 적당한 때

approximately, around ADV yak 약: *around 30 people* yak samsimmyeong 약 30명

April N sawol 사월

archetypal ADJ jeonhyeongjeogida/-jeogin 전형적이다/-적인

archipelago N yeoldo 열도

architecture N geonchuk 건축

ardent, passionate ADJ yeollyeolhada 열렬하다

area, place N badak 바닥: *the market area* sijang badak 시장 바닥

area, region N jiyeok 지역

arena N gyeonggijang 경기장

Argentina N areuhentina 아르헨티나

argue, to V nonjaenghada 논쟁하다

argue over, to V ...e daehae nonjaenghada ...에 대해 논쟁하다

argument N nonjaeng 논쟁

argument, quarrel N eonjaeng 언쟁

arithmetic, calculation N sansu 산수

arm N pal 팔: *raise one's arm* pareul deulda 팔을 들다

armchair, recliner N allak uija 안락 의자

army N yukgun 육군

around here, nearby ADV geuncheoe
근처에

around, nearby ADV ...gakkai(e) ...가
까이(에)

around, surrounding ADV ...juwie
...주위에

arrange, organize, clean up, to ADJ
jeongnihada 정리하다

arrange, prepare, to V maryeonhada
마련하다: *arrange a solution* bangbeobeul maryeonhada 방법을 마련하다

arranged blind date N seon 선

arrangement N maryeon 마련

arrangement *(music)* N pyeongok 편곡

arrival N dochak 도착

arrive at, get to V ireuda 이르다

arrow N hwasal 화살

art N yesul 예술

article *(in newspaper)* N gisa 기사:
write an article gisareul sseuda 기사를
쓰다

artificial, man-made ADJ
in.gongjeogida, in.gongjeogin 인공적
이다/-적인: *artificial beauties* ingongjeogin areumdaum 인공적인 아름다움

artificial flower N johwa 조화

artificial leg N uijok 의족

artist N yesulga 예술가

artistic talent, entertainments N
yeneung 예능

as it is ADV idaero 이대로

**as many as, to the prodigious
number of** ADV muryeo 무려

as one might say PHR ireul temyeon
이를 테면

as one pleases, at one's *(own)* **discretion** ADV maeumdaero 마음대로

as well ADV ...do ttohan ...도 또한

ashamed, embarrassed ADJ
bukkeureopda 부끄럽다, bukkeureoun
부끄러운

ashamed, shy, bashful, to be V
bukkeureowohada 부끄러워하다: *be
ashamed of one's mistakes* silsue daehae bukkeureowohada 실수에 대해
부끄러워하다; *be shy to speak* malhagi bukkeureowohada 말하기 부끄러
워하다; *ashamed of oneself* bukkeureopda 부끄럽다

Asia N asia 아시아

ask, greet *(honorific form)*, **to** V
yeojjuda 여쭈다

ask about, to V ...e daehae mureoboda
...에 대해 물어보다

ask for, request *(informally)*, **to** V
butakhada 부탁하다

asleep ADJ jago itda 자고 있다

aspiration N yeomwon 염원

aspire, desire, to V yeolmanghada
열망하다: *desire to become a singer*
gasuga doegireul yeolmanghada
가수가 되기를 열망하다

assault, attack, rape N pokhaeng 폭행

assemble, gather, to V mo.euda 모으
다: *gather data* jaryoreul moeuda 자료
를 모으다

assemble, put together, to V joriphada 조립하다

assign, entrust, to V matgida 맡기다

assist, help, to V dopda 돕다

assistance, help N doum 도움

association N yeonsang 연상

asthma N cheonsik 천식

astray, to go V eonnagada 엇나가다

astronomy N cheonmunhak 천문학

at least ADV jeogeodo 적어도

at night ADV bame 밤에

at once, immediately, soon ADV got
곧

at once, promptly ADV inae 이내

at the latest ADV neujeodo 늦어도

atmosphere, ambience N bunwigi
분위기

atomic bomb N wonjapoktan
원자폭탄

atomic energy N wonjaryeok 원자력

attachment, affection N aechak 애착

attack *(in war)*, **assault** N gonggyeok
공격

attain, achieve, accomplish, to V
dalseonghada 달성하다: *achieve one's
goal* mokpyoreul dalseonghada 목표를
달성하다

attempt I N sido 시도 II V sidohada
시도하다, chamseokhada 참석하다

attend, work for, to V danida 다니다:
attend school hakgyoe danida 학교에
다니다; *work for a reputable company*
joeun jikjange danida 좋은 직장에
다니다

attic, loft N darak 다락

attitude N taedo 태도

attract, invite, to V yuchihada 유치
하다: *attract foreign tourists* oegugin

A

gwangwanggaegeul yuchihada 외국인 관광객을 유치하다

attractive ADJ maeryeokjeogida, mae-ryeokjeogin 매력적이다/–적인

auction, to V gyeongmaehada 경매하다

auctioned off, to be V gyeongmaero pallida 경매로 팔리다

August N parwol 팔월

aunt N imo 이모

aunt, ma'am *(married female)* N ajumeoni 아주머니

Australia N hoju 호주: *Australian (nationality)* hoju saram 호주 사람

authority *(power)* N gwonhan 권한: *give sb the authority to (do)* gwon-haneul buyeohada 권한을 부여하다

autograph, signature N seomyeong 서명

automatic ADJ jadonggui 자동의

automobile, car, motor vehicle N jadongcha 자동차

autonomy N jayul 자율

autumn, fall N ga.eul 가을

average N botong 보통

average *(numbers)* N pyeonggyun 평균

aviation, flying N hanggong 항공

avoid, get away, to V myeonhada 면하다

awake ADJ kkae.eo itda 깨어 있다

awake, wake up, to V kkae.eo nada 깨어나다

awareness, realization N insik 인식

awfully pleasant ADJ tongkwaehada 통쾌하다

awkward ADJ eosaekhada 어색하다

awkward, difficult, embarrassing ADJ nancheohada 난처하다, nancheo-han 난처한

B

baby N agi 아기

back *(part of body)* N deung 등

back, rear, tail N dwi 뒤

backflow N yeongnyu 역류

background N batang 바탕

backward ADV dwiro 뒤로

backyard N dwinmadang 뒷마당

bacteria N bakteria 박테리아, segyun 세균

bad luck N burun 불운

bad mood, under the weather N jeogiap 저기압

bad, wrong, poor, ill-natured, unpleasant ADJ nappeuda 나쁘다, nappeun나쁜: *bad weather* nappeun nalssi 나쁜 날씨; *poor quality product* pumjiri nappeun sangpum 품질이 나쁜 상품; *ill-natured* maeumssiga nappeun 마음씨가 나쁜; *unpleasant* gibuni nappeun 기분이 나쁜

bag N baek 백 (가방), gabang 가방

baggage, package, load N jim 짐: *bear a load* jimeul jida 짐을 지다

bake, roast, grill, to V gupda 굽다: *bake cookies* kukireul gupda 쿠키를 굽다

balance N gyunhyeong 균형

balance, to V gyunhyeongeul japda 균형을 잡다

bald ADJ daemeoriin 대머리인

ball N gong 공

ballpoint pen N bolpen 볼펜

balloon N pungseon 풍선

ballot N mugimyeong tupyoyongji 무기명 투표용지

banana N banana 바나나

bandage N bungdae 붕대

bank N 1 *(finance)* eunhaeng 은행 2 *(of river)* duk 둑

bankbook N tongjang 통장

bankruptcy N pasan 파산: *The hospital bill drove him into bankruptcy* geuneun byeongwonbi ttaemune pasanhal jigyeonge ireureotda 그는 병원비 때문에 파산할 지경에 이르렀다

banquet N yeonhoe 연회

banter N nollim 놀림

bar, pub N suljjip 술집

barber N ibalsa 이발사: *barbershop* ibalso 이발소

barely ADV gyeo.u 겨우

barely, hardly ADV gansinhi 간신히: *barely finished one's work* ireul gan-sinhi kkeunmachida 일을 간신히 끝마치다

barely, narrowly ADV gakkaseuro 가까스로: *barely finished work* ireul gak-kaseuro kkeunnaeda 일을 가까스로 끝내다

bargain, haggle, to V heungjeonghada 흥정하다: *bargain with sb over the price (of)* gagyeogeul heungjeonghada 가격을 흥정하다

barn N heotgan 헛간

barrel N tong 통

barren, infertile ADJ memareun 메마른: *a barren land* memareun ttang 메마른 땅

base, foundation, bottom N gicho 기초

baseball N yagu 야구

based on ADJ ...e gichohan ...에 기초한

basement N jihacheung 지하층, jihasil 지하실

basic ADJ gibonjeogida 기본적이다, gibonjeogin 기본적인

basis N geun.geo 근거

basket N baguni 바구니: *basketball* nonggu 농구

bat N 1 bangmangi 방망이 2 bakjwi 박쥐

bath N mogyok 목욕

bathe, take a bath, to V mogyokhada 목욕하다

bathroom N mogyoksil 목욕실

battery N geonjeonji 건전지, baeteori 배터리

battle N jeontu 전투

bay N man 만

be absorbed, be deeply occupied, to V yeonyeom 여념

be absorbed, be immersed, to V molduhada 몰두하다

be accomplished, come true, to V irueojida 이루어지다; *a dream comes true* kkumi irucojida 꿈이 이루어지다

be accused of, to V mollida 몰리다

be allayed, to V pullida 풀리다

be at a loss for words with anger, to V makhida 막히다

be beaten, to V eodeomatda 얻어맞다

be belated, be delayed, to V yeonchakhada 연착하다: *a delayed train* yeonchakdoen gicha 연착된 기차

be bereaved, to V yeouida 여의다

be born with, to V tagonada 타고나다: *an inborn talent* tagonan jaeneung 타고난 재능

be born, to V tae.eonada 태어나다

be bound, to V eongmaeida 얽매이다

be buried in, to V pamuchida 파묻히다

be careful!, look out! INTERJ josimhaseyo! 조심하세요!

be connected, to V ieojida 이어지다: *The road is connected to the highway*

i gireun gosokdorowa ieojinda 이 길은 고속도로와 이어진다

be continued, to V ieojida 이어지다: *Past traditions continue to this day* gwageoui jeontongi hyeonjaekkaji ieojida 과거의 전통이 현재까지 이어지다

be cornered, be pushed, to V mollida 몰리다

be cut *(off)*, **be chopped, to** V jallida 잘리다

be desirable, to V tamnada 탐나다

be discouraged, be bummed out, to V nakdamhada 낙담하다

be dispirited ADJ uigisochimhada 의기소침하다

be embarrassed ADJ changpihada 창피하다/changpihan 창피한

be enthusiastic ADJ yeoljunghada 열중하다

be enthusiastic, go wild, to V yeolgwanghada 열광하다

be faithful ADJ uiriga itda 의리가 있다

be filial to parents, to V hyodohada 효도하다

be free, have nothing to do, to ADJ hangaropda 한가롭다

be full of ambition ADJ manmanhada 만만하다

be full of self-confidence ADJ manmanhada 만만하다

be hard of hearing, *(amblyacousia)*, **to** V ganeungwimeokda 가는귀먹다

be in harmony with, blend in, to V johwadoeda 조화되다

be infected, catch something from sb, to V omda 옮다: *catch a cold from a friend* chinguege gamgiga omda 친구에게 감기가 옮다

be inferior to, to V cheojida 처지다

be installed, to V noida 놓이다

be kept down, to V nullida 눌리다

be located, be situated, to V wichihada 위치하다

be locked in, to V gachida 갇히다

be obstructed, be blocked, to V garomakhida 가로막히다

be omitted, to V tallakhada 탈락하다

be on the watch for, pay sharp attention to, to V se.uda 세우다

be overwhelmed, to V nullida 눌리다

be past, go by, go through, to V

B

ENGLISH–KOREAN

jinada 지나다: *past midnight* jajeongi
jinada 자정이 지나다
be placed in, to V noida 놓이다
be placed on, be laid on, to V eonchida 얹히다
be plastered, to V manchwihan 만취한
be pompous, be inflated, to V ujjulhada 우쭐하다
be pushed out, to V millyeonada
밀려나다
be reached, be made, to V irueojida
이루어지다
be removed, be untied, to V pullida
풀리다: *shoelaces came undone* sinbalkkeuni pullida 신발끈이 풀리다
**be rolling in the dough, sit on a
pile of money, to** V donbangseoge
anda 돈방석에 앉다
be seen, come in sight, to V boida
보이다: *a sign came into sight* pyojipani nune boida 표지판이 눈에 보이다
be sick and tired of, to V yeomjeungnada 염증나다: *I am tired of this job*
naneun i ire yeomjeungi nanda 나는
이 일에 염증이 난다
be smoothed down, lie down, to V
jamjada 잠자다
be sold, to V pallida 팔리다: *be sold
at a giveaway price* heolgapse pallida
헐값에 팔리다
be squashed, to V nullida 눌리다: *a
loaf of bread squashed flat* napjakhage nullin ppang 납작하게 눌린 빵
be taken off, come off, to V beotgyeojida 벗겨지다
be the same ADJ dareumeopda
다름없다
be touched by, be moved, to V
gamdonghada 감동하다
**be under unfair/false accusation,
to** ADJ eogulhada 억울하다: *be
unjustly accused* eogulhan numyeongeul sseuda 억울한 누명을 쓰다
be, exist, to V itda 있다: *There are
birds that can't fly* nalji motaneun
saedo itda 날지 못하는 새도 있다
beach, coast, seashore N badatga
바닷가
bean N kong 콩
bean curd, tofu N dubu 두부
bear, endure, stand, to V chamda
참다: *endure hardship* gonaneul

chamda 고난을 참다
beard N teoksuyeom 턱수염
beat, hit, to V paeda 패다: *beat sb to a
pulp* heumssin dudeulgyeo paeda 흠씬
두들겨 패다
beat, rhythm N bakja 박자
beat, strike, to V ttaerida 때리다:
strike one's head meorireul ttaerida
머리를 때리다
beat, win, defeat, to V igida 이기다:
win a game geimeseo igida 게임에서
이기다
beautiful, pretty ADJ yeppeuda 예쁘다,
yeppeun 예쁜; areumdapda 아름답다,
areumdaun 아름다운: *a beautiful artwork* areumdaun yesul jakpum 아름다
운 예술 작품
beauty N minyeo 미녀
became alone, widowed ADJ honjadoen 혼자된
because, since CONJ -gi ttaemune
-기 때문에
become, to V doeda 되다
**become acquainted, familiar with,
to** V ikhida 익히다: *be familiarized
with (faces)* eolgureul rikhida 얼굴을
익히다
become clear, be ascertained, to V
panmyeongnada 판명나다
become dark, to V eoduwojida
어두워지다
become estranged, to V teureojida
틀어지다: *become estranged from*
saiga teureojida 사이가 틀어지다
become feverish, to V yeollada 열나다
become proficient, master, to V
ikhida 익히다: *master the technique
of* gisureul ikhida 기술을 익히다
become sulky, to V torajida 토라지다
become thin/lean, to V yeowida 여위다
become unemployed, to V siljikhada,
siljikan 실직하다, 실직한
bed N chimdae 침대
bed, bedstead N jamjari 잠자리: *go to
bed* jamjarie deulda 잠자리에 들다
bedroom N chimsil 침실
beef N soegogi 쇠고기
beer N maekju 맥주
befall, come near, to V dakchida 닥치다
before, ago, earlier ADV jeone 전에
before, in front of PREP ...ape(seo)
...앞에(서)

before one knows ADV eoneudeot 어느덧

beforehand, in advance ADV miri 미리

beg, entreat, to V ganguhada 간구하다

begin, start, to V sijakhada 시작하다: *beginning, start* sijak 시작

beginning of the year N yeoncho 연초, yeonsi 연시: *the end and the beginning of the year* yeonmaryeonsi 연말연시

behave V cheosinhada 처신하다

behave like a spoiled child, to V eungseokburida 응석부리다

behind *(space)* ADV dwie 뒤에

belief, faith N mideum 믿음

believe, trust, to V mitda 믿다

bellow, howling N pohyo 포효

belly, abdomen, tummy, stomach N bae 배: *a fat tummy* ttungttunghan bae 뚱뚱한 배

belong to V ...e sokada ...에 속하다

below, under ADV arae.e 아래에

below zero temperature N yeongha 영하

belt N belteu 벨트

bench N benchi 벤치

benefactor N eunin 은인

benefit, boon N hyetaek 혜택

besides, in addition ADV gedaga 게다가

best ADJ jeil jota/jo.eun 제일 좋다/좋은: *best friend* danjjak 단짝

bet, wager N naegi 내기: *place a bet* naegireul hada 내기를 하다, naegireul geolda 내기를 걸다

better ADJ deo jota/jo.eun 더 좋다/좋은: *like winter better* gyeouri deo jota 겨울이 더 좋다; *a better choice* deo joeun seontaek 더 좋은 선택

better, cured, recovered, to be *(get)* V hoebokdoeda 회복되다

between PREP ...saie ...사이에: *between you and me* neowa na saie 너와 나 사이에

between times ADV teumteumi 틈틈이

beyond one's power ADJ beokchada 벅차다: *This is beyond my power* i iri naegeneun neomu beokchada이 일이 나에게는 너무 벅차다

bib, pinafore N teokbaji 턱받이

bicker, squabble, to V tigyeoktae-gyeokhada 티격태격하다

bicycle, bike N jajeon.geo 자전거

big, large ADJ keuda 크다, keun 큰: *big snowflakes* hambangnun 함박눈

bill N gyesanseo 계산서

bill *(currency)*, **bank note** N jipye 지폐

billion NUM sibeok 십억

bind, tie, to V eongmaeda 얽매다

bird N sae 새: *a flock of birds* sae tte 새 떼

birth, nativity N tansaeng 탄생

birth, to give V nata 낳다

birthday N saeng.il 생일

biscuit N biseuket 비스켓

bite, to V mulda 물다

bitter ADJ sseuda 쓰다, sseun 쓴: *bitter feeling, grudge* wonmang 원망

bitter, resentful ADJ wontonghada 원통하다

black ADJ kkamata 까맣다, kkaman 까만

black beans N kkaman kong 까만 콩

blade *(of knife)* N kallal 칼날

blame, accuse, to V binanhada 비난하다

bland ADJ mumigeonjohada/-han 무미건조하다/-한

blank N kan 칸: *Please fill in the blanks* bin kaneul chaeuseyo 빈 칸을 채우세요

blank, margin N yeobaek 여백

blanked, outcast, to be V wangtta 왕따: *be treated as an outcast* wangttareul danghada 왕따를 당하다

blanket N damnyo 담요, ibul 이불: *cover with a blanket* ibureul deopda 이불을 덮다

bleaching N pyobaek 표백

bless, to V chukbokhada 축복하다

blessing N chukbok 축복

blind ADJ nunmeon 눈먼

blind, to become V nunmeolda 눈멀다

blinded *(by greed)* ADJ eodupda 어둡다, eoduun 어두운: *be blinded by greed (power)* yoksim (gwollyeok)e nuni eodupda 욕심 (권력)에 눈이 어둡다

blindly, thoughtlessly ADV mujak-jeong 무작정

blister, to V bureuteuda 부르트다: *blistered lips from fatigue* piroro ipsuri bureuteuda 피로로 입술이 부르트다

B

block, cut-off N chadan 차단
blood N hyeoraek 혈액, pi 피
blood pressure N hyeorap 혈압
blood vessel N hyeolgwan 혈관
bloodcurdling, hair-raising ADJ
  ossakhada 오싹하다
blouse N beullauseu 블라우스
blue I ADJ parata 파랗다, paran 파란 II
  N (color) parang 파랑
blue jean N cheongbaji 청바지
bluefin tuna N darangeo 다랑어
blunt, gruff, abrupt ADJ tungmyeongseureopda 퉁명스럽다
boarding N tapseung 탑승
boarding house N hasukjip 하숙집
boast, show off N jarang 자랑
boat N bae 배, boteu 보트
body N mom 몸
body, flesh N yukche 육체
boil, cook, to V samda 삶다
boil, heat, simmer, to V kkeurida
  끓이다: boil water mureul kkeurida
  물을 끓이다
boiled ADJ kkeurin 끓인, salmeun 삶은
boiled, cooked, to be V ikda 익다:
  the meat is not cooked yet gogiga
  deol igeotda 고기가 덜 익었다
bomb N poktan 폭탄: atomic bomb
  wonjapoktan 원자폭탄; bombing
  pokgyeok 폭격
bomb, to V pokpahada 폭파하다
bombing, bombardment N pokgyeok
  폭격
bon voyage! PHR yeohaeng jal
  danyeo.oseyo! 여행 잘 다녀오세요!
bone N ppyeo 뼈
book N chaek 책
bookshelf N chaekkkochi 책꽂이
bookstore N seojeom 서점
bookworm N chaekbeolle 책벌레
border, edge N gajangjari 가장자리
bored ADJ jiruhada 지루하다,
  jiruhaehada 지루해하다; simsimhada
  심심하다, simsimhan 심심한; jiruhada
  지루하다, jiruhan 지루한: a boring
  movie jiruhan yeonghwa 지루한 영화
borrow, to V billida 빌리다: borrow
  money from a person doneul billida
  돈을 빌리다
boss N boseu 보스
botanic gardens N singmurwon
  식물원

both I ADV dul da 둘 다 II N yangjjok
  양쪽 III PRON yang 양: cut both ends
  yangjjok kkeucheul da jareuda 양쪽
  끝을 다 자르다
bother, disturb, hinder, to V banghaehada 방해하다
bother, disturbance, hindrance N
  banghae 방해
bottle N byeong 병: a juice bottle juice
  byeong 쥬스 병
bottom, the N ...arae ...아래
bottom, buttocks N eongdeong.i
  엉덩이
bounce, to V twigida 튀기다: bounce
  a ball gongeul twigida 공을 튀기다
boundary, border (between countries)
  N gyeonggye 경계
bowl N sabal 사발
box, chest, crate, case N sangja 상자
boy N so.nyeon 소년: boyfriend namja
  chin.gu 남자 친구
bra N beuraejieo 브래지어
bracelet N paljji 팔찌
brain N noe 뇌
brainstorm, to V jjada 짜다: brainstorm ideas aidieoreul jjada 아이디어
  를 짜다
brake N beureikeu 브레이크
brakes, to step on V beureikeu bapda
  브레이크 밟다
branch N jijeom 지점
branch (of tree) N gaji 가지: break a
  branch gajireul kkeokda 가지를 꺾다;
  branches (of tree) namutgaji 나뭇가지
brand, stigma N nagin 낙인: be
  branded as nagini jjikhida 낙인이
  찍히다
brandish, swing, to V hwidureuda
  휘두르다
brave, daring ADJ yonggamhada/-han
  용감하다, 용감한
brazen, thick-skinned, shameless
  ADJ cheonnyeondeokseureopda 천연덕
  스럽다
breach N wibae 위배
bread N ppang 빵
break, to V kkaejida 깨지다
break, chop, to V paeda 패다: chop
  firewood jangjageul paeda 장작을 패다
break, crush, destroy, to V kkaetteurida 깨뜨리다
break, to V bureojida 부러지다: break

one's ankle balmogi bureojida 발목이 부러지다

break *(promise, rules)*, **to** v eogida 어기다: *break one's promise (word)* yaksogeul eogida 약속을 어기다

break apart, to v jjogaeda 쪼개다

break down *(car, machine)*, **to** v gojangnada 고장나다

break open, to v teuda 트다

break up, divorce, to v gallaseoda 갈라서다: *divorced after a year of marriage* gyeolhonhan ji 1nyeon mane gallaseotda 결혼한 지 1년 만에 갈라 섰다

break up a fight, to v mallida 말리다

breakfast, morning meal N achim siksa 아침 식사: *to eat breakfast* achim siksahada 아침 식사하다

breathe out, spurt out, to v naeppumda 내뿜다

breathtaking, suffocating, to be v makhida 막히다: *breathtakingly beautiful* sumi makhige yeppeuda 숨이 막히게 예쁘다; *be suffocated with heat* deowiro sumi makhida 더위로 숨이 막히다

breeze N sandeulbaram 산들바람: *The grass is swaying in the breeze* puri sandeulbarame nabukkinda 풀이 산들 바람에 나부낀다

brick N byeokdol 벽돌

bride N sinbu 신부

bridegroom N sillang 신랑

bridge N dari 다리: *cross over a bridge* darireul geonneoda 다리를 건너다

brief, short, simple ADJ gandanhada 간단하다, gandanhan 간단한

briefcase N seoryu gabang 서류 가방

briefs, panties, underpants N paenti 팬티

bright, promising ADJ changchanghada 창창하다: *a promising future* changchanghan amnal 창창한 앞날

brilliant, splendid ADJ challanhada 찬란하다

brimful ADJ gadeukhada 가득하다

bring, fetch, carry, to v gajyeo.oda 가져오다

bring down, lower, cut down, to v naerida 내리다: *lower a price* gagyeogeul laerida 기격을 내리다

bring up *(topic)*, **mention, to** v geo-

ronhada 거론하다

bring up, nurse a child, to v kiuda 키우다

British ADJ yeonggukui 영국의

broadcast I N bangsong 방송 II v bangsonghada 방송하다

broccoli N beurokeolli 브로컬리

broken ADJ bureojin 부러진: *a broken arm* bureojin pal 부러진 팔

broken, shattered ADJ kkaejin 깨진

bronze N cheongdong 청동

broom N bijjaru 빗자루

broth, soup N guk 국

brother, sibling N hyeongje 형제

brother and sister N nammae 남매, onui 오누이

brother-in-law N 1 *(elder sister's husband)* hyeongbu 형부 2 *(wife's brother)* cheonam 처남 3 *(younger sister's husband)* maeje 매제

brown I ADJ galsaekui 갈색의 II N galsaek 갈색

bruise N meong 멍

brush I N but 붓, sol 솔: *a toothbrush* chitsol 칫솔 II v soljilhada 솔질하다

bubble N geopum 거품

bucket N yangdong.i 양동이

Buddhism N bulgyo 불교: *Buddhist* bulgyosinja 불교신자

budget N yesan 예산 : *Long-term budget deficits are a problem* janggi yesan jeokjaneun munjega doenda 장기 예산 적자는 문제가 된다

buffalo *(water buffalo)* N mulso 물소

build, make, construct, to v jitda 짓다: *build a house* jibeul jitda 집을 짓다

build, open, to v teuda 트다

build up, to v kiuda 키우다: *build up muscles* geunnyugui himeul kiuda 근육의 힘을 키우다

building N bilding 빌딩

bulky, brawny, beefy ADJ uramhada 우람하다: *a bulky frame* uramhan chegyeok 우람한 체격

bulky, heavy, massive ADJ yukjunghada 육중하다

bull N hwangso 황소

bullet N chongal 총알

bully, browbeat, to v eukbakjireuda 윽박지르다

bundle, bunch, sheaf *(counting unit)*

N dan 단: *three bunches of spinach* sigeumchi se dan 시금치 세 단

burglar N gangdo 강도, doduk 도둑

burglarize, to V teolda 털다

burn *(flare, blaze, flame)* **up, to** V taoreuda 타오르다

burn I N *(injury)* hwasang 화상 II V *(blaze)* tada 타다: *burn well* jal tada 잘 타다

burn, emblaze, to V tae.uda 태우다: *burn the rice* babeul taeuda 밥을 태우다

burned down, out ADJ da tada 다 타다: *The house was burned down* jibi da tabeoryeotda 집이 다 타버렸다

burning, combustion N yeonso 연소

burning, stinging ADJ eoreolhada 얼얼하다

burst of laughter N pokso 폭소

bury, to V 1 mutda 묻다 2 *(entomb)* pamutda 파묻다

bus N beoseu 버스: *bus station* beoseu jeonggeojang 버스 정거장

bush N gwanmok 관목, deombul 덤불

busily, briskly ADV bappi 바삐

business N 1 *(enterprise)* sa.eop 사업 2 *(sales)* yeongeop 영업: *opens for business* yeongeobeul sijakada 영업을 시작하다 3 *(trade)* bijeuniseu 비즈니스

business, task *(to do)* N yongmu 용무

businessperson N sa.eopga 사업가

bustling, busy ADJ busanhan 부산한

busy, crowded ADJ bokjaphada 복잡하다, bokjapan 복잡한: *crowded streets* bokjapan geori 복잡한 거리

busy *(doing something)* ADJ bappeuda 바쁘다, bappeun 바쁜: *be busy* bappeuda 바쁘다; *busy people* bappeun saramdeul 바쁜 사람들

but, however ADV geureochiman 그렇지만

but, only, merely ADV dan 단

butcher and eat, devour, to V jabameokda 잡아먹다

butter N beoteo 버터

butterfly N nabi 나비

button N danchu 단추

buy, to V sada 사다

buyer N gumaeja 구매자, baieo 바이어

by ADV ...e uihae ...에 의해: *by accident* uyeonhi 우연히: *meet by chance* uyeonhi mannada 우연히 만나다; *by*

itself (naturally) jeojeollo 저절로; *by rail* gicharo 기차로; *by the way* geureonde 그런데

C

cab N taeksi 택시

cabbage N yangbaechu 양배추

cabin N 1 odumakjip 오두막집 2 seonsil 선실

cabinet N jang 장

cable N keibeul 케이블

caddie *(golf)* N kaedi 캐디

Cadillac N kaedillak 캐딜락

café, coffee house N kape 카페

caféteria, canteen N maejeom 매점

caffeine N kapein 카페인

cage in, shut in, lock in, to V gaduda 가두다

cake N keikeu 케이크

calcium N kalsyum 칼슘

calculate, to V gyesanhada 계산하다: *calculation* yeonsan 연산; *calculator* gyesan.gi 계산기

calendar N dallyeok 달력

call, summon, to V bureuda 부르다: *call a friend* chingureul bureuda 친구를 부르다

called, named, to be V bullida 불리다, bullineun 불리는: *a fruit called coffee-cherry* keopicherira bullineun yeolmae 커피체리라 불리는 열매

called to account, found to be blameable, to be V chaekjapida 책잡히다

calm, relaxed, quiet ADJ chabunhada 차분하다

calorie N kallori 칼로리

Cambodia N kambodia 캄보디아

camcorder N kaemkodeo 캠코더

cameo N kameo 카메오

camera N kamera 카메라, sajingi 사진기

cameraman N kameramaen 카메라맨

camouflage, disguise N wijang 위장: *disguise oneself as* wijanghada 위장하다

campaign N kaempein 캠페인

camping N kaemping 캠핑

campus N kaempeoseu 캠퍼스

can, be able to, be capable of ADJ -(eu)l su itda -(으)ㄹ 수 있다

can, tin N kkangtong 깡통: *canned food* tongjorim 통조림
Canada N kaenada 캐나다
cancel, to V chwisohada 취소하다
cancer N am 암: *She has been battling cancer for years* geunyeoneun yeoreo hae dongan amgwa tubyeongeul hago itda 그녀는 여러 해 동안 암과 투병을 하고 있다
candidate N huboja 후보자, jiwonja 지원자: *The senator is the leading candidate for President* geu sangwonuiwoni gajang yuryeokhan daetongnyeong huboida 그 상원의원이 가장 유력한 대통령 후보이다
candle N yangcho 양초
candy N kaendi 캔디, *(sweets)* satang 사탕
Cannes N kan 칸
cannot, be unable to ADJ -rsueopda –ㄹ수없다: *The work cannot be done on time* ireul je sigane kkeunnael su eopda 일을 제 시간에 끝낼 수 없다
canoe N kanu 카누
can't, not ADV mot 못: *can't sing* noraereul mot handa 노래를 못 한다
can't bear to ADV chama 차마
canvas N kaenbeoseu 캔버스, hwapok 화폭
cap, hat N moja 모자
capital N jabon 자본
captain N seonjang 선장
captivate, enslave, bewitch, to V nogida 녹이다: *captivate (men's) heart* aeganjangeul nogida 애간장을 녹이다
capture, catch I N pochak 포착: *catch a chance* gihoereul pochakhada 기회를 포착하다 II V japda 잡다: *catch a ball* gongeul japda 공을 잡다
car N cha 차: *new-model car* sinhyung cha 신형 차; *car pool system* kapulje 카풀제
caramel N kaereomel 캐러멜
carat N kaereot 캐럿
carbohydrate N tansuhwamul 탄수화물
cardboard N panji 판지
cards, game N kadeu(nori) 카드(놀이)
care for, look after, to V chaenggida 챙기다: *take great care of one's health* geongangeul kkeumjjigi chaengginda 건강을 끔찍이 챙긴다; *Take good care of your mother!* eomeonireul jal chaenggyeodeuryeora 어머니를 잘 챙겨드려라
career N keorieo 커리어
career, work experience N gyeongnyeok 경력
careful, to be V josimhada 조심하다
caricature N kaerikeocheo 캐리커처
carnation N kaneisyeon 카네이션
carnival N kanibal 카니발
carpet N kapeteu 카페트
carrier N 1 susonggi 수송기 2 bogyunja 보균자
carrot N danggeun 당근
carry, to V gajyeogada 가져가다
carry, put in, to V sitda 싣다
carsickness N chameolmi 차멀미
cart N sure 수레, kateu 카트
cartoon N manhwa 만화
carve, sculpt, to V jogakhada 조각하다
carving, sculpture N jogak 조각
case N 1 gyeong.u 경우 2 *(criminal)* sakkeon 사건
cash, money N hyeon.geum 현금: *cash a check* hyeon.geumeuro bakkuda 현금으로 바꾸다
casino N kajino 카지노
cassette N kaseteu 카세트
cast N baeyeok 배역
cast, to V 1 deonjida 던지다 2 beorida 버리다: *A fisherman cast a net into the water* eobuga mulsogeuro geumureul deonjyeotda 어부가 물속으로 그물을 던졌다
casualty N sasangja 사상자, pihaeja 피해자: *The train was derailed, causing many casualties* yeolchaga talseonhayeo maneun sasangjareul naeeotda 열차가 탈선하여 많은 사상자를 내었다
cat N goyang.i 고양이
catalog N katallogeu 카탈로그
catch alive, capture, to V sarojapda 사로잡다: *capture one's heart* maeumeul sarojapda 마음을 사로잡다
category N kategori 카테고리
Catholicism N cheonjugyo 천주교
cattle N so 소
caught, captured, to be V japida 잡히다
cauliflower N keollipeullawo 컬리플라워
cause N wonin 원인: *the cause of the accident* sagoui wonin 사고의 원인

cautious, prudent ADJ sinjunghada 신중하다, sinjunghan 신중한

cave N donggul 동굴

cave over, to V dwijibeojida, 뒤집어지다

CD N ssidi 씨디: *CD-ROM* ssidi-rom 씨디-롬

cease, to V jungdandoeda 중단되다, geuchida 그치다: *They voted to cease strike action immediately* geudeureun paeobeul jeuksi jungdansikigi wihae tupyoreul haetda 그들은 파업을 즉시 중단시키기 위해 투표를 했다

ceiling N cheonjang 천장

celebrate, to V chukhahada 축하하다

celery N saelleori 샐러리

cell phone, mobile phone N haendeupon 핸드폰: *try calling her (his) cell phone* haendeuponeuro yeollakhae boseyo 핸드폰으로 연락해 보세요

cemetery N myoji 묘지: *His parents are buried in a cemetery near the center of town* geuui bumonimeun dosim gakkaie inneun myojie muchisyeotda 그의 부모님은 도심 가까이에 있는 묘지에 묻히셨다

center, middle N jung.ang 중앙, jungsim 중심

central ADJ jung.ang(ui) 중앙의

century N segi 세기

ceremony N (ye)sik (예)식: *wedding ceremony* gyeolhon yesik 결혼 예식

certain, sure ADJ hwaksilhada 확실하다, hwaksilhan 확실한: *a sure method* hwaksilhan bangbeop 확실한 방법

certainly, surely, without fail ADV bandeusi 반드시

certainly! PHR teullimeopseoyo! 틀림없어요!

certificate N jeungmyeongseo 증명서

chaffer, discount N enuri 에누리

chain, links N yeonswae 연쇄

chair N uija 의자

challenge N dojeon 도전

chamber N bang 방

chameleon N kamelleon 카멜레온

champion N chaempi.eon 챔피언

chance, opportunity N chanseu 찬스, gihoe 기회

change, switch, to V bakkuda 바꾸다

change *(money, coin)* N jandon 잔돈

change jobs, to V ijikhada 이직하다

change one's mind, to V ma.eumeul bakkuda 마음을 바꾸다

change, exchange *(money)*, **to** V hwanjeonhada 환전하다

change, switch *(clothes)*, **to** V garaipda 갈아입다

channel N 1 chaeneol 채널 2 gyeongno 경로

chaos, bedlam N nanjangpan 난장판

chap, to V teuda 트다

chapter, lesson N gwa 과: *chapter 12* sibigwa 12과

character N 1 kaerikteo 캐릭터 2 *(written)* geuljja 글자 3 *(personality)* seongkkyeok 성격

characteristic N teukjing 특징

charisma N kariseuma 카리스마

charity N jaseon 자선

charming, attractive ADJ maeryeokjeogin 매력적인

charms, winsomeness N aegyo 애교

chase, run after, to V jjotda 쫓다

chase away, chase out, to V jjochanaeda 쫓아내다

chastise, to V eungjinghada 응징하다

cheap, inexpensive ADJ ssada 싸다, ssan 싼

check, verify, to V chekeuhada 체크하다

checked *(pattern)* N chekeumunui(ui) 체크무늬(의)

cheek N ppyam 뺨: *be slapped* ppyameul matda 뺨을 맞다

cheer N 1 eungwon 응원: *cheerleading squad* eungwondan 응원단 2 *(ovation)* hwanho 환호

cheer, root for, support, to V eungwonhada 응원하다

cheers! INTERJ geonbae! 건배!

cheese N chijeu 치즈

chemistry N hwahak 화학

cheque, check N supyo 수표

cherish, value, hold *(sth)* **dear, to** V akkida 아끼다

cherish, preserve, to V ganjikhada 간직하다

chess N cheseu 체스

chest *(breast)* N gaseum 가슴

chew, to V ssipda 씹다

chicken N dak 닭: *chicken meat* dakgogi 닭고기; *chicken roasted whole* tongdak 통닭

chief N wonjang 원장

chief, boss, head N udumeori 우두머리

child N 1 *(young person)* eorini 어린이 2 *(offspring)* ai 아이

childcare, baby care N yuga 육아

childish, infantile ADJ yuchihada 유치하다

chilled, refrigerated ADJ naengjang-han 냉장한

chilli paste N gochujang 고추장

chilli pepper N gochu 고추

chin, jaw N teok 턱

China N jungguk 중국: *Chinese (language)* junggugeo 중국어; *Chinese (nationality)* N jungguk saram 중국 사람

Chinese cabbage N baechu 배추

chocolate N chokollet 초콜렛

choice N seontaek 선택

choose, pick, select, to V seon-taekhada 선택하다

choose between two, either–or N yangjataegil 양자택일

chopsticks N jeotgarak 젓가락

chorus N koreoseu 코러스

Christian N gidokgyosinja 기독교신자: *Christianity* gidokgyo 기독교

Christmas N keuriseumaseu 크리스마스: *Christmas carol* kaereol 캐럴

chubby ADJ 1 odongtonghada 오동통하다 2 *(plump)* tongtonghada 통통하다

church N gyohoe 교회

cider N saida 사이다

cigar N siga 시가

cigarette N dambae 담배

circle N won 원: *draw a circle* woneul geurida 원을 그리다

circulate, bruit, spread, to V yupohada 유포하다: *circulate a fabricated rumor* jojakdoen sasireul yupohada 조작된 사실을 유포하다

cite, to V 1 eongeupada 언급하다 2 innyonghada 인용하다

citizen N simin 시민

citizenship N simingwon 시민권

citrus N gamgyullyu 감귤류

city N dosi 도시: *city hall* sicheong 시청

claim, demand, to V yoguhada 요구하다

clap, applause, to V baksuchida 박수치다

class N ban 반: *What class are you in?* museun banini? 무슨 반이니?

classic N keullaesik 클래식

classify, to V bullyuhada 분류하다: *Please classify the document by date* seoryureul naljja byeollo bullyuhaeju-seyo 서류를 날짜 별로 분류해주세요

classroom N gyosil 교실

clean I ADJ kkaekkeuthada 깨끗하다, kkaekkeutan 깨끗한 II V cheongsohada 청소하다

cleanliness N cheonggyeol 청결

clear, plain, obvious ADJ yeongnyeo-khada 역력하다: *It looks obvious that ~* yeongnyeokhae boida 역력해 보이다

clear, pure, clean ADJ makda 맑다, malgeun 맑은: *clear eye* malgeun nun 맑은 눈; *clear water* malgeun mul 맑은 물

clear, vivid ADJ seonmyeonghada 선명하다

clear one's throat, catch one's breath, to V gadadeumda 가다듬다: *clear one's throat* moksorireul gada-deumda 목소리를 가다듬다; *catch one's breath* hoheubeul gadadeumda 호흡을 가다듬다

clear oneself of a false charge, to V beotda 벗다: *clear oneself of a false charge* numyeongeul beotda 누명을 벗다

clerical work, office work N samu 사무

clever, bright ADJ yeongnihada 영리하다, yeongnihan 영리한: *a clever puppy* yeongnihan gangaji 영리한 강아지

climate N gihu 기후

climb up *(hills, mountains)*, **to** V ...e oreuda ...에 오르다

cling to, stick to, to V yeonnyeonhada 연연하다

clock, watch N sigye 시계

clogged, blocked, plugged, to be V makhida 막히다: *the sink is clogged* singkeuga makhida 싱크가 막히다

close, shut, to I V dachida 닫히다, datda 닫다 II ADJ dachin닫힌: *a closed door* dachin mun 닫힌 문

close in upon, to V yukbakhada 육박하다

cloth N 1 otgam 옷감 2 *(fabric)* cheon 천

C

ENGLISH–KOREAN

clothes, clothing, garment N ot 옷

cloudy, overcast, dull ADJ heurida 흐리다, heurin 흐린: *the water is cloudy* muri heurida 물이 흐리다; *the sky is overcast* haneuri heurida 하늘이 흐리다

club *(night)* N keulleop 클럽

club, group N dongari 동아리: *club member* gateun dongari membeo 같은 동아리 멤버

clumsy, fumbling, sloppy ADJ eoseolpeuda 어설프다

co-worker, colleague N dongnyo 동료

coat N 1 *(jacket)* jaket 자켓 2 *(overcoat)* koteu 코트

cocktail N kakteil 칵테일

coconut N kokoneot 코코넛

coffee N keopi 커피

coin N dongjeon 동전

cola N kolla 콜라

cold N chupda 춥다, chuun 추운: *feel cold (or it is cold)* chupda 춥다; *a cold area* chuun jiyeok 추운 지역; *cold area, cold region* hanji 한지; *cold water* chanmul 찬물

cold wind N chanbaram 찬바람: *The cold wind wailed* chanbarami ssaeng-ssaeng bulda 찬바람이 쌩쌩 불다

cold, chilly ADJ chada 차다: *The wind is as cold as ice* barami eoreumjang-gachi chada 바람이 얼음장같이 차다

cold, flu N gamgi 감기

cold, harsh ADJ maemolchada 매몰차다

cold, icy, frosty ADJ chagapda 차갑다

collect payments, to V sugeumhada 수금하다

college student N daehaksaeng 대학생

collide, to V chungdolhada 충돌하다: *collision* chungdol 충돌

color N saekkal 색깔: *color pencil* saegyeonpil 색연필

color blindness N saengmaeng 색맹

colorful, diversified ADJ dachaeropda 다채롭다

comb N bit 빗

combine, unite, to V hapchida 합치다

come, to V oda 오다

come at, jump at, spring at, to V deombida 덤비다

come back, return, to V doraoda 돌아오다: *return to one's native country* goguke dola oda 고국에 돌아오다

come closer, approach, to V dagaoda 다가오다

come in, to V deureo.oda 들어오다

come into view, be in sight, to V baraboida 바라보이다

come on!, let's go! hurry! INTERJ eoseoyo! 어서요!

come-from-behind victory N eokjeonseung 역전승: *win a come-from-behind victory* yeokjeonseungeul geodueotda 역전승을 거두었다

comfort, console, to V wirohada 위로하다

comfortable ADJ pyeonanhada, pyeonanhan 편안하다, 편안한

comical ADJ iksalseureopda 익살스럽다

command, order N myeongnyeong 명령

commendation *(official)* N pyochang 표창

common, familiar ADJ heunhada 흔하다, heunhan 흔한: *a traffic jam is common in this area* i jiyeogui gyo-tongjeongcheneun heunhada 이 지역의 교통정체는 흔하다; *a familiar scene* heunhan jangmyeon 흔한 장면

commoner N pyeongmin 평민

communication N keomyunikeisyeon 커뮤니케이션

community N keomyuniti 커뮤니티

commute to school, to V tonghakhada 통학하다

company, firm N hoesa 회사

compare, to V bigyohada 비교하다

compare to, compare with, to V ...wa/gwa bigyohaeseo ...와/과 비교해서: *compared to last year* jangnyeon-gwa bigyohaeseo 작년과 비교해서; *as compared with her* geunyeowa bigyo-haeseo 그녀와 비교해서

compensation, indemnification N bosang 보상: *obtain a compensation* bosangeul batda 보상을 받다

compete, to V gyeongjaenghada 경쟁하다: *competition* gyeongjaeng 경쟁

competitive spirit, refusal to yield N ogi 오기

compilation, edit N pyeonjip 편집

complain, to V bulpyeonghada 불평하다: *complaint* bulpyeong 불평

complaint, murmur N wonseong 원성

complete, to v wanseonghada 완성하다: *complete plan* gyehoegeul wanseonghada 계획을 완성하다

complete, end, finish, close, to v kkeunnaeda 끝내다, wallyohada 완료하다

complete, thorough ADJ cheoljjeohada/-han 철저하다, 철저한: *thorough in everything* modeun ire cheoljeohada 모든 일에 철저하다; *thorough inspection* cheoljeohan geomsa 철저한 검사

completely ADV bassak 바싹, wanjeonhi 완전히: *completely different* wanjeonhi dareun 완전히 다른; *achieve a complete mastery* wanjeonhi seupdeukhada 완전히 습득하다

completely, closely ADV bajjak 바짝

complicated ADJ 1 bokjaphada 복잡하다, bokjapan 복잡한 2 kkadaropda 까다롭다, kkadaroun 까다로운: *a complicated matter* kkadaroun munje 까다로운 문제

comply with, to v eunghada 응하다

compose (music), to v jakgokhada 작곡하다

composite, synthetic ADJ hapseong(ui) 합성(의): *composite photograph* hapseong sajin 합성 사진; *synthetic textiles* hapseong seomnyu 합성 섬유

composition N 1 *(music)* jakgok 작곡 2 *(writings)* jangmun 작문

composure N yeoyu 여유

comprehension N ihaeryeok 이해력: *listening comprehension* cheongchwi ihaeryeok 청취 이해력

compromise N tahyeop 타협

compulsory, mandatory, indispensable ADJ pilsu.ida, pilsu(ui) 필수이다, 필수(의)

computer N keompyuteo 컴퓨터: *computer illiterate* keommaeng 컴맹

conceal, cover up, to v eunpyehada 은폐하다

conceit, pride N jaman 자만

concentrate, to v jipjunghada 집중하다

concentrate, dedicate, to v jeonnyeomhada 전념하다: *concentration of mind* jeonnyeom 전념

concert N konseoteu 콘서트

conclude, close, to v jitda 짓다: *draw a conclusion* gyeolloneul jitda 결론을 짓다

condition N 1 *(state of being)* sangtae 상태: *one's physical condition* geongang sangtae 건강 상태 2 *(terms)* jokgeon 조건

confectionery, biscuit, cookie, cracker N gwaja 과자

confession N jabaek 자백

confide, to v teoreonota 털어놓다: *confide in friends* chinguege bimireul teoreonota 친구에게 비밀을 털어놓다

confidence N jasin 자신: *to be confident* jasin itda 자신 있다

Confucianism N yugyo 유교

confuse, to v hollansikida 혼란시키다: *confusing* hollansikineun 혼란시키는

congested with heavy traffic, to be v makhida 막히다: *the road is congested* giri makhida 길이 막히다

congested, jammed, to be v bumbida 붐비다: *congested with people* saramdeullo bumbida 사람들로 붐비다

conglomerate, chaebol N jaebeol 재벌

congratulations! PHR chukhahaeyo! 축하해요!

connect, to v yeon.gyeolhada 연결하다

conscience V yangsim 양심: *conscienceless, shamelessness* paryeomchihan 파렴치한

conscious of, to be v ...eul/reul uisikhada ...을/를 의식하다, ...reul/eul uisikhada ...를/을 의식하다

consecutively ADV yeongeopu 연기푸

consider, ponder, think over, to v sukgohada 숙고하다

considerate ADJ gipda 깊다, gipeun 깊은

consideration N 1 saryeo 사려: *He's very considerate* geuneun maeu saryeo gipda 그는 매우 사려 깊다 2 *(considered judgment)* saryo 사료

consignment, trust N witak 위탁

consist of, be made up of, to v irueojida 이루어지다

consolation, comfort N wiro 위로: *offer words of consolation to* wiroui mareul hada 위로의 말을 하다

consult, discuss, to v sanguihada 상의하다

contact, call N yeollak 연락

C

contact, get in touch with, to v
yeollakhada 연락하다

contact lens N kontenteurenjeu
콘텐트렌즈

content with, satisfied with, to be
ADJ manjokhada 만족하다

contest N konteseuteu 콘테스트

continent N daeryuk 대륙

continue, to v gyesokhada 계속하다

continuity N yeonsok 연속

contribute to, to v ibajihada
이바지하다

convenient, handy ADJ pyeollihada
편리하다, pyeollihan 편리한

conversation N daehwa 대화

cook, to v 1 jitda 짓다: cook rice
babeul jitda 밥을 짓다 2 yorihada
요리하다

cook, boil, to v ikhida 익히다: boil
(cook) food eumsigeul ikhida 음식을
익히다

cook, chef N yorisa 요리사

cooked ADJ yoriga doeda/doen 요리가
되다/된

cookie, sweet biscuit N kuki 쿠키

cooking, cuisine, dish N yori 요리

cooking for oneself (living alone) N
jachwi 자취

cool, chilly ADJ seoneulhada 서늘하다,
seoneulhan 서늘한

cool off, cool down, to v sikhida
식히다

cooperation, collaboration N hyeopdong 협동

cope with, handle with, to v gamdanghada 감당하다

copper N guri 구리

copy, photocopy I N boksa 복사 II v 1
boksahada 복사하다 2 (transcribe)
bekkida 베끼다

coral N sanho 산호

cornea N gangmak 각막

corner N koneo 코너

correct, rectify, to v 1 barojapda 바로
잡다: correct typos otareul barojapda
오타를 바로잡다 2 gochida 고치다:
correct one's shortcomings danjeomeul gochida 단점을 고치다

correct, right, suitable ADJ matda
맞다, manneun 맞는

correspond, write letters, to v
pyeonji yeollakhada 편지 연락하다

corridor, hall N bokdo 복도

cosmos N koseumoseu 코스모스

cost I v (be worth, weigh) nagada 나가
다 II N (expense, fee) biyong 비용

cost, price N gap 값

cotton N myeon 면

cough I N gichim 기침 II v gichimhada
기침하다

could, might ADJ -(eu)l sudo itda -(으)
ㄹ 수도 있다: It could (might) rain biga
ol sudo itda 비가 올 수도 있다

counselor N kaunseulleo 카운슬러

counter (for paying, buying tickets) N
kaunteu 카운터

counter effect N yeokhyogwa 역효과

counterattack N yeokseup 역습,
bangyeok 반격

country N 1 (nation) nara 나라 2 (rural
area) sigol 시골

country of origin N wonsanji 원산지

coupon N kupon 쿠폰

cover I v 1 (close sth) deopda 덮다 2
(plaster over sth) bareuda 바르다 II N
(as protection) eomho 엄호

covert, furtive ADJ eunmilhada
은밀하다

covet, to v neomboda 넘보다

cow N amso 암소

cowboy N kauboi 카우보이

coyly, well-behaved ADJ yamjeonhada 얌전하다

cozy, comfy ADJ obutada 오붓하다

CPR N ingonghoheup 인공호흡

crab N ge 게

crack, rift N teumsae 틈새

crack, split, fracture, to v geumi gada
금이 가다: have a fracture on a bone
ppyeoe geumi gada 뼈에 금이 가다

crack down, bust, to v dansokhada
단속하다: There was a big drug bust
daedaejeogin mayak dansogi iseotda
대대적인 마약 단속이 있었다

cracked ADJ geumi gan 금이 간: a
cracked vase geumi gan kkotbyeong
금이 간 꽃병

cracker, salty biscuit N keuraekeo
크래커

crafts N gong.ye 공예: craftsman gong.
yega 공예가

crawling, go on all fours ADV
eonggeumeonggeum 엉금엉금

create, to v changjohada 창조하다:

creation (writing, composition) chang-jak 창작

creditor, money lender N bitjaengi 빚쟁이

credulous, naïve ADJ eosurukhada 어수룩하다

criminal N beomin 범인

crisis N wigi 위기

crisscross, to V nubida 누비다

critical, dodgy ADJ witaeropda 위태롭다

criticism N binan 비난

cross, cut across, to V garojireuda 가로지르다: cut across the street gireul garojilleogada 길을 가로질러가다

cross, go over, to V geonneoda 건너다: cross the street gireul geonneoda 길을 건너다

crouch, huddle oneself up, to V ungkeurida 웅크리다

crowded, busy ADJ bumbineun 붐비는: the busiest hour gajang bumbineun sigan 가장 붐비는 시간

crown N wanggwan 왕관

cruel ADJ janinhada 잔인하다, janinhan 잔인한: cruelty, brutality janhok 잔혹

crumbs, chip N buseureogi 부스러기

crunch, crispy ADJ basakhan 바삭한: crunchy cookies basakbasakhan kuki 바삭바삭한 쿠키

crush, mash, to V eukkaeda 으깨다

cry, weep, to V ulda 울다

cry out, to V bureujitda 부르짖다: cry out (roar) with pain gotongeuro bureujitda 고통으로 부르짖다

crybaby N ulbo 울보

cucumber N oi 오이

cultivate, grow, raise, to V gakkuda 가꾸다: grow flowers kkocheul gakkuda 꽃을 가꾸다

culture N munhwa 문화

cup N keop 컵

cup noodles N kalguksu 칼국수

cupboard N chanjang 찬장

currency N tonghwa 통화

curriculum N keorikyulleom 커리큘럼

curry N kare 카레

curse N akdam 악담

curtail, shorten, reduce, to V danchukhada 단축하다

curtain N keoteun 커튼

custom, tradition N gwanseup 관습

cut, to V jareuda 자르다

cut, chop, to V kaljilhada 칼질하다

cut from a sword, a N kaljaguk 칼자국

cute ADJ gwiyeopda 귀엽다, gwiyeo.un 귀여운

cutting N kaljil 칼질

D

dad N appa 아빠

daily I ADJ haru.ui 하루의 II N ilgan 일간: daily newspaper ilgan sinmun 일간 신문

dairy products N yujepum 유제품

damage, harm, to V sonsangsikida 손상시키다

damage, loss N sonhae 손해

damp ADJ chukchukhada/-han 축축하다, 축축한: the floor is wet (damp) badagi chukchukhada 바닥이 축축하니; damp clothes chukchukhan ot 축축한 옷

dance I N chum 춤 II V chumchuda 춤추다

danger N wiheom 위험: danger zone wiheomjiyeok 위험지역

dangerous ADJ wiheomhada 위험하다, wiheomhan 위험한: All great ideas are dangerous modeun widaehan aid-ieoneun wiheomhada 모든 위대한 아이디어는 위험하다

daring, bold, plucky ADJ dangdol-hada 당돌하다

dark, gloomy, bleak, dim ADJ eodupda 어둡다, eoduun 어두운: It's dark outside bakki eodupda 밖이 어둡다; dark colors eoduun saekkkal 어두운 색깔; have a gloomy face pyojeongi eodupda 표성이 이듭다; a bleak future eoduun mirae 어두운 미래; a dim light eoduun bulbit 어두운 불빛

dark brown N dagalsaek 다갈색

darkish ADJ gamuseureumhada 가무스름하다

darkness N eodum 어둠: She was lost in the darkness geunyeoneun eodum sogeseo gireul ireotda 그녀는 어둠 속에서 길을 잃었다

database N deiteobeiseu 데이터베이스

date (going out) N yeonae 연애

date, day N naljja 날짜

D

ENGLISH–KOREAN

daughter N ttal 딸
daughter-in-law N myeoneuri 며느리
dawn N saebyeok 새벽
day N nal 날: *an exam day* siheom nal 시험 날; *New Year's day* seollal 설날; *day after tomorrow* more 모레; *day before yesterday* geujeokke 그저께; *day of the week* yoil 요일; *day off* bibeon 비번
day, daytime N nat 낮
daydream, to V gongsanghada 공상하다
dead ADJ jugeun 죽은
deadline N saseon 사선
deadly pale look, a N sasaek 사색: *turn to a deadly pale look* eolgulbichi sasaegi doeda 얼굴빛이 사색이 되다
deadly situation N sagyeong 사경
deaf ADJ gwiga meogeun 귀가 먹은
deaf, to become V gwiga meokda 귀가 먹다
death N jugeum 죽음
death penalty N sahyeong 사형
debate N toron 토론: *That is still a matter of debate* geugeoseun nyeojeonhi toronui yeojiga itda 그것은 여전히 토론의 여지가 있다
debate, to V toronhada 토론하다
debone, to V bareuda 바르다: *(de)bone fish* saengseonui ppyeoreul bareuda 생선의 뼈를 바르다
debris N janhae 잔해, papyeon 파편
debt N bit 빚, buchae 부채
debt, liabilities N chaemu 채무
debut N debwi 데뷔, cheot churyeon 첫출연: *She made herself known after the debut* geunyeoneun debwi hue yumyeonghaejyeotda 그녀는 데뷔 후에 유명해졌다
decade N sip nyeongan 십 년간: *The anniversary marked a decade in business* geu ginyeomsigeun changsa sip junyeoneul ginyeomhaetda 그 기념식은 창사 십 주년을 기념했다
decease, death N samang 사망
deceive, cheat, to V sogida 속이다
December N sibiwol 십이월
decent ADJ 1 gwaenchaneun 괜찮은 2 yeui bareun 예의 바른: *He impresses me as a decent man* geuneun yeui bareun namjaraneun insangeul junda 그는 예의 바른 남자라는 인상을 준다

decide, to V gyeoljjeonghada 결정하다: *decision* gyeoljjeong 결정
decision (judicial), judgment N pangyeol 판결
deck N gappan 갑판
declamation N yeolbyeon 열변
declaration, spelling N pyogi 표기
declare, to V seoneonhada 선언하다
decline, decay, to V soetoehada 쇠퇴하다
decline, refuse, reject, to V geojeolhada 거절하다
decorate, to V kkumida 꾸미다
decorative, fancy ADJ jangsigi doen 장식이 된
decrease, reduce, to V julda 줄다
decrease, reduce, cut down, downsize, narrow down, to V jurida 줄이다
dedicate, consecrate, to V bachida 바치다
deduct, take away, to V chagamhada 차감하다: *deduction, subtraction* chagam 차감
deem, to V saenggakhada 생각하다: *We deem her honest* urineun geunyeoga jeongjikhadago saenggakhanda 우리는 그녀가 정직하다고 생각한다
deep ADJ gipda 깊다, gipeun 깊은: *a deep well* gipeun umul 깊은 우물
deer N saseum 사슴
defeat, to V chyeobusuda 쳐부수다
defect N gyeolham 결함: *a physical defect* sinchejeok gyeolham 신체적 결함
defend, to V bang.eohada 방어하다
defendant N pigo 피고: *The defendant faced the death penalty* pigoneun sahyeong seongoreul badatda 피고는 사형 선고를 받았다
defender N bangeoja 방어자
deficit N bujok 부족, gyeolson 결손
definite ADJ myeonghwakhada, myeonghwakan 명확하다/-한
definitely, by far ADV dannyeonko 단연코: *It will definitely not happen* dannyeonko geureon ireun eopseul geonnida 단연코 그런 일은 없을 것이다; *By far, this place has the best food* dannyeonko igot eumsigi gajang matsitda 단연코 이곳 음식이 가장 맛있다

degrade, become depraved, to v tarakhada 타락하다

degree, level N deunggeup 등급

degree, limit N jeongdo 정도: *a matter of degrees* jeongdoui munje 정도의 문제

degrees N 1 (*level, standard*) do 도 2 (*temperature*) do 도: *3 degrees below zero* yeongha 3do 영하 3도

dejected, dispirited, to be v heotalhada 허탈하다

delay I N jiyeon 지연 II v (*postpone, put off*) yeon.gihada 연기하다: *delay one's wedding* gyeolhoneul yeongihada 결혼은 연기하다

delayed, postponed ADJ jiyeondoen 지연된

delayed, to be v jiyeondoeda 지연되다

deliberately ADV 1 sinjunghi 신중히 2 gouiro 고의로

delicate, feeble, fragile ADJ yeonnyakhada 연약하다

delicate, soft, subdued ADJ euneunhada 은은하다

delicious, tasty ADJ masitda 맛있다, masinneun 맛있는

delightful, cheerful, merry ADJ yukwaehada 유쾌하다

deliver, to v baedalhada 배달하다

deliver, transfer, to v indohada 인도하다

delusion, fantasy N mangsang 망상

demeanour N momgajim 몸가짐

democracy N minjuju.i 민주주의

demonstrate, display, to v boida 보이다: *demonstrate courage* yonggireul boida 용기를 보이다

denial N buin 부인

dense ADJ 1 (*dull, slow*) mudida 무디다: *a dense person* mudin saram 무딘 사람 2 (*thick*) jaukhada 자욱하다

density N mildo 밀도

dentist N chikkwa(uisa) 치과(의사)

denture N teulli 틀니

deny, to v buinhada 부인하다: *The mayor did not deny that he lied* sijangeun geuga geojinmareul haetdaneun geoseul bujeonghaji anatda 시장은 그가 거짓말을 했다는 것을 부정하지 않았다

department N bu 부, gwa 과

department store N baekhwajeom 백화점

departure N chulbal 출발

depend on, to v uijonhada 의존하다: *depend on medication* yage uijonhada 약에 의존하다

depleted, run out, to be v badaknada 바닥나다: *running out of patience* innaesimi badangnada 인내심이 바닥나다

deposit into savings, to make a v yegeumhada 예금하다

depravity, corruption N tarak 타락

depressed, gloomy, blue ADJ uulhada 우울하다

depth N gipi 깊이: *The lake is more than a mile in depth* geu hosuneun gipiga il mail isangida 그 호수는 깊이가 일 마일 이상이다

deputy N daeriin 대리인

descendant, offspring N jason 자손

describe, to v myosahada 묘사하다

desert (*arid land*) N samak 사막

desire I N yongmang 욕망 II v (*hope, wish*) barada 바라다

desk N chaeksang 책상

desolate, sorrowful ADJ cheoryanghada 처량하다

desperately, eagerly ADV ganjeolhi 간절히

despicable, detestable ADJ gajeungseureopda 가증스럽다

dessert, sweets N dijeoteu 디저트

destination N mokjeokji 목적지

destiny, fate N unmyeong 운명, palja 팔자

destroy, to v pagoehada 파괴하다

destroyed, demolished, to be v pagoedoeda, pagoedoen 파괴되다, 파괴된

destruction N pagoe 파괴

detective N tamjeong 탐정

detention, interment N eongnyu 억류

detergent N seje 세제

determined, stubborn, firm ADJ hwakgohada/-han 확고하다/-한: *stand firm in one's resolution* gyeolsimhi hwakgohada 결심히 확고하다

develop, to v 1 baljjeonsikida 발전시키다: *develop technology* gisureul baljeonsikida 기술을 발전시키다 2 (*film*) hyeonsanghada 현상하다:

D

develop a film (pictures) filleum (sajin)eul hyeonsanghada 필름 (사진)을 현상하다 3 *(advance, grow)* baljjeonhada 발전하다

development N 1 *(growth)* balttal 발달 2 *(progress)* baljjeon 발전

device N jangchi 장치

devil N angma 악마

diagonal I ADJ daegakseonui 대각선의: *diagonal line* saseon 사선 II N daegakseon 대각선

diagonally ADV daegakseoneuro 대각선으로

diagram, graph, chart N pyo 표: *draw a graph* pyoreul geurida 표를 그리다

dialect N saturi 사투리

diamond N daiamondeu 다이아몬드

diary N 1 *(daybook)* ilgi 일기 2 *(journal)* iljji 일지

dictionary N sajeon 사전

didn't pass PHR andwaetda 안됐다: *didn't pass one's promotion test* seungjine andwaetda 승진에 안됐다

die, to V jukda 죽다

diet N daieoteu 다이어트

difference *(in quality)* N chai 차이

difference, margin, the difference between two prices N cha.aek 차액

different ADJ dareuda 다르다, dareun 다른: *different in size* keugiga dareuda 크기가 다르다; *a different kind* dareun jongnyu 다른 종류

difficult, hard ADJ eoryeopda 어렵다, eoryeo.un 어려운, heomnanhada 험난하다

dig, to V pada 파다: *dig in the ground* ttangeul pada 땅을 파다

dig into, to V pagodeulda 파고들다: *dig into inside details of an issue* munjereul gipi pagodeulda 그 문제를 깊게 파고들었다

dig up, dig out, to V kaenaeda 캐내다: *dig out secrets* bimireul kaenaeda 비밀을 캐내다

dig up, turn up, to V hejipda 헤집다

dignity, class N pumgyeok 품격

digress, wander off, to V binnagada 빗나가다

dilemma N dillema 딜레마, jintoeyangnan 진퇴양난

dim, faint, vague ADJ aryeonhada 아련하다: *dim recollection* aryeonhan

yet chueok 아련한 옛 추억; *a vague moonlight* aryeonhan dalbit 아련한 달빛

dimension, level N chawon 차원

dimly, vaguely ADV eoryeompussi 어렴풋이

dining together *(workplace)* N hoesik 회식

dinner, evening meal N jeonyeok siksa 저녁 식사: *to eat dinner* jeonyeok siksahada 저녁 식사하다

diplomat N oegyogwan 외교관

dipper, ladle N gukja 국자

direct, produce, to V yeonchulhada 연출하다

direction N banghyang 방향

direction, production N yeonchul 연출

dirty ADJ deoreopda 더럽다, deoreo.un 더러운

disagreeable, not to one's liking ADJ monmattanghada 못마땅하다

disappear, to V eopseojida 없어지다

disappointed, to be V silmanghada, silmanghan 실망하다, 실망한

disaster N jaenan 재난

discipline, punish, to V daseurida 다스리다: *discipline a law breaker with punishment* joeineul maero daseurida 죄인을 매로 다스리다

disclose, reveal, to V bakhida 밝히다: *reveal the fact* sasireul bakhida 사실을 밝히다

discount N diseukaunteu 디스카운트

discover, to V balgyeonhada 발견하다

discovery, revelation N tanno 탄로: *a conspiracy has been revealed* eummoga tannonada 음모가 탄로나다

discuss, to V uinonhada 의논하다: *discussion* uinon 의논

disease, illness N byeong 병: *an incurable illness* bulchiui byeong 불치의 병

disguise N gajang 가장: *disguise oneself as an enemy* jeokguneuro gajanghada 적군으로 가장하다

disgusting ADJ yeokgyeopda 역겹다, yeokgyeo.un 역겨운

dish, platter N jeopsi 접시

dish cloth, saucer N jeopsibatchim 접시받침

dishonorable, shameful ADJ biyeolhada/biyeolhan 비열하다/비열한, mangsinseureopda 망신스럽다

disk N wonban 원반

diskette N diseuket 디스켓

dislike, to ADJ sireohada 싫어하다

dismal ADJ 1 *(hopeless)* kamkamhada 캄캄하다: *I feel hopeless* nunapi kamkamhada 눈앞이 캄캄하다 2 *(somber, dark)* ujungchunghada 우중충하다

dismiss V haesansikida 해산시키다

disordered, untidy ADJ eosuseonhada 어수선하다

dispatch N pagyeon 파견

display I N jeonsi 전시, jinyeol 진열 II V jinyeolhada 진열하다

disregard, overlook, to V gangwahada 간과하다: *won't overlook even a small mistake* jageun silsudo gangwahaji aneul geotsida 작은 실수도 간과하지 않을 것이다

dissolve, melt down, to V nogida 녹이다: *dissolve sugar* seoltangeul nogida 설탕을 녹이다

dissuasive ADJ mallyuhanuen 만류하는

distance N geori 거리

distinguish, discriminate, differentiate, to V chabyeolhada 차별하다

distinguishing ADJ teukjingjeogin 특징적인

distort, twist, to V waegokhada 왜곡하다

distribution N yutong 유통

district, borough N gu 구: *Yongsan-gu (district)* yongsangu 용산구

diversity, variety N dayang 다양

divide, to V 1 *(share, segment, dissect)* nanuda 나누다· *divide equally* ttokgachi nanuda 똑같이 나누다; *division (math)* nanutsem 나눗셈 2 *(split, pull apart)* gallanota 갈라놓다

divided ADJ nanu.eojin 나누어진

divided into, divided by, to be V nanu.eojida 나누어지다

divorce, to V ihonhada 이혼하다: *divorce by mutual agreement* habui ihonhada 합의 이혼하다

divorced ADJ ihonhan 이혼한

dizzy, giddy ADJ eojireopda 어지럽다

do one's best, to V choeseoneul dahada 최선을 다하다

do up and down, to V oreunaerida 오르내리다

do, perform an action, to V hada 하다: *to study* gongbuhada 공부하다; *to work* ilhada 일하다

doctor N uisa 의사

document, letter N munseo 문서

dog N gae 개

dolphin N dolgorae 돌고래

dominate V jibaehada 지배하다: *He tried to dominate other people* geuneun dareun saramdeureul jibaeharyeogo haetda 그는 다른 사람들을 지배하려고 했다

don't do that! PHR geureoji maseyo! 그러지 마세요!

don't mention it!, you're welcome! It's alright! PHR gwaenchanayo! 괜찮아요

door, gate N mun 문

dork, jerk N eolgani 얼간이

double N du bae 두 배

doubt, suspect, to V uisimhada 의심하다: *doubtful* uisimseureopda 의심스럽다

down, downward ADV araero 아래로

downstairs N araecheung 아래층

downtown N sinae jungsimji 시내 중심지

dragonfly N jamjari 잠자리: *a flying dragonfly* naraganeun jamjari 날아가는 잠자리

draw, paint (a painting), to V geurida 그리다

draw near, to V dagaseoda 다가서다

drawer N seorap 서랍

dream I N kkum 꿈 II V kkumkkuda 꿈꾸다

dress, attire, outfit N otcharim 옷차림: *tidy outfit, proper attire* danjeonghan otcharim 단정한 옷차림

dress, frock N deureseu 드레스

dress up, to V charyeoipda 차려입다

dressing gown N sillaebok 실내복

drift, drifting N pyoryu 표류

drifter, wanderer N nageune 나그네

drink I N *(refreshment)* eumnyo 음료 II V masida 마시다

drinking N eumju 음주: *Never drink and drive* eumjuunjeoneul hamyeon an doenda 음주운전을 하면 안 된다

drive (a car), to V unjeonhada 운전하다

drive, hammer, to V bakda 박다: *hammer a nail* moseul bakda 못을 박다

D

drive out, expel, to V moranaeda 몰아내다

driven, carried away, to be V ikkeullida 이끌리다: *be driven by emotions* gamjeonge ikkeullida 감정에 이끌리다

drizzle N iseulbi 이슬비

drizzle, mist N garangbi 가랑비

droop, sag, to V cheojida 처지다

drop, to V tteoreotteurida 떨어뜨리다

drop in, come by, stop by, to V danyeogada 다녀가다: *My friend stopped by and then left* chinguga uri jibe danyeogatda 친구가 우리 집에 다녀갔다

drought N gamum 가뭄

drown, to V iksahada 익사하다

drug, medicine N yak 약: *cold medicine* gamgi yak 감기 약; *drugstore, pharmacy* yakguk 약국

drunk, to be V sul chwihada 술 취하다

dry I ADJ 1 mareun 마른: *dried snack, bar snack* mareun anju 마른 안주 2 *(humidity)* geonjohada 건조하다, geonjohan 건조한: *dried fruit* geonjohan gwail 건조한 과일 II V mallida 말리다, mareuda 마르다, mareun 마른

duck N ori 오리

duel, quarrel, fight N datum 다툼

dull, blunt ADJ mudida 무디다: *a dull blade* mudin kallal 무딘 칼날

dull-witted ADJ udunhada 우둔하다

dumbfounded ADJ eoanibeongbeonghada 어안이병병하다

dumpling N mandu 만두

during, for ...dong.an ...동안

dusk, twilight years N hwanghon 황혼

dusky, dim ADJ eodukhada 어둑하다

dust N meonji 먼지

dust off, to V teolda 털다

duty 1 N *(obligation)* uimu 의무: *a duty to pay tax* segeumeul naeneun uimu 세금을 내는 의무 2 *(responsibility)* chaegim 책임 3 *(import tax)* gwanse 관세

DVD N dibidi 디비디

dwarf, pigmy N nanjaengi 난쟁이

dye, get dyed, to V muldeulda 물들다

dyeing N yeomsaek 염색: *dye the hair purple* meorireul borasaegeuro yeomsaekhada 머리를 보라색으로 염색하다

E

each, every, separate ADJ gakgakui 각각의

ear N gwi 귀: *earrings* gwigeori 귀걸이

early ADJ ireun 이른: *early morning* ireun achim 이른 아침; *early in the morning* achim iljjik 아침 일찍

earn, to V beolda 벌다

earnest, eager ADJ ganjeolhada 간절하다: *earnest request* gangu 간구

earphone N ieopon 이어폰

earth N 1 *(soil)* heuk 흙 2 *(Earth, the world)* jigu 지구

earthquake N jijin 지진

easily ADV swipge 쉽게: *A long thread is easily entangled* gin sireun swipge eokhinda 긴 실은 쉽게 얽힌다

east N dongjjok 동쪽

eastern ADJ dongjjogui 동쪽의

easy ADJ 1 *(comfortable)* pyeonhada 편하다 2 *(light)* gappunhada 가뿐하다 3 *(woman's character)* hepeuda 헤프다: *she's easy* geunyeoneun haengsiri hepeuda 그녀는 행실이 헤프다

eat, to V meokda 먹다: *eating out, dining out* oesik 외식

eat one's heart out PHR aetaeuda 애태우다

eavesdrop, to V yeotdeutda 엿듣다

economical ADJ gyeongjejeogida/-jeogin 경제적이다/-적인: *an economical vehicle* gyeongjejeogin seungyongcha 경제적인 승용차

economist N gyeongjehakja 경제학자

economy N gyeongje 경제

edge N gajangjari 가장자리, kkeut 끝

edgy, sensitive ADJ yeminhada 예민하다: *extremely sensitive* geukdoro yeminhada 극도로 예민하다

edit, to V pyeonjipada 편집하다: *I need to edit the draft by Friday* naneun geumnyoilkkaji chogoreul pyeonjipaeya handa 나는 금요일까지 초고를 편집해야 한다

edition N pan 판: *The stamp is a special edition* i upyoneun teukbyeolpanida 이 우표는 특별판이다

editor N pyeonjipjang 편집장

educate, to V gyoyukhada 교육하다: *education* gyoyuk 교육

effect I N *(result)* gyeolgwa 결과 II V

(has effect) jagyonghada 작용하다

efficiency N neungnyul 능률

effort N noryeok 노력: *to make an effort* noryeokhada 노력하다

egg N gyeran 계란, al 알

eggplant, aubergine N gaji 가지

ego, self N jaa 자아

Egypt N ijipteu 이집트

eight NUM 1 yeodeol 여덟: *eight o'clock* yeodeol si 여덟 시 2 pal 팔: *eight times two equals sixteen* pal gopagi ineun sibyuk 팔 곱하기 이는 십육

eighteen NUM 1 sip.pal 십팔 2 yeolyeodeol 열여덟

eighty NUM 1 palsip 팔십: *eighty eight* palsip pal 팔십 팔 2 yeodeun 여든

elastic, springy ADJ tallyeoginneun 탄력있는: *elasticity* tallyeok 탄력

elbow N palkkumchi 팔꿈치

elder N 1 *(older)* sonwi(ui) 손위 2 *(ranking)* yeonjangja 연장자

elderly N noin 노인

elect, to V seonchulhada 선출하다: *They met to elect a president* geudeureun uijangeul seonchulhagi wihae moyeotda 그들은 의장을 선출하기 위해 모였다

election N seon.geo 선거

electric ADJ jeon.gi(ui) 전기의: *electric home appliances* gajeonjepum 가전제품

electricity N jeon.gi 전기: *electricity generation* baljjeon 발전

electromagnetic wave N jeonpa 전파

electron N jeonja 전자

electronic, electromagnetic ADJ jeonja(ui) 전자(의)

electronics, electronic products N jeonja jepum 전자 제품

elegant ADJ uahada 우아하다, uahan 우아한: *an elegant figure* uahan jatae 우아한 자태

elegant, graceful ADJ danahada 단아 하다: *elegance, grace* dana 단아

element N yoso 요소

elephant N kokkiri 코끼리

elevator N ellibeiteo 엘리베이터

eleven NUM 1 sibil 십일 2 yeolhana 열하나

eligible ADJ jeokgyeogui 적격의

elite N elliteu 엘리트

else, anything else ADV geubakke 그밖에

e-mail, email I N jeonjaupyeon 전자우 편, i meil 이 메일: *check one's email* imeireul hwaginhada 이메일을 확인하 다 II V *sending email* i meil bonaeda 이 메일 보내다

embarrassed, taken aback, flustered, to be V danghwanghada/ -haehada 당황하다/-해하다

embassy N daesagwan 대사관

embrace, hug I N poong 포옹 II V kkyeo.anda 껴안다

embraced, to be V angida 안기다

embroidered ADJ suno.eun 수놓은: *a dress embroidered with flowers* kkocheul sunoeun ot 꽃을 수놓은 옷; *embroidery* (ja)su (자)수

embryo N taea 태아

emerge, rise, to V busanghada 부상 하다: *emerge as a big star* ingiseutaro busanghada 인기스타로 부상하다

emergency N bisang(satae) 비상(사태), eunggeup 응급

emission N bangsa 방사

emotion N gamjeong 감정

emotional ADJ gamjeongjeogin 감정적인

emotionally ADV gamjeongjeogeuro 감정적으로

emphasis N gangjo 강조

employ, hire, to V goyonghada 고용하다: *hire an employee* jigwoneul goyonghada 직원을 고용하다: *employee* jigwon 직원, pigoyong.in 피고용인

employer N goyongju 고용주

employment N chwijik 취직

empty, hollow, vacant ADJ teong bin 텅 빈

empty out, to V teolda 털다: *to be emptied out* teong bida 텅 비다

empty talk, flummery N binmal 빈말

encirclement N powi 포위

encourage, to V gyeongnyeohada 격려하다

end of the month N wolmal 월말

endure, to V innaehada 인내하다

enemy N jeok 적, wonsu 원수: *enemy of my father* nae abeojiui wonsu 내 아버지의 원수

energy N eneoji 에너지

E

enforce, to V 1 sihaenghada 시행하다
2 gangyohada 강요하다: *Some cities
enforce a 10 pm curfew for teenagers*
ilbu dosieseoneun yeolsi ihu cheongsonyeon tonggeumeul sihaenghanda
일부 도시에서는 열시 이후 청소년 통
금을 시행한다

enforcement N 1 sihaeng 시행
2 gangje 강제

engaged, to get V yakhonhada
약혼하다

engagement N yakhon 약혼

engine N enjin 엔진

engineer N gisa 기사: *an electrical
engineer* jeongi gisa 전기 기사

England N yeongguk 영국: *English*
yeong.eo 영어

engrave, to V saegida 새기다

enhance, to V ganghwahada 강화하다:
We need to enhance patient rights
urineun hwanjaui gwollireul gang-
hwasikyeoya handa 우리는 환자의
권리를 강화시켜야 한다

enjoy, to V jeulgida 즐기다

enjoy oneself, to V jeulgeopge
bonaeda 즐겁게 보내다

enjoy to the fullest, to V mankkik
만끽하다: *enjoy one's freedom to the
fullest* jayureul mankkikhada 자유를
만끽하다

enjoyable, happy, pleasant ADJ
jeulgeopda 즐겁다, jeulgeo.un 즐거운

enjoyment, pleasure N hyangnak 향락

enlarge, to V hwakdaehada 확대하다:
enlarge a photo sajineul hwakdaehada
사진을 확대하다

enough ADJ chungbunhada 충분하다,
chungbunhan 충분한: *This is enough* i
jeongdomyeon chungbunhada 이 정도
면 충분하다; *enough evidence* chungbunhan jeunggeo 충분한 증거

enquire, ask, to V mureoboda 물어보다

enroll, to V deungnokhada 등록하다:
I want to enroll as a member here
yeogi hoewoneuro deungnokhago
sipseumnida 여기 회원으로 등록하고
싶습니다

ensure, to V 1 anjeonhage hada
안전하게 하다 2 hwaksilhagehada
확실하게 하다

enter, to V deureogada 들어가다

enterprise N gieop 기업

entertainer, celebrity N yeonyein
연예인

enthusiasm N yeolgwang 열광

entire, whole, all of ADJ jeonche(ui)
전체(의): *entirety, whole* jeonche 전체

entrance, way in N ipgu 입구

entrepreneur N gieopga 기업가

enumerate, to V yeolgeohada 열거하다

enunciate, to V bakhida 밝히다

envelope N bongtu 봉투

envious ADJ bureopda 부럽다: *I envy
you* dangsini bureopda 당신이 부럽다

environment, the N hwan.gyeong 환경

envy, to V bureo.um 부러움, bureowohada 부러워하다: *envy one's success*
seonggongeul bureowohada 성공을
부러워하다

epidemic ADJ yuhaengseongui
유행성의

epidermis N pyopi 표피

equal, identical, same, alike ADJ
gatda 같다, gateun 같은

equality N pyeongdeung 평등: *treat
(persons) equally* pyeongdeunghage
daehada 평등하게 대하다

equation N 1 bangjeongsik 방정식
2 dongilhwa 동일화

equivalent ADJ dongdeunghan 동등한:
*The two computers are equivalent in
speed* geu du keompyuteoneun sok-
doga dongdeunghada 그 두 컴퓨터는
속도가 동등하다

equivocate, prevaricate, to V
eomulgeorida 어물거리다

eradication, extermination N bangmyeol 박멸

error N ereo 에러, oryu 오류

escalator N eseukeolleiteo
에스컬레이터

escape N 1 talchul 탈출 2 *(refuge)*
pisin 피신

escape from, to V talchulhada
탈출하다

essay N esei 에세이

**establish, set up, elect, stand,
found, to** V seolliphada 설립하다,
se.uda 세우다: *establish a factory*
gongjangeul seuda 공장을 세우다

establish privately, to V saseol 사설

eternity, perpetuity N yeongwon 영원

ethical ADJ yullijeogin 윤리적인: *There
are serious ethical issues* simgakhan

yullijeogin munjedeuri itda 심각한 윤
리적인 문제들이 있다
ethics, morals N yulli 윤리
ethics, moral philosophy N yullihak
윤리학
ethnic group N minjok 민족
etiquette N etiket 에티켓
Europe N yureop 유럽
evacuate, withdraw, to V cheolsuhada
철수하다
evaluation N pyeongga 평가
even, flat, smooth, level ADJ
pyeongpyeonghada/-han 평평하다/
–한: *level ground* pyeongpyeonghan
ttang 평평한 땅; *a flat nose* pyeongpyeonghan ko 평평한 코
even *(also)* ADV ...jochado ...조차도
even less, much less ADV hamulmyeo
하물며
even though, though CONJ birok-
jiman 비록 –지만: *although It's cold*
birok nalssiga chupjiman 비록 날씨가
춥지만
evening N jeonyeok 저녁
event N haengsa 행사
eventful, full of difficulties ADJ
dananhada 다난하다
ever, to have done ADJ -(eu)n jeogi
itda -(으)ㄴ 적이 있다
every, each ADJ mae 매: *every month,
each month* mae dal 매 달
every day N maeil 매일
every kind of ADJ modeun jongnyu.ui
모든 종류의
every time N maebeon 매번
everybody, everyone PRON modeun
saram 모든 사람
everyday ADJ pyeongso 평소
everything PRON modeun geot 모든
것, ontong 온통
everywhere ADV modeun got 모든 곳
evidence N jeunggeo 증거: *The evidence was in my favor* geu jeunggeoneun naege yurihaetda 그 증거는
나에게 유리했다
evident ADJ bunmyeonghan 분명한
evoke, arouse, to V jaanaeda 자아내
다: *evoke one's sympathy* dongjeongsimeul jaanaeda 동정심을 자아내다
evolution N jinhwa 진화
evolve, to V seoseohi baljeonsikida
서서히 발전시키다

ex-convict N jeongwaja 전과자
exact, accurate ADJ jeonghwakhada
정확하다, jeonghwakan 정확한
exactly, precisely ADV jeonghwakhi
정확히
exactly! just so! that's it! PHR baro
geugeoyeyo! 바로 그거예요!
exaggerate pain, make a fuss, to V
eomsalburida 엄살부리다: *make a fuss
about trifles* eomsareul burida 엄살을
부리다; *exaggeration of pain* eomsal
엄살
exam, test N siheom 시험
examine, to V geomtohada 검토하다
examine, check up, to V jinchalhada
진찰하다
example N ye 예: *for example* yereul
deureo 예를 들어
excellence, superiority N tagwol 탁월
excellent ADJ usuhada/usuhan 우수하
다/우수한, tagwolhada 탁월하다:
Excellent choice! tagwolhan seontaegida 탁월한 선택이다
excellent, magnificent ADJ hullyunghada 훌륭하다
except ... PREP ...reul/eul je.oehago
...를/을 제외하고: *except in the event
of...* han gyeongureul jeoehago 한
경우를 제외하고
exception N yeoe 예외: *There is an
exception to all rules* modeun ireneun
yeoega itda 모든 일에는 예외가 있다
excessive profits N pongni 폭리:
make excessive profits budanghage
pongnireul chwihada 부당하게 폭리를
취하다
exchange *(money, opinions)*, **to** V
gyohwanhada 교환하다
excited, gleeful ADJ sini nada 신이
나다, sini nan 신이 난
exciting, cheerful ADJ sinnada 신나다,
sinnaneun 신나는
exclusive, solo, independent ADJ
dandokui 단독의
excrete, to V baeseolhada 배설하다
excuse, pretext N pinggye 핑계: *make
excuses* pinggyereul daeda 핑계를
대다
excuse me! PHR sillyehamnida! 실례
합니다!
exertion of the mind N nosimchosa
노심초사

E

exhibition N bangnamhoe 박람회, jeonsihoe 전시회

exhilaration N kwaegam 쾌감

exist, to V jonjaehada 존재하다: *Many forms of life exist on the ocean floor* haejeoeneun maneun jongnyuui saengmuri jonjaehanda 해저에는 많은 종류의 생물이 존재한다

exit I N *(way out)* chulgu 출구 II V *(get out of)* jonjaehada 존재하다

exorbitant ADJ eomcheongnada 엄청나다

expand, to V 1 *(grow bigger)* hwak-daehada 확대하다: *expand the scope of an investigation* susaui beomwireul hwakdaehada 수사의 범위를 확대하다; *expand employment* goyongeul hwakdaehada 고용을 확대하다 2 *(make larger)* hwakjanghada 확장하다: *expand one's influence* seryeogeul hwakjanghada 세력을 확장하다

expect, to V gidaehada 기대하다: *expectation* yesang 예상

expelled from school, to be V toe-hakhada 퇴학하다

expenses N jichulgeum 지출금

expensive ADJ bissada 비싸다, bissan 비싼: *an expensive dress* bissan deureseu 비싼 드레스

experience I N gyeongheom 경험 II V gyeongheomhada 경험하다

expert N jeonmun.ga 전문가

expert, master N darin 달인

expiration date N yuhyogigan 유효기간

explain, to V seolmyeonghada 설명하다

explosion N pokbal 폭발

export I N *(goods)* suchul(pum) 수출(품) II V suchulhada 수출하다

exposure, disclosure N nochul 노출, pongno 폭로

express, state, to V pyohyeonhada 표현하다

express train N teukgeubyeolcha 특급열차

expression *(on face)* N pyojeong 표정

extend, to V 1 yeonjanghada 연장하다: *extension* yeonjang 연장; *telephone extension* naeseon 내선 2 *(stretch)* neureonada 늘어나다

extensive reading N dadok 다독

extra ADJ chuga(ui) 추가의

extradite, to V indohada 인도하다

extravagance, luxury N hosa 호사: *live a luxurious life* hosareul nurida 호사를 누리다

extremely ADV geukdoro 극도로

eye N nun 눈: *close one's eyes* nun reul gamda 눈을 감다

eye disease, oculopathy N nun-byeong 눈병

eyebrow N nunsseop 눈썹

eyeglasses, spectacles N an.gyeong 안경

eyelid N nunkkeopul 눈꺼풀: *heavy eyelids from fatigue* pigoneuro mugeoun nunkkeopul 피곤으로 무거운 눈꺼풀

F

fabric, textile N jingmul 직물

face I N eolgul 얼굴 II V jingmyeonhada 직면하다

facial features, looks N imokgubi 이목구비: *have well-defined features* imokgubiga tturyeotada 이목구비가 뚜렷하다

facilitate, to V chokjinhada 촉진하다: *The company offered to facilitate an international conference in the following year* geu hoesaneun daeum haee gukje hoeuireul chokjinhagetdago malhaetda 그 회사는 다음 해에 국제 회의를 촉진하겠다고 말했다

facility N siseol 시설, seolbi 설비

fact N sasil 사실

factor N yoin 요인: *A bit on the side is a main factor of divorce* bullyuneun ihonui judoen yoinida 불륜은 이혼의 주된 요인이다

factory N gongjang 공장

faculty N 1 neungnyeok 능력 2 gyosu-jin 교수진, hakbu 학부

fade *(away)*, discolor, to V baraeda 바래다: *a faded photo* saek baraen sajin 색 바랜 사진

fail, flunk I N nakje 낙제 II V 1 *(flunk, not pass)* nakjehada 낙제하다 2 *(not succeed)* silpaehada 실패하다: *fail in one's attempt* gyehoegi silpaehada 계획이 실패하다

fail to recognize, to V mollaboda 몰라보다

failure N silpae 실패: *a humiliating fail-*

ure guryokjeogin silpae 굴욕적인 실
패; *failure in an examination* nakbang
낙방; *failure to notice* gangwa 간과
faint(ly), indistinct(ly) ADJ, ADV
huimihage 희미하게
fairy N yojeong 요정
faith N mideum 믿음
fake, false *(imitation)* ADJ gajjaida
가짜이다, gajja(ui) 가짜(의)
fall, to V 1 *(drop)* tteoreojida 떨어지다:
fall off a bike jajeongeoeseo tteoreojida 자전거에서 떨어지다 2 *(trip, tumble)* neomeojida 넘어지다
fall asleep, sink into a slumber, to
V jamdeulda 잠들다
fall behind, to V cheojida 처지다: *fell
behind in the race* gyeongjuseo dwiro
cheojyeotda 경주에서 뒤로 처졌다
fall down, tumble, to V jappajida 자빠
지다: *The bread always falls buttered
side down* dwiro jappajyeodo koga
kkaejinda 뒤로 자빠져도 코가 깨진다
fall foliage N danpung 단풍
fall through, to V teureojida 틀어지다:
The plan has fallen through gyehoegi
teureojida 계획이 틀어지다
false *(not true)* ADJ geojisida/geojit(ui)
거짓이다/거짓(의): *false name,
assumed name* gamyeong 가명
fame N myeongseong 명성
familiar with, not to be ADJ eodupda
어둡다, eoduun 어두운: *not familiar
with the area* jirie eodupda 지리에
어둡다
family N gajok 가족
famine N gigeun 기근
famous ADJ yumyeonghada 유명하다,
yumyeonghan 유명한: *be famous for
the scenery* gyeongchiro yumyeonghada 경치로 유명하다; *a famous singer*
yumyeonghan gasu 유명한 가수
fan I N 1 *(admirer)* paen 팬 2 *(for cooling)* buchae 부채 II V buchida 부치다:
fan oneself buchaereul buchida 부채를
부치다
fantastic ADJ hwansangjeogin 환상적
인: *The film was fantastic from start
to finish* yeonghwaneun cheoeumbuteo kkeutkkaji hwansangjeogieotda
영화는 처음부터 끝까지 환상적이었다
far from it!, absurd!, not a chance!
PHR eorimeopda 어림없다

far-sighteded ADJ wonsi 원시
far, distant, long way ADJ meolda
멀다, meon 먼; adeukhada 아득하다,
adeukhan 아득한: *an island far in the
distance* adeukhan seom 아득한 섬
fare, rate, tariff N yogeum 요금: *base
rate* gibon yogeum 기본 요금
farewell, parting N jakbyeol 작별: *say
farewell* jakbyeoreul gohada 작별을 고
하다
farm N nongjang 농장: *farmland, fields
and paddies* nonbat 논밭
farmer N nongbu 농부
fascinating ADJ maehokjeogin
매혹적인
fashion, vogue, trend N yuhaeng
유행: *follow the trend* yuhaengeul
ttareuda 유행을 따르다
fast, fasting N dansik 단식: *He fasted
for 3 days* geuneun samil dongan dansikhaetda 그는 3일 동안 단식했다
fast, to V dansikhada 단식하다
fasten, button up, to V jamgeuda
잠그다: *button up* danchureul
jamgeuda 단추를 잠그다
fat I N *(grease)* jibang 지방 II ADJ
(plump, stout) ttungttunghada/-han
뚱뚱하다/-한 III V *(to get fat)* jjida
찌다: *get fat* sari jjida 살이 찌다
fatal ADJ 1 chimyeongjeogin 치명적인
2 unmyeongui 운명의
fate N 1 unmyeon 운명 2 jugeum 죽음:
My fate hangs upon his decision naui
unmyeongeun geuui gyeoljeonge
dallyeoitda 나의 운명은 그의 결정에
달려있다
father N abeoji 아버지: *father-in-law*
jang.in 장인; *father-in-law (husband's
father)* siabeoji 시아버지
fatigue N piro 피로: *She showed no
signs of fatigue* geunyeoneun pirohan
gisaegeul boiji anatda 그녀는 피로한
기색을 보이지 않았다
fault, mistake, error N jalmot 잘못
favor N houi 호의
favor, to V houireul boida 호의를
보이다
fax I N 1 *(machine)* paekseu 팩스: *Do
you have a fax machine?* paekseu
iseuseyo? 팩스 있으세요? 2 *(message)* paekseu 팩스: *Did you get a
fax?* paekseu badeusyeoseoyo? 팩스

받으셨어요? II v *(sent by fax)* paekseu bonaeda 팩스 보내다: *send a fax* paekseu bonaeda 팩스를 보내다

fear N museo.um 무서움

feather N gitteol 깃털

February N iwol 이월

federal ADJ yeonbangui 연방의

fee N susuryo 수수료

fee-charging N yuryo 유료

feeble, slender ADJ ganyalpeuda 가냘프다

feed, to V meogida 먹이다

feedstuff N saryo 사료: *feed a pig* dwaejiege saryoreul juda 돼지에게 사료를 주다

feel, to V neukkida 느끼다

feel at ease, feel at home, to V ma.eum pyeon hada 마음 편히하다

feel down, to V garaanda 가라앉다: *feeling down* gibuni garaanda 기분이 가라앉다

feel guilty, to V joechaekgameul neukkida 죄책감을 느끼다

feel jealous, envy, to V jiltuhada 질투하다

feel ticklish ADJ ganjireopda 간지럽다

feel uncomfortable with, to V eoryeowohada 어려워하다

feel uneasy *(out of guilty conscience),* **to** V kenggida 켕기다

feeling N neukkim 느낌

feeling thirsty ADJ keolkeolhada 컬컬하다: *feel thirsty* mogi keolkeolhada 목이 컬컬하다

female, woman N yeoseong 여성: *a single woman* mihon yeoseong 미혼 여성; *a married woman* gihon yeoseong 기혼 여성

fence N 1 ultari 울타리 2 *(wall)* dam 담

fencing N pensing 펜싱

ferment, ripen, to V sakhida 삭히다: *ferment rice juice* sikhyeoreul sakhida 식혜를 삭히다

ferocity, brutality N pyodok 표독

fertile ADJ biokhada 비옥하다, biokan 비옥한

festival N chukje 축제, janchi 잔치

fever N 1 yeol 열: *have a fever* yeori nada 열이 나다 2 *(febrile disease)* yeolbyeong 열병

few, little, almost none ADJ geo.i eopda/eomneun 거의 없다/없는

fiancé N yakhonja 약혼자

fiancée N yakhonnyeo 약혼녀

fiber N seomnyu 섬유, seomnyujil 섬유질

fiction, fabrication N heogu 허구

fidelity, loyalty N uiri 의리: *be loyal to* uirireul jikida 의리를 지키다

field N 1 *(ground)* deul 들: *work in the fields* deure naga ilhada 들에 나가 일하다 2 *(type of business)* badak 바닥 3 *(empty space)* gongteo 공터

fierce, wild, nasty ADJ sanapda 사납다, sanaun 사나운: *a fierce dog* sanaun gae 사나운 개; *fierce fight* yeoljeon 열전

fifteen NUM 1 sibo 십오 2 yeoldaseot 열다섯

fifty NUM 1 osip 오십 2 swin 쉰

fight, to V 1 *(physical blows)* ssauda 싸우다 2 *(quarrel)* eureureonggeorida 으르렁거리다

fighting spirit, morale N sagi 사기: *boost morale* sagireul bukdotda 사기를 북돋다

figure, number N sujja 숫자

figure, shape *(of body)* N mommae 몸매

fill, stuff, pack, to V chae.uda 채우다

fill out, prepare, to V jakseonghada 작성하다

filled, full ADJ gadeuk chan 가득 찬

filled *(space),* **full, crowded, to be** V chada 차다: *a bus full of passengers* seunggaegeuro gadeuk chan beoseu 승객으로 가득 찬 버스

film N 1 *(for camera)* pilleum 필름: *rewind the film* pilleumeul gamda 필름을 감다 2 *(movie)* yeonghwa 영화

final, last ADJ majimakui 마지막의

finally ADV machimnae 마침내

find, seek, look for, search for, to V chatda 찾다

find fault with, to V chaekjapda 책잡다: *(be) found fault with* chaegeul japida 책을 잡히다

fine, penalty *(punishment)* N beolgeum 벌금

finger N sonkkarak 손가락

finish, completion N mamuri 마무리: *complete a work* ireul mamuri jitda 일을 마무리 짓다

finished ADJ kkeunnan 끝난

fire, dismiss, terminate *(job),* **to** V

haegohada 해고하다: *dismiss an employee* jongeobwoneul haegohada 종업원을 해고하다

fire N bul 불: *put out a fire* bureul kkeuda 불을 끄다; *fireworks* bulkkonnori 불꽃놀이

firm ADJ 1 *(stern)* danhohada 단호하다 2 *(free of wrinkles (skin))* paengpaenghada 팽팽하다: *firm skin* paengpaenghan pibu 팽팽한 피부

first N cheot beonjjae 첫 번째

first, earlier, beforehand ADV meonjeo 먼저

first, first of all N useon 우선

first, first time, beginning N cheoeum 처음: *first impression* cheonninsang 첫인상

first, for now ADV ilttan 일단

first aid, emergency treatment N eunggeupchiryo 응급치료

fish I N mulkkogi 물고기, saengseon 생선 II V gogi japda 고기 잡다

fisherman N eobu 어부

fishery N eoeop 어업

fishing N naksi 낚시

fishy ADJ birida 비리다

fistfight N nantu 난투

fit perfectly, to V kkok matda 꼭 맞다

fitting, suitable ADJ eo.ullineun 어울리는

five NUM 1 daseot 다섯 2 o 오: *five senses* ogam 오감; *five-way crossing* ogeori 오거리

fix, to V 1 *(adjust clothes)* gadadeumda 가다듬다 2 *(decide, determine)* jeonghada 정하다 3 *(prepare, set up)* charida 차리다: *set the table* bapsangeul charida 밥상을 차리다 4 *(repair, mend)* gochida 고치다: *fix a computer* keompyuteoreul gochida 컴퓨터를 고치다

fixate, gaze, to V eungsihada 응시하다

flag N gippal 깃발: *flags of all nations* mangukgi 만국기

flashlight, torch N sonjeondeung 손전등

flat I ADV napjak 납작 II ADJ *(plain)* minmitada 밋밋하다

fleet N hamdae 함대

flesh, fat N sal 살: *you look fat* sari mani jjyeoboinda 살이 많이쪄보인다

flexible ADJ yungtongseongi inneun 융통성이 있는: *a flexible person* yungtongseongi inneun saram 융통성이 있는 사람

flight N bihaeng 비행

float, to V buyuhada 부유하다: *float on the water* murwie buyuhada 물위에 부유하다

flock, be swamped with, to V mollida 몰리다: *be swamped with people* inpaga mollida 인파가 몰리다

flood N hongsu 홍수

floor N 1 maru 마루 2 cheung 층: *second floor* icheung 이층 3 *(the bottom)* badak 바닥: *a slippery floor* mikkeureoun badak 미끄러운 바닥

flour N milkkaru 밀가루

flower N kkot 꽃

flu N dokgam 독감: *a flu shot* dokgam jusa 독감 주사

fluent ADJ yuchanghada 유창하다, yuchanghan 유창한: *speak English fluently* yeongeoga yuchanghada 영어가 유창하다

fluid ADJ yudongseongui 유동성의

fluorescent light N hyeonggwangdeung 형광등

flute N peulluteu 플루트

flutter, flap, to V pallanggeorida 팔랑거리다: *flutter softly* napulgeorida 나풀거리다

fly I N *(insect)* pari 파리 II V 1 *(move in the air)* nalda 날다, nallida 날리다 2 nallida 날리다: *fly a paper airplane* jongibihaenggireul nallida 종이비행기를 날리다 3 *(flee, run away)* daranada 달아나다

fly away, take wings, to V naragada 날아가다: *a flying airplane* naraganeun bihaenggi 날아가는 비행기

fog, mist N an.gae 안개

fold, to V jeopda 접다

folks, everybody *(audience)* N yeoreobun 여러분

follow, go after, obey, to V ttareuda 따르다

follow along, to V jjuk ttaragada 쭉 따라가다

follow behind, to V dwittaragada 뒤따라가다

following N da.eum 다음

following year, the N ideumhae 이듬해

food N eumsik 음식

F

food, clothing and shelter N uisikju 의식주

fool, moron N babo 바보

foot N bal 발

for a moment, a while ADV jamkkan 잠깐, jamsi 잠시

for instance, for example ADV yekeondae 예컨대

for oneself, by oneself ADV seuseuro 스스로

forbid, to V geumhada 금하다: geumjidoen 금지된

forbidden, prohibited, restricted, to be V geumjidoeda 금지되다: *be prohibited by law* beobeuro geumjidoeda 법으로 금지되다

force, power, strength N him 힘

force, compel, to V gang.yohada 강요하다

forcibly, unwillingly ADV eokjiro 억지로: *work unwillingly* eokjiro ireul hada 억지로 일을 하다

forehead N ima 이마

foreign ADJ oeguk(ui) 외국(의): *foreign country* taguk 타국; *foreigner* oegugin 외국인

forest N sup 숲: *forest fire* sanbul 산불

forever I ADV yeong.wonhi 영원히 II ADJ *(always)* mannyeon 만년: *a forever section chief* mannyeon gwajang 만년 과장

forge, counterfeit, to V wijohada 위조하다: *forgery, fabrication* wijo 위조

forget, to V itda 잊다: *forget the past* gwageoreul itda 과거를 잊다

forgetfulness N manggak 망각: *Lethe* manggagui gang 망각의 강

forgive, to V yongseohada 용서하다

forgiveness, mercy N youngseo 용서: *forgiveness of sin* sajoe 사죄

forgotten ADJ ichyeojin 잊혀진: *a forgotten memory* ityeojin gieok 잊혀진 기억

forgotten, to be V ichyeojida, ichyeojin 잊혀지다, 잊혀진

fork N pokeu 포크

forked road, crossroad N gallimgil 갈림길

form, shape N moyang 모양

formation N pyeonseong 편성

former I ADJ jinan 지난 II N *(previous)* jeonja 전자: *the former and the latter* jeonjawa huja 전자와 후자

fortress N yosae 요새

fortunately ADV dahaenghi 다행히

forty NUM 1 maheun 마흔 2 sasip 사십

forward ADV apeuro 앞으로

foul-mouthed, be rough in speech ADJ geolda 걸다

four NUM 1 net 넷 2 sa 사: *four seasons* sagye 사계

fourteen NUM 1 sipsa 십사 2 yeolnet 열넷

fox N yeou 여우

fraction N bunsu 분수

fracture, give way, snap, to V bureojyeo nagada 부러져나가다: *The pillars gave way* gidungi bureojyeonagatda 기둥이 부러져나갔다

fragrant, aromatic ADJ hyanggiropda 향기롭다

frankly ADV soljikhi 솔직히: *Do you mind if I speak frankly?* soljikhage malsseum deuryeodo doelkkayo? 솔직하게 말씀 드려도 될까요?

fraud N sagi 사기

free, independent ADJ dongnipan 독립한

free of charge ADV muryo(ui) 무료의

free of restraints ADV jayuropda 자유롭다, jayuroun 자유로운

freedom, liberty N jayu 자유

freeze, to V eoreobutda 얼어붙다, eollida 얼리다: *freeze water* mureul eollida 물을 얼리다

French I N 1 peurangseuin 프랑스인 2 peurangseueo 프랑스어 II ADJ peurangseuui 프랑스의

frequency N bindo 빈도

frequent I ADJ binbeonhada 빈번하다, binbeonhan 빈번한 II V *(patronize)* danida 다니다

frequently ADV jaju 자주, binbeonhi 빈번히: *He flies frequently for his business* geuneun saeopsang jaju bihaengeul handa 그는 사업상 자주 비행을 한다

fresh ADJ sinseonhada 신선하다, sinseonhan 신선한

freshman N sinipsaeng 신입생: *A welcome party was held for freshmen* sinipsaeng hwannyeongpatiga yeollyeotda 신입생 환영파티가 열렸다

friction, rubbing N machal 마찰

Friday N geumyoil 금요일

fried ADJ twigin 튀긴: *fried food* twigim 튀김

friend N chin.gu 친구: *friendship* ujeong 우정

frightened ADJ geommeogeun 겁먹은: *a frightened child* geommeogeun ai 겁먹은 아이

from, of, through PREP ...hanteseo ...한테서: *a letter from a friend* chinguhanteseo on pyeonji 친구한테서 온 편지; *hear news from an employee* jigwonhanteseo sosigeul deutda 직원 한테서 소식을 듣다

from (starting point) PREP ...eseo ...에서

from (time) PREP ...buteo ...부터: *free from now* jigeumbuteo jayuda 지금부터 자유다

front, façade N jeongmyeon 정면

frown, to V jjinggeurida 찡그리다

frozen ADJ eon 언: *frozen shoulder* osipgyeon 오십견

frozen, to be V eolda 얼다: *have frozen feet* bari eolda 발이 얼다

frugality, saving N jeoryak 절약

fruit N gwail 과일, yeolmae 열매

fry, to V twigida 튀기다: *deep-fry* gireume twigida 기름에 튀기다

fuel N yeollyo 연료

fuel efficiency N yeonbi 연비: *have good fuel efficiency* jadongcha yeonbiga jota 자동차 연비가 좋다

fulfill, accomplish, to V suhaenghada 수행하다

full moon N boreumdal 보름달

full, stuffed ADJ baebureuda 배부르다

full, to be V gadeuk chada 가득 차다

full of (emotion), **filled with** (emotion), **to be** V chada 차다: *be filled with joy* gippeumeuro gadeuk chada 기쁨으로 가득 차다

fun, to have V jaemiitge bonaeda 재미있게 보내다

function, effect N jagyong 작용

funds, funding N gigeum 기금

funeral N jangnyesik 장례식

fungus N gompang.i 곰팡이

funny, interesting ADJ jaemiitda, jaemiinneun 재미있다, 재미있는: *What fun!* jeongmal jaemiitda! 정말 재미있다!

furniture N gagu 가구

further, additional ADJ geu isang 그 이상

fusion, blending N yunghap 융합

fussy, picky, difficult (character) ADJ kkadaropda 까다롭다, kkadaroun 까다로운: *a man difficult to please* kkadaroun saram 까다로운 사람

future, tomorrow N jangnae 장래: *in future* mirae 미래

G

gain N iik 이익: *The gain is estimated at 2 million dollars* geu iigeun ibaengman bullo chujeongdoenda 그 이익은 이백만 불로 추정된다

gain, to V eotda 얻다: *We have everything to lose and nothing to gain* urineun ireul ppun eonneun geoseun eopda 우리는 잃을 뿐 얻는 것은 없다

galaxy N eunhagye 은하계, eunhasu 은하수

gallery N misulgwan 미술관

gamble N dobak 도박

game N geim 게임

gap, space N sai 사이

garage (for parking) N chago 차고

garbage N sseuregi 쓰레기

garden, yard N jeong.won 정원

gardens, park N gong.won 공원

garlic N maneul 마늘

gas station N juyuso 주유소

gasoline N 1 gasollin 가솔린 2 (petrol) hwiballyu 휘발유

gastric cancer, cancer of the stomach N wiam 위암: *have stomach cancer* wiame geollida 위암에 걸리다

gather, flock, to V moida 모이다: *gather from all over the country* jeongugeseo moida 전국에서 모이다

gaze N jusi 주시

gaze, to V ttureojige boda 뚫어지게 보다: *People are gazing at the billboards* saramdeuri gwanggopaneul ttureojige bogo itda 사람들이 광고판을 뚫어지게 보고 있다

gear N 1 gieo 기어, jangchi 장치 2 tobnibakwi 톱니바퀴

gender N seongbyeol 성별

gene N yujeonja 유전자

general, all-purpose ADJ ilbanjeogida/-jeogin 일반적이다/-적인

generally ADV 1 ilbanjeogeuro 일반적 으로 2 (mostly) daechero 대체로

generation N sadae 세대

generous ADJ neogeureopda 너그럽다, neogeureoun 너그러운: *generous attitude* neogeureoun taedo 너그러운 태도

genetic ADJ yujeonui 유전의: *This is called a genetic disorder* igeoseul yujeonjeok jilhwanirago handa 이것을 유전적 질환이라고 한다

genius N cheonjae 천재

gentle ADJ 1 *(affectionate)* sangnyanghada 상냥하다 2 *(mild)* onnyuhada 온유하다 3 *(respectable)* jeomjanta 점잖다, jeomjaneun 점잖은

genuine, real, authentic ADJ jinjjaui 진짜의

geography N jiri(hak) 지리(학)

germ, virus N se.gyun 세균

German I N 1 dogirin 독일인 2 dogireo 독일어 II ADJ dogirui 독일의

gesture N jeseucheo 제스처

get, receive, obtain, to V eotda 얻다

get a walloping, to V wanpaehada 완패하다

get an assurance from sb, to V dajimbatda 다짐받다

get better, improve, to V joajida 좋아지다

get bitten, to V mullida 물리다: *bitten by a mosquito* mogie mullida 모기에 물리다

get dressed, to V ot ipda 옷 입다

get intertwined, to V eokhida 얽히다

get into, board, to V tapseunghada 탑승하다

get lost *(can't find way)*, **to** V gireul ilta 길을 잃다

get off, disembark, to V naerida 내리다: *get off a car* chaeseo naerida 차에서 내리다

get on, board, ride *(transport)*, **to** V tada 타다: *get in(to) a car* chareul tada 차를 타다

get out of, get over, get through, free from, to V heeonada 헤어나다: *get out from poverty* bingoneseo heeonada 빈곤에서 헤어나다

get rid of, eliminate, remove, to V jegeohada 제거하다

get seized, be snatched, to V garochaeida 가로채이다

get stabbed, to V kalmatda 칼맞다

get tired of, to V mullida 물리다: *get*

sick and tired of candies satange mullida 사탕에 물리다

get treated to, be called names, to V eodeomeokda 얻어먹다

get undressed, to V ot beotda 옷 벗다

get up *(from bed)*, **to** V ireonada 일어나다: *get up in the morning* achime ireonada 아침에 일어나다

get well soon! PHR got hoebokhaseyo! 곧 회복하세요!

ghost N gwisin 귀신, yuryeong 유령

ghostly, spooky ADJ euseuseuhada 으스스하다

giant N geo.in 거인

giddiness, frivolity N odobangjeong 오도방정

giddy, dizzy, faintish ADJ ajjilhada 아찔하다

giggle, chuckle, to V kikkikgeorida 킥킥거리다

ginger N saenggang 생강

girl N so.nyeo 소녀: *girlfriend* yeojachin.gu 여자 친구

gist, main point N yojeom 요점

give, to V bachida 바치다, juda 주다

give *(a person)* **a piggyback, to** V eopda 업다

give a ride, to V taewojuda 태워주다

give an answer, to V eungdapada 응답하다

give extra, to V eonjeojuda 얹어주다: *give one extra* hanareul deo eonjeojuda 하나를 더 얹어주다

give up on oneself, to V japojagihada 자포자기하다

giving a look N nunchori 눈초리: *an angry look* seongnan nunchori 성난 눈초리; *a scornful look* gyeongmyeorui nunchori 경멸의 눈초리; *a look of suspicion* uisimui nunchori 의심의 눈초리; *a look of dissatisfaction* monmattanghan nunchori 못마땅한 눈초리

glacier N bingha 빙하

glad, happy, welcome ADJ gippeun 기쁜, bangapda 반갑다: *Nice to meet you* mannaseo bangapseumnida 만나서 반갑습니다

glare, to V bureuptteuda 부릅뜨다

glass *(material)* N yuri 유리

glimmer, flicker, to V areungeorida 아른거리다

G

glimpse N heulkkeut bom 흘끗 봄

gloat over *(somebody's misfortune)*, **to** V gosohada 고소하다

glorious, honorable ADJ yeong-gwangseureopda 영광스럽다

glossy, shiny ADJ yunnada 윤나다

gloves N janggap 장갑

glutinous rice N chapssal 찹쌀

go, to V gada 가다

go and return, to V danyeooda 다녀오다: *My husband went on a trip and returned* nampyeoni chuljangeul danyeowatda 남편이 출장을 다녀왔다

go around in groups, to V mollyeo-danida 몰려다니다

go around, visit, to V gaboda 가보다

go astray, to V binnagada 빗나가다

go back, return, to V doragada 돌아가다: *go back home* jibeuro doragada 집으로 돌아가다

go berserk with *(anger, joy)* V peoljjeokttuida 펄쩍 뛰다: *go berserk with anger* hwaga naseo peoljjeok ttwida 화가 나서 펄쩍 뛰다

go home, to V jibe gada 집에 가다

go missing *(person)* ADJ haengbang-bulmyeongdeon 행방불명된: *a missing girl* haengbangbulmyeongdoen sonyeo 행방불명된 소녀

go off, power out, to V nagada 나가다

go out, to V 1 *(exit, leave, go forth)* nagada 나가다 2 *(be extinguished, be blown out)* kkeojida 꺼지다

go to bed, to V jareogada 자러가다

go up, climb, lift, to V ollagada 올라가다: *go up to the 3rd floor* sam-cheunge ollagada 3층에 올라가다

go wide, miss, to V binnagada 빗나가다: *go wide off the mark* gwanyeo-geul binnagada 과녁을 빗나가다

goal N mokpyo 목표

goat N yeomso 염소

gobble, to V peomeokda 퍼먹다

God N hananim 하나님: *the grace of God* hananimui eunhye 하나님의 은혜

god N sin 신

goddess N yeosin 여신: *the goddess of love* sarangui yeosin 사랑의 여신

gold N geum 금

golf N golpeu 골프

good luck! PHR haeng.uneul bimnida! 행운을 빕니다!

good ADJ 1 *(fair, pretty)* wenmanhada 웬만하다 2 *(fine, nice)* jota 좋다, jo.eun 좋은, chakhada 착하다 3 *(nice and pretty)* chamhada 참하다

goodbye PHR 1 *(said to a person leaving (in honorific form))* annyeonghi gaseyo 안녕히 가세요 2 *(said to a person staying (in honorific form))* annyeonghi gyeseyo 안녕히 계세요

goodness, virtue N seon 선: *do good* seoneul haenghada 선을 행하다

goods, products N sangpum 상품

goose N geowi 거위

gourd *(dipper)*, **calabash** N bagaji 바가지

govern, rule, to V daseurida 다스리다: *govern a nation* narareul daseurida 나라를 다스리다

government N jeongbu 정부

governor N jujisa 주지사

grab, to V butjapda 붙잡다: *I have to grab that opportunity* naneun geu gihoereul butjabaya handa 나는 그 기회를 붙잡아야 한다

grabbed, to be V japida 잡히다

grace, *(divine)* **blessing** N eunchong 은총

gradually ADV jeomchajeogeuro 점차적으로

grain N 1 goksik 곡식 2 *(cereal)* gong-mul 곡물

grammar N munpeopp 문법

grandchild N *(granddaughter)* sonnyeo 손녀, *(grandson)* sonja 손자

grandfather N harabeoji 할아버지, jobu 조부

grandmother N halmeoni 할머니, jomo 조모

grandparents N jobumo 조부모

grapes N podo 포도

grasp, understanding N paak 파악

grass N pul 풀

grateful ADJ gomapda 고맙다, gomaun 고마운

grave N mudeom 무덤, sanso 산소

gravel, pebble N jagal 자갈

gravity N jungnyeok 중력

great, impressive, magnificent ADJ daedanhada 대단하다, daedanhan 대단한

Great Wall of China, the N mallijang-seong 만리장성

green ADJ pureuda 푸르다, pureun 푸른

greenhouse N onsil 온실

greens, vegetables N yachae 야채: *vegetable stir-fried rice* yachae bok-keumbap 야채 볶음밥

greet, to V 1 insahada 인사하다: *greet politely* kkakduetsi insahada 깍듯이 인사하다 2 *(welcome)* bangida 반기다 3 *(welcome, receive)* matda 맞다, manneun 맞는: *welcome (greet) a guest* sonnimeul matda 손님을 맞다

greetings N insamal 인사말: *say hi (to)* insamareul geonneda 인사말을 건네다

grey ADJ hoesaek(ui) 회색(의)

grief N bitan 비탄: *Her heart was numbed with grief* geunyeoui maeumeun bitane jinnullyeotda 그녀의 마음은 비탄에 짓눌렸다

ground, earth, land N ttang 땅

groundless rumor N heotsomun 헛소문: *spread a false rumor* heotsomuneul peotteurida 헛소문을 퍼뜨리다

group N geurup 그룹, muri 무리

grow, to V 1 *(cultivate)* jaebaehada 재배하다: *grow crops* nongjang-mureul jaebaehada 농작물을 재배하다 2 *(grow up)* jarada 자라다: *grow up quickly and healthy* mureongmureok jarada 무럭무럭 자라다 3 *(develop)* seongjanghada 성장하다

grow dark, to V jeomulda 저물다

grow desperate, have a fit of anger, to V batchida 받치다: *have a fit of anger* age batchida 악에 받치다

grow haggard, to V sanghada 상하다: *look haggard from fatigue* piroro eolguri sanghada 피로로 얼굴이 상하다

grow hoarse, to V jamgida 잠기다: *get hoarse* mogi jamgida 목이 잠기다

grow larger, to V keojida 커지다

grow old, to V neukda 늙다

gruesome, horrendous ADJ chamhokhada 참혹하다

guarantee I N 1 bojang 보장, bojeung 보증 2 *(talk big, boast)* jangdam 장담: *big talk, loud boast* hoeonjangdam 호언장담 II V bojeunghada 보증하다

guard, to V 1 *(keep)* jikida 지키다 2 *(control)* dansokhada 단속하다

guess, to V chucheukhada 추측하다

guesstimate N I ganeum 가늠 II V *(judge)* ganeumhada 가늠하다

guest N sonnim 손님: *guest of honor* gwibin 귀빈

guide, lead I N gaideu 가이드 II *(lead)* indohada 인도하다

guidebook N annaeseo 안내서

guilt N yujoe 유죄: *There is no evidence of his guilt* geuga yujoeraneun jeunggeoneun eopda 그가 유죄라는 증거는 없다

guilty *(of crime)* ADJ yujoe.ida 유죄이다, yujoe.in 유죄인

guitar N gita 기타

gull *(sea)* N galmaegi 갈매기

gun N chong 총

gush out, well up, to V saemsotda 샘솟다

guy N nyeoseok 녀석, namja 남자

gym N cheyukgwan 체육관

H

habit N beoreut 버릇

habitat N seosikji 서식지

hail I N ubak 우박 II V *(rain)* bitbalchida 빗발치다

hair N 1 meori(karak) 머리(가락) 2 *(fur)* teol 털

half N 1 ban 반: *Please give me half* banman juseyo 반만 주세요 2 jeolban 절반

halfway ADJ eojungganhada 어중간하다

hall N hol 홀

hallway N bokdo 복도

hammer N mangchi 망치

hanbok, Korean dress N hanbok 한복

hand N son 손

hand out, distribute, pass out, to V nanu.eojuda 나누어주다

hand over, pass on, to V neomgyeo-juda 넘겨주다

handcart, wheelbarrow N sonsure 손수레

handful N 1 han umkeum 한 움큼: *He drew a handful of coins from his pocket* geuneun geuui jumeonieseo han umkeumui dongjeondeureul kkeonaetda 그는 그의 주머니에서 한 움큼의 동전들을 꺼냈다 2 myeot an doeneun saram 몇 안 되는 사람: *a handful of men* sosuui inwon 소수의 인원 3 darugi himdeun saram 다루기 힘든 사람: *Her children are a real* *handful* geunyeoui aideureun darugi eoryeopda 그녀의 아이들은 다루기 어렵다

handicap N jang.ae 장애

handicraft N sugong.ye 수공예

handkerchief N sonsugeon 손수건

handle N sonjabi 손잡이

handrail, railing N nangan 난간

handsome, good-looking ADJ jalsaenggida 잘생기다, jalsaenggin 잘생긴

hang, to V 1 *(on the wall)* geolda 걸다: *hang a picture on the wall* byeoge geurimeul geolda 벽에 그림을 걸다 2 *(spread out)* neolda 널다; *hang laundry to dry* ppallaereul neolda 빨래를 널다

hang out with, go around with, to V danida 다니다: *hang out with club friends* dongari chingudeulgwa eoullyeo danida 동아리 친구들과 어울려 다니다

hanger *(for coats)* N otgeori 옷걸이

happen, occur, to V ireonada 일어나 다: *a miracle happens* gijeogi ireonada 기적이 일어나다

happily ADV haengbokhage 행복하게: *I hope they live happily* naneun geudeuri haengbokhage salgi baranda 나는 그들이 행복하게 살기 바란다

happy ADJ haengbokhada 행복하다, haengbokhan 행복한: *be as happy as can be* deo eopsi haengbokhada 더 없이 행복하다; *a happy marriage* haengbokhan gyeolhon 행복한 결혼; *happiness* haengbok 행복

happy birthday! PHR saeng.il chukhahamnida! 생일 축하합니다!

happy new year! PHR saehae bok mani badeuseyo! 새해 복 많이 받으세요!

happy occasion, a N gyeongsa 경사

harassment N goeropim 괴롭힘, aemeogeum 애먹음

harbor, port N hanggu 항구

hard, solid, firm ADJ dandanhada 단단하다, dandanhan 단단한

hard disk N hadeudiseukeu 하드디스크

hard-hearted ADJ maejeonghada 매정 하다

hard liquor N dokhan sul 독한 술

hardly, rarely, seldom ADV geoui -ji anta 거의 -지 않다

hardship N eoryeoum 어려움, *(adversity)* heomnan 험난

hardware N cheolmul 철물

hardworking, industrious ADJ geunmyeonhan 근면한

harm N hae 해: *do harm* haereul kkichida 해를 끼치다

harmful ADJ haeropda 해롭다, haero.un 해로운: *a harmful environment* haeroun hwangyeong 해로운 환경

harmony N 1 *(balance)* johwa 조화: *harmonious* johwadoen 조화된 2 *(concord)* hwahap 화합

harsh ADJ gahokhan 가혹한: *The punishment was too harsh for such a young child* geu cheobeoreun eorinaiegeneun neomu gahokhan geotsieotda 그 처벌은 어린아이에게는 너무 가혹한 것이었다

harshly, severely ADV toktokhi 톡톡 히: *pay severely for one's sin* joetgapseul toktokhi chireuda 죗값을 톡톡히 치르다

harvest N suhwak 수확: *Last year's harvest fell short of the average* jangnyeonui suhwageun pyeonggyune bihae tteoreojinda 작년의 수확은 평균에 비해 떨어진다

harvest, to V suhwakhada 수확하다

hat N moja 모자

hate, to ADJ miwohada 미워하다

hateful, detestable ADJ yalmipda 얄밉다

hatred N jeung.o 증오

haughty, proud, arrogant ADJ dodohada 도도하다

haul *(a person)* **in, to** V yeonhaenghada 연행하다

have, to V 1 *(own sth)* itda 있다: *We have a garden in our house* uri jibeneun jeongwoni itda 우리 집에는 정원이 있다; *have money* doni itda 돈이 있다 2 *(take, hold)* gajida 가지다

have a haircut *(male hair)*, **to** V ibalhada 이발하다

have been to somewhere, to V ga bonjeogi itda 가 본적이 있다

have disagreement, to V eotgallida 엇갈리다

have done something, to V da haetda 다 했다: *have done one's homework* sukjereul da haetda 숙제를 다 했다

H

have indigestion, to v eonchida 얹히다

have mixed feelings, to v eotgallida 엇갈리다: *mixed feelings of joy and sadness* huibiga eotgallida 희비가 엇갈리다

hawk N mae 매

hay N geoncho 건초

hazard N wiheom 위험

he, him PRON geu 그

head N meori 머리

head *(counter for cabbage)* N pogi 포기: *buy a head of cabbage* baechu han pogireul sada 배추 한 포기를 사다

head for, toward, to v ...(eu)ro hyanghada ...(으)로 향하다

head of household, breadwinner N gajang 가장: *a child-headed household* sonyeon sonyeo gajang 소년 소녀 가장

head-butt N bakchigi 박치기

headache N dutong 두통

heading, title N pyoje 표제

headline N hedeu rain 헤드 라인, pyoje 표제

headquarters N bonbu 본부

heal, to v amulda 아물다

health center N bogeonso 보건소

healthy ADJ geon.ganghada 건강하다, geon.ganghan 건강한: *be in good physical health* sinchejeogeuro geon.ganghada 신체적으로 건강하다; *health foods* geongang sikpum 건강 식품

heap, pile N sandeomi 산더미

hear, listen, to v deutda 듣다

hearing N 1 cheongnyeok 청력, cheong-gak 청각 2 gongcheonghoe 공청회

heart N ma.eum 마음, simjang 심장

heat I N *(excitement)* yeolgi 열기 II v de.uda 데우다: *heat up the soup* jji-gaereul deuda 찌개를 데우다

heatstroke N yeolsabyeong 열사병

heaven N cheon.guk 천국

heavily ADV 1 simhage 심하게 2 mu-geopge 무겁게

heavy ADJ 1 mugeopda 무겁다, mugeo. un 무거운: *heavy snow* pokseol 폭설 2 *(vital, critical)* makjunghan 막중한

heel N bal dwikkumchi 발 뒤꿈치

height, level N nopi 높이

helicopter N hellikopteo 헬리콥터

hello, hi, how are you? *(in honorific form)* PHR annyeonghaseyo 안녕하세요

hello! *(on phone)* INTERJ yeoboseyo! 여보세요!

helmet N helmet 헬멧, anjeonmo 안전모

help, aid N bojo 보조: *receive government aid* jeongbu bojoreul batda 정부 보조를 받다

help! INTERJ dowajuseyo! 도와주세요!

hem N dan 단: *hem of a skirt* chimaui dan 치마의 단

hepatitis N gannyeom 간염

her PRON geu yeoja-ui 그 여자의

her *(hers)* PRON geu yeoja.ui (geot) 그 여자의 (것)

here I N yeogi 여기 II *(to this way)* ADV iri(ro) 이리(로): *Come here* iriro wa 이리로 와

heritage N yusan 유산

hero, heroine N yeongung 영웅

hesitate, to v jujeohada 주저하다

hexahedron N yungmyeonche 육면체

hey! you! *(impolite)* INTERJ eoi 어이

hidden, to be v sumgyeojida, sum-gyeojin 숨겨지다, 숨겨진

hide, conceal, to v 1 garida 가리다 2 sumgida 숨기다 3 *(go into hiding)* sumda 숨다

hideout N eunsincheo 은신처

high ADJ nopda 높다, nopeun 높은

highway N gosokdoro 고속도로

hijack, kidnapping N napchi 납치

hill N eondeok 언덕

hippopotamus N hama 하마

his PRON geu.ui 그의

historical N yeoksajeok 역사적

history N yeoksa 역사

hit, to v 1 *(strike)* chida 치다 2 *(crash, bump)* bakda 박다

hit, struck, beaten, slapped, to be v matda 맞다, manneun 맞는

hobby N chwimi 취미

hold, to v 1 *(grasp)* butjapda 붙잡다 2 *(rank)* chajihada 차지하다

hold back, restrain, to v eokjehada 억제하다

hold up, support, to v batchida 받치다: *hold up the wall with a post* byeogeul gidungeuro batchida 벽을 기둥으로 받치다

holding back an urge N anganhim 안간힘

hole N gumeong 구멍

holiday N 1 *(a day off)* hyu.il 휴일

2 *(festival)* myeongjeol 명절: *observe a holiday* myeongjeoreul soeda 명절을 쇠다 3 *(vacation)* hyu.ga 휴가

holy, sacred ADJ sinseonghada 신성하다, sinseonghan 신성한

home, house N jip 집

homesickness N hyangsuppyeong 향수병

homicide, murder N tasal 타살

honest, honorable, truthful ADJ jeongjikhada 정직하다, jeongjikan 정직한

honestly ADV soljikhi 솔직히

honey N kkul 꿀

Hong Kong N hongkong 홍콩

honor N 1 *(reputation)* myeong.ye 명예 2 *(glory)* yeonggwang 영광

hope I N *(probability)* gamang 가망: *no hope for full recovery* wankwaedoel gamangi eopda 완쾌될 가망이 없다 II V neomboda 넘보다

hopefully ADV barageonde 바라건대

horizon N jipyeongseon 지평선, supyeongseon 수평선

hormone N hormon 호르몬

horse N mal 말

horsepower N maryeok 마력

hospital N byeong.won 병원

host N ju.in 주인

hostile ADJ jeokdaejeogin 적대적인: *Both countries are hostile to each other* du naraneun jeokdaejeogin gwangyee itda 두 나라는 적대적인 관계에 있다

hot ADJ 1 *(temperature)* deopda 덥다, deo.un 더운: *hot air balloon* yeolgigu 열기구; *hot spring* oncheon 온천 2 *(spicy)* maekomhada 매콤하다, maepda 맵다, mae.un 매운

hot-blooded, short-tempered ADJ dahyeoljillui 다혈질의

hotel N hotel 호텔

hour N sigan 시간: *four hours* ne sigan 네 시간

housekeeping N sallim 살림

housemaster N sagam 사감

housewife N jubu 주부

how ADV eotteoke 어떻게

how dare...? PHR eongamsaengsim 언감생심

how long? PHR eolmana oraeyo? 얼마나 오래요?

how many? how much? PHR eolmana maniyo? 얼마나 많아요?

how many? how old? what time? PHR meot 몇

how much is it? PHR eolmayeyo? 얼마예요?

how much, how many ADJ eolmana 얼마나

how old? PHR myeot sarieyo? 몇 살이에요?

how, why ADV eoi 어이

however, but CONJ geureona 그러나

huge ADJ geodaehada 거대하다, geodaehan 거대한, keodarata 커다랗다

human N in.gan 인간: *human rights* ingwon 인권; *human voice* yukseong 육성

humming N konnorae 콧노래

humor N yumeo 유머: *have a great sense of humor* yumeoga neomchida 유머가 넘치다

humorous ADJ 1 yumeoreoseuhada 유머러스하다 2 *(funny, hilarious)* utgineun 웃기는

hundred NUM baek 백

hundred thousand NUM simman 십만

hungry ADJ baegopeuda 배고프다, baegopeun 배고픈: *a hungry lion* baegopeun saja 배고픈 사자; *hunger* heogi 허기

hunting, hunt N sanyang 사냥: *hunter* sanyangkkun 사냥꾼

hurry up! INTERJ ppalliyo! 빨리요!

hurt, to be V dachida 다치다

hurt (cause pain), to V apeuge hada 아프게 하다

hurt, injured ADJ i dachin 다친: *an injured person* dachin saram 다친 사람

husband N nampyeon 남편

hut, shack N odumak 오두막

hydrochloric acid N yeomsan 염산

hymn, psalm N chansongga 찬송가

hypocritical ADJ wiseonjeogin 위선적인: *hypocrisy* wiseon 위선

I

I am sorry! excuse me! *(apology)* PHR mianhamnida! 미안합니다!

I have nothing to do with it, I don't care, it doesn't matter PHR sang-gwaneopda 상관없다

I, me PRON 1 *(humble form)* jeo 저: *I am ten years old* jeoneun nyeol sal imnida 저는 열 살 입니다 2 na 나: *I am a student.* naneun haksaengimnida 나는 학생입니다; *Please pick me* nareul ppobajuseyo 나를 뽑아주세요

I, my N, ADJ 1 *(humble form)* je 제: *I will do it* jega hagetseumnida 제가 하겠습니다; *She is my girlfriend* je yeoja chingu imnida 제 여자 친구 입니다 2 nae 내: *I am the best* naega jeil jalhaeyo 내가 제일 잘해요; *My brother is bigger* nae dongsaengi deo keoyo 내 동생이 더 커요

I'm so ashamed! PHR changpihada! 창피하다!

ice N eoreum 얼음

ice cream N aiseu keurim 아이스크림

icon N aikon 아이콘

icy ground N eoreumpan 얼음판

idea N aidieo 아이디어

idea, thoughts, mind N saenggak 생각

ideal N isang 이상: *The actual is often contradictory to the ideal* hyconsilgwa isangeun jongjong mosundoenda 현실과 이상은 종종 모순된다

ideal ADJ isangjeogin 이상적인: *My wife has been my ideal companion through 30 years of marriage* nae anaeneun samsimnyeonui gyeolhonsaenghwal dongan naui isangjeogin dongbanjayeotda 내 아내는 삼십년의 결혼생활 동안 나의 이상적인 동반자였다

identical ADJ dongilhan 동일한, ttokgachin 똑같은: *It's impossible for people to have identical fingerprints* jimuni wanjeonhi ttok gateun saramdeureun iseul su eopda 지문이 완전히 똑 같은 사람들은 있을 수 없다

identification N sinwon hwagin 신원 확인, sinbun jeungmyeong 신분 증명

identify, to V hwaginhada 확인하다

identity N sinwon 신원, sinbun 신분

ideological ADJ inyeomjeogin 이념적인

ideology N ideollogi 이데올로기, inyeom 이념

idol N usang 우상; *cast an idol* usangeul mandeulda 우상을 만들다

if need be ADV yeochahamyeon 여차하면

igloo N igeullu 이글루

ignorant ADJ musikhada 무식하다, musikan 무식한

ignore, to V musihada 무시하다

ill, sick, sore, painful ADJ apeuda 아프다, apeun 아픈

illegal ADJ bulppeobida 불법이다, bulppeop(ui) 불법(의)

illness N *(disease)* byeong 병

illusion N 1 hwangak 환각 2 *(delusion)* chakgak 착각

illustrate, to V 1 sapwareul sseuda 삽화를 쓰다 2 inyonghada 인용하다

image N imiji 이미지, yeongsang 영상

imagination N sangsangnyeok 상상력, sangsang 상상

imagine, to V sangsanghada 상상하다

immature, infantile ADJ cheoreopda 철없다: *still immature* ajik cheori eopda 아직 철이 없다

immediate ADJ jeukgakjeogin 즉각적인

immediately ADV jeuksi 즉시: *I have to finish the report immediately* naneun geu bogoseoreul jeuksi kkeunnaeya handa 나는 그 보고서를 즉시 끝내야 한다

immersion, devotion N morip 몰입

immigrant ADJ ijuhae oneun 이주해 오는

immigrant N imin 이민

immigration N 1 iju 이주, imin 이민 2 churipguk gwalliso 출입국 관리소

immovable, motionless, stationary ADJ umjigiji anneun 움직이지 않는: *an immovable object* umjigiji anneun mulche 움직이지 않는 물체

immune ADJ myeonnyeokseongi inneun 면역성이 있는

impact N yeonghyang 영향, chunggyeok 충격

implement, to V sihaenghada 시행하다: *We've decided to implement the system* urineun geu jedoreul sihaenghagiro gyeoljeonghaetda 우리는 그 제도를 시행하기로 결정했다

implementation N ihaeng 이행, silhaeng 실행

implication N 1 hamchuk 함축 2 *(involvement)* yeollu 연루

imply, to V amsihada 암시하다, uimihada 의미하다: *What does the speaker imply about herself?* hwajaneun jasine daehae mueoseul amsihaneunga? 화자는 자신에 대해 무엇을 암시하는가?

impolite, rude ADJ muryehada 무례하다, muryehan 무례한

import, to V su.iphada 수입하다

important ADJ jung.yohada 중요하다, jung.yohan 중요한: *importance* jung. yoseong 중요성

importantly ADV jungyohage 중요하게

imported goods N su.ippum 수입품

impose, to V 1 doipada 도입하다 2 bugwahada 부과하다

impossible ADJ bulganeunghada/-han 불가능하다/-한

impression, to make an V insang.eul juda 인상을 주다: *make a strong impression* gangnyeolhan insangeul juda 강렬한 인상을 주다

impressive ADJ insangjeogida 인상적이다, insangjeogin 인상적인: *an impressive (memorable) scene* insang jeogin jangmyeon 인상적인 장면

imprison, to V gamgeumhada 감금하다: *imprisonment* gamgeum 감금

improve one's appearance, to V gakkuda 가꾸다

improvement of illness N chado 차도: *showing improvements in an illness* byeongsega chadoreul boigo itda 병세가 차도를 보이고 있다

impulse N chungdong 충동

in *(time, years)* PREP ...e ...에

in a calm and orderly way ADV chageunchageun 차근차근

in a moment of bewilderment ADV conggeopgyeore 엉겁결에

in addition, besides, at the same time ADV aulleo 아울러

in an instant ADV eontteut 언뜻

in flames, aflame, to be V bultago itda 불타고 있다: *be aflame with love* sarangeuro bultada 사랑으로 불타다

in need of, to be V piryohada, piryohan 필요하다, 필요한

in one breath, in one sitting ADV dansume 단숨에

in order that, so that CONJ -gi wihaeseo -기 위해서

in order to ADV -(eu)reo -(으)러

in-laws N sadon 사돈

in, at, on *(location of action)* PREP ...eseo ...에서

in, at, on *(location)* PREP ...e ...에

in, by PREP inae 이내: *Be there in 30 minutes* samsipbun inaero gagetseumnida 30분 이내로 가겠습니다

inarticulate ADJ eonulhada 어눌하다

incense, fragrance, aroma N hyang 향: *burn incense* hyangeul piuda 향을 피우다

incentive N jangnyeochaek 장려책

incident, affair, event N sakkeon 사건

included, including ADJ pohamdoen 포함된, pohamhaeseo 포함해서: *including myself* nareul pohamhaeseo 나를 포함해서

income N su.ip 수입

incorrect answer N odap 오답

increase I N jeungga 증가 II V 1 *(rise)* jeunggahada 증가하다 2 neullida 늘리다: *increase one's fortune* jaesaneul neullida 재산을 늘리다

increasing ADJ jeunggahaneun 증가하는: *It is difficult to provide housing for the rapidly increasing population* geupsokhi jeunggahaneun ingue jutaegeul gonggeupagiran eoryeopda 급속히 증가하는 인구에 주택을 공급하기란 어렵다

increasingly ADV jeomjeom deo 점점 더

incredible ADJ mideul su eomneun 믿을 수 없는, nolaun 놀라운

incredibly ADV mideul su eopseul jeongdoro 믿을 수 없을 정도로

incur, suffer, to V ipda 입다: *suffer a great damage* keun sonhae (pihae)reul ipda 큰 손해 (피해)를 입다

indebted to, favored with, to be V ipda 입다: *be indebted to, receive groat kindness* eunhyereul ipda 은혜를 입다

indeed! INTERJ geureomyo! 그럼요!

independence N dongnip 독립

independent ADJ dongnipui 독립의

independent, to become V dongniphada 독립하다: *achieve financial independence* gyeongjejeogeuro dongnipada 경제적으로 독립하다

index N saegin 색인

India N indo 인도: *a trip to India* indo yeohaeng 인도 여행

Indian I ADJ indoui 인도의 II N indoin 인도인

indicate, to V natanaeda 나타내다: *The*

ENGLISH–KOREAN

facts indicate a need for action geu sasildeureun haengdongi piryohameul latanaenda 그 사실들은 행동이 필요함을 나타낸다
indication N mal 말
indicator N jipyo 지표
indifference N mugwansim 무관심
indigenous, native ADJ tochakui 토착의
indigestion N sohwabullyang 소화불량
individual I N gaein 개인: *the freedom of the individual* gaeinui jayu 개인의 자유 II ADJ *(personal, private)* gaein(ui) 개인의
Indonesia N indonesia 인도네시아
induce, to V yudohada 유도하다
induction N yudo 유도: *induced labor* yudobunman 유도분만
industrial ADJ saneobui 산업의
industry N saneop 산업
inevitable ADJ bulgapihan 불가피한: *He maintains that war is inevitable* geuneun jeonjaengi bulgapihadago jujanghanda 그는 전쟁이 불가피하다고 주장한다
inevitability, necessity N piryeon 필연
inevitably ADV anina dareulkka 아니나 다를까, bulgapihage 불가피하게
inexperience N saengso 생소
infant N yua 유아
infect, to V gamyeomsikida 감염시키다
infection N gamnyeom 감염
inferior, of poor quality ADJ yeoldeunghada 열등하다: *inferiority* yeoldeung 열등
infinity, limitless N muhan 무한
inflammation N yeomjueng 염증
inflation N inpeulleisyeon 인플레이션
influence N yeonghyang 영향
influential ADJ yeonghyangnyeok inneun 영향력 있는: *He was young but very influential* geuneun eorijiman maeu yeonghyangnyeok inneun saramieotda 그는 어리지만 매우 영향력 있는 사람이었다
inform, let someone know, to V allida 알리다
informal ADJ 1 gyeoksige eongmaeiji anneun 격식에 얽매이지 않는 2 pyeongsangbogui 평상복의
information N jeongbo 정보
information booth N annaeso 안내소

infrastructure N sahoe giban siseol 사회 기반 시설
infuriated, aggavated, to be V hwanada 화나다
ingredient N jaeryo 재료
inherent ADJ naejaehaneun 내재하는
inherit, to V sangsokbatda 상속받다: *He inherited a large fortune from his father* geuneun geuui abeojirobuteo maneun jaesaneul sangsokbadatda 그는 그의 아버지로부터 많은 재산을 상속받았다
inheritance N yusan 유산
initial ADJ cheoeumui 처음의
initially ADV cheoeume 처음에
initiate, strike up a conversation, to V geolda 걸다: *initiate a conversation* mareul geolda 말을 걸다
initiative N 1 gyehoek 계획 2 gyeoldallyeok 결단력
inject, to V jusahada 주사하다: *injection* jusa 주사
injured, to be V ipda 입다
injury, wound N busang 부상: *a minor injury* gabyeoun busang 가벼운 부상
inmate N sugamja 수감자
ink N ingkeu 잉크
inn, motel N yeogwan 여관
inner ADJ naebuui 내부의
innocence N mujoe 무죄
innocent ADJ gyeolbaekhada 결백하다, gyeolbaekan 결백한
innovation N hyeoksin 혁신
innovative ADJ hyeoksinjeogin 혁신적인, hoekgijeogin 획기적인: *It is a bold and innovative plan* igeoseun daedamhago hyeoksinjeogin gyehoegida 이것은 대담하고 혁신적인 계획이다
input N 1 tuip 투입 2 imnyeok 입력
inquiry N 1 yeongu 연구 2 jilmun 질문
insect N beolle 벌레
insert, to V sabiphada 삽입하다
inside N anjjok 안쪽
inside of ADV ...ane(seo) ...안에(서)
insight N tongchallyeok 통찰력
insist, persist, to V ugida 우기다, jujanghada 주장하다
inspection N sachal 사찰, jeomgeom 점검, josa 조사
inspector N josagwan 조사관
inspiration N yeonggam 영감; *be inspired* yeonggameul batda 영감을 받다

install, to v seolchihada 설치하다
installation N seolchi 설치
instance N sarye 사례, gyeongu 경우
instant, moment N challa 찰나: *at that very moment* baro geu challae 바로 그 찰나에
instant noodle, ramen N ramyeon 라면
instantly ADV jeuksi 즉시: *I recognized her instantly* naneun geunyeoreul jeuksi araboatda 나는 그녀를 즉시 알아보았다
instead of PREP ...daesine ...대신에: *use forks instead of chopsticks* jeotgarak daesine pokeureul sayonghada 젓가락 대신에 포크를 사용하다
instigate, incite, to v buchugida 부추기다
instinct N bonneung 본능
institution N gigwan 기관
instruct, direct, to v jisihada 지시하다
instruction N 1 seolmyeong 설명 2 jisi 지시
instructor N gangsa 강사
instrument *(musical)* N akgi 악기
insult I N moyok 모욕 II v moyokhada 모욕하다
insurance N boheom 보험
intact, sound, whole ADJ onjeonhada 온전하다
integral, complete ADJ wonmanhada 원만하다
integrate, join, to v hamnyuhada 합류하다: *integration* hamnyu 합류
Integration N tonghap 통합
integrity N jinsilseong 진실성
intellectual ADJ jijeogin 지적인: *If you read more books, you will have more intellectual power* dokseoreul mani halsurok jijeogin neungnyeogi hyangsangdoel geonnida 독서를 많이 할수록 지적인 능력이 향상될 것이다
intelligence N jineung 지능
intelligent ADJ chongmyeonghan 총명한
intend, mean, to v -(eu)ryeogo hada -(으)려고 하다
intended for, to be v ...wihae goandoeda ...위해 고안되다
intensity N gangnyeolham 강렬함
intent N uiji 의지, uihyang 의향
intention N 1 uido 의도: *an intention to cheat* sogiryeoneun uido 속이려는

의도 2 uihyang 의향: *an intention to meet* mannal ruihyang 만날 의향
interest *(money)* N ija 이자: *pay back interest* ijareul gapda 이자를 갚다
interested in, to be v gwansimi itda/inneun 관심이 있다/있는
interesting ADJ heungmiinneun 흥미있는
interfere in, to v naseoda 나서다
interference, meddling N chamgyeon 참견
interior ADJ naebuui 내부의, anjjogui 안쪽의
intermission N makgan 막간: *break during an intermission* makganui hyusik 막간의 휴식
internal ADJ naebuui 내부의: *This is an internal matter* igeoseun naebuui munjeda 이것은 내부의 문제다
international ADJ gukjejeogida, gukje(jeogin) 국제적이다/국제(적인)
international student N yuhaksaeng 유학생
Internet N inteonet 인터넷
interpret, translate, to v tongyeokhada 통역하다: *interpretation* tongyeok 통역; *interpreter* tong.yeoksa 통역사
interrelated, intimate ADJ miljeophada 밀접하다
interrogate, to v kaemutda 캐묻다
interrupt, obstruct, block, to v garomakda 가로막다
intersection N gyocha(ro) 교차(로)
interval N sai 사이
interview N myeonjeop 면접: *an individual interview* gaebyeol myeonjeop 개별 면접
intimate with, friends with, close with, to become v gakkawojida 가까워지다: *become intimate with each other* seoro gakkawojida 서로 가까워지다
intimate, close together ADJ chinhada 친하다, chinhan 친한: *be close to someone* nuguwa chinhada 누구와 친하다; *a close friend* chinhan chingu 친한 친구
into PREP ...aneuro ...안으로
introduce, to v sogaehada 소개하다
introduction N 1 sogae 소개 2 doip 도입
inured to, sick of, to be v igollada

이골나다: *I'm inured to this kind of work* ireon iriramyeon igori natda 이런 일이라면 이골이 났다; *I'm sick of eating ramen* ramyeoniramyeon igori nanda 라면이라면 이골이 난다

invade, to v chimipada 침입하다: *When did the Romans invade Britain?* roma gundaega eonje yeonggugeul chimnyakhaennayo? 로마 군대가 언제 영국을 침략했나요?

invasion N chimip 침입, chimnyak 침략

invalidity, nullity N muhyo 무효

invent, to v balmyeonghada 발명하다

invention N balmyeong 발명

inventory N 1 mongnok 목록 2 jaego 재고

invest, to v tujahada 투자하다: *We get back as much as we had invested* urineun tujahan mankeum dollyeobanneunda 우리는 투자한 만큼 돌려받는다

investigate, research, to v josahada 조사하다

investigation N susa 수사, josa 조사

investment N tuja 투자

invisible ADJ boiji anneun 보이지 않는: *Many stars are invisible to human eyes* maneun byeoldeureun saramui nune boiji anneunda 많은 별들은 사람의 눈에 보이지 않는다

invitation N chodae 초대

invite, to v 1 *(formally)* chodaehada 초대하다 2 *(casual, verbal)* oragohada 오라고하다

invoice, bill N cheongguseo 청구서

involve, to v gwallyeondoeda/-doen 관련되다/-된

involve, include, incorporate, to v pohamhada 포함하다

involvement N gwallyeon 관련, gaeip 개입

Ireland N aillaendeu 아일랜드

iron I N *(equipment)* cheol 철 II v *(to iron clothes)* darida 다리다

irony N aireoni 아이러니

irresolute, indecisive ADJ uyubudanhada 우유부단하다

Islam N iseullamgyo 이슬람교

Islamic ADJ iseullamgyoui 이슬람교의

island N seom 섬

isolated, deserted ADJ oettan 외딴

isolation N gorip 고립

Israeli I N iseuraerin 이스라엘인 II ADJ iseuraerui 이스라엘의

issue N isyu 이슈

It is nothing PHR amugeotdo anida 아무것도 아니다

it is nowhere... PHR eodiedo eopda 어디에도 없다

Italian I N 1 italliain 이탈리아인 2 itallia eo 이탈리아 어 II ADJ italliaui 이탈리아의

item, piece *(counting unit)* N ...gae ...개: *two pieces of chocolate* chokollet du gae 초콜렛 두 개

ivory N sang.a 상아

J

jacket N jaekit 재킷, sangui 상의

jail, prison N gamok 감옥

jam N jaem 잼

January N irwol 일월

Japan N ilbon 일본

Japanese *(language)* N ilboneo 일본어: *Japanese (nationality)* ilbon saram 일본 사람

jar N byeong 병

jaw N teok 턱

jawbone N teokppyeo 턱뼈

jazz N jazz 재즈

jealousy N jiltu 질투

jeans N cheongbaji 청바지

Jesus Christ N Yesu Geuriseudo 예수 그리스도

jet N jeteugi 제트기, bunsa 분사

Jew N yudaein 유대인

jewellery N boseok 보석

Jewish ADJ yudaeinui 유대인의

job, occupation, profession N jigeop 직업, il 일

join, go along, to v gaiphada 가입하다

join in, participate in, to v chamyeohada 참여하다: *join in an election campaign* seongeo undonge chamnyeohada 선거 운동에 참여하다

joint ADJ gongdongui 공동의: *Would you like to open a joint account?* gongdong yegeum gyejwareul yeosigetseumnikka? 공동 예금 계좌를 여시겠습니까?

joke N nongdam 농담

journal N ilji 일지

journalism N jeoneollijeum 저널리즘
journalist N eollonin 언론인
journey N yeohaeng 여행
joy N gippeum 기쁨
judge N pansa 판사: *The judge sentenced the criminal to life in prison* pansaneun geu beominege jongsinhyeongeul seongohaetda 판사는 그 범인에게 종신형을 선고했다
judge, to V jaepanhada 재판하다, pandanhada 판단하다 *Don't judge people by the way they look* oemoro sarameul pandanhaji mara 외모로 사람을 판단하지 마라
judgment N pandan 판단
judicial ADJ sabeobui 사법의
Judo N yudo 유도: *a judo player* yudoseonsu 유도선수
jug, pitcher N jujeonja 주전자
juice N jyuseu 쥬스
July N chirwol 칠월
jump, to V jeompeuhada 점프하다
June N yuwol 유월
jungle N jeonggeul 정글
junior ADJ sonaraeui 손아래의, hubaeui 후배의
jurisdiction N sabeopgwon 사법권
juror N baesimwon 배심원
jury N baesimwon 배심원
just, fair ADJ gongjeonghada/-han 공정하다/-한
just, fair, legal ADJ jeongdanghan 정당한
just, only, merely ADV danji 단지
just a moment!, wait please! INTERJ jamkkanmanyo! 잠깐만요!
just in time ADV machim 마침
just now, right now ADV baro jigeum 바로 지금
justice N jeong.ui 정의
justify, to V jeongdanghwahada 정당화 하다: *The end does not justify the means* mokjeogi sudaneul jeongdanghwahajineun anneunda 목적이 수단을 정당화하지는 않는다
juvenile delinquent N bihaeng cheongsonyeon 비행 청소년

K

kangaroo N kaenggeoru 캥거루
karma N eopbo 업보

KATUSA *(Korean Augmentation of the US army)* N katusa 카투사
keep cool, refrigerate, to V naengjanghada 냉장하다
keep hacking, coughing, to V kollokgeorida 콜록거리다
keep still, to V umjigiji anta/anneun 움직이지 않다/않는다
key N ki 키 (열쇠)
key *(to room)* N yeolsoe 열쇠
keyboard *(of computer)* N kibodeu 키보드
khaki *(color)* N kakisaek 카키색
kick, to V chada 차다: *kick a ball* gongeul ballo chada 공을 발로 차다
kick, storm out, to V bakchada 박차다
kid N ai 아이
kidney N sinjang 신장
kidney beans N gangnangkong 강낭콩
kill, murder, to V jugida 죽이다
killer N sarinja 살인자
killing N sarin 살인
kilogram N killogeuraem 킬로그램
kilometer N killomiteu 킬로미터
kind *(of)*, **sort** *(of)*, **variety** *(of)* N 1 gaji 가지: *various kinds of books* yeoreogajiui chaek 여러가지의 책 2 jongnyu 종류
kind, friendly ADJ chinjeolhada 친절하 다, chinjeolhan 친절한: *be kind to everyone* moduege chinjeolhada 모두에게 친절하다; *a friendly person* chinjeolhan saram 친절한 사람
kind and sensitive ADJ dajeongdagamhan 다정다감한
kindness, favor, grace N eunhye 은혜
king N wang 왕: *kingdom* wangguk 왕국
kiss I N kiseu 키스 II V kiscuhada 키스 하다
kit N joribyongpum seteu 조립용품 세트
kitchen N bu.eok 부엌
kiwi fruit N kiwi 키위
knee N mureup 무릎
kneel, to V mureup kkulta 무릎 꿇다: *He kneeled down on the ground as a sign of surrender* geuneun hangbogui pyosiro mureupeul kkureotda 그는 항복의 표시로 무릎을 꿇었다
knife N kal 칼
knight N gisa 기사: *a knight in armor* gabot ibeun gisa 갑옷 입은 기사

knock, tap, to v dudeurida 두드리다

know, be acquainted with, to v ...e iksukhada ...에 익숙하다

know, to v alda 알다: *know the answer for a question* munjeui dabeul alda 문제의 답을 알다

know how to v -(eu)l jul alda -(으)ㄹ 줄 알다

know...well, to ikhi 익히: *Her name is well known* geunyeoui ireumeul ikhi algo itda 그녀의 이름을 익혀 알고 있다

knowledge N jisik 지식

known ADJ allyeojin 알려진

koala N koalla 코알라

Korea N 1 daehanminguk 대한민국 2 hanguk 한국: *a Korean War* hanguk jeonjaeng 한국 전쟁

Korean N 1 (*language*) han.gugeo 한국어 2 (*nationality*) han.guk saram 한국 사람

Korean paper (*traditional*) N hanji 한지

L

lab N silheomsil 실험실

label N rabel 라벨

labor N nodong 노동

laboratory N yeongusil 연구실

lace, lacework N reiseu 레이스: *a lace-trimmed skirt* reiseuga dallin chima 레이스가 달린 치마

lack N bujok 부족, gyeolpip 결핍: *A lack of sleep had worn her out* geunyeoneun sumyeon bujogeuro pigonhae haetda 그녀는 수면 부족으로 피곤해 했다

lack, to v ...i eopda ...이 없다

lacking ADJ 1 (*missing*) -ga/i eopda/eomneun -가/이 없다/없는 2 (*non-existing*) i/ga eopda/eomneun ...이/가 없다/없는

ladder N sadari 사다리

lady N sungnyeo 숙녀

lake N hosu 호수

lamb, mutton N yanggogi 양고기

lamp N deung 등, ramp 램프

land, shore I N yukji 육지 II v (*land a plane*) changnyukhada 착륙하다

landing N changnyuk 착륙

landmark N juyo jihyeongjimul 주요 지형지물, raendeumakeu 랜드마크: *Is there any landmark around your office?* samusil guncheoe juyo jihyeongjimuri itseumnikka? 사무실 근처에 주요 지형지물이 있습니까?

landscape N punggyeong 풍경

lane (*traffic*) N chaseon 차선

language N eoneo 언어, mal 말

languid ADJ 1 (*drowsy*) nareunhada 나른하다: *a drowsy voice* nareunhan moksori 나른한 목소리 2 (*exhausted*) nogonhada 노곤하다

lap, splash, to v challanggeorida 찰랑 거리다

large ADJ keun 큰: *They pitched a large tent over the floor* geudeureun badak gwie keun cheonmageul chyeotda 그들은 바닥 위에 큰 천막을 쳤다

largely ADV 1 keuge 크게 2 juro 주로: *What he says is largely false* geuga malhaneun geoseun juro geojinnida 그가 말하는 것은 주로 거짓이다

larva, caterpillar N aebeolle 애벌레

laser N reijeo 레이저

last month of pregnancy, the N mansak 만삭

last, continue, endure, to v jisokhada 지속하다

last night N jinan bam 지난 밤

last week N jinan ju 지난 주

last year N jangnyeon 작년

late ADJ neutda 늦다, neujeun 늦은: *late lunch* neujeun jeomsim 늦은 점심; *late at night* bamneukke 밤 늦게; *late summer heat* neutdeowi 늦더위

late child (*of old parents*) N neutdungi 늦둥이: *have a late child at age 40* sasibe neutdungireul boda 40에 늦둥 이를 보았다

lately ADV choegeun(e) 최근(에)

later ADV najung.e 나중에

Latin ADJ ratinui 라틴의

laugh, to v utda 웃다

laugh at, to v biutda 비웃다

laughable ADJ gasoropda 가소롭다; useupda 우습다

laughter N useum 웃음

launch N balsa 발사: *The launch of the space shuttle was a great success* uju wangbokseonui balsaneun daeseong-gongieotda 우주 왕복선의 발사는 대성공이었다

launch, to v 1 sijakhada 시작하다 2 chulsihada 출시하다: *Click Finish to*

L

launch the recovery application bokgu eungyongpeurogeuraemeul sijakharyeomyeon machimeul keullikhasipsio 복구 응용프로그램을 시작하려면 마침을 클릭하십시오

laundry, dry cleaner N setakso 세탁소

lava N yongam 용암

lavender N rabendeo 라벤더

lawful ADJ matda 맞다, manneun 맞는

lawmaker N ipbeopja 입법자

lawn, meadow N pulbat 풀밭

laws, legislation N beop 법

lawsuit N sosong 소송: *I'm sure he will lose this lawsuit* geuga ibeon sosongseo jil geotsira hwaksinhanda 그가 이번 소송에서 질 것이라 확신한다

lawyer N byeonhosa 변호사

lax, slack ADJ heosulhada 허술하다

lay, to V nupida 눕히다

layer N cheung 층: *ozone layer* ojon cheung 오존 층

lazy ADJ ge.eureuda 게으르다, ge.eureun 게으른

lead, to V 1 *(take the lead)* rideuhada 리드하다 2 *(guide)* annaehada 안내하다

leader N jidoja 지도자

leadership N jidoryeok 지도력

leading ADJ 1 gajang jungyohan 가장 중요한 2 seonduui 선두의

leading question N yudosinmun 유도신문

leaf N ip 잎

league, federation, union N yeonmaeng 연맹

leak, to V saeda 새다

lean, rely on, to V uijihada 의지하다: *rely on a friend* chingureul uijihada 친구를 의지하다

leap *(up)***, jump, to** V nalttwida 날뛰다

learn, to V bae.uda 배우다

learned, educated ADJ yusikhada 유식하다

learning N hakseup 학습

least *(smallest amount)* N choeso 최소

leather N gajuk 가죽

leave, depart, to V tteonada 떠나다

leave, put, check *(in)***, deposit, to** V matgida 맡기다

leave, save, set aside, to V namgida 남기다

leave alone, to V gamanduda 가만두다: *I won't leave him alone. I'll give it to*

him geureul gamanduji anketda 그를 가만두지 않겠다

leave behind and come, to V dugo oda 두고 오다

leave behind and go, to V dugo gada 두고 가다

lecture, classes *(at university)* N gang. ui 강의: *lecturer (at university)* gangsa 강사

led, guided, to be V ikkeullida 이끌리다: *led to school by mom's hand* eomeoni sone ikkeullyeo hakgyoe gatda 어머니 손에 이끌려 학교에 갔다

left, remaining ADJ namda 남다, nameun 남은: *leftover (food)* nameun eumsik 남은 음식

left-hand side N oenjjok 왼쪽

leg N dari 다리: *sprain one's legs* darireul ppida 다리를 삐다

legacy N yusan 유산

legal, legitimate ADJ hapbeopjeogida 합법적이다, hapbeopjeogin 합법적인: *a legitimate government* hapbeopjeok jeongbu 합법적 정부

legally ADV beomnyuljeogeuro 법률적으로: *They are employed legally* geudeureun beomnyuljeogeuro goyongdoeeotda 그들은 법률적으로 고용되었다

legend N jeonseol 전설

legislative ADJ ipbeobui 입법의

legislator N ipbeopja 입법자

legislature N ipbeopbu 입법부

leisure-sports N repocheu 레포츠

lemon, citrus N remon 레몬: *lemonade* remoneideu 레모네이드

lend, to V billyeojuda 빌려주다: *lend money to a person* doneul billyeojuda 돈을 빌려주다

length N giri 길이

lens N renjeu 렌즈

less *(smaller amount)* ADJ deo jeokda/jeogeun 더 적다/적은

lessen, lighten, ease, to V deolda 덜다

lesson N reseun 레슨, *(class)* su.eop 수업

let, allow, to V -ge hada -게 하다

let go, leave behind, to V teolda 털다: *leave one's worry behind* geunsim geokjeongeul teolda 근심 걱정을 털다

let's learn PHR bae-uja 배우자: *Let's*

L

learn Korean hangugeoreul baeuja 한 국어를 배우자

letter N pyeonji 편지

lettuce N sangchu 상추

level I N 1 *(equality)* pyeongjun 평준 2 *(standard)* sujun 수준: *an economical level* gyeongje sujun 경제 수준 II ADJ *(even)* panpanhada 판판하다

liability N 1 chaegim 책임 2 buchae 부채

liberal N jayujuuija 자유주의자

liberal ADJ jayujuuiui 자유주의의

liberty N jayu 자유: *They are longing for liberty* geudeureun jayureul galmanghago itda 그들은 자유를 갈망하고 있다

library N doseogwan 도서관: *librarian* saseo 사서

licence, permit N heoga 허가, myeon-heojjeung 면허증, raisenseu 라이센스

lick, to V haltta 핥다: *lick a plate* jeop-sireul halda 접시를 핥다

lid N ttukkeong 뚜껑

lie, tell a falsehood, to V geojinmal-hada 거짓말하다

lie down, to V nupda 눕다

lie face down, prostrate, to V eop-deurida 엎드리다

life N insaeng 인생, saengmyeong 생명

life, breath of life N moksum 목숨

lifestyle N saenghwal yangsik 생활 양식

lifetime N pyeongsaeng 평생

lift I N *(elevator)* seungganggi 승강기 II V *(raise)* (deureo)ollida (들어)올리다

light I N 1 bit 빛 2 *(lamp)* bul 불: *turn off the light* bureul kkeuda 불을 끄다; *turn on the light* bureul kyeoda 불을 켜다 II ADJ 1 *(not heavy/severe)* gabyeopda 가볍다, gabyeo.un 가벼운 2 *(bright)* bakda 밝다, balgeun 밝은: *a bright light* balgeun bul 밝은 불 3 *(casual)* gatteunhada 가뜬하다

light up, to V bakhida 밝히다

lighter N raiteo 라이터

lightly ADV gatteunhi 가뜬히

lightning N beon.gae 번개

lightweight *(boxer)* N raiteu 라이트

like, as PREP ...cheoreom ...처럼: *like an angel* cheonsa cheoreom 천사처럼

like, care for, be fond of, be pleased by, to V joahada 좋아하다

likelihood N ganeungseong 가능성,

gamang 가망: *There is no longer the likelihood of a World War* deo isang segyedaejeonui ganeungseongeun eopda 더 이상 세계대전의 가능성은 없다

likewise, alike ADV machan.gajiro 마찬 가지로

lilac N raillak 라일락

limb N 1 pal 팔 2 lalgae 날개

limit I N 1 *(boundary)* hangye 한계 2 *(restriction)* jehan 제한 II *(restrict)* jehanhada 제한하다

limitation N hangye 한계, jeyak제약: *Disability is a physical limitation on your life* jangaeneun saenghwalhaneun de mullijeogin jeyagi doenda 장애는 생활하는 데 물리적인 제약이 된다

limited, finite ADJ yuhanhada 유한하다

limousine N rimujin 리무진

line *(mark)* N seon 선: *a straight line* jikseon 직선

line *(telephone's)* **is busy!** PHR tong-hwajung.ida 통화중이다

line up, queue, to V julseoda 줄서다

lingering imagery N yeoun 여운

linguistics N eohak 어학

link N ringkeu 링크: *link blog* beullo-geureul lingkeuhada 블로그를 링크하다

lion N saja 사자

lip-sync N ripsingkeu 립싱크

lips N ipsul 입술: *full lips* dotomhan ipsul 도톰한 입술

lipstick N ripseutik 립스틱

liquid N aekche 액체

liquid ADJ aekcheui 액체의

list I N riseuteu 리스트 II V myeongdan 명단

listen attentively to, to V saegyeo-deutda 새겨듣다

listener N deunneun saram 듣는 사람, cheongchwija 청취자

literally ADV munja geudaero 문자 그대 로: *The beach was literally a sea of people* haebyeoneun munja geudaero insaninhaeyeotda 해변은 문자 그대로 인산인해였다

literary ADJ munhagui 문학의

literature N munhak 문학

little ADJ 1 *(not much)* jeokda 적다, jeogeun 적은 2 *(small, tiny, short in height)* jakda 작다, jageun 작은

L

live, be alive, to v salda 살다

live off, to v eonchyeosalda 얹혀살다

lively motion, vividness N saeng-dong 생동

liver N gan 간

living, livelihood N saenggye 생계

load, to v sitda 싣다: *load a truck* teureoge mulgeoneul sitda 트럭에 물건을 싣다

loan N daebu 대부

lobby N robi 로비, hol 홀

local ADJ jiyeogui 지역의, hyeonjiui 현지의: *The doctors have been warmly welcomed by local people* geu uisadeureun hyeonjiui jumindeurege ttatteutan hwannyeongeul badatda 그 의사들은 현지의 주민들에게 따뜻한 환영을 받았다

locate, to v 1 (wichie)duda (위치에)두다 2 (wichireul)chajanaeda (위치를)찾아내다

location N jangso 장소

lock I N jamulsoe 자물쇠 II v jamgeuda 잠그다: *lock the door* muneul jamgeuda 문을 잠그다

locked, fastened, to be v jamgida 잠기다: *The door is locked* muni jamgida 문이 잠기다

lodging N sukso 숙소

log N tongnamu 통나무

logic N nolli 논리

logical adj nollijeogin 논리적인: *I think men are more logical than women* naneun namjaga yeojaboda deo nollijeogirago saenggakhanda 나는 남자가 여자보다 더 논리적이라고 생각한다

loiter (about), **wander, to** v baehoehada 배회하다

London N reondeon 런던

loneliness N oeroum 외로움: *She can't stand loneliness* geunyeoneun oeroumeul gyeondiji motanda 그녀는 외로움을 견디지 못한다

lonely ADJ oeropda 외롭다, oeroun 외로운

long (length) ADJ gilda 길다, gin 긴

long distance N janggeori 장거리

long for, thirst for, to v galguhada 갈구하다

long holidays N yeonhyu 연휴

longing, yearning N samo 사모

longtime ADJ orae, oraen 오래, 오랜

look after, take care of, to v dolboda 돌보다: *take care of a child* aireul dolboda 아이를 돌보다

look after oneself, to v apgarim hada 앞가림하다

look at, to v 1 (watch, see, view) boda 보다 2 (watch) baraboda 바라보다

look down upon, to v eopsinnyeogida 업신여기다

look into, to v araboda 알아보다: *look into the market value* sisereul raraboda 시세를 알아보다

look like I ADJ -rmoyangida -ㄹ모양이다 II v ...cheoreom boida ...처럼 보이다: *look like an angel* cheonsacheoreom boida 천사처럼 보이다

lookout N mang 망: *keep a lookout* mangeul boda 망을 보다

lookout shed N wondumak 원두막

look up, to v chajaboda 찾아보다

look, seem, appear, to v -ge boida -게 보이다, ...(eu)ro boida ...(으)로 보이다

look, seem, be likely, to ADJ -rgeot gatda -ㄹ것 같다: *It looks like it's going to rain* biga ol geot gatda 비가 올 것 같다

look! PHR boseyo! 보세요!

loop N gori 고리

loose ADJ 1 (baggy) heolgeopda 헐겁다 2 (wobbly) heundeulheundeulhada/-han 흔들흔들하다/-한

Los Angeles N roseuaenjelleseu 로스앤젤레스

lose, be defeated, to v jida 지다

lose, mislay, to v ireobeorida 잃어버리다: *lose a bag* gabangeul ireobeorida 가방을 잃어버리다; *lost (missing)* ireobeorin 잃어버린

lose, suffer a loss, to v mitjida 밑지다, sonhaeboda 손해보다

lose weight, become thin, become slim, to v mareuda 마르다

loss, forfeiture N sangsil 상실

lost property N bunsilmul 분실물

lost, missing, to be ADJ eopseojin 없어진

lotion N rosyeon 로션

lots of ADJ maneun 많은

lottery N bokgwon 복권

loud ADJ soriga keuda/keun 소리가 크다/큰

L

lounge N raunji 라운지
love I N sarang 사랑 II V saranghada 사랑하다
lovely, adorable, endearing ADJ sarangseureopda, sarangseureo.un 사랑스럽다/–스러운
lover N yeonin 연인
low ADJ natda 낮다, najeun 낮은: *low (atmospheric) pressure* jeogiap 저기압
low form of speech, casual form of speech N banmal 반말
lower *(half of the)* **body** N habansin 하반신
lower class N hageup 하급
loyal ADJ chungseongseureoun 충성스러운, chungsilhan 충실한: *He was loyal to me* geuneun naege chungseongseureowotda 그는 나에게 충성스러웠다
loyalty N chungseongsim 충성심, chungseong 충성
luck N un 운: *luck for (in) business* saeop bun 사업 운; *luck with (on) exam* siheom un 시험 운
lucky, fortunate ADJ un jota/jo.eun 운 좋다/좋은
luggage, suitcase N yeohaenggabang 여행가방
lullaby N jajangga 자장가
lumber N gangmok 각목
lump N eungeori 응어리: *lumps in dough* banjuk eungeori 반죽 응어리
lunch N 1 reonchi 런치 2 *(mid-day meal)* jeomsim siksa 점심 식사: *to eat lunch* jeomsim siksahada 점심 식사하다
lungs N pye 폐: *lung capacity* pye-hwallyang 폐활량
luxurious, extravagant ADJ sachiseu-reopda, sachiseureo.un 사치스럽다/–스러운

M

machine N gigye 기계
machinery N gigyeryu 기계류
mad, crazy, insane ADJ michida, michin 미치다
madam *(term of address)* N bu.in 부인
magazine N japji 잡지
magic N mabeop 마법, *(witchcraft)* yosul 요술

magnet N jaseok 자석: *magnetism* jaryeok 자력
magnetic ADJ jaseongui 자성의
magnificent, grand ADJ eurieurihada 으리으리하다
magnify, blow up, to V hwakdaehada 확대하다: *magnify an object with a microscope* hyeonmigyeongeuro hwakdaehada 현미경으로 확대하다
magnitude N 1 gyumo 규모 2 jijin gyumo 지진 규모
mahjong N majak 마작
maid, maidservant N hanyeo 하녀
maiden, girl, wife, bride N saekksi 색시
mail, post N upyeonmul 우편물
main, major, primary ADJ juyohan 주요한
mainstream ADJ juryuui 주류의
maintain, to V yujihada 유지하다
maintenance N yuji 유지
major ADJ juyohan 주요한
majority vote N dasugyeol 다수결
make, form, to V iruda 이루다
make, produce, to V mandeulda 만들다
make a compromise, to V tahyeopada 타협하다
make a mess, to N eojireuda 어지르다
make efforts, struggle, to V aesseuda 애쓰다
make light of, look down on, to V yatboda 얕보다
make light of a person V manmanha-geboda 만만하게 보다
make sb cry, to V ullida 울리다
makeup N meikeueop 메이크업
Malaysia N malleisia 말레이시아
male N namseong 남성
male, man N sanai 사나이
malicious, spiteful, vicious ADJ dokhada 독하다: *She is vicious* geu yeojaneun dokhada 그 여자는 독하다
malign, slander, to V eumhaehada 음해하다
mall N shopping mol 쇼핑 몰
malnutrition N yeongyangsiljo 영양실조
man N namja 남자, sanae 사내
man and woman N namnyeo 남녀
manage, to V 1 *(handle)* burida 부리다 2 *(succeed)* cheorihaenaeda 처리해내다: *manage to bring sth to a success*

eoryeoun ireul cheorihaenaeda 어려운
일을 처리해내다

management N gyeongyeong 경영

manager N bujang 부장, *(person in
charge)* gwallichaegimja 관리책임자

managing ADJ cheorihaneun 처리하는

mandate N gwonhan 권한

mango N manggo 망고

manipulate, to V jojonghada 조종하다

manners N yei 예의

manners, etiquette N yejeol 예절:
table manners siktagyejeol 식탁예절

mansion N 1 daejeotaek 대저택 2
maensyeon 맨션

manual N seolmyeongseo 설명서

manual ADJ sudongui 수동의

manufacture, produce, make, to V
jejohada 제조하다

manufacturer N jejosa 제조사

manufacturing N jejoeop 제조업

many, much ADJ manta 많다, maneun
많은

map N jido 지도: *a map of the world*
segyejido 세계지도

maple *(tree)* N danpungnamu 단풍나무

marathon N maraton 마라톤

marble N 1 daeriseok 대리석 2 guseul
구슬

March N samwol 삼월

margin N yeobaek 여백, majin 마진

marine N haebyeong 해병

mark, stain N jaguk 자국

marker N makeo 마커

market N sijang 시장

marketing N maketing 마케팅

marketplace N sijang 시장

marking, grading N chaejeom 채점

marksman, shooter N sasu 사수

marriage N gyeolhon saenghwal 결혼
생활

marry, get married, to V gyeolhonhada 결혼하다, gyeolhonhan 결혼한

marsh, swamp N neup 늪

mask N gamyeon 가면, maseukeu 마스
크, tal 탈: *wear a mask* tareul sseuda
탈을 쓰다

mass N deongeori 덩어리, muri 무리: *A
mass of rock fell down the mountain*
bawideongeoriga san araero gulleo
tteoreojyeotda 바위덩어리가 산 아래
로 굴러 떨어졌다

mass ADJ maneun 많은

massage, to V masajihada 마사지하다

massive ADJ geodaehan 거대한

master N 1 juin 주인 2 darin 달인: *He is
a servant true to his master* geuneun
geuui juinege chungjikhan hainida
그는 그의 주인에게 충직한 하인이다

mat N kkalgae 깔개

match, game N sihap 시합

matches N seongnyang 성냥

mate N chingu 친구

material, ingredient N jaeryo 재료:
natural materials cheonyeonjaeryo 천연재료

materiality N yuhyeong 유형

math, mathematics N suhak 수학:
I have a math exam today at school
naneun oneul hakgyoeseo suhaksi-
heomi iseoseo 나는 오늘 학교에서
수학시험이 있었어

matter, substance N muljil 물질

mattress N maeteuriseu 매트리스

mature ADJ eoreunseureopda 어른스럽
다: *mature for one's age* naie bihaeseo eoreunseureopda 나이에 비해서
어른스럽다

maximum ADJ choegoui 최고의

May N owol 오월

may *(might)* **be** V -rneunjido moreuda
-ㄹ는지도 모르다: *That may be pos-
sible* ama geureolleunjido moreunda
아마 그럴는지도 모른다

may, can, be allowed to I ADJ -eo/
ado jota -어/아도 좋다 II V -a/eodo
jota -아/어도 좋다: *you may eat* meogeo
도 좋다; *you may look* boado 좋다

may, would *(conjecture)* V -get- -겠-

mayor N sijang 시장

meal N siksa 식사

mean, signify, to V uimihada 의미하다:
Red light means 'stop' ppalgan
bureun jeongjireul uimihanda 빨간 불
은 '정지'를 의미한다

meaning N uimi 의미

meaningful ADJ uimi inneun 의미 있는

meantime N geudongan 그동안

meanwhile N geu dong.an 그 동안

measure, to V jaeda 재다

measurement, size N chisu 치수

meat N gogi 고기: *meatball* gogi wanja
고기 완자; *meat juice* yukjeup 육즙

mechanic N 1 jeongbigong 정비공 2
gigyehak 기계학

mechanical ADJ gigyejeogin 기계적인

M

mechanism N 1 gigye jangchi 기계 장치 2 bangbeop 방법

medal N medal 메달: *This medal is to honor the winner* i medareun useungjareul pyochanghagi wihan geotsida 이 메달은 우승자를 표창하기 위한 것이다

meddle in, butt in, to V chamgyeonhada 참견하다

meddlesome, nosy ADJ ojirap 오지랖: *be nosy* ojirapi neolda 오지랖이 넓다

media N maeche 매체: *The corporations control the media* daegieopdeuri maechereul keonteurolhanda 대기업들이 매체를 컨트롤한다

medical ADJ uihakui 의학의: *medical insurance* uiryoboheom 의료보험; *medical school* uidae 의대

medication N yak 약: *This medication did not help him at all* i yageun jogeumdo geuege doumi doeji anatda 이 약은 조금도 그에게 도움이 되지 않았다

medicine N 1 uihak 의학 2 yak 약

meditation, contemplation N sasaek 사색: *be absorbed in meditation* sasaege jamgida 사색에 잠기다

medium N sudan 수단, maegaemul 매개물

medium ADJ jungganui 중간의, botongui 보통의

meek, docile ADJ onsunhada 온순하다

meet, to V 1 majuchida 마주치다 2 mannada 만나다

meeting N moim 모임: *a regular meeting* jeonggi moim 정기 모임

melon N chamoe 참외

melt, thaw, to V nokda 녹다

member N hoewon 회원: *honorary member* myeongyehoewon 명예회원; *life member* pyeongsaenghoewon 평생회원

member, employee N sawon 사원: *an employee of a company* hoesaui sawon 회사의 사원

membership N hoewon 회원, membeosip 멤버십

memories N chu.eok 추억, gi.eok 기억

memorization N amgi 암기

memory *(one's power of)* N amgiryeok 암기력

menstruate, to V saengnihada 생리하다: *menstruation* wolgyeong 월경

mental ADJ 1 jeongsinui 정신의 2 michin 미친

mentally ADV jeongsinjeogeuro 정신적으로

mention N eongeup 언급

mention, to V eongeupada 언급하다

mentor N mento 멘토: *Mentor and mentee meet weekly for a year* mentowa mentineun illyeon dongan maeju mannanda 멘토와 멘티는 일년 동안 매주 만난다

menu N menyu 메뉴

merchant N sangin 상인

mercy N jabi 자비: *show mercy to* jabireul bepulda 자비를 베풀다

mere ADJ gyeou 겨우

merely, simply ADV ojik 오직, daman 다만: *I simply wish his happiness* naneun daman geuga haengbokhagil baral ppunida 나는 다만 그가 행복하길 바랄 뿐이다

merger of political parties N hapdang 합당

merit N gachi 가치

mess, wreck N eongmang 엉망

message N mesiji 메시지

messy, chaotic ADJ eongmang.ida, eongmang.in 엉망이다, 엉망인

metal N geumsok 금속

metaphor N eunnyu 은유, biyu 비유

meter N 1 miteo 미터 2 gyeryanggi 계량기

method N bangbeop 방법: *He worked out a new method* geuneun saeroun bangbeobeul jjanaetda 그는 새로운 방법을 짜냈다

meticulous, precise *(character)* ADJ binteumeopda/binteumeomn eun 빈틈없다/빈틈없는: *a meticulous character* binteumeomneun kkomkkomhan seonggyeok 빈틈없는 꼼꼼한 성격

metropolitan ADJ daedosiui 대도시의

Mexican ADJ meksikoui 멕시코의

microphone N maikeu 마이크

middle, center N gaunde 가운데, junggan 중간

middle: in the middle of doing something ADV -neun jung -는 중

midnight N 1 hanbamjjung 한밤중 2 jajeong 자정

midst N jungang 중앙

migraine N pyeondutong 편두통

migration N iju 이주

migratory bird N cheolsae 철새

mild, gentle, tame, meek ADJ sunhada 순하다, sunhan 순한: *mild cigarettes* sunhan dambae 순한 담배

military ADJ gunsa(ui) 군사(의)

milk N uyu 우유

million NUM baengman 백만

mind, bother, notice, to V sin.gyeong sseuda 신경 쓰다

mind, thought N yeomdu 염두: *keep a thought in mind* saenggageul yeomdue duda 생각을 염두에 두다

mine N nae geot 내 것

mineral N gwangmul 광물, mineral 미네랄

minibus N minibeoseu 미니버스

minimal ADJ choesoui 최소의

minimize, to V choesohwahada 최소화 하다, chuksohada 축소하다

minimum ADJ choesohanui 최소한의

minimum N choesohando 최소한도

minister N janggwan 장관: *The story is about the new minister* geu iyagineun saeroun janggwane daehan geotsida 그 이야기는 새로운 장관에 대한 것이다

minor ADJ jageun 작은

minority N sosu 소수

minor role N dannyeok 단역

minus N maineoseu 마이너스

minute N bun 분: *It's 20 (minutes) past three* sesi isipbun 3시 20분

miracle N gijeok 기적: *It's a miracle that he wasn't killed* geuga jukji aneun geoseun gijeogida 그가 죽지 않은 것은 기적이다

mirror N geo.ul 거울

miscarry *(a baby)*, **to** V yusanhada 유산하다: *have a miscarriage* aireul yusanhada 아이를 유산하다

mischief, fun N jangnan 장난

misconception N oin 오인

misery N bicham 비참

misfortune, unhappiness N bulhaeng 불행

mishap, accident N ibyeon 이변

miss, to V I *(thinking of loved ones)*, geuriwohada 그리워하다 2 *(not to meet)* eotgallida 엇갈리다: *missed each other on the way* giri eotgallida

길이 엇갈리다 3 *(cutting class, attendance, etc)* gyeolseokhada 결석 하다 4 *(feel the absence)* aswiwohada 아쉬워하다 5 *(lose an opportunity)* nochida 놓치다

miss, young female adult N 1 agassi 아가씨 2 yang 양: *Ms. Kim!* gim nyang! 김 양!

missile N misail 미사일: *The missile homed in on the target* misairi pyojeogeul hyanghae naagago iseotda 미 사일이 표적을 향해 나아가고 있었다

missing ADJ 1 eopseojin 없어진 2 ppajin 빠진

mission, calling N samyeong 사명

missionary N seongyosa 선교사

mistake N silssu 실수, chago 착오

mistake A for B, delude oneself, to V chakgakhada 착각하다

mistake A for B, be confused, to V hondonghada 혼동하다

misunderstanding N ohae 오해

mix together, to V beomurida 버무리다

mix, blend, to V seokda 섞다: *mix paints* mulgameul seokda 물감을 섞다

mixed, blended, mingled, to be V seokkida, seokkin 섞이다, 섞인

moan, pour out, to V hasoyeonhada 하소연하다: *moan in tears* nunmullo hasoyeoneul hada 눈물로 하소연을 하다

mobile ADJ 1 idonghaneun 이동하는 2 umjigimi jayuroun 움직임이 자유로운

mode N bangsik 방식

model, example N mobeom 모범

moderate ADJ botongui 보통의, jungganui 중간의

modern ADJ hyeondae(ui) 현대(의)

modest ADJ 1 *(simple, unostentatious)* susuhada 수수하다, susuhan 수수한 2 *(courteous)* dasogotada 다소곳하다

modestly, shyly ADV dasogosi 다소곳이

modify, to V sujeonghada 수정하다

molar *(tooth)* N eogeumni 어금니

molecule N bunja 분자

mollusks N yeonchedongmul 연체동물

mom N eomma 엄마: *Mom is an ordinary housewife* eommaneun pyeongbeomhan jubuda 엄마는 평범한 주부다

moment, instant N sun.gan 순간: *a*

M

crucial moment gyeoljeongjeogin sungan 결정적인 순간

momentum N tallyeok 탄력

Monday N woryoil 월요일

money N don 돈

monitor *(of computer)* N moniteo 모니터

monkey N wonsungi 원숭이: *The monkey fell off the tree* geu wonsungineun namueseo tteoreojyeotda 그 원숭이는 나무에서 떨어졌다

monopolize, to V doksikhada 독식하다

monopoly N doksik 독식

monster, goblin N yogoe 요괴

month N dal 달: *next month* daeum dal 다음 달

month to *(by)* **month, monthly** ADV dadari 다달이: *pay rent monthly* jipsereul dadari naeda 집세를 다달이 내다

monthly rent N wolse 월세

monthly salary N wolgeup 월급: *pay monthly salary* wolgeubeul juda 월급을 주다

monument N ginyeommul 기념물

mooch off, sponge off, to V bilbutda 빌붙다

mood N gibun 기분

moon N dal 달: *a full moon* boreumdal 보름달

moral ADJ dodeokjeogin 도덕적인

more *(comparative)* ADV deo 더

more of *(quantity)* ADJ deo maneun 더 많은

(more) than *(comparison)* ADV ...boda (deo) ...보다 (더): *Friendship is more valuable than money* ujeongeun don boda deo gwihada 우정은 돈 보다 더 귀하다

morning N achim 아침, ojeon 오전: *8 in the morning* ojeon yeodeolsi 오전 8시

mortality N jugeumeul pihal su eopseum 죽음을 피할 수 없음, samang 사망

mortgage N dambo daechul 담보 대출

mortuary N binso 빈소

mosaic N mojaikeu 모자이크

mosquito N mogi 모기

moss, liverwort N ikki 이끼

most *(superlative)* ADV gajang 가장

most *(superlative)*, **number 1** ADV jeil 제일: *most important thing* jeil jun-gyohan geot 제일 중요한 것

most *(the most of)* N daebubun 대부분

mostly, mainly ADV juro 주로

moth N nabang 나방

mother N eomeoni 어머니: *mother-in-law* jangmo 장모; *mother-in-law (husband's mother)* sieomeoni 시어머니

motion sickness N meolmi 멀미

motivate, to V donggi buyeohada 동기 부여하다

motivation N donggibuyeo 동기부여: *Most people said that pay was their main motivation for working* maneun saramdeureun bosuga geudeurui judoen donggibuyeora malhanda 많은 사람들은 보수가 그들의 주된 동기부여라 말한다

motive N donggi 동기, iyu 이유: *The spiritual strength is just the motive power of victory* jeongsillyeogi baro seungniui iyuida 정신력이 바로 승리의 이유이다

motor, engine N moteo 모터

motorcycle N otobai 오토바이

moult N teolgari 털갈이

mount, stud, to V bakda 박다: *mount a ruby onto a necklace* mokgeorie rubireul bakda 목걸이에 루비를 박다

mountain N san 산

mouse N 1 *(animal)* saengjwi 생쥐 2 *(of computer)* mauseu 마우스

moustache N kossuyeom 콧수염

mouth N ip 입: *have a big mouth* ibi ssada 입이 싸다

move, to V isahada 이사하다

move, shift, to V omgida 옮기다: *move to a different department* buseoreul omgida 부서를 옮기다

movement, motion N dongjak 동작

movie N yeonghwa 영화: *The movie has been showing for three months* geu yeonghwaneun sam gaewol jjae sangyeongdoego itda 그 영화는 삼 개월 째 상영되고 있다

movie theater N yeonghwagwan 영화관

Mr N *(namja)...ssi* (남자)...씨, ...nim ...님

Mrs N *(yeoja)...buin* (여자)...부인

Ms N *(yeoja)...ssi* ...씨

much, quite ADV dabunhi 다분히

mud N jinheuk 진흙: *We tugged her*

car that was stuck in the mud urineun jinheulge ppajin geunyeoui chareul kkeureonaetda 우리는 진흙에 빠진 그 녀의 차를 끌어냈다

muddy, turbid ADJ takhada 탁하다

multinational N dagukjeok 다국적

multiple ADJ 1 maneun 많은 2 bokhap-jeogin 복합적인

multipurpose ADJ damokjeok 다목적

municipal ADJ jibang jachijeui 지방 자치제의, siui 시의

murder N sarin 살인

murder, to V salhaehada 살해하다

muscle N geunyuk 근육

museum N bangmulgwan 박물관

mushroom N beoseot 버섯

music N eumak 음악

musical ADJ eumakjeogin 음악적인

musician N eumakga 음악가, myu-jisyeon 뮤지션: *The musician played the song again at the request* yocheonge uihaeseo geu eumakganeun gyesokhaeseo gogeul yeonjuhaetda 요청에 의해서 그 음악가는 계속해서 곡을 연주했다

Muslim N iseullamgyodo 이슬람교도

must, have to, ought to V -a/eoya hada −아/어야 하다, -eo/aya hada −어/아야 하다

mutter, to V 1 jungeolgeorida 중얼거리다 2 tudeolgeorida 투덜거리다

mutual ADJ seoroui 서로의: *I met him through a mutual friend of ours* geuwa naneun seoroui chingureul tonghaeseo alge dwaetda 그와 나는 서로의 친구를 통해서 알게 됐다

my goodness! INTERJ eomeona, sesang.e! 이머나, 세상에!

my, mine PRON na.ui 나의 (것): *my room* naui bang 나의 방; *it's mine* naui geonnida 나의 것이다

myriad years *(ten thousand years)* N mannyeon 만년

mysterious phenomenon N johwa 조화

mystery N susukkekki 수수께끼, miseuteori 미스터리: *The mystery novel has an intricate plot* i miseuteori soseoreun guseongi bokjapada 이 미스터리 소설은 구성이 복잡하다

myth N sinhwa 신화

nag, henpeck, to V bagajiguelda 바가지 긁다

nail *(finger)* N sontop 손톱

nail *(spike)* N mot 못

naive, innocent ADJ cheonjin-nanmanhada 천진난만하다

naked ADJ beolgeobeoseun 벌거벗은

naked eye N yugan 육안: *too small to tell with the naked eye* neomu jagaseo yuganeuroneun sikbyeori eoryeopda 너무 작아서 육안으로는 식별이 어렵다

naked, to be V beolgeobeotda 벌거벗다

naked, to get V balgabeotda 발가벗다

name, given name N ireum 이름

name tag N ireumpyo 이름표

narcotics, drug N mayak 마약

narrative N myosa 묘사

narrow ADJ jopda 좁다, jobeun 좁은

narrow-minded ADJ 1 *(petty)* ongjol-hada 옹졸하다: *a narrow-minded man, a petty man* ongjolhan saram 옹졸한 사람 2 *(inflexible, stubborn)* makhida/makin 막히다/막힌

nasty ADJ 1 yeokgyeoun 역겨운 2 mot-doen 못된: *A nasty smell greeted my nose as I entered there* geu gose deureoseoja yeokgyeoun naemsaega punggyeotda 그 곳에 들어서자 역겨운 냄새가 풍겼다

nation, country N gukga 국가

national ADJ gukga(ui) 국가(의)

nationality N gukjeok 국적

nationwide ADV jeongukjeogeuro 전국적으로: *A nationwide hunt is under way to find the killer* sarinjareul japgi wihan susaga jeongukjeogeuro jinhaeng jungida 실인지 를 잡기 위한 수사가 전국적으로 진행 중이다

native N wonjumin 원주민

natural ADJ jayeon(ui) 자연의: *natural sciences* igwa 이과

naturally ADV jayeonseureopge 자연스럽게

nature N jayeon 자연

naughty, rude ADJ beoreuteopda, beo-reuteomneun 버릇없다, 버릇없는: *be rude* beoreuseopda 버릇없다

nauseous, sick, to be V meseukke-opda 메스껍다

naval ADJ haegunui 해군의

N

near ADJ gakkaun 가까운
near ADV gakkai 가까이
nearby ADJ gakkaun 가까운
nearby ADV gakkaie 가까이에
nearly ADV eolchu 얼추: *nearly the same* eolchu biseutada 얼추 비슷하다
neat, tidy ADJ 1 danjeonghada 단정하다, danjeonghan 단정한 2 jeongdondoen 정돈된
necessity, need N piryo 필요
neck N mok 목
neckband, collar N otgit 옷깃: *pull up one's collar* otgiseul seuda 옷깃을 세우다
necklace N mokgeori 목걸이: *a pearl necklace* jinju mokgeori 진주 목걸이
necktie, tie N nektai 넥타이
need, to V piryohada 필요하다
needle N baneul 바늘
negative ADJ 1 bujeongjeogin 부정적인 2 sogeukjeogin 소극적인: *He answered in a negative way* geuui daedabeun bujeongjeogieotda 그의 대답은 부정적이었다
negotiation N hyeopsang 협상
neighbor N iut(saram) 이웃(사람)
neighborhood N iut 이웃, geuncheo 근처
neighboring ADJ iusui 이웃의, geuncheoui 근처의
neither ADJ eoneu jjokdo -ji anta 어느 쪽도 -지 않다, eoneu jjokdo ..anida 어느 쪽도....아니다
neither...nor CONJ ...do ...do -ji anta ...도 ...도 -지 않다: *neither big nor small* keujido jakjido anta 크지도 작지도 않다; ...do ...do anida ...도 ...도 ...아니다: *neither money nor power* dondo myeongyedo anida 돈도 명예도 아니다
nephew N joka 조카
nerve N singyeong 신경
nervous ADJ chojohaehada, cojohaehaneun 초조해하다/-하는
nest N dungji 둥지
net N geumul 그물, mang 망, neteu 네트
network N neteuwokeu 네트워크
neutral ADJ jungnipjeogin 중립적인: *Journalists are supposed to be politically neutral* eonnonineun jeongchijeogeuro jungnipjeogieoya handa 언론인은 정치적으로 중립적이어야 한다

never ADJ gyeolko -ji anta 결코 -지 않다, gyeolko ...anida 결코 ...아니다
never mind! don't worry about it! PHR sin.gyeong sseuji maseyo! 신경 쓰지 마세요!
nevertheless ADV geuraedo 그래도
new ADJ sae 새: *a new car* sae cha 새 차
new, fresh ADJ saeropda 새롭다, saeroun 새로운
New Zealand N nyujillaendeu 뉴질랜드
newly ADV saero 새로, choegeune 최근에
news N nyuseu 뉴스: *newspaper* sinmun 신문
next (in line, sequence) ADJ da.eumui 다음의
next day N igil 익일, iteunnal 이튿날
next month N igwol 익월
next to, beside ADV ...yeope ...옆에: *right next to* baro yeope 바로 옆에
next week N da.eumju 다음 주
next year N naenyeon 내년
nice ADJ joeun 좋은, meotjin 멋진
nicotine N nikotin 니코틴
niece N jokattal 조카딸
night N bam 밤: *night guard* yagan gyeongbi 야간 경비
nightly ADJ yagan 야간
nightmare N angmong 악몽: *have a nightmare* angmongeul kkuda 악몽을 꾸다
nine NUM ahop 아홉, gu 구: *one ninth* gubunui il 구분의 일
nineteen NUM sipgu 십구, yeorahop 열아홉
ninety NUM aheun 아흔
no ADV 1 (in honorific form, when answering) anio 아니오 2 (in honorific form) anieyo 아니에요
no, not (with nouns) ADJ ...anida ...아니다: *not a book* chaegi anida 책이 아니다; *It's not the (that) book* geu chaegi anida 그 책이 아니다
no, not (with verbs and adjectives) ADJ -ji anta -지 않다
no, not, don't (with verbs and adjectives) ADV an 안: *not go (don't go)* an gada 안 가다; *not do (don't do)* an hada 안 하다; *a book one hasn't read* an ilgeun chaek 안 읽은 책

no matter how ADV amuri 아무리: *no matter how hard it is* amuri eoryeowodo 아무리 어려워도

no wonder ADV eojjeonji 어쩐지: *No wonder you look happy* eojjeonji gibuni joa boideora 어쩐지 기분이 좋아 보이더라

no. 2, second in rank N chaseok 차석

nobody is ... PHR amudo ...anida 아무도 ...아니다: *Nobody is as much as I am* amudo namankeumeun anida 아무도 나만큼은 아니다

nobody is ...-ing PHR amudo -ji anta 아무도 -지 않다: *Nobody is seeking* amudo chatji anta 아무도 찾지 않다

nod, to V kkeudeogida 끄덕이다: *His head was starting to nod* geuneun meorireul kkeudeogigi sijakhaetda 그는 머리를 끄덕이기 시작했다

noise N so.eum 소음

noisy, loud, troublesome ADJ sikkeureopda 시끄럽다, sikkeureoun 시끄러운: *loud music* sikkeureoun eumak 시끄러운 음악; *a noisy street* sikkeureoun geori 시끄러운 거리; *a troublesome situation* sikkeureoun munje 시끄러운 문제

nomination N jimyeong 지명

nominee N jimyeongdoen saram 지명된 사람, hubo 후보

non-existent, nothing, none ADJ ...eopda ...없다, ...eomneun ...없는

noncommittal ADJ eojeongjjeonghada 어정쩡하다

nonetheless ADV geureokineun hajiman 그렇기는 하지만

nonprofit ADJ biyeongnijeogin 비영리적인

nonsense N 1 *(not logical)* neonsenseu 넌센스 2 *(sham)* eongteori 엉터리

noodles N guksu 국수, sari 사리

noon, midday N jeong.o 정오

noose, snare N olgami 올가미

nor CONJ ...do ttohan -ji anta ...도 또한 -지 않다; ...do ttohan ...anida ...도 또한 ...아니다

norm N pyojun 표준

normal ADJ jeongsangjeogida 정상적이다, jeongsangjeogin 정상적인

normally ADV botongeun 보통은: *Sharks do not normally hunt people* sangeoneun botong sarameul sanyanghaji anneunda 상어는 보통 사람을 사냥하지 않는다

north N bukjjok 북쪽

North Korea N bukhan 북한

north-east N bukdongjjok 북동쪽

north-west N bukseojjok 북서쪽

northern ADJ bukjjogui 북쪽의

nose N ko 코

nostril N kokkumeong 콧구멍

not know how to V -(eu)l jul moreuda -(으)ㄹ 줄 모르다

not really, not particularly ADV byeollo 별로: *not particularly busy today* oneureun byeollo bappeuji anta 오늘은 별로 바쁘지 않다

note N 1 *(message, memo)* memo 메모 2 *(musical)* eumpyo 음표

notebook N gongchaek 공책

note down, write down, to V jeokda 적다

notice N tongji 통지, yego 예고: *without notice* yego eopsi 예고 없이

notice, realize, be aware of, to V arachaeda 알아채다: *notice a danger* wiheomeul arachaeda 위험을 알아채다

notion N gwannyeom 관념

novel N soseol 소설: *a full-length novel* jangpyeonsoseol 장편소설

November N sibirwol 십일월

nowhere ADV amudedo 아무데도: *The old man has nowhere to live* geu noineun amudedo sal gosi eopda 그 노인은 아무데도 살 곳이 없다

nuclear ADJ wonjaryeogui 원자력의

nude N nache 나체

numb ADJ gamgagi eopda/eomneun 감각이 없다/없는

number N beonho 번호

numerical figure, value N suchi 수치

numerous ADJ dasuui 다수의, sumaneun 수 많은: *Numerous people attended the concert* su maneun saramdeuri geu konseoteue chamseokhaetda 수 많은 사람들이 그 콘서트에 참석했다

nurse N I ganhosa 간호사 II V *(care for)* ganhohada 간호하다: *nursing, care* ganho 간호

nut N 1 gyeongwa 견과 2 neoteu 너트, amnasa 암나사

nutrient N yeongyangso 영양소

nutrition N yeongyang 영양: *well-balanced nutrition* gyunhyeonginneun yeongyang 균형있는 영양

nutritive value N yeongyangga 영양가

nylon N naillon 나일론

O

oak *(tree)* N chamnamu 참나무

oath, vow, pledge N maengse 맹세

obedient ADJ sunjonghaneun 순종하는

obesity N biman 비만

obey, to V sunjonghada 순종하다

object N samul 사물, mulche 물체

object, oppose, protest, to V bandaehada 반대하다

objection N iui 이의: *raise an objection* iuireul jegihada 이의를 제기하다

objective N mokjeok 목적, mokpyo 목표

observe, to V gwanchalhada 관찰하다: *He was able to observe the process of the film production* geuneun yeonghwa jejak gwajeongeul gwanchalhal su iseotda 그는 영화 제작 과정을 관찰할 수 있었다

observer N 1 gwanchalja 관찰자 2 mokgyeokja 목격자

obstacle N jangae(mul) 장애(물), banghae(mul) 방해(물)

obstinate, insistent ADJ eokjiseureopda 억지스럽다

obtain, to V eotda 얻다: *You must obtain approval to build a high-rise in this area* i jiyeoge gocheunggeonmureul jieuryeomyeon seungineul eodeoya handa 이 지역에 고층건물을 지으려면 승인을 얻어야 한다

obvious ADJ myeongbaekhada 명백하다, myeongbaekan 명백한

occasion N 1 gyeongu 경우, ttae 때 2 teukbyeolhan il 특별한 일

occasional ADJ gakkeumui 가끔의

occupancy N chaji 차지

occupation N jigeop 직업

occupy, take up, to V chajihada 차지하다: *The desk takes up half of the space in the room* chaeksangi bangui baneul chajihanda 책상이 방의 반을 차지한다

occur, to V ireonada 일어나다, bal-

saenghada 발생하다

ocean N daeyang 대양, bada 바다

October N siwol 시월

odd, eccentric ADJ yubyeollada 유별나다

odor, smell N naemsae 냄새

of course ADV mullon 물론

of, from PREP ...eseo ...에서

off: switch off, turn off, to V kkeuda 끄다

offend, to V gibun sanghage hada 기분 상하게 하다

offended, displeased, to be V gibuni sanghada 기분이 상하다

offended, hurt, to get V sanghada 상하다: *be distressed, take offense at* maeumi sanghada 마음이 상하다

offender N beomjoeja 범죄자

offense, crime N beomjoe 범죄

offer, suggest, to V je.uihada 제의하다

offering N heon.geum 헌금

office N samusil 사무실

officer N 1 janggyo 장교 2 gongmuwon 공무원, gyeonggwan 경관

official, formal ADJ gongsik(ui) 공식(의)

officials *(government)* N gongmuwon 공무원

often ADV jaju 자주

oh dear! INTERJ jeoreon 저런, won 원: *oh my goodness* won sesange 원 세상에

oil N gireum 기름

ointment N yeongo 연고: *apply ointment* yeongoreul bareuda 연고를 바르다

okay ADJ gwaenchanta 괜찮다

old *(of things)* ADJ oraedoeda 오래되다, oraedoen 오래된

old, outdated, old-fashioned ADJ mukda 묵다, mukeun 묵은: *old (well-fermented) kimchi* mugeun gimchi 묵은 김치; *a timeworn idea* mugeun saenggak 묵은 생각; *old customs* mugeun gwanseup 묵은 관습

old age ADJ nai manta/maneun 나이 많다/많은

old days, the N yennal 옛날

older N yeonsang 연상: *an older girlfriend* yeonsangui yeojachingu 연상의 여자친구

older brother N 1 *(female's)* oppa 오빠 2 *(male's)* hyeong 형

older sister N *(female's)* eonni 언니

2 *(male's)* nuna 누나

Olympics N gukjejeok gyeonggi dae-hoe 국제적 경기 대회

omission N tallak 탈락

omission, ellipsis N saengnyak 생략

omnipotence, being almighty N manneung 만능

on, at ADV ...wie ...위에

on *(of dates)* PREP ...e ...에

on *(turned on, left on)* ADJ kyeojyeo itda 켜져 있다

on foot ADV georeoseo 걸어서: *go on foot* georeoseo gada 걸어서 가다

on the opposite side of ADJ majeun pyeonui 맞은 편의

on the way ADV ganeun gire 가는 길에, oneun gire 오는 길에

on time ADV je sigane 제 시간에: *arrive on time* je sigane dochakhada 제 시간에 도착하다

on: switch on, turn on, to V kyeoda 켜다: *turn on the radio* radioreul kyeoda 라디오를 켜다

one NUM hana 하나: *one of the two* dul jung hana 둘 중 하나

one more, another ADJ hana deo 하나 더

one way N pyeondo 편도: *one-way ticket* pyeondopyo 편도표

one's family *(clan)* N gamun 가문

one's house N jataek 자택

one's later years N malnyeon 말년

one's manner of speaking N malbeoreut 말버릇

one's own efforts N jaryeok 자력

one's own expense N sabi 사비

one's date of birth *(birth date, month, year)* N saengnyeonworil 생년월일: *Please write down your date of birth* saengnyeonworireul jeogeuseyo 생년월일을 적으세요

one's remnant existent N yeosaeng 여생

onion N yangpa 양파

online ADJ ollain 온라인로, ollainui 온라인의

only ADV man 만

open, to V yeolda 열다: *open the door* muneul yeolda 문을 열다 2 yeollida 열리다: *a door (flies) open* muni (hwak) yeollida 문이 (확) 열리다

open, stretch, to V beollida 벌리다;

open your mouth wide ne ibeul keuge beollyeora 네 입을 크게 벌려라

open one's heart up, to V teonota 터놓다

opening N 1 sijak bubun 시작 부분, gaemak 개막 2 gumeong 구멍 3 binjari 빈자리

opera N opera 오페라

operate, to V 1 jakdongdoeda 작동되다 2 gadonghada 가동하다

opinion N uigyeon 의견

opponent, other party N sangdaebang 상대방

opportunity N gihoe 기회

oppose, to V bandaehada 반대하다: *He did not dare to oppose me* geuneun gamhi naege bandaehaji anatda 그는 감히 나에게 반대하지 않았다

opposite side N majeun pyeon 맞은 편

opposite, contrary N bandae(ui) 반대(의)

oppressed, repressed, to be V eongnullida 억눌리다

opt, to V taekhada 택하다

optimism N nakcheon 낙천: *be optimistic* nakcheonjeok 낙천적

option N seontaekgwon 선택권

optional, selective, sectional ADJ seontaekjeogida, seontaekjeogin 선택적이다, 선택적인

or ADV ttoneun 또는

or else, otherwise ADV geureochi aneumyeon 그렇지 않으면

oral ADJ guduui 구두의, ibui 입의: *An oral agreement is not enough* gudu habuironeun chungbunhaji anta 구두 합의로는 충분하지 않다

orange (color) I ADJ orenjisaekui 오렌지색의 II N orenjisaek 오렌지색

orange, citrus N orenji 오렌지

order I N 1 *(placed for food, goods)* jumun 주문 2 *(sequence, turn)* sunseo 순서: *be out of order* sunseoga bakkwida 순서가 바뀌다; charye 차례 II V 1 *(command)* myeongnyeonghada 명령하다 2 *(place an order)* jumunhada 주문하다

orderly, organized, to be V jeongdondoeda 정돈되다

ordinary, plain, common ADJ pyeongbeomhada/-han 평범하다/-한:

O

ordinary times, the usual pyeong-sangsi 평상시

organ N 1 janggi 장기 2 oreugan 오르간

organization, group, team N danche 단체

organic ADJ 1 yuginongui 유기농의 2 janggiui 장기의

oriental *(herb)* **medicine** N hannyak 한약

origin, source N chulcheo 출처

original N wonbon 원본

originally, primarily ADV wollae 원래

originate, come from, to V yuraehada 유래하다

ornament N jangsik(mul) 장식(물)

orphan N goa 고아

ostentatious ADJ hosaseureopda 호사스럽다

otolaryngology, ENT N ibiinhugwa 이비인후과

ought V ...haeya hada ...해야 하다, ...hal ruimuga itda ...할 의무가 있다

our ADJ uri(ui) 우리(의)

ourselves PRON uri jasin 우리 자신

out ADV ...bakke ...밖에

out of order, broken ADJ gojangnan 고장난

out of order, broken, to be V manggajida 망가지다

out-toed gait N palja 팔자

outcome N gyeolgwa 결과: *Their opinions are reflected in the outcome* geudeurui uigyeoneun gyeolgwae bannyeongdoeeotda 그들의 의견은 결과에 반영되었다

outdoor ADJ jip bakkui 집 밖의, yaoeui 야외의: *People are sitting at an outdoor cafe* saramdeuri yaoeui kapee anjaitda 사람들이 야외의 카페에 앉아 있다

outer ADJ bakkachi 바깥의, oebuui 외부의

outing, excursion, picnic N nadeuri 나들이

outlet *(electric)* N konsenteu 콘센트

outline N yungwak 윤곽

output N saengsan 생산, sanchul 산출

outside N bakkat(jjok) 바깥(쪽)

outside of... ADV ...ui bakkate ...의 바깥에

outsider N autsaideo 아웃사이더

outstanding ADJ ttwieonan 뛰어난: *He was an outstanding athlete* geuneun ttwieonan seonsuyeotda 그는 뛰어난 선수였다

oval *(shape)* N tawonhyeong(ui) 타원형

oven N obeun 오븐

over there ADV jeogi 저기

over, finished, done, complete, gone, to be V kkeunnada 끝나다

overall ADJ jeonbuui 전부의

overall ADV jeonbanjeogeuro 전반적으로

overcharged, ripped off, to be V bagajisseuda 바가지 쓰다: *I've been ripped off* bagajireul sseotda 바가지를 썼다

overcoat N oetu 외투: *put on an overcoat* oetureul ipda 외투를 입다

overcome, to V igyeonaeda 이겨내다

overlook, to V gangwahada 간과하다: *We can't overlook his wild words* urineun geuui pogeoneul gangwahal su eopda 우리는 그의 폭언을 간과할 수 없다

overpass, overpass bridge N yukgyo 육교: *cross the overpass* yukgyoreul geonneoda 육교를 건너다

overseas ADJ hae.oe(ui) 해외(의): *overseas market* haeoe sijang 해외 시장; *overseas travel* haeoe yeohaeng 해외 여행

oversee, to V gamdokhada 감독하다: *Her job is to oversee all the company's advertising* geunyeoui ireun hoesaui modeun gwanggoreul gamdokhaneun geotsida 그녀의 일은 회사의 모든 광고를 감독하는 것이다

overthrow, to V eopda 엎다: *overthrow the present government* hyeon jeongbureul eopda 현 정부를 엎다

overturned, upside down ADJ dwijibeojin 뒤집어진

overwhelmed ADJ beokchada 벅차다: *overwhelmed by joy* gippeumeuro gaseumi beokchada 기쁨으로 가슴이 벅차다

owe, to V bitjida 빚지다

owl N olppaemi 올빼미

own, personal ADJ jasinui 자신의

owner N juin 주인, soyuju 소유주

oxygen N sanso 산소

oyster N gul 굴

P

pace N sokdo 속도

pack, to V 1 *(get ready)* chaenggida 챙기다: *pack for a trip* yeohaenggal jimeul chaenggida 여행갈 짐을 챙기다 2 *(wrap)* ssada 싸다

package N pojangmul 포장물

packing, pack *(up)* N, V pojang 포장

pad N paedeu 패드

page N peiji 페이지

paid ADJ jibuldoen 지불된: *paid in full* wannap 완납

paid, to be V jibuldoeda 지불되다

pain N 1 gotong 고통 2 golchitgeori 골칫거리: *The pain in my shoulder abated after two days* eokkaeui tongjeungi iteul hue gasyeotda 어깨의 통증이 이틀 후에 가셨다

painful ADJ 1 apeun 아픈 2 golchi apeun 골치 아픈: *Unrequited love is often very painful* jjaksarangeun ttaeron maeu apeun geotsida 짝사랑은 때론 매우 아픈 것이다

paint I N peinteu 페인트: *a can of paint* peinteu han tong 페인트 한 통; *a coat of paint* peinteu chil 페인트 칠 II V *(house, furniture)* chilhada 칠하다

painting N geurim 그림

pair of, a N han ssang 한 쌍: *a pair of lovers* han ssangui yeonin 한 쌍의 연인

pajamas N jamot 잠옷, pajama 파자마

palace N gung 궁: *Deoksu Palace* deoksugung 덕수궁

pale, pallid ADJ changbaekhada 창백하다

palm N 1 sonbadak 손바닥 2 yajanamu 야자나무

pan, pot N naembi 냄비

panorama N panorama 파노라마

panic N gonghwang 공황, gongpo 공포: *A panic attack can occur any time, and anywhere* gonghwang sangtaeneun eonje eodiseodeun ireonal su itda 공황 상태는 언제 어디서든 일어날 수 있다

pants, trousers N baji 바지

paper N jong.i 종이, peipeo 페이퍼

paper *(counting unit)* N mae 매: *100 sheets of paper* jongi baengmae 종이 100 매

parade N peoreideu 퍼레이드, haengjin 행진

parallel, parallelism N pyeonghaeng 평행

parcel N sopo 소포

pardon me? what did you say? PHR mworago hasyeosseoyo? 뭐라고 하셨어요?

parents N bumo 부모

park *(car)*, **to** V juchahada 주차하다

parking N jucha 주차

parliament N gukhoe 국회

part *(not whole)* N bubun 부분

part, component *(of machine)* N busok 부속

part from, separate, to V heeojida 헤어지다

part one's hair, to V gareumaareultada 가르마를 타다

part-time job N areubaiteu 아르바이트

participant N chamgaja 참가자: *He is the oldest participant in this marathon* geuneun ibeon maratonui choegoryeong chamgajada 그는 이번 마라톤의 최고령 참가자다

participate, to V chamgahada 참가하다

particular, especial ADJ gakbyeolhada 각별하다: *a(n) (extra) special relationship* gakbyeolhan sai 각별한 사이

particularly ADV gakbyeolhi 각별히, *(especially)* teukhi 특히

parting, farewell N ibyeol 이별

partition, divider N kanmagi 칸막이

partly ADV bubunjeogeuro 부분적으로

partner N 1 *(in business)* dong.eopja 동업자 2 *(spouse)* bae.uja 배우자

partnership N dongeop 동업, pateuneosip 파트너십

party N 1 *(social event)* pati 파티 2 *(political)* jeongdang 정당

pass *(exam)*, **to** V hapgyeokhada 합격하다: *pass with flying colors* usuhan seongjeogeuro hapgyeokhada 우수한 성적으로 합격하다

pass, adopt, approve, select, to V chaetaekhada 채택하다

pass, go past, to V tonggwahada 통과하다

pass, transit N tonghaeng 통행

pass away, die, to V unmyeonghada 운명하다: *His grandfather passed away today* geuui harabeojiga oneul unmyeonghasyeotda 그의 할아버지가 오늘 운명하셨다

pass on, switch, turn, to

P

pass on, switch, turn, to v dollyeoboda 돌려보다

pass through, to v tonghaenghada 통행하다

passage, passageway N tongno 통로

passenger N seunggaek 승객

passing ADJ tonggwahaneun 통과하는, jinaganeun 지나가는: *I hailed a passing cab* naneun jinaganeun taeksireul keun soriro bulleotda 나는 지나가는 택시를 큰 소리로 불렀다

passing N 1 gyeonggwa 경과 2 tonggwa 통과 3 jugeum 죽음: *Congrats on passing your exam* siheome tonggwahan geoseul chukahanda 시험에 통과한 것을 축하한다

passion N jeongnyeol 정열

passion, adoration N yeoljeong 열정

passionate love N yeorae 열애

passport N yeokkwon 여권

password, code N amho 암호

pasta N paseuta 파스타

pastime, timekiller N soilkkeori 소일거리

pastor, minister N moksa 목사

pat, comfort, console, to v dadokgeorida 다독거리다

patent N teukheo 특허

path N gil 길

pathetic ADJ hansimhada 한심하다

patient I ADJ *(calm)* innaesimitda/inneun 인내심 있다/-있는 II N *(medical)* hwanja 환자

patrol N sunchal 순찰

pattern, design N dijain 디자인

patterned ADJ munuiui 무늬의: *floral patterned* kkonmunuiui 꽃무늬의

pause N ilsijeongji 일시정지: *Press "pause" to stop the tape* teipeureul jungdansikiryeomyeon ilsijeongjireul nureuseyo 테이프를 중단시키려면 일시정지를 누르세요

pause, to v jungdanhada 중단하다: *Don't pause in writing a letter* pyeonji sseuneun geoseul jungdanhaji mara 편지 쓰는 것을 중단하지 마라

pay, to v jibulhada 지불하다

pay attention, to v jumokhada 주목하다

pay dearly, to v keunkodachida 큰코다치다

pay one's tribute of praise, ladle out praise, pay a high compliment to, to v chansareul bonaeda 찬사를 보내다

payment N jibul 지불, jiburaek 지불액

peace N pyeonghwa 평화

peaceful ADJ pyeonghwaropda, pyeonghwaroun 평화롭다, 평화로운 taepyeonghada 태평하다

peak, summit N jeongsang 정상

peanut N ttangkong 땅콩

pearl N jinju 진주

peas, green beans N wandukong 완두콩

peasant N sojangnong 소작농

peculiar, eccentric, odd ADJ namdareuda 남다르다

pedal N pedal 페달

pedestrian N haengin 행인

peek, watch for *(an opportunity)*, **to** v yeotboda 엿보다: *sneak peek* mollae yeotboda 몰래 엿보다

peel, to v kkeopjireul beotgida 껍질을 벗기다

pen N pen 펜

penal regulations N beolchik 벌칙

penalty N cheobeol 처벌, beolgeum 벌금

pencil N yeonpil 연필

penetrate into, to v pagodeulda 파고들다

penis N *(namja)* seonggi (남자) 성기

penniless, to become v teong bida/bin 텅 비다/빈: *become penniless* jumeoniga teong bida 주머니가 텅 비다

pentagon N ogakhyeong 오각형

people N saramdeul 사람들

pepper *(black)* N huchu 후추

perceive, to v gamjihada 감지하다

percent N peosenteu 퍼센트

percentage, ratio N biyul 비율

perception N jigak 지각

perfect ADJ wanbyeokhada, wanbyeokhan 완벽하다, 완벽한: *perfect (thorough) knowledge* wanbyeokhan jisik 완벽한 지식

perform, conduct, to v suhaenghada 수행하다

performance N 1 *(acting)* yeon.gi 연기: *give the best performance of one's career* insaeng choegoui yeongireul boida 인생 최고의 연기를 보이다 2 *(musical, recital)* yeonju 연주

P

performer N yeongija 연기자

perfume N hyangsu 향수

perhaps, maybe, possibly, probably ADV ama 아마

period N 1 *(of time)* gigan 기간 2 *(menstrual)* saengni 생리 3 *(end of a sentence)* machimpyo 마침표

perjury, false witness N wijeung 위증

permanence N yeonggu 영구

permanent ADJ yeonggujeogida, yeonggujeogin 영구적이다, 영구적인: *permanent residency* yeongjugwon 영주권

permission, tolerance N heoyong 허용

permit N heogajeung 허가증: *This is my parking permit* ige nae jucha heogajeungiya 이게 내 주차 허가증이야

permit, to V heogahada 허가하다: *The law does not permit the sale of this book* beobeun i chaegui panmaereul heogahaji anneunda 법은 이 책의 판매를 허가하지 않는다

persecution N pipbak 핍박

person N 1 *(in honorific form)* bun 분: *one person* han bun 한 분 2 *(human being)* saram 사람

personal ADJ gaeinjeogin 개인적인: *Can I ask you a personal question?* naega gaeinjeogin jilmun hana haedo dwae? 내가 개인적인 질문 하나 해도 돼?

persuade, to V seoldeukhada 설득하다: *Don't try to persuade me* nareul seoldeukharyeogo hajima 나를 설득하려고 하지마

perusal, reading N yeollam 열람

pester, importune, ride, to V bokda 볶다: *importune a person* sarameul bokda 사람을 볶다

pet *(animal)* N aewandongmul 애완동물

petrified, to be V jajireojida 자지러지다

phase N dangye 단계

Philippines N pillipin 필리핀

philosophy N cheolhak 철학

phlegm, sputum N garae 가래: *have phlegm in one's throat* moge garaega kkeulta 목에 가래가 끓다

phone N jeonhwa 전화

photograph I N sajin 사진 II V *(take a picture)* sajin jjikda 사진 찍다

photographer N sajin jakga 사진 작가

phrase N gu 구

physical ADJ 1 yukcheui 육체의 2 muljirui 물질의

physician N naegwa uisa 내과 의사

piano N piano 피아노

pick up, lift, find, to V jupda 줍다

pickled radish N danmuji 단무지

pickpocket I N *(person)* somaechigi 소매치기 II V *(steal)* somaechigihada 소매치기하다

picture N 1 *(drawing, painting)* geurim 그림 2 *(image)* yeongsang 영상

pie N pai 파이

piece of cloth N heonggeop 헝겊

piece, item, unit N nat gae 낱개

piece, portion, section, cut, slice N jogak 조각

pierce, penetrate, to V ttulta 뚫다

pig N dwaeji 돼지

pig out, snarf down, to V cheomeokda 처먹다

pile N deomi 더미: *I have to finish this pile of work by next week* naneun i il deomireul daeumjukkaji kkeunnaeya handa 나는 이 일 더미를 다음주까지 끝내야 한다

pile, to V ssaa ollida 쌓아 올리다: *She is piling the boxes on the shelves* geunyeoneun bakseudeureul seonbane ssaa olligo itda 그녀는 박스들을 선반에 쌓아 올리고 있다

pillow N begae 베개

pills, tablets N allyak 알약

pilot N jojongsa 조종사

pimple, zit N yeodeureum 여드름: *pop a pimple* yeodeureumeul jjada 여드름을 짜다

pin N pin 핀

pineapple N painaepeul 파인애플

pinetree N sol 솔

pink N pingkeusaek 핑크색

pipe N gwan 관, paipeu 파이프

pit N gudeongi 구덩이

pitch-dark, dark ADJ kamkamhada 캄캄하다: *It's dark outside* bakki kamkamhada 밖이 캄캄하다

pitcher N tusu 투수

piteous ADJ garyeonhada 가련하다

pitiable ADJ bulssanghada 불쌍하다

pitiful ADJ aecheoropda 애처롭다

pivot, capital, center N jungsimji 중심지

149

pizza N pija 피자

place N jangso 장소

place, to V 1 *(put on, lay)* eonda 얹다 2 *(put, place, release)* nota 놓다: *place a book on a desk* chaegeul chaeksange nota 책을 책상에 놓다

plain *(not fancy),* **simple, naïve** ADJ dansunhada 단순하다, dansunhan 단순한: *the situation is simple* sanghwangeun dansunhada 상황은 단순하다; *a simple-minded person* dansunhan saram 단순한 사람

plaintive, ominously sorrowful ADJ cheongseungmatda 청승맞다

plan I N gyehoek 계획 II V *(form, map out)* gyehoekhada 계획하다, se.uda 세우다: *lay out a plan* gyehoegeul seuda 계획을 세우다

plane N pyeongmyeon 평면

planet N haengseong 행성

plant I N *(vegetable)* singmul 식물 II V *(grow)* simda 심다

plastic N peullaseutik 플라스틱

plate N jeopsi 접시

platform N peullaetpom 플랫폼

play I N yeongcuk 연극 II V 1 *(a game)* gyeonggireulhada 경기를 하다 2 *(video, audio)* jaesaeng 재생하다: *play a video* bidioreul jaesaenghada 비디오를 재생하다 3 *(musical instruments)* kyeoda 켜다: *play the violin* baiollineul kyeoda 바이올린을 켜다 4 nolda 놀다

play around, to V gajigo nolda 가지고 놀다

play innocent, to V jabatteda 잡아떼다

play it both ways, play a double game, sit on the fence, to V yangdari 양다리

play the baby to, to V eorigwang 어리광

playground N noriteo 놀이터

plead, to V tanwonhada 탄원하다

plead, defend *(with words),* **to** V byeonhohada 변호하다

pleasant ADJ gibun jota/jo.eun 기분 좋다/좋은

please *(request for help)* PHR butakhamnida 부탁합니다

please *(request for something)* PHR -eo/a juseyo −어/아 주세요, -a/eo juseyo −아/어 주세요

please do so *(go ahead)* PHR geureoke haseyo 그렇게 하세요

Please don't INTERJ -ji maseyo −지 마세요: *Please do not speak (please be quiet)* malhaji maseyo 말하지 마세요

pleased, to be V gippeuda 기쁘다, gippeohada 기뻐하다

pleasure, amusement N jaemi 재미, orak 오락

pleasure, enjoyment N kwaerak 쾌락

pledge, assure, to V dajimhada 다짐하다

plenty ADV chungbunhi 충분히: *We have plenty of time* urineun chungbunhi sigani itda 우리는 충분히 시간이 있다

plot N 1 guseong 구성 2 eummo 음모

plug *(electric)* N peulleogeu 플러그

plum N jadu 자두

plus N peulleoseu 플러스

pocket N hojumeoni 호주머니

pocket money, pin money N yongdon 용돈: *receive pin money after doing chores* simbureumeul hago yongdoneul batda 심부름을 하고 용돈을 받다

poem, poetry N si 시: *recite a poem* sireul nangsonghada 시를 낭송하다

point, dot N jeom 점

point of view N sijjeom 시점

point out, to V jijeokhada 지적하다

point to *(at),* **to** V garikida 가리키다: *point at a destination* mokjeokjireul garikida 목적지를 가리키다

poison N dok(yak) 독(약)

poisonous ADJ dogi itda/inneun 독이 있다/있는: *poisonous mushroom* N dokbeoseot 독버섯

pole N 1 gidung 기둥 2 geuk 극

police N gyeongchal 경찰: *police officer* gyeongchalgwan 경찰관; *police station* gyeongchalseo 경찰서

policeman N gyeongchalgwan 경찰관

polish, to V 1 *(furbish, shine)* yunnaeda 윤내다 2 *(revise)* dadeumda 다듬다 3 *(shoes, table)* dakda 닦다: *polish one's shoes* gudureul dakda 구두를 닦다

polite ADJ gongsonhada 공손하다, gongsonhan 공손한

political science N jeongchihak 정치학

politics N jeongchi 정치

poll N yeoronjosa 여론조사

pollution N oyeom 오염

pond N yeonmot 연못

pool N 1 suyeongjang 수영장 2 ungdeongi 웅덩이 3 gongdongchulja 공동출자

poop, crap N ttong 똥

poor ADJ 1 *(impoverished)* gananhada 가난하다, gananhan 가난한 2 *(careless)* eongseonghada 엉성하다: *poorly written script* eongseonghan geukbon 엉성한 극본

poor, unskilled, to be V seotureuda 서투르다

poor sense of direction, bad with directions ADJ eodupda 어둡다, eoduun 어두운: *be bad with directions* gil nuni eodupda 길 눈이 어둡다

popular ADJ inkki itda/inneun 인기 있다/있는: *a popular song* yuhaengga 유행가

popularity N ingi 인기

population N in.gu 인구

porch N hyeongwan 현관

pork N dwaejigogi 돼지고기

port N hanggu 항구

portion, serving N ...inbun ...인분: *a double order (portion) of bulgogi* bulgogi iinbun 불고기 2인분

portrait N chosanghwa 초상화

pose a question, to V uimuneul jegihada 의문을 제기하다

position N 1 wich 위치 2 jase 자세

position, to V 1 duda 두다 2 wichireul jeonghada 위치를 정하다

positive ADJ geungjeongjeogin 긍정적인

possess, own, to V soyuhada 소유하다

possession, reserve N boyu 보유

possessions, belongings N soyumul 소유물

possibility N ganeungseong 가능성

possible ADJ ganeunghada 가능하다, ganeunghan 가능한

post, column N gidung 기둥

post, mail, to V buchida 부치다: *mail a package* soporeul buchida 소포를 부치다

postcard N yeopseo 엽서

post office N ucheguk 우체국

poster N poseuteo 포스터

postponed, to be V yeon.gidoeda 연기되다: *be postponed indefinitely* mugihan yeongidoeda 무기한 연기되다

pot N hwabun 화분

potato N gamja 감자

potent, pungent, strong ADJ dokhada 독하다: *strong medicine* dokhan yak 독한 약; *potent smell* hyangi dokhada 향이 독하다

potentiality N jamjaeryeok 잠재력

poultry N gageum(nyu) 가금(류)

pound N paundeu 파운드

pound, to V magu chida 마구 치다

pour, to V butda 붓다: *pour water* mureul butda 물을 붓다

powder N garu 가루

powerful ADJ 1 *(influential)* himitda 힘있다, himinneun 힘있는: *an influential person* himitneun saram 힘있는 사람 2 *(strong)* yuryeokhada 유력하다

practical ADJ 1 siryongjeogin 실용적인 2 hyeonsiljeogin 현실적인: *They produced pottery for practical uses* geudeureun siryongjeogin yongdoro dojagireul saengsanhaetda 그들은 실용적인 용도로 도자기를 생산했다

practice I N yeonseup 연습 II V yeonseuphada 연습하다

praise I N 1 *(good report)* chingchan 칭찬 2 *(eulogization, high compliment)* chansa 찬사 II V chingchanhada 칭찬하다

pray, to V gidohada 기도하다

prayer N gidomun 기도문: *the Lord's Prayer* jugidomun 주기도문

preach, to V seolgyohada 설교하다

preaching, sermon N seolgyo 설교

precious ADJ gwijunghada 귀중하다, gwijunghan 귀중한

predict, to V yecheukhada 예측하다: *It is hard to predict the future* miraereul yecheukhaneun geoseun eoryeopda 미래를 예측하는 것은 어렵다

prefer, to V seonhohada 선호하다

preference N seonho 선호

pregnancy N imsin 임신

pregnant, to be V imsinhada 임신하다: *be pregnant with one's first baby* cheosaireul rimsinhada 첫아이를 임신하다

prejudice, bias N pyeongyeon 편견

prenatal education N taegyo 태교

preparation N junbi 준비: *preparation of lessons* yeseup 예습

prepare, to V 1 *(arrange, get ready)* junbihada 준비하다, junbisikida 준비시키다 2 *(fix, make (a meal))* siksa junbihada 식사 준비하다

prepared, ready ADJ junbideon 준비된

prepared, ready, to be V junbidoeda 준비되다

preposterous, ridiculous ADJ eocheogunieopda 어처구니없다

preschool, kindergarten N yuchiwon 유치원

prescription N cheobang(jeon) 처방(전)

presence N 1 jonjae 존재 2 chamseok 참석

present I N *(gift)* seonmul 선물 II ADJ 1 *(now)* hyeonjae 현재 2 *(here)* chulseokhada 출석하다 III V 1 *(give)* seonmulhada 선물하다 2 *(submit)* jechulhada 제출하다

presently, nowadays ADV yojeum 요즘

preserved, stored, to be V jeojangdoeda 저장되다

president N daetongnyeong 대통령, sajang 사장

press, journalism N eollon 언론

press, to V 1 *(push sth)* nureuda 누르다 2 *(urge, push)* dageuchida 다그치다: *press (chase) for answers* dageuchida 다그치다

pressing, urgent ADJ dageupada 다급하다

pressure N amnyeok 압력, apbak 압박

pretend to know, to V aneunchehada 아는체하다

pretty ADV 1 yeppeun 예쁜 2 *(very)* sangdanghan 상당한

pretty ADJ jeokdanghi 적당히

prevent, to V bangjihada 방지하다, yebanghada 예방하다

prevention N yebang 예방

preview *(movie)* N yego 예고: *The preview is too long* yegopyeoni neomu gilda 예고편이 너무 길다

previous life N jeonsaeng 전생

previous, former ADJ ijeon(ui) 이전의; *previous experience* ijeonui gyeongheom 이전의 경험

previously, formerly ADV ...jeone ...전에

price, value *(cost)* N gagyeok 가격

pride N jajonsim 자존심

pride, self-respect N jabusim 자부심: *have much pride in oneself* jabusimi ganghada 자부심이 강하다

priest N sinbu 신부

primary factor, cause N yoin 요인

prime ADJ 1 judoen 주된 2 choegoui 최고의

prime minister N susang 수상

primitive, primeval ADJ wonsi 원시

prince N wangja 왕자

principal N juyeok 주역

principal ADJ judoen 주된: *His principal reason for studying was to please his parents* geuga gongbureul haneun judoen iyuneun geuui bumonimeul gippeuge haedeurigi wihaeseo yeotda 그가 공부를 하는 주된 이유는 그의 부모님을 기쁘게 해드리기 위해서 였다

principle N 1 *(basic tenet)* wonchik 원칙: *ironclad rule, principle* cheolchik 철칙 2 *(theory)* wolli 원리

print, to V inswaehada 인쇄하다

priority N useongwon 우선권

prison N gamok 감옥

prisoner N 1 joesu 죄수 2 poro 포로

private, personal ADJ sajjeogida 사적이다, sajjeogin 사적인: *personal affairs* sajeogin eommu 사적인 업무; *private loan* sachae 사채

private establishment N sarip 사립

private school, (educational) institute N hagwon 학원

privilege N teukgwon 특권

prize N posang 포상, sang 상: *give sb a prize* sangeul juda 상을 주다; *prize money* sanggeum 상금

problem N 1 *(sth troublesome)* tal 탈: *cause problems* tareul ireukida 탈을 일으키다 2 *(question, issue, matter)* munje 문제

procedure N jeolcha 절차: *It's just a matter of procedure* geugeoseun danji jeolchasangui munjeida 그것은 단지 절차상의 문제이다

proceed, to V jinhaenghada 진행하다

process N gwajeong 과정

process, to V gagonghada 가공하다, cheorihada 처리하다

processor N peuroseseo 프로세서
produce, to V saengsanhada 생산하다
product N saengsanmul 생산물, sang-pum 상품, jepum 제품
profession N jigeop 직업, jeonmunjik 전문직
professor, lecturer N gyosu 교수
profit, returns N iik 이익, iyun 이윤
profit, to make a V beollida 벌리다
profitable, favorable, beneficial ADJ iropda 이롭다
profound ADJ gipda 깊다, gipeun 깊은: *a deep (profound) meaning* gipeun tteut 깊은 뜻
program N peurogeuraem 프로그램
programming N peurogeuraeming 프로그래밍
progress N jinjeon 진전
prohibit, to V geumhada 금하다: *Many countries prohibit marriage between close relatives by law* maneun nara-deuri geunchinhoncul beobeuro geum-hago itda 많은 나라들이 근친혼을 법으로 금하고 있다
project N gihoek 기획, saeop 사업
project, to V gihoekhada 기획하다
prolongation of life N yeonmyeong 연명
prominent, distinguished ADJ jaeng-jaenghada 쟁쟁하다
promise, to V yaksokhada 약속하다, yukseonghada 육성하다
promote, to V 1 chokjinhada 촉진하다 2 hongbohada 홍보하다 3 seungjin-sikida 승진시키다: *Our mission is to promote peace among the nations* gukje pyeonghwareul chokjinhaneun geotsi uriui samyeongida 국제 평화를 촉진하는 것이 우리의 사명이다
promotion N 1 seungjin 승진 2 hongbo 홍보
prompt ADJ jeukgakjeogin 즉각적인: *Prompt treatment is critical* jeukgak-jeogin cheojiga jungyohada 즉각적인 처지가 중요하다
pronounce, to V bareumhada 발음하다
proof N jeunggeo 증거
prop, support N batchim 받침
proper ADJ jeokjeolhan 적절한: *To maintain your health proper nutrition is essential* jeokjeolhan yeonyang-seopchwineun geongang yujie pilsuda

적절한 영양섭취는 건강 유지에 필수다
property, wealth N jaesan 재산: *public property* gonggongjaesan 공공재산
proposal N 1 jean 제안 2 cheonghon 청혼: *He turned down the proposal* geuneun geu jeaneul geojeolhaetda 그는 그 제안을 거절했다
propose, to V 1 jeanhada 제안하다 2 cheonghonhada 청혼하다: *He will pro-pose a new plan at the meeting* geuneun moimeseo sae gyehoegeul jeanhal geotsida 그는 모임에서 새 계획을 제안할 것이다
prosaic ADJ memareun 메마른: *a pro-saic person* gamjeongi memareun saram 감정이 메마른 사람
protect, to V bohohada 보호하다
protection N boho 보호
protein N danbaekjil 단백질
protest, complain, to V hang.uihada 항의하다
proud, boastful ADJ jarangseureopda, jarangseureon 사랑스럽다, 자랑스런
prove, to V jeungmyeonghada 증명하다
provide, to V gonggeuphada 공급하다
province N jibang 지방
provision N 1 gonggeup 공급 2 daebi 대비
provisional contract N gagyeyak 가계약
provoke, irritate, to V yagollida 약올리다
prowl, saunter, loiter, to V eoseulleonggeorida 어슬렁거리다
prune, clean, to V dadeumda 다듬다: *prune a tree* namutgajireul dadeumda 나뭇가지를 다듬다; *clean a cabbage (for kimchi)* baechureul dadeumda 배추를 다듬다
psychologist N simnihakja 심리학자
public ADJ gonggong(ui) 공공(의)
public opinion N yeoron 여론
publication N chulpan 출판, chulpan-mul 출판물
publish, to V chulpanhada 출판하다, pyeonaeda 펴내다: *publish a book* chaekeul pyeonaeda 책을 펴내다다
publisher N chulpansa 출판사
pull, to V danggida 당기다
pull, draw, to V jabadanggida 잡아당기다

pull oneself together, to v gada-deumda 가다듬다

pulse N maekbak 맥박

pump N peompeu 펌프

punch, to v 1 jumeogeuro chida 주먹으로 치다 2 gumeongeul ttulta 구멍을 뚫다

punctual, to be v siganeul jal jikida/jikineun 시간을 잘 지키다/지킨

punctual, not to be v eogida 어기다: *not to be punctual, not to be on time* siganeul reogida 시간을 어기다

punish, to v cheobeolhada 처벌하다: *We are here to punish you* urin neo-reul cheobeolhagi wihae watda 우린 너를 처벌하기 위해 왔다

punishment N cheobeol 처벌

pupil N donggong 동공

purchase N gumae 구매: *It's included in the purchase price* gumae gagye-oge pohamdoeeo itseumnida 구매 가격에 포함되어 있습니다

purchase, to v gumaehada 구매하다: *Would you like to purchase both books?* chaek du gwoneul modu gumaehasigetseumnikka? 책 두 권을 모두 구매하시겠습니까?

pure ADJ sunsuhada 순수하다, sunsuhan 순수한: *pure hearted* cheongsun-hada 청순하다

purple N jajusaek(ui) 자주색(의)

purpose N mokjeok 목적: *a sense of purpose* mokjeok guisik 목적 의식

push, to v milda 밀다

push out, stick out, to v naemilda 내밀다: *stick out hands for reconciliation* hwahaeui soneul laemilda 화해의 손을 내밀다

put arms around each other's shoulders, side by side eokkae-dongmu 어깨동무

put blame upon, to v tatada 탓하다: *blame others* nameul tatada 남을 탓하다

put into action, to v omgida 옮기다: *put one's ideas into action* saengga-geul haengdonge omgida 생각을 행동에 옮기다

put off, postpone, to v yeongihada 연기하다

put on, wear, to v chada 차다: *wear a watch* sigyereul chada 시계를 차다

puzzled ADJ eoridungjeolhada/-hae-hada 어리둥절하다/-해하다

qualification N jagyeok 자격: *hold qualification* jagyeogeul gatchuda 자격을 갖추다

qualify, to v jagyeogeul eotda 자격을 얻다: *I think I qualify myself for the job* naneun naega geu ire daehan jag-yeogeul gatchueotdago saenggakhanda 나는 내가 그 일에 대한 자격을 갖추었다고 생각한다

quantity N yang 양

quarrel I N maldatum 말다툼 II v datuda 다투다

quarter N sa bunui il 4 분의 1

queen N yeowang 여왕

quest N tamgu 탐구

question N jilmun 질문

questionnaire N jilmunsahang 질문사항

queue, line, rope, string N jul 줄

quick, agile ADJ nalssaeda 날쌔다

quick, fast, rapid ADJ ppareuda 빠르다, ppareun 빠른

quickly ADV eoseo 어서, ppalli 빨리, *(immediately)* naengkeum 냉큼, *(right away)* eolleun 얼른

quiet ADJ joyonghada 조용하다, joyonghan 조용한

quietly ADV joyonghi 조용히: *I got out of the back door quietly* naneun dwin-muneuro joyonghi nagatda 나는 뒷문으로 조용히 나갔다

quilt, to v nubida 누비다: *quilt a blanket* ibureul lubida 이불을 누비다

quit, to v geumanduda 그만두다: *He quit his job immediately* geuneun gap-jagi ireul geumandwotda 그는 갑자기 일을 그만뒀다

quite, enough, if possible ADV enganhada 엔간하다: *quite stubborn* enganhaeseoneun mareul deutji anne-unda 엔간해서는 말을 듣지 않는다; *Enough is enough* enganhi jom haera 엔간히 좀 해라; *Please attend if at all possible* enganhamyeon chamseokhagi baranda 엔간하면 참석하기 바란다

quite, fairly, considerably ADV sang-danghi 상당히

quite big ADJ keumjikhada 큼직하다
quote N innyongmun 인용문
quote, to V innyonghada 인용하다:
This instance was quoted as important i yega jungyohan geoseuro innyongdoeeotda 이 예가 중요한 것으로 인용되었다
quiz N kwijeu 퀴즈

R
rabbit N tokki 토끼
race *(sports)* N reiseu 레이스: *a car race* jadongcha reiseu 자동차 레이스
racism N injong chabyeol 인종 차별
rack N batchimdae 받침대, seonban 선반: *The man is looking at postcards on the rack* geu namjaneun seonban wie inneun yeopseoreul bogo itda 그 남자는 선반 위에 있는 엽서를 보고 있다
radiate, to V balgwanghada 발광하다
radiation N bangsaseon 방사선: *It absorbs radiation emitted by the sun* geugeoseun taeyangeseo naeppumneun bangsaseoneul heupsuhanda 그것은 태양에서 내뿜는 방사선을 흡수한다
radio N radio 라디오
rafting N raepeuting 래프팅
rage N bunno 분노: *He was seized with a sudden rage* geuneun gapjagi bunnoe sarojapyeotda 그는 갑자기 분노에 사로잡혔다
rail N 1 reil 레일 2 nangan 난간: *The train is puffing out on the rail* reil wieseo gichaga yeongireul naeppumgo itda 레일 위에서 기차가 연기를 내뿜고 있다
railroad, railway N cheoltto 칠도
rain I N bi 비: *rainy season, monsoon* jangma 장마 II V biga oda 비가 오다
raincoat N reinkoteu 레인코트
raise, to V 1 *(nuture)* yang.yukhada 양육하다: *raise one's children* janyeoreul yangyukhada 자녀를 양육하다 2 *(lift, increase)* ollida 올리다: *raise wages* imgeumeul rollida 임금을 올리다
rally N 1 jipoe 집회 2 raelli 랠리
ram, shove, stuff, to V cheobakda 처박다
rampage N nandong 난동

rampant, prevalent ADJ mannyeonhada 만연하다
random ADJ mujagwiui 무작위의: *We did a random telephone survey* urineun mujagwiui jeonhwajosareul haetda 우리는 무작위의 전화조사를 했다
range N beomwi 범위: *The talks embraced a wide range of issues* geu hoedameun gwangbeomwihan munjedeureul pumeotda 그 회담은 광범위한 문제들을 품었다
range, to V jeongnyeolhada 정렬하다
rank N 1 *(class)* gyegeup 계급 2 *(status, position)* jiwi 지위
ranking, placing N sunwi 순위
rap N raep 랩: *raps while singing* noraehamyeo raebeul hada 노래하며 랩을 하다
rape N ganggan 강간: *A rape was committed in the park last night* jinan bame gongwoneseo ganggan sageoni iseotda 지난 밤에 공원에서 강간 사건이 있었다
rapid ADJ ppareun 빠른: *His rapid speech is difficult to understand* geuui ppareun mareun ihaehagi himdeulda 그의 빠른 말은 이해하기 힘들다
rare, scarce ADJ deumulda 드물다, deumun 드문
rarely ADV deumulge 드물게
rat N jwi 쥐
rate of exchange *(for foreign currency)* N hwannyul 환율
rather, rather than ADV charari 차라리: *I'd rather die* charari jukgo sipda 차라리 죽고 싶다
rather than... ADV ...boda ohiryeo ...보다 오히려
rating N 1 sunwi 순위 2 deunggeup 등급
ratio N biyul 비율: *We are uneasy about our debt ratio* urineun uriui buchaebiyul ttaemune buranhada 우리는 우리의 부채비율 때문에 불안하다
rave with fury, to V nalttwida 날뛰다
ravine, gorge N sangoljjagi 산골짜기
raw, uncooked ADJ nal (geosui) 날 (것의): *raw fish* nal saengseon 날 생선
raw material N wonjajae 원자재
reach, to V 1 *(arrive, get)* dochakhada 도착하다 2 *(deduce)* ireuda 이르다: *reach a conclusion* gyeollone ireuda 결론에 이르다

R

react, respond, reply, to v baneung-hada 반응하다

reaction, response N baneung 반응

read, to v 1 *(printed materials)* ikda 읽다: *read a book* chaegeul ikda 책을 읽다 2 *(study in details)* yeollamhada 열람하다

reader N dokja 독자, ingneun saram 읽는 사람: *The poetry evoked a feeling of love in the reader* geu sineun dokjadeurege sarangui gamjeongeul bulleo ireukyeotda 그 시는 독자들에게 사랑의 감정을 불러 일으켰다

readily ADV sonswipge 손쉽게

ready ADJ junbiga doen 준비가 된

real ADJ jinjjaui 진짜의

realism N rieollijeum 리얼리즘

reality N siljje(ui) 실제

realize, recognize, to v insikhada 인식하다: *recognize danger* wiheomeul insikhada 위험을 인식하다

really, truly ADV jeongmal 정말

really? INTERJ jeongmaryo? 정말요?

rear ADJ dwijjok 뒤쪽

reason N iyu 이유, sayu 사유

reasonable, rational ADJ hamnijeogida/-jeogin 합리적이다/ -적인: *a rational choice* hamnijeogin seontaek 합리적인 선택

rebate, kickback N ribeiteu 리베이트

rebound N ribaundeu 리바운드

rebuild, to v dasi seuda 다시 세우다, dasi joripada 다시 조립하다

recall N rikol 리콜

receipt N yeongsujeung 영수증

receive, to v batda 받다: *receive a letter* pyeonjireul batda 편지를 받다

receiver N 1 banneun saram 받는 사람, suchwiin 수취인 2 susingi 수신기

recent ADJ choegeunui 최근의: *His recent conduct has estranged many of his friends* geuui choegeunui haengdong ttaemune maneun chingudeuri geuegeseo doraseotda 그의 최근의 행동 때문에 많은 친구들이 그에게서 돌아섰다

recently ADV choegeune 최근에

reception N risepsyeon 리셉션

recipe N joribeop 조리법

reckless driving N pokju 폭주

recognize, to v araboda 알아보다: *recognize a person* sarameul araboda

사람을 알아보다

recommend, to v chucheonhada 추천하다

record, disc N eumban 음반

recording N 1 nogeum 녹음 2 girok 기록

recover completely, to v wankwaehada 완쾌하다

recovered ADJ hoebokhada, hoebokan 회복하다, 회복한

recovery, retrieval N manhoe 만회

recovery from illness N kwaeyu 쾌유: *wish a person a full recovery* kwaeyureul bilda 쾌유를 빌다

recruit, to v mojipada 모집하다: *His task is to recruit new members for the club* geuui immuneun sinipsawoneul mojipaneun irida 그의 임무는 신입사원을 모집하는 일이다

rectangle N jiksagakhyeong 직사각형

recycling N risaikeulling 리사이클링

red ADJ ppalgata 빨갛다, ppalgan 빨간: *red bean* pat 팥

reddish, rosy, flushed ADJ balgeurehada 발그레하다

reduce, to v jurida 줄이다: *The leaves on trees reduce pollution* namunnipeun oyeomeul jurinda 나뭇잎은 오염을 줄인다

reduction N chukso 축소

refer to, consult, to v chamgohada 참고하다

reference, consultation N chamgo 참고

reference, mention N eongeup 언급

reference book, study-aid book N chamgoseo 참고서

refill, to v ripilhada 리필하다: *refill drinks* eumnyosureul lipilhaetda 음료수를 리필했다

reflect, to v 1 *(light)* bansahada 반사하다 2 *(feedback)* bannyeonghada 반영하다: *reflect public opinion* yeoroneul bannyeonghada 여론을 반영하다

reflection N bansa 반사

reform, amend, restore, to v barojapda 바로잡다: *amend one's conduct* haengsireul barojapda 행실을 바로잡다

refrain, suppress, to v eongnureuda 억누르다

refreshments N dagwa 다과

refrigerator N naengjanggo 냉장고

refund N hwanbul 환불

refuge N pinan 피난

refugee N nanmin 난민: *She took a year off and worked at a refugee camp* geunyeoneun il nyeoneul swigo pinanmin kaempeueseo ilhaetda 그녀는 일 년을 쉬고 피난민 캠프에서 일했다

refusal N 1 *(objection)* geojeol 거절 2 *(denial)* sajeol 사절

refuse, deny, to V sajeolhada 사절하다

regard, consider, treat, to V yeogida 여기다: *treat a child (person) as one's own* chinjasikcheoreom yeogida 친자식처럼 여기다

regarding, concerning ADV ...e gwanhayeo ...에 관하여

regardless ADV gaeuichi anko 개의치 않고

region N jibang 지방

regional ADJ jibangui 지방의

register, to V deungnokhada 등록하다: *registered post* deunggi upyeon 등기 우편

regret, to V huhoehada 후회하다

regretful, sorry, to be V yugamseureopda/-seureo.un 유감스럽다/-스러운

regrettable, unfortunate ADJ akkapda 아깝다: *a regrettable failure* akkaun silpae 아까운 실패

regrettably ADV yugamseureopgedo 유감스럽게도

regular *(customer)* N dangol 단골: *a regular customer* dangol sonnim 단골 손님

regular, normal, average ADJ botong(ui) 보통(의)

regularly ADV jeonggijeogeuro 정기적으로: *We changed the monitor oil in our car regularly* urineun jeonggijcogeuro jadongcha enjinoireul garajunda 우리는 정기적으로 자동차 엔진오일을 갈아준다

regulation N gyujeong 규정, gyuje 규제: *The regulation have been tightened up recently* gyujeongi choegeune eomhage dwaetda 규정이 최근에 엄하게 됐다

rehabilitation N gaengsaeng 갱생

rehearsal N riheoseol 리허설

reinforce, to V ganghwahada 강화하다: *We intend to reinforce that position* urineun geu ipjangeul ganghwaha-ryeoneun uidoreul gajigo itda 우리는 그 입장을 강화하려는 의도를 가지고 있다

reject, refuse, to V chada 차다

rejection, refusal N toejja 퇴짜

relate, to V gwallyeonsikida 관련시키다

relation, connection N yeongo 연고: *have no connections in Korea* hangugeneun amu yeongoga eopda 한국에는 아무 연고가 없다

relations N sai 사이: *relations between friends* chingu sai 친구 사이; *relations between husband and wife* bubu sai 부부 사이

relationship N gwan.gye 관계

relatives, family N chincheok 친척

relax, to V ginjang.eul pulda 긴장을 풀다

relay N rillei 릴레이

release N 1 seokbang 석방 2 gaebong 개봉

release, to V 1 noajuda 놓아주다 2 gaebonghada 개봉하다

relevant ADJ gwallyeon inneun 관련 있는

reliability N silloeseong 신뢰성

reliable ADJ 1 *(dependable)* mideumjikhada 믿음직하다 2 *(solid, trustworthy)* chaksilhada 착실하다

relic N 1 *(antiquity)* yumul 유물 2 *(article left by the deceased)* yupum 유품

relief N ansim 안심: *But for now at least the relief is palpable* hajiman jigeumeun jeogeodo ansimi doenda 하지만 지금은 적어도 안심이 된다

relieve, to V 1 andohage hada 안도하게 하다 2 wanhwahada 완화하다

religion N jonggyo 종교

religious ADJ jonggyoui 종교의

reluctant ADJ kkeorineun 꺼리는, majimotan 마지못한: *They are reluctant to embark on it* geudeureun geugeose seungseonhagireul kkeoryeohaetda 그들은 그것에 승선하기를 꺼려했다

rely, to V uijihada 의지하다

remain dormant, to V jambokhada 잠복하다

remain still, to V gamanitda 가만있다

remaining ADJ nama inneun 남아 있는

remark N juui 주의

remark, to V 1 juuihada 주의하다 2 malhada 말하다

R

remarkable ADJ nollaun 놀라운, jumokhal manhan 주목할 만한
remember, to V gi.eokhada 기억하다
remind, to V sanggisikida 상기시키다
reminder N sanggisikineun geot 상기시키는 것
remote ADJ 1 (far, distant) gipda 깊다, gipeun 깊은: a remote mountain gipeun san sok 깊은 산 속 2 (dim, faint) adeukhada 아득하다, adeukhan 아득한: remote past adeukhan yennal 아득한 옛날
remote control N rimokeon 리모컨
remove, to V chiuda 치우다, jegeohada 제거하다: Remove foil, bake 5 more minutes or until firm hoireul jegeo-hago obun deo gupgeona ttakttakhae jil ttaekkaji gumneunda 호일을 제거하고 오분 더 굽거나 딱딱해 질 때까지 굽는다
Renaissance, the N reunesangseu 르네상스
rent, to V imdaehada 임대하다
rent out, to V sejuda 세주다
rental car N renteoka 렌터카
repair N suri 수리: This building is in need of repair i geonmureun suriga piryohada 이 건물은 수리가 필요하다
repair, to V surihada 수리하다
repairs shop, service center N jeongbiso 정비소
repay, requite, to V bodaphada 보답하다
repeat, to V banbokhada 반복하다
repeatedly, often ADV jakku 자꾸
repent, confess, to V chamhoehada 참회하다
replace, to V daechehada 대체하다: replace A with B Areul Bro daeche-hada A를 B로 대체하다
report I N bogo 보고 II V bogohada 보고하다
reporter N gija 기자, ripoteo 리포터
represent, to V daepyohada 대표하다
representative N daepyoja 대표자, daeriin 대리인
repress (emotion), **swallow, control, to** V chamda 참다: control one's temper hwareul chamda 화를 참다
reproachful, hateful ADJ wonmang-seureopda 원망스럽다
reproduction N jaesaeng 재생

reptiles N pachungnyu 파충류
republic N gonghwaguk 공화국
reputation N pyeongpan 평판, myeongseong 명성
request, ask, to V yocheonghada 요청하다
require, to V 1 piryohada 필요하다 2 yoguhada 요구하다
requirement N piryo 필요, yogeon 요건
rescue, to V gujohada 구조하다
research I N tamgu 탐구, yeon.gu 연구: research institute yeonguso 연구소 II V tamguhada 탐구하다, yeon.guhada 연구하다
resemble, to V damda 닮다
resentment N ulhwa 울화
resentment, bitterness (deeply rooted) N eungeori 응어리
reserve, to V yeyakhada 예약하다: reservation yeyak 예약
resident, inhabitant N jumin 주민
residential ADJ jugeoui 주거의
resign, to V sajikhada 사직하다
resignation N satoe 사퇴
resist, to V jeohanghada 저항하다
resistance, defiance N banbal 반발
resolution N dajim 다짐
resolve, solve, to V haegyeolhada 해결하다: solve a problem munjereul haegyeolhada 문제를 해결하다
resort N rijoteu 리조트
resources N jawon 자원
respect I N jon.gyeong 존경 II V jon.gyeonghada 존경하다
respectable, decent, honorable ADJ eoyeotada 어엿하다
responsible ADJ chaegim itda/inneun 책임 있다/있는: be responsible for chaegim itda 책임이 있다; a responsible answer chaegim inneun dapbyeon 책임 있는 답변
rest, relax, to V swida 쉬다
rest, remainder, leftover N nameoji 나머지
restaurant N eumsikjeom 음식점, reseutorang 레스토랑, sikdang 식당
restrict, to V jehanhada 제한하다
restriction N jehan 제한
result N gyeolgwa 결과
resulting from, as a result ADV gyeolgwaroseo 결과로서

resume, to v jaegaehada 재개하다

retail ADJ somae 소매, somaeui 소매의

retailer N somaeeopja 소매업자, somaeeop 소매업

retain, to v yujihada 유지하다

retire, to v toejikhada 퇴직하다: *retirement* euntoe 은퇴

retreat, to v hutoehada 후퇴하다

return, to v 1 *(give back)* dollyeojuda 돌려주다 2 *(home)* jibe doraoda 집에 돌아오다

return, turn-in N bannap 반납

return ticket N wangbokpyo 왕복표

reveal, expose, to v pongnohada 폭로 하다: *expose injustice* bujeongeul pongnohada 부정을 폭로하다

revenge, retaliation N anggapeum 앙갚음

revenue N suik 수익: *Tourism is this town's main source of revenue* gwangwangsaeobeun i dosiui ju suig-ida 관광사업은 이 도시의 주 수익이다

reverse, back up, to v dwiro gada 뒤로 가다

reverse, reversal N banjeon 반전

reversed, backwards ADJ geokkuroui 거꾸로의

review N ribyu 리뷰

revive, bring back, to v sallida 살리다

revolution N hyeongmyeong 혁명: *That paved the way for the revolution* geugeonni hyeongmyeongui giuneul joseonghaetda 그것이 혁명의 기운을 조성했다

reward, compensation N sarye 사례

rhino N koppulso 코뿔소

rhythm N rideum 리듬

rhythmic movement, dance N yul-dong 율동

rhythmical ADJ rideumikeolhada 리드미컬하다

rib N galbi 갈비

ribbon N ribon 리본

rice N 1 *(cooked meal)* bap 밥 2 *(plant)* byeo 벼 3 rice *(uncooked grains)* ssal 쌀

rice fields N non 논

rich, wealthy, well off ADJ buyuhan 부유한: *a wealthy family* buyuhan jiban 부유한 집안

richness, abundance N pungyo 풍요

rid, to v eopsaeda 없애다, jegeohada 제거하다

ride N talgeot 탈것

ride, to v tada 타다

ridiculous ADJ maldo an doeneun 말도 안 되는

rifle N raipeulchong 라이플총, sochong 소총

right I N *(privilege)* jagyeok 자격: *have a right to demand* yoguhal jagyeogi itda 요구할 자격이 있다; *right of autonomy* jachigwon 자치권; *right of freedom* jayugwon 자유권 II ADJ 1 *(correct)* olta 옳다, oreun 옳은 2 *(rightful, entitled)* olbareuda 올바르다

right now ADV jigeum dangjang 지금 당장

right path, right method N jeongdo 정도: *stray from the right path* jeong-doeseo beoseonada 정도에서 벗어나다

right-hand side N oreunjjok 오른쪽

righteous, rightful ADJ uiropda 의롭다

rights N gwolli 권리

ring I N *(jewellery)* banji 반지 II v 1 *(bell)* ullida 울리다: *ring a bell* jongeul ullida 종을 울리다 2 *(call, dial on the telephone)* jeonhwahada 전화하다

rinse N rinseu 린스

riot N pokdong 폭동: *The riot was nipped in the bud* pokdongeun keuge beonjigi jeone jinapdoeeotda 폭동은 크게 번지기 전에 진압되었다

rip, to v jjitda 찢다

ripe, to grow v ikda 익다: *the rice is ripening* byeoga ikda (igeoganda) 벼가 익다 (익어간다)

ripen, to v ikhida 익히다

ripple, water ring N pamun 파문

rise, ascend, to v oreuda 오르다

risk N riseukeu 리스크

risky, close, critical, dangerous ADJ aseuraseulhada 아슬아슬하다

ritual, formality N eurye 의례

rival N gyeongjaengsangdae 경쟁상대, raibeol 라이벌

river N gang 강

road N doro 도로

roadway, highway N chado 차도: *roadway full of cars* chadoe chaga manta 차도에 차가 많다

R

roast, stir-fry to v bokda 볶다: *stir-fry meat with oil* gireume gogireul bokda 기름에 고기를 볶다

robot N robot 로봇

rock N bawi 바위

rocket N roket 로켓

rod N makdae 막대

rodeo N rodeo 로데오

role N yeokhal 역할

roll N 1 durumari 두루마리 2 myeongbu 명부

roll, to v gureuda 구르다, gullida 굴리다

roller coaster N rolleo koseuteo 롤러 코스터

roller skates N rolleo skate 롤러 스케이트

romance N nangman 낭만, romang 로망, romaenseu 로맨스: *a holiday romance* hyugajieseoui romaenseu 휴가지에서의 로맨서

romantic ADJ romaentikhada 로맨틱하다: *He's very romantic* geuneun maeu romaentikhada 그는 매우 로맨틱하다

Rome N roma 로마: *When in Rome, do as Romans do* romaeseoneun nomaui beobeul ttaraya handa 로마에서는 로마의 법을 따라야 한다

romp about, to v jangnanchida 장난치다

roof N jibung 지붕

room N bang 방, kan 칸, rum 룸

room *(counting unit)* N kan 칸: *How many rooms?* bangi myeot kanieyo? 방이 몇 칸이에요?

room, cabin *(hotel/boat)* N gaeksil 객실

room, margin N yeoji 여지

room, space N gonggan 공간

root N 1 *(origin, source)* woncheon 원천 2 *(of plant)* ppuri 뿌리

rope N batjul 밧줄

rose N jangmi 장미

rotation N jajeon 자전

rotten ADJ sseokda 썩다, sseogeun 썩은

rough ADJ 1 *(crude, coarse)* tubakhada 투박하다 2 *(wild)* geochilda 거칠다, geochin 거친

roughly, approximately ADV daegang 대강

roulette N rullet 룰렛

round *(shape)* ADJ dunggeulda 둥글다, dunggeun 둥근

rouse up, burst forth, to v ukhada 욱하다

route N ruteu 루트: *investigate a purchase route* guip nuteureul josahada 구입 루트를 조사하다

routine N teul 틀, ilsang 일상

row N yeol 열, jul 줄: *Our seats are on the fifth row* uri jarineun daseot beonjae jure itda 우리 자리는 다섯 번째 줄에 있다

row, to v noreul jeotda 노를 젓다

royal ADJ gugwangui 국왕의

rub, to v munjireuda 문지르다

rubber N gomu 고무

rubbish N 1 *(filth)* omul 오물 2 *(nonsense, silly talk)* jamkkodae 잠꼬대: *Stop talking rubbish* jamkkodae gachin sori haji mara 잠꼬대 같은 소리 하지 마라

ruby N rubi 루비

rude, abrupt, forward ADJ dangdolhada 당돌하다

rugby N reokbi 럭비

ruin, to v mangchida 망치다

rule, reign N tongchi 통치

rule over, to v tongchihada 통치하다

ruler N ja 자

rules N gyuchik 규칙

ruling N jibae 지배, tongchi 통치

ruling party and opposition party, the N yeoya 여야

rumor N somun 소문: *a rumor gets started* somuni nada 소문이 나다

run, to v dallida 달리다

run away, to v 1 *(flee)* domanggada 도망가다. tokkida 토끼다 2 *(from home)* gachulhada 가출하다

run into, bump into, to v majuchida 마주치다: *bump into an old friend* bump into an old friend yet chingureul uyeonhi majuchida 옛 친구를 우연히 마주치다

run mad, go crazy, to v balgwanghada 발광하다

run out, to v tteoreojida 떨어지다: *run out of money* doni tteoreojida 돈이 떨어지다

rural ADJ sigorui 시골의, jibangui 지방의

rush N doljin 돌진

rush, to v 1 doljinhada 돌진하다 2 seodureuda 서두르다

Russia N reosia 러시아

S

sack N budae 부대, jaru 자루

sacred, holy ADJ seongseureopda 성스 럽다, seongseureo.un 성스러운

sacrifice I N hisaeng 희생 II v hisaeng-hada 희생하다

sad ADJ seulpeuda 슬프다, seulpeun 슬픈

safety N anjeon 안전: *People use air-bags for safety reasons* saram-deureun anjeonui mokjeogeuro eeobaegeul sayonghanda 사람들은 안 전의 목적으로 에어백을 사용한다

sail, to v hanghaehada 항해하다

sake N 1 iik 이익 2 mokjeok 목적

salad N saelleodeu 샐러드

salary N bonggeup 봉급

sale *(discounted prices)* N seil 세일

sale, for ADV panmae jung 판매 중

sales assistant, shopkeeper N jeomwon 점원

salmon N yeoneo 연어

salt N sogeum 소금

salt seasoning N gan 간: *be well-seasoned* gani matda 간이 맞다

salty ADJ jjada 짜다, jjan 짠: *salt is salty* sogeumeun jjada 소금은 짜다

sample N gyeonbon 견본

sand N morae 모래: *a sand castle* moraeseong 모래성

sandals N saendal 샌달

sandwich N saendeuwichi 샌드위치

sanitation N wisaeng 위생

sarcastic, to be v binjeonggeorida 빈정거리다

satellite N ingongwiseong 인공위성

satisfied, to be v manjokhada, manjokhaehada 만족하나, 만족해하다

satisfied with, content with, to be v chada 차다: *prove (be) unsatisfactory* maeume chaji anneunda 마음에 차지 않는다

satisfy, to v manjoksikida 만족시키다

saturate oneself with *(sunshine or moonlight)*, **to** v batda 받다: *saturate oneself with sunlight* haetbicheul (heumppeok) batda 햇빛을 (흠뻑) 받다

Saturday N toyoil 토요일

Saturn N toseong 토성

sauce N soseu 소스

save, to v 1 *(economize, conserve)* akkida 아끼다: *conserve water* mureul rakkida 물을 아끼다 2 *(keep)* bogwan-hada 보관하다

saving N jeochuk 저축

savory aroma, tasty flavor N goso-hada 고소하다

saw N top 톱

say, speak, talk, tell, to v malhada 말하다

say goodbye, to v jal garago jeonhada 잘 가라고 전하다

say hello, to v anbujeonhada 안부전하다

say sorry, to v mianhadago jeonhada 미안하다고 전하다

say thank you, to v gomapdago jeonhada 고맙다고 전하다

scales N jeo.ul 저울

scan, to v 1 salpida 살피다 2 josahada 조사하다

scandal N seukaendeul 스캔들, chumun 추문: *Her scandal is reported in a newspaper* geunyeoui chumuni sin-mune ollatda 그녀의 추문이 신문에 올랐다

scared, frightened, to be v geom-meokda 겁먹다

scarf, muffler N mokdori 목도리

scary, frightening ADJ museopda 무섭다, museo.un 무서운

scatter, to v heutppurida 흩뿌리다

scene N jangmyeon 장면, sin 신

scenery, view N gyeongchi 경치

scent N naemsae 냄새

schedule N seukejul 스케줄

scheme N gyehoek 계획, chaengnyak 책략

scholar N hakja 학자

scholarship N janghakgeum 장학금

school N hakgyo 학교: *(senior) high school* godeunghakgyo 고등학교

science N gwahak 과학

scientist N gwahakja 과학자

scissors N gawi 가위

scold, to v 1 *(rebuke)* pinjanhada 핀잔 하다 2 *(blame)* namurada 나무라다: *scold a student* haksaengeul namu-rada 학생을 나무라다

score N deukjeom 득점

Scotland N seukoteullaendeu 스코틀랜드

S

scratch, to V halkwida 할퀴다, geukda 긁다

scream, to V sorichida 소리치다: *You don't have to scream at me* nahante sorichil piryo eopseo 나한테 소리칠 필요 없어

screen *(of computer)* N seukeurin 스크린

screening N simsa 심사

screw N nasa 나사

scribble I N *(graffiti)* nakseo 낙서 2 V galgyeosseuda 갈겨쓰다

script N 1 daebon 대본 2 geulssi 글씨

scrub, to V munjireuda 문지르다: *scrub lightly* salsal munjireuda 살살 문지르다

sculpture N jogakpum 조각품

sea N bada 바다

seafood N haemul 해물: *seafood medley* haemul japtang 해물 잡탕; *seafood plate* haemul yori 해물 요리

seal, to V bonghada 봉하다

search N susaek 수색

search, to V chatda 찾다

seashore N haebyeon 해변

season N gyejeol 계절

seat, room, space, position, location, site N jari 자리

secede from, to V taltoehada 탈퇴하다

second ADJ du beonjjaeui 두 번째의: *second-largest* dubeonjjaero keun 두 번째로 큰; *second daughter* chanyeo 차녀; *second son* chanam 차남

secondary ADJ ichajeogin 이차적인: *A question like that is a secondary importance* geureon ireun ichajeogin munjeda 그런 일은 이차적인 문제다

secret N bimil 비밀

secret, to keep a V bimireul jikida 비밀을 지키다

secretary N biseo 비서

secure, safe ADJ anjeonhada 안전하다, anjeonhan 안전한: *a safe shelter* anjeonhan pinancheo 안전한 피난처; *a secure job* anjeonhan jikjang 안전한 직장

see, to V boda 보다

seek, to V chatda 찾다

see you later! PHR tto bopsida! 또 봅시다!, najung.e bopsida! 나중에 봅시다!

seed N ssi 씨

seed money N mitcheon 밑천

seem, to V boida 보이다: *You seem busy these days* neo yosae bappa boinda 너 요새 바빠 보인다

seize, to V butjapda 붙잡다: *He tried to seize at straws* geuneun jipuragirado butjabeuryeogo haetda 그는 지푸라기라도 붙잡으려고 했다

seldom ADV jomcheoreom...anneun 좀처럼…않는

select, to V goreuda 고르다

selected ADJ seontaekdoen 선택된

selection N seonbal 선발, seontaek 선택

self N jagi 자기

self-control N jaje 자제

self-education N dokhak 독학

self-esteem N jabusim 자부심: *The problem is low levels of self-esteem* munjeneun najeun jabusimida 문제는 낮은 자부심이다

self-examination N banseong 반성

self-interest N sari 사리

self-portrait N jahwasang 자화상

self-reliance N jarip 자립

sell, to V palda 팔다: *sell sth cheap* ssage palda 싸게 팔다

seller N panmaein 판매인

Senate N sangwon 상원

send, to V bonaeda 보내다: *send a letter* pyeonjireul bonaeda 편지를 보내다

send back, return, to V dollyeobonaeda 돌려보내다

senior ADJ sangwiui 상위의, sonwiui 손위의

senior N yeonjangja 연장자, seonbae 선배

sensation N gamgak 감각

sense N gamgak 감각

sense, to V neukkida 느끼다

sense of duty N uimugam 의무감

sense of hearing N cheonggak 청각

sensible ADJ bunbyeollyeok itda/inneun 분별력 있다/있는

sentence N 1 *(grammar)* munjang 문장 2 *(judgment)* seon.go 선고

separate, to V bullihada 분리하다

separation by death N sabyeol 사별

September N guwol 구월

sequence N yeonsok 연속

series N sirijeu 시리즈, yeonsongmul 연속물

serious ADJ 1 *(stern)* simgakhada 심각하다, simgakan 심각한 2 *(grave, important)* jungdaehada 중대하다, jungdaehan 중대한

servant N hain 하인: *treat sb like a servant* hain burideut tada 하인 부리듯 하다

serve, to V mosida 모시다

service N seobiseu 서비스

serving N jeopdae 접대

sesame oil N chamgireum 참기름

sesame seeds N chamkkae 참깨

set N 1 seteu 세트 2 *(assemble)* matchuda 맞추다

set down, take down, to V naeryeonota 내려놓다

set off, to V naseoda 나서다

setback, snag N chajil 차질

settle, to V nota 놓다

settlement N jeongchak 정착

seven NUM 1 ilgop 일곱 2 chil 칠: *the 7th* je chirui 제 칠의

seventeen NUM 1 sipchil 십칠 2 yeorilgop 열일곱

seventy NUM 1 chilsip 칠십 2 ilheun 일흔

severe ADJ 1 *(heavy, harsh)* simhada 심하다, simhan 심한 2 *(strict)* eomhada 엄하다

severely ADV simhage 심하게: *Our profits will be severely reduced* uriui iyuni simhage gamsohal geonnida 우리의 이윤이 심하게 감소할 것이다

sew, to V baneujilhada 바느질하다, bakda 박다

sewing machine N jaebongteul 재봉틀

sex N 1 *(gender)* seong 성 2 *(intercourse)* sekseu 섹스

sexual ADJ seongjeogin 성적인

sexy ADJ seksihan 섹시한

shack N panjajip 판자집

shade N geuneul 그늘: *shaded ground* eumji 음지

shadow N geurimja 그림자

shake, to V 1 *(shiver)* tteolda 떨다: *shake one's legs* darireul tteolda 다리를 떨다 2 *(swing, wave)* heundeulda 흔들다

shake hands, to V aksuhada 악수하다: *shake hands with the president* daetongnyeonggwa aksuhada 대통령과 악수하다

shall V ...il geotsida …일 것이다

shallow ADJ yatda 얕다, yateun 얕은: *shallow water* yateun mul 얕은 물

shame N 1 *(disgrace)* mangsin 망신 2 *(disgrace, humiliation)* suchi 수치

shameless, brazen N yeomchi 염치

shampoo N syampu 샴푸

shape, form, to V hyeongseonghada 형성하다

share N mok 몫: *He claimed his share of the property* geuneun yusanui jagi mokseul yoguhaetda 그는 유산의 자기 몫을 요구했다

share, to V nanuda 나누다: *Couples share joys and sorrows of life* keopeureun insaengui gorageul hamkke nanunda 커플은 인생의 고락을 함께 나눈다

shark N sang.eo 상어

sharp, keen ADJ nalkaropda 날카롭다, nalkaroun 날카로운: *a sharp knife* nalkaroun kal 날카로운 칼; *keen insight* nalkaroun tongchallyeok 날카로운 통찰력

shave, to V myeondohada 면도하다: *shaved ice (with syrup)* bingsu 빙수

she PRON geu yeoja 그 여자

shed, to V heullida 흘리다: *She shed tears* geunyeoneun nunmureul heullyeotda 그녀는 눈물을 흘렸다

sheep N yang 양: *a stray sheep* gil ireun yang 길 잃은 양

sheet N 1 *(for bed)* siteu 시트 2 *(of paper)* jang 장

shelf N seonban 선반

shell N kkeopdegi 껍데기

shelter N jugeoji 주거지

shepherd, lead, to V ikkeulda 이끌다: *lead an arrny* gundaereul ikkculda 군대를 이끌다

shift N byeonhwa 변화

shift, to V banghyangeul bakkuda 방향을 바꾸다

shine, sparkle, to V binnada 빛나다

shiny ADJ binnaneun 빛나는

ship, boat, ferry N bae 배: *a fishing boat* gogijabi bae 고기잡이 배

shirt N syeocheu 셔츠: *shirts* sangui 상의

shock N chunggyeok 충격

shoes N sinbal 신발

shoot, to V ssoda 쏘다

S

shooting N sagyeok 사격

shop I N *(store)* gage 가게, maejang 매장 II *(go shopping)* syopinghada 쇼핑하다

shopping N shopping 쇼핑

short ADJ jjalbeun 짧은

short ADV gapjagi 갑자기

short distance N dangeori 단거리

short film N danpyeonyoenghwa 단편 영화

short pants N banbaji 반바지

short sketch, short novel N danpyeonsoseol 단편소설

shortening, reduction N danchuk 단축

short piece, fragment N danpyeon 단편

shorts N banbaji 반바지

short-term ADJ dangiui 단기의

shot N balpo 발포

shoulder N eokkae 어깨

shout, yell, to V oechida 외치다

show I N *(entertainment)* syo 쇼 II V *(display)* boyeojuda 보여주다: *show an ID* sinbunjeungeul boyeojuda 신분증을 보여주다

show program N syopeuro 쇼프로

shower N 1 *(for washing)* syawo 샤워 2 *(of rain)* sonagi 소나기

shrewd, clever ADJ yeongakhada 영악하다

shriek with laughter, to V jajireojida 자지러지다

shrimp, prawn N sae.u 새우

shrink, to V ogeuradeulda 오그라들다: *Her heart seemed to shrink with fear* geunyeoui simjangi gongporo ogeuradeuneun geot gatatda 그녀의 심장이 공포로 오그라드는 것 같았다

shrivel *(up),* **to** V ogeuradeulda 오그라들다: *shriveled up legs* ogeuradeun dari 오그라든 다리

shudder, shiver N jeonnyul 전율

shut, to V datda 닫다: *The door does not shut well* muni jal dachiji anneunda 문이 잘 닫히지 않는다

shut up *(impolite)* V dakchida 닥치다: *Shut your mouth!* ip dakchyeo! 입 닥쳐!

shy ADJ sujubeun 수줍은

sibling N hyeongje jamae 형제 자매

sick ADJ byeongdeun 병든

sickening, disgusting ADJ yeokhada 역하다

sickness, illness N tal 탈: *get ill* tari nada 탈이 나다

side N jjok 쪽, yeopguri 옆구리

sidewalk N indo 인도: *The vehicle drove into the sidewalk* chaga indokkaji deureowatda 차가 인도까지 들어왔다

sigh, to V hansum swida 한숨 쉬다

sight N sigak 시각

sightseeing N *(sinae)* gwangwang (시내) 관광

sign I N *(mark)* pyosi 표시 II V *(a document)* sainhada 사인하다

signal N sinho 신호

signature, autograph N sain 사인

signboard N ganpan 간판

significant ADJ jungyohan 중요한

silence N goyo 고요, jeongjeok 정적

silent, still, quiet, calm ADJ goyohada 고요하다, goyohan 고요한

silk N silkeu 실크

silly ADJ eoriseogeun 어리석은: *There is no such thing as a silly offer* eoriseogeun jeaniraneun geoseun eopda 어리석은 제안이라는 것은 없다

silver N eun 은, *(color)* eunsaek 은색

silver hair N eunbal 은발

similar, alike ADJ biseuthada 비슷하다, biseutan 비슷한: *have similar interests* gwansimsaga biseutada 관심사가 비슷하다; *similar faces* biseutan saenggimsae 비슷한 생김새

similarity N yusaseong 유사성

simple, easy ADJ swipda 쉽다, swiun 쉬운

simply ADV gandanhi 간단히, dansunhage 단순하게

sin N joe 죄

since, after ADV ...ihu ...이후: *since that day* geu nal ihu 그 날 이후; *after 5 o'clock* daseotsi ihu 5시 이후

sing, to V noraehada 노래하다: *singer* gasu 가수

Singapore N singgapol 싱가폴

single N 1 *(not married)* doksin 독신 2 *(solitary, lonely person)* oetori 외톨이

single game, singles N dansik 단식: *mens singles (games)* namja dansik gyeonggi 남자 단식 경기

single room, solitary cell N dokbang
독방

singular N dansu 단수

sink, go under, to V garaanda 가라
앉다: the boat has sunk baega garaanjatda 배가 가라앉았다

sir N seonsaengnim 선생님

siren N sairen 사이렌

sister N jamae 자매

sister-in-law N 1 (brother's wife) olke
올케 2 (husband's younger sister)
sinu.i 시누이 3 (wife of one's elder
brother) hyeongsu 형수

sit down, to V an(j)da 앉다

situated, located, to be V itda 있다:
The river is located south of the city
geu gangeun dosi namjjoge itda 그
강은 도시 남쪽에 있다

situation, conditions N sanghwang
상황

six NUM 1 yeoseot 여섯 2 yuk 육

sixteen NUM 1 simnyuk 십육 2 yeolyeoseot 열여섯

sixth sense, hunch N yukgam 육감

sixty NUM 1 yesun 예순: be over sixty
yesuni neomda 예순이 넘다 2 yuksip
육십

size N keugi 크기, saijeu 사이즈

skating rink N ringkeu 링크: ice-rink
aiseuringkeu 아이스링크

skewer N kkochaeng.i 꼬챙이

ski N seuki 스키

skill N 1 gisul 기술, gineung 기능
2 sungnyeon 숙련, noryeon 노련

skilled, experienced ADJ ikda 익다:
be skilled in sone ikda 손에 익다

skillful, dexterous ADJ yonghada
용하다

skillful, experienced ADJ neungsukhada 능숙하다, neungsukan 능숙한

skin N pibu 피부

skinny, thin, slim ADJ mareun 마른:
(too) skinny bijjeok mareun 비쩍 마른

skip, to V 1 ttwida 뛰다 2 georeuda
거르다: It is easy to skip workouts
when traveling yeohaengeul hal ttaeneun undongeul georeugi swipda
여행을 할 때는 운동을 거르기 쉽다

skirt N chima 치마

skull N dugaegol 두개골, haegol 해골

sky N haneul 하늘: blue sky pureun
haneul 푸른 하늘

slander, speak ill of sb, to V heoltteutda 헐뜯다: always speak ill of
someone neul nameul heoltteunneunda 늘 남을 헐뜯는다

slang N euneo 은어

slap, to V 1 ttaerida 때리다 2 buditchida
부딪치다: I'll slap him in the face
naneun geuui eolgureul ttaeril geonnida 나는 그의 얼굴을 때릴 것이다

slave N noye 노예

sleep, go to bed, to V jada 자다: go
to bed early iljjik jada 일찍 자다

sleep talking N jamkkodae 잠꼬대

sleepy, drowsy ADJ jollin 졸린

sleepy, tired, to feel V jollida 졸리다

sleeve N somae 소매

slender ADJ ganeudarata 가느다랗다,
ganeudaran 가느다란

slice N (yalge sseon) jogak (얇게 썬)
조각

slice, to V yalge sseolda 얇게 썰다

slide N mikkeureomteul 미끄럼틀

slight ADJ yakganui 약간의

slim, slender, lean ADJ nalssinhada
날씬하다, nalssinhan 날씬한

slip (petticoat, underskirt) N seullip
슬립

slippers N seullipeo 슬리퍼

slippery ADJ mikkeureobda 미끄럽다

slope N gyeongsa 경사

slow ADJ neurida 느리다, neurin 느린:
be a slow walker georeumi neurida
걸음이 느리다

slowly ADV cheoncheonhi 천천히

sly ADJ neungcheong 능청

smack of (flavor, taste), to V masi nada
맛이 나다

small ADJ jageun 작은

small salary, poor pay N bakbong
박봉

smart, clever ADJ ttokttokhada 똑똑
하다, ttokttokan 똑똑한

smell, to V naemsaematda 냄새맡다

smile I N miso 미소 II V misojitda
미소짓다

smile with one's eyes, to V nunuseum
눈웃음

smoke I N yeon.gi 연기: cigarette
smoke dambae yeongi 담배 연기 II V
(tobacco) dambae pida 담배 피다

smooth ADJ 1 (easy) sunjoropda, sunjoroun 순조롭다, 순조로운: a smooth

S

ENGLISH—KOREAN

start sunjoroun chulbal 순조로운 출발
2 *(silky)* maekkeunhada 매끈하다, mae-
kkeureopda/-reo.un 매끄럽다/-러운

smuggle, to V milsuhada 밀수하다

snail N dalpaengi 달팽이

snake N baem 뱀

snarl, growl, roar, to V eureureonggeorida 으르렁거리다

snatch, steal, intercept, to V garochaeda 가로채다: *intercept a ball* gongeul garochaeda 공을 가로채다

sneak, to V 1 salgeumsalgeum deureo-
oda 살금살금 들어오다 2 sumda
숨다: *Don't sneak up like that* geureoke salgeumsalgeum deureooji mara
그렇게 살금살금 들어오지 마라

sneeze I N jaechaegi 재채기: *hold a
sneeze* jaechaegireul chamda 재채기
를 참다 II V jaechaegihada 재채기하다

sniff, sneer N kouseum 코웃음

snore, to V kogolda 코 골다

snow I N nun 눈: *snow-covered streets*
nun deogin geori 눈 덮인 거리 II V
nuni oda 눈이 오다

snowman N nunsaram 눈사람

snug ADJ pogeunhada 포근하다, aneukhada 아늑하다, aneukhan 아늑한:
cozy space aneukhan gonggan 아늑한
공간

snuggle into, to V pagodeulda 파고들
다: *The baby snuggled into mom's
arms* agiga eomma pumeul pagodeureotda 아기가 엄마 품을 파고들었다

so, therefore, thus CONJ geuraeseo
그래서

soak, wet, humidify, to V jeoksida
적시다: *wet a towel* sugeoneul jeoksida 수건을 적시다

soak out, come off, to V ureonada
우러나다

soap N binu 비누

soar, to V geupjeunghada 급증하다

soccer N chukgu 축구

sociable, gregarious, outgoing ADJ
sagyojeogda/-jeogin 사교적이다/-적인

social ADJ sahoejeogin 사회적인

**socialize with, associate with, get
along with, to** V eo.ullida 어울리다:
get along with anyone nuguwado jal
eoullida 누구와도 잘 어울리다

society, community N sahoe 사회

socket *(electric)* N soketeu 소케트

socks N yangmal 양말

sofa, couch N sopa 소파

soft ADJ 1 *(to the senses)* budeureopda
부드럽다, budeureo.un 부드러운: *have
soft skin* pibuga budeureopda 피부가
부드럽다; *soft wind* budeureoun
baram 부드러운 바람 2 *(cushiony)*
puksinhada 푹신하다 3 *(mild, genial)*
yuhada 유하다 4 *(pliable)* yuyeonhada
유연하다 5 *(tender, tender-hearted)*
yeorida 여리다

soft drink N eumnyosu 음료수

soft persimmon N hongsi 홍시,
yeonsi 연시

software N software 소프트웨어

sol *(music scale)* N sol 솔

solar ADJ taeyangui 태양의

sold out ADJ maejindoen 매진된

soldier N gunin 군인

sole, only ADJ yu.ilhan 유일한: *only
friend* yuilhan chingu 유일한 친구

solely ADV 1 *(only)* oroji 오로지
2 *(particularly)* yudok 유독

solid I N goche 고체 II ADJ tantanhada
탄탄하다

solve, to V 1 haegyeolhada 해결하다
2 pulda 풀다: *We did solve the problem in a very real sense* sireun uriga
geu munjereul pureotda 실은 우리가
그 문제를 풀었다

some ADJ eotteon 어떤, yakgan(ui)
약간(의)

some, several, a few ADJ meot 몇: *a
few people* myeot saram 몇 사람

somebody, someone PRON eotteon
saram 어떤 사람

somehow ADV eojjeonji 어쩐지: *I feel
sad somehow* eojjeonji seulpeuda
어쩐지 슬프다

something PRON eotteon geot 어떤 것

**sometimes, from time to time,
occasionally** ADV gakkeum 가끔

somewhat, a bit ADV daso 다소: *feel a
bit unpleasant* daso bulkwaehada 다소
불쾌하다

somewhere ADV eodin.ga 어딘가

son N adeul 아들: *sons and daughters*
janyeo 자녀

son-in-law N sawi 사위

song N norae 노래

sonorous ADJ ureongchada 우렁차다

soon, finally ADV ieukgo 이윽고:

Finally, the night falls ieukgo bami doeeotda 이윽고 밤이 되었다

soothe, pacify, to v dallaeda 달래다: *pacify a crying baby* uneun agireul dallaeda 우는 아기를 달래다

sorrow N seulpeum 슬픔

sort out, to v 1 *(assort, classify)* garyeonaeda 가려내다: *sort out an imitation* gajjareul garyeonaeda 가짜를 가려내다 2 *(deal with)* cheorihada 처리하다

soul, spirit N yeonghon 영혼

sound, noise N sori 소리

soup *(spicy stew)* N jjigae 찌개

sour ADJ sida 시다, sin 신

south N namjjok 남쪽

South Gate, the namdaemun N namdaemun 남대문

South Korea N namhan 남한

South Pole, the N namgeuk 남극

southeast N namdongjjok 남동쪽

southwest N namseojjok 남서쪽

souvenir N ginyeompum 기념품

sovereign, ruler N wonsu 원수

soy sauce N ganjang 간장

spare *(oneself)*, **to** v akkida 아끼다: *be sparing of oneself* momeul akkida 몸을 아끼다

speak ambiguously, equivocate, to v eolbeomurida 얼버무리다

speaker N yeonseolja 연설자, malhaneun saram 말하는 사람

special ADJ teukbyeolhada/-han 특별하다/-한

specially ADV teukbyeolhi 특별히

spectacular ADJ janggwaneul iruneun 장관을 이루는

speculation N eokcheuk 억측

speech N yeonseol 연설: *to make a speech* yeonseolhada 연설하다

speech and behavior N eonhaeng 언행

speed N sokdo 속도

spell, to v cheoljjahada 철자하다

spend, to v 1 *(money)* sseuda 쓰다: *spend money recklessly* doneul hamburo sseuda 돈을 함부로 쓰다; *spend the last penny* teoreomeokda 털어먹다 2 *(time)* bonaeda 보내다: *spend time* siganeul bonaeda 시간을 보내다

spices N hyangnyo 향료, yangnyeom 양념

spices and condiments N hyangsillyo 향신료

spicy beef soup N yukgaejang 육개장

spill, to v heullida 흘리다, ssotda 쏟다

spinach N sigeumchi 시금치

spine N cheokchu 척추

spiral ADJ naseonhyeong(ui) 나선형의

splash, spit, to v twigida 튀기다: *splash water* mureul twigida 물을 튀기다

split, divide, to v gareuda 가르다

spoilt, stale, rotten, to be v sanghada 상하다: *the milk has gone bad* uyuga sanghada 우유가 상하다

sponge N seupeonji 스펀지

sponge cake N kaseutella 카스텔라

sponsor N huwonin 후원인, seuponseo 스폰서

spoon N sukkarak 숟가락

sports N seupocheu 스포츠

spot N 1 jeom 점 2 eolluk 얼룩 3 jangso 장소

spot, to v deoreopyeojida 더럽혀지다

spotted *(pattern)* ADJ jeommuneuui 점무늬의

spouse N baeuja 배우자

spray N seupeurei 스프레이

spread, to v 1 *(diffuse)* peotteurida 퍼뜨리다 2 *(open, unfold, stretch)* pyeoda 펴다: *birds spread their wings* saega nalgaereul pyeoda 새가 날개를 펴다 3 *(propagate)* jeonpahada 전파하다

spread on, to v bareuda 바르다: *spread jam on bread* ppange jaemeul bareuda 빵에 잼을 바르다

spring N 1 *(metal piece)* yongsucheol 용수철 2 *(season)* bom 봄

sprout, bud, to v teuda 트다

spy I N gancheop 간첩 II v yeomtamhada 염탐하다: *spy on an opposing team* dareun timeul yeomtamhada 다른 팀을 염탐하다

squander, to v teoreomeokda 털어먹다

square N 1 *(shape)* jeongsagakhyeong 정사각형 2 *(town square)* gwangjang 광장

squeeze *(press)* **oil, to** v jjada, jjan 짜다

squid N ojing.eo 오징어

squirrel N daramjwi 다람쥐

stable ADJ anjeongdoen 안정된, anjeongjeogin 안정적인: *His blood pressure is now stable* geuui hyeorabi ijeneun anjeongjeogida 그의 혈압이 이제는 안정적이다

stadium, sports arena N gyeonggi-jang 경기장

staff N jigwon 직원, seutaepeu 스태프

stage N 1 dangye 단계 2 mudae 무대

stain N eolluk 얼룩

stairs, steps N gyedan 계단

stakeout N jambok 잠복

stall *(car)*, **die, to** V seo(beori)da 서(버리)다

stall, stand *(market)* N panmaedae 판매대

stamp N 1 *(ink)* seutaempeu 스탬프 2 *(postage)* upyo 우표

stand, to V seoda 서다

stand something up, to V se.uda 세우다

stand up, to V ireoseoda 일어서다

standard N pyojun 표준, gijun 기준

standard ADJ pyojunui 표준의

star N byeol 별

stare, to V ppanhi chyeodaboda 빤히 쳐다보다, eungsihada 응시하다: *Don't stare at me like that* geureoke ppanhi chyeodaboji ma 그렇게 빤히 쳐다보지 마

start N chulbal 출발, sijak 시작

start, to V chulbalhada 출발하다, sijakhada 시작하다

starting point, the N wonjeom 원점

starved, famished ADJ heogijida 허기지다

state, to V jinsulhada 진술하다

state N 1 sangtae 상태 2 gukga 국가, nara 나라 3 ju 주

statement, enunciation N nonsul 논술

station N yeok 역

stationery N mun.guryu 문구류

statue N dongsang 동상

statute N beopgyu 법규

stay, to V 1 *(lodge)* mukda 묵다: *stay at a hotel* hotere mukda 호텔에 묵다 2 *(remain)* meomureuda 머무르다

stayout, sleepout N oebak 외박

stay up all night, to V saeuda 새우다: *stay up all night* bameul saeuda 밤을 새우다

steady ADJ kkujunhan 꾸준한

steak N seuteikeu 스테이크

steal, to V humchida 훔치다

stealthily, surreptitiously ADV mollae 몰래

steam I N jeunggi 증기 2 V jjida 찌다: *steam sweet potatoes* gogumareul jjida 고구마를 찌다

steamed ADJ jjin 찐

steel N gangcheol 강철

steep, sharp ADJ gapareuda 가파르다: *a steep cliff* gapareun jeolbyeok 가파른 절벽

steer, spin, to V dollida 돌리다

step N dan.gye 단계

sterilization N salgyun 살균

stick, pole N makdaegi 막대기

stick out, bulge, protrude, pop out, to V twi.eonaoda 튀어나오다

stick to, to V butda 붙다

sticky ADJ kkeunjeok.kkeunjeokhada/-han 끈적끈적하다/-한: *sticky rice* ilbanmi 일반미

stiff, rigid, unfriendly, starchy ADJ ppeotppeothada/-han 뻣뻣하다/-한: *stiff shoulders* ppeotppeotan eokkae 뻣뻣한 어깨; *a rigid person, an inflexible person* ppeotppeotan saram 뻣뻣한 사람

still I ADJ *(tranquil)* janjanhada 잔잔하다 II ADV 1 *(calmly)* gamanhi 가만히: *sit still* gamanhi anjaitda 가만히 앉아 있다 2 *(even now)* ajik 아직: *It's still one o'clock* ajik han siya 아직 한 시야

stimulate, excite, incite, to V dotguda 돋구다

stimulation N jageuk 자극

stingy, tight-fisted ADJ jjada 짜다, jjan 짠: *a stingy person* jjan saram 짠 사람

stink, smell, to V naemsaenada 냄새나다

stir, to V jeotda 젓다, seokda 섞다: *Stir in the milk one cup at a time* han beone uyu han keopssigeul jeoeora 한 번에 우유 한 컵씩을 저어라

stock N 1 jaegopum 재고품 2 gachuk 가축 3 jabongeum 자본금

stock in on, buy *(in)*, **to** V sadeurida 사들이다

stomach N wijang 위장

stone N dol 돌

stool, chair N geolsang 걸상

stop I N (bus or train station) jeongnyujang 정류장 II v 1 (cease, quit) geumanduda 그만두다 2 (fill, plug) teureomakda 틀어막다 3 (halt) meomchuda 멈추다 4 (pull over) se.uda 세우다

stop by, pay a visit, to v deulleuda 들르다

stop it! PHR geumanduseyo! 그만두세요!

stopper, cork, plug N magae 마개

store, save, reserve, to v jeojanghada 저장하다

storm N pokpung 폭풍

story (of a building) N cheung jjari 층 짜리: a 10-story building 10cheung jjari geonmul 10층 짜리 건물

story (tale) N iyagi 이야기: an old story, a bedtime story, a fairy tale yennal iyagi 옛날 이야기

stove, cooker N seutobeu 스토브

straight ADJ 1 (correct, right) ttokbareuda 똑바르다, ttokbareun 똑바른 2 (square, neat) bandeutada 반듯하다

straight, directly ADV baro 바로

straight ahead ADV ttokbaro 똑바로

straighten, adjust, to v barojapda 바로잡다

strain, bear down, to v yongsseuda 용쓰다: strain oneself to, struggle yongeul sseuda 용을 쓰다

strait N haehyeop 해협: the Korea Strait daehan haehyeop 대한 해협

strand, yarn, string N gadak 가닥: a piece of string sil han gadak 실 한 가닥

strange ADJ isanghada 이상하다, isanghan 이상한

stranger N natseon saram 낯선 사람

strategic ADJ jeollyakjeogin 전략적인

strategy N jakjeon 작전

straw N 1 jip 짚 2 ppaldae 빨대

straw rope N saekki 새끼

stream N 1 gaeul 개울 2 julgi 줄기

street N geori 거리

street light N garodeung 가로등

strength N him 힘

stress N apbak 압박, seuteureseu 스트레스

stress, to v amnyeogeul gahada 압력 을 가하다

stretch oneself, to v kyeoda 켜다: stretch oneself gijigaereul kyeoda 기지개를 켜다

strict ADJ eomgyeokhada, eomgyeokan 엄격하다, 임격한

strictly, exactly ADV eommilhage 엄밀하게

strike, to go on v pa.eophada 파업하다

string N kkeun 끈

stripe N julmunui 줄무늬: striped patterned julmunuiui 줄무늬의

stroke, pat, to v eorumanjida 어루만지다

stroller N yumocha 유모차

strong ADJ 1 (muscular) himseda 힘세다, himsen 힘센 2 (solid, healthy) teunteunhada 튼튼하다

struggle, wriggle, flounder, to v beodunggeorida 버둥거리다

strut, shrug, to v eusseukgeorida 으쓱거리다

stubborn, determined ADJ gojip sen 고집 센

student N haksaeng 학생

studio N seutyudio 스튜디오

study, learn, to v gongbuhada 공부하다

study abroad, to v yuhakhada 유학하 다: go to study abroad at an early age eoryeoseul ttae yuhageul gada 어렸을 때 유학을 가다

study by oneself, to v dokhakhada 독학하다

stuff N jaeryo 재료, mulgeon 물건

stuff, to v ...e chaeuda …에 채우다: Don't stuff anything else into the bag gabange dareun geoseun chaeuji mara 가방에 다른 것은 채우지 마라

stumble, to v bari geollida 발이 걸리나

stunned, dazed, to be v eolppajida 얼빠지다

stupefaction, bewilderment N honmihada 혼미하다

stupid ADJ 1 (dull-witted) adunhada 아둔하다, adunhan 아둔한 2 (silly, foolish) eoriseokda 어리석다, eoriseogeun 어리석은

sty (of the eyes), **hordeolum** N daraekki 다래끼

style N seutail 스타일

subdue, control, to v daseurida 다스 리다: control one's anger hwareul daseurida 화를 다스리다

subject of discussion N nonje 논제

S

submerged, flooded, to be v jamgida, jamgin 잠기다, 잠긴: *submergence* jamsu 잠수

submit, to v 1 jechulhada 제출하다 2 hangbokhada 항복하다

subside, calm down, to v garaanda 가라앉다: *the storm has subsided* pokpungi garaanjatda 폭풍이 가라앉 았다

substance N muljil 물질, silche 실체

subtract, deduct from, take off, to v deolda 덜다

suburban ADJ 1 gyooeui 교외의 2 pyeongbeomhan 평범한

subway train N jeoncheol 전철

succeed, to v seonggonghada 성공하다

success N seonggong 성공

successful ADJ seonggonghan 성공한, seonggongjeogin 성공적인: *He turned out successful after all* geuneun gyeolguk seonggonghage doeeotda 그는 결국 성공하게 되었다

succession, inheritance N sangsok 상속

such ADV geureon 그런

suck, to v ppalda 빨다

sudden ADJ gapjakseureoun 갑작스러운

suddenly ADV gapjagi 갑자기

sue, to v gosohada 고소하다

suffer, undergo, to v gyeokda 겪다

suffering N gotong 고통

sufficient ADJ chungbunhan 충분한: *He has sufficient qualifications for a team captain* geuneun timui jujangeuroseo chungbunhan jagyeogi itda 그는 팀의 주장으로서 충분한 자격이 있다

sugar N seoltang 설탕

sugarcane N satangsusu 사탕수수

suggest, to v je.anhada 제안하다

suggestion N je.an 제안

suicide N jasal 자살

suit, formal dress N jeongjang 정장

suit one's taste *(palate)*, **to** v batda 받다

suitable ADJ jeokhapan 적합한: *You should wear clothes suitable for the occasion* neoneun geu haengsae jeokhapan oseul ibeoya hae 너는 그 행사에 적합한 옷을 입어야 해

sum N hap 합, hapgye 합계

summary N yoyak 요약

summer N yeoreum 여름: *summer break* yeoreumbanghak 여름방학

sun N taeyang 태양, hae 해

sunbeams N haetsal 햇살

Sunday N iryoil 일요일

sunflower N haebaragi 해바라기

sunlight N haeppit 햇빛

sunny, clear, bright *(weather)* ADJ hwachanghada/-han 화창하다/-한: *It's sunny and clear* nalssiga hwachanghada 날씨가 화창하다

sunrise N haedoji 해돋이, ilchul 일출

sunset N ilmol 일몰: *sunset glow* noeul 노을

supermarket N supeomaket 수퍼마켓

supervise, guide, to v jidohada 지도하다

supervisor N gamdokgwan 감독관

supplies, article N yongpum 용품

support I N jijihada 지지하다 II v gajeonghada 가정하다, *(back up)* sitda 싣다

suppose, to v saenggakhada 생각하다, chujeonghada 추정하다

suppress, hold back, restrain, to v chamda 참다

surely, certainly ADV yeongnageopda 영락없다

surf, wave *(in sea)* N pado 파도

surface N pyomyeon 표면: *the surface of the moon* dal pyomyeon 달 표면

surgery N susul 수술

surname N seong 성

surplus N yeoyu 여유

surprised, astonished, to be v nollada, nollawohada 놀라다, 놀라와하다

surprising ADJ nollapda 놀랍다, nollaun 놀라운

surrender N hangbok 항복

surround, enclose, to v ewossada 에워싸다

surroundings N juwibaegyeong 주위배경

survive, to v saranamda 살아남다

suspect N yonguija 용의자: *He is interrogating the suspect now* geuneun jigeum yonguijareul simmunhago itda 그는 지금 용의자를 심문하고 있다

suspension of water supply N dansu 단수

suspicion N 1 *(charge)* hyeomui 혐의 2 *(doubt)* uihok 의혹

suspicious, smell fishy ADJ naemsaenada 냄새나다

swagger, show off, boast, to V euseudaeda 으스대다

swallow, to V samkida 삼키다

swallowtail *(butterfly)* N horangnabi 호랑나비

swarm, be crowded, to V ugeulgeorida 우글거리다

sway, swing, to V haneulgeorida 하늘거리다

swear, curse N yok 욕

sweat I N ttam 땀 II V *(perspire)* ttam heullida 땀 흘리다

sweater N seuweteo 스웨터

sweep, to V sseulda 쓸다

sweet ADJ dalda 달다, dan 단, dalkomhada 달콤하다

sweet and sour ADJ saekomdalkomhada/-han 새콤달콤하다/-한

sweet corn N oksusu 옥수수

sweet persimmon N dangam 단감

sweetfish N euneo 은어

swell, puff up, to V butda 붓다: *have a swollen face* eolguri butda 얼굴이 붓다

sweltering, muggy ADJ mudeopda 무덥다, mudeo.un 무더운

swim, to V suyeonghada 수영하다

swim in the sea, to V haesuyok 해수욕

swimming N heeom 헤엄

swimming pool N suyeongjang 수영장

swimsuit N suyeongbok 수영복

swindler, crook, con man N sagikkun 사기꾼

switch N seuwichi 스위치

sword N kal 칼, geom 검

sworn brothers N uihyeongje 의형제

symbol N 1 sangjing 상징 2 buho 부호

symptom N jeungsang 증상

system N jedo 제도, cheje 체제, siseutem 시스템

T

t-shirt N tisyeocheu 티셔츠

table N teibeul 테이블, sang 상: *clear the table* sangeul chiuda 상을 치우다

tablespoon N teibeulseupun 테이블스푼

table tennis, ping-pong N takgu 탁구

tablecloth N teibeul bo 테이블 보

tacitly, implicitly ADV eunnyeonjunge 은연중에

tactic, strategy N jeollyak 전략: *establish a strategy* jeollyageul jjada 전략을 짜다

tadpole, polliwog N olchaengi 올챙이

taekwondo N taegwondo 태권도

taffy N yeot 엿

tag N kkoripyo 꼬리표

tail N kkori 꼬리

take, to V 1 *(haul off)* jabagada 잡아가다 2 *(remove)* gajyeogada 가져가다

take a shower, to V syawohada 샤워하다

take a U-turn, to V yuteonhada 유턴하다

take away, snatch away, to V asagada 앗아가다

take action, to V naseoda 나서다

take back, return, to V mullida 물리다

take care of, look after, to V bosalpida 보살피다

take dictation, take down, to V badasseuda 받아쓰다

take down, unload, to V naerida 내리다: *unload a truck* teureogeseo jimeul nacrida 트럭에서 짐을 내리다

take off *(clothes, glasses, hat, socks)*, **to** V beotda 벗다: *take off one's glasses* angyeongeul beotda 안경을 벗다

taking notes, note N pilgi 필기

tale N iyagi 이야기

talent N jaeneung 재능: *She has a talent for golf* geunyeoneun golpeue jaeneungi itda 그녀는 골프에 재능이 있다

talented ADJ jaeneungi inneun 재능이 있는

talk about, to V ...e daehae malhada ...에 대해 말하다

talk privately, have a private talk, to V sadam 사담: *have a private talk* sadameul nanuda 사담을 나누다

tall ADJ ki keuda/keun 키 크다/큰

tame ADJ gildeuryeojin 길들여진

tangle, get tangled, to V eongkida 엉키다

tank N taengkeu 탱크, jeoncha 전차

tanned ADJ gamujapjapada 가무잡잡하다: *tanned skin* gamujapjapan pibu 가무잡잡한 피부

Taoism N dogyo 도교

tap, to V gabyeopge dudeurida 가볍게 두드리다

tape *(scotch, adhesive)* N teipeu 테이프

tape recording N nogeum 녹음

target N mokpyo 목표, pyojeok 표적: *The bullet hit the target right in the center* chongari pyojeogui han gaunde majatda 총알이 표적의 한 가운데 맞았다

task N jingmu 직무, gwaje 과제: *The task absorbed all my time* geu jingmu ttaemune nae siganeul modu ppaetgyeotda 그 직무 때문에 내 시간을 모두 뺏겼다

taste I N mat 맛 II V 1 *(sample)* matboda 맛보다 2 *(to see if it's properly seasoned)* ganboda 간보다

taut, tight ADJ paengpaenghada 팽팽하다: *a tightrope* paengpaenghan batjul 팽팽한 밧줄

tax N segeum 세금

taxi N taeksi 택시

taxpayer N napseja 납세자

tea N cha 차: *a cup of tea* han janui cha 한 잔의 차

teach, to V gareuchida 가르치다

teacher N seonsaengnim 선생님

teaching N gareuchigi 가르치기, gareuchim 가르침: *The teaching of the school is in chime with the thought of the founder* geu hakgyoui gareuchimeun seollipjaui saenggakgwa ilchihanda 그 학교의 가르침은 설립자의 생각과 일치한다

team N tim 팀

teamwork N timwokeu 팀워크, hyeopdong jageop 협동작업

tear, rip, to V jjitda 찢다

tears N nunmul 눈물

tears, to scream in V jajireojida 자지러지다

tears, to shed V jitda 짓다: *dabbing tears from one's eyes* nunmureul jitda 눈물을 짓다

tears, to squeeze out V jjada, jjan 짜다, 짠: *squeeze out tears* nunmureul jjada 눈물을 짜다

teary, to get V jeoksida 적시다

teaspoon N tiseupun 티스푼

technician N gisulja 기술자

technology N gwahak gisul 과학 기술

teenager N sipdae 십대

telephone N jeonhwagi 전화기: *telephone number* jeonhwabeonho 전화번호

telescope N mangwongyeong 망원경

television N tellebijeon 텔레비전

tell, say, to … V ireuda 이르다: *make sure to tell sb not to do (something)* haji mallago dandanhi ireuda 하지 말라고 단단히 이르다

tell on, tattle on, to V ireuda 이르다: *tattle on sb to sb* jalmoseul ireuda 잘못을 이르다

tell the truth, to V isiljikgohada 이실직고하다

temperature N ondo 온도

temple N jeol 절, sachal 사찰

temple *(Buddhist)*, **church** N sawon 사원: *walk in the temple* sawoneul geonilda 사원을 거닐다

temporary ADJ imsi(ui) 임시의

temptation, lure N yuhok 유혹

ten NUM 1 sip 십 2 ycol 열: *ten fingers* songarak yeol gae 손가락 열 개

ten days N yeolheul 열흘

ten thousand NUM man 만

tend, decorate, to V gakkuda 가꾸다: *decorate one's house* jip baneul jal gakkuda 집 안을 잘 가꾸다

tension N ginjang 긴장: *Warm milk will lessen the tension* ttatteutan uyuneun ginjangeul wanhwahae jul geotsida 따뜻한 우유는 긴장을 완화해 줄 것이다

tendon N himjjul 힘줄

tennis N teniseu 테니스

tens *(of)*, **dozens** *(of)* N susibui 수십의

tense ADJ ginjanghan 긴장한

tense, to become V ginjanghada 긴장하다

tent N tenteu 텐트, cheonmak 천막

term N gigan 기간: *The term of redemption is ten years* sanghwan giganeun sip nyeonida 상환 기간은 십 년이다

terminal N teomineol 터미널

terrace N teraseu 테라스

terrible ADJ 1 *(dreadful)* hyeongpyeoneopda 형편없다 2 *(tragic)* chamdamhada 참담하다

terrific ADJ goengjanghan 굉장한

territory N 1 *(dominion)* ycongto 영토 2 *(turf)* yeongyeok 영역: *mark one's territory* yeongyeogeul pyosihada 영역을 표시하다

terror N gongpo 공포, tereo 테러

terrorism N tereorijeum 테러리즘

terrorist N tereoriseuteu 테러리스트, tereobeom 테러범

test, to V geomsahada 검사하다, teseuteuhada 테스트하다

test, to take a V (siheom) boda (시험) 보다

testicles N gohwan 고환

text N bonmun 본문, geul 글: *What kind of text is this?* igeoseun eotteon jongnyuui geuringa? 이것은 어떤 종류의 글인가?

textbook N gyogwaseo 교과서

textile N jingmul 직물

text message N munja 문자

Thailand N taeguk 태국

than I CONJ ...boda ...보다 II PREP ...boda ...보다

thank, to V gamsahada 감사하다

Thanksgiving N chusugamsajeol 추수감사절

thank you! PHR gamsahamnida! 감사합니다!

that I PRON 1 jeo geot 저 것 2 *(near listener)* geu (geot) 그(것) II CONJ *(introducing a quotation)* ...go hada ...고 하다

that, those PRON jeo 저: *that person* jeo saram 저 사람

that serves you right! PHR gosohada 고소하다

thaw N haedong 해동

the best, the top N eutteum 으뜸: *the best of schools* eutteum ganeun hakgyo 으뜸 가는 학교

the second best *(plan)* N chaseon 차선: *Go for the second best if you can't have the best* choeseoni animyeon chaseoneul taekhara 최선이 아니면 차선을 택하라

theater *(drama)* N geukjang 극장

their (theirs) PRON geudeurui (geot) 그들의 (것)

then I ADV geureomyeon 그러면 II PRON geuttae 그때

theology N sinhak 신학

theory N iron 이론

there PRON geogi 거기

thereby ADV geugeose uihayeo 그것에 의하여

therefore CONJ geureomuro 그러므로

these PRON igeotdeul 이것들: *These are useless* igeotdeureun sseulmoeopda 이것들은 쓸모없다

they, them PRON geudeul 그들

thick ADJ 1 *(of things)* dukkeopda 두껍다, dukkeo.un 두꺼운 2 *(strong)* jinhada 진하다, jinhan 진한: *Blood is thicker than water* pineun mulboda jinhada 피는 물보다 진하다

thief N doduk 도둑

thigh N heobeokji 허벅지

thin ADJ 1 *(light)* yeolda 엷다: *light colors* yeolbeun saek 엷은 색 2 *(watery)* mukda 묽다, mulgeun 묽은: *thin sauce* mulgeun soseu 묽은 소스

thin coat of ice N sareoreum 살얼음

thing N mulgeon 물건

think, consider, contemplate, reckon, suppose, to V saenggakhada 생각하다

thinly, haggardly ADV bassak 바싹

third N se beonjjae 세 번째

thirst, craving N galgu 갈구

thirsty ADJ mongmareun 목마른

thirteen NUM 1 sipsam 십삼 2 yeolset 열셋

thirty NUM 1 samsip 삼십 2 seoreun 서른

this PRON igeot 이것: *This is mine* igeoseun naegeonnida 이것은 내것이다

this, these PRON i 이: *this person* i saram 이 사람

this much, like this ADV itorok 이토록

thoroughly, carefully ADV chanchanhi 찬찬히

those PRON jeo geotdeul 저 것들

though, although CONJ birok-(eu)l jirado 비록 –(으)ㄹ 지라도: *though it's raining, though it might rain* birok biga ol jirado 비록 비가 올 지라도

thought N saenggak 생각

thousand NUM cheon 천: *a thousand apples* cheon gaeui sagwa 천 개의 사과

thread N sil 실: *thread a needle* baneure sireul kkweda 바늘에 실을 꿰다

threat N 1 (blackmail) hyeopbak 협박 2 (intimidation) eureumjang 으름장

threaten, to V wihyeophada 위협하다: threaten one's health geongangeul wihyeopada 건강을 위협하다

three NUM 1 sam 삼 2 set 셋

thrill N tongkwae 통쾌

throat N mok(gumeong) 목(구멍)

throb with pain, to V uksingeorida 욱신거리다

through, past ADV ...eul/reul tong-hayeo ...을/를 통하여

through, past, by way of PREP ...reul/eul tonghayeo ...를/을 통하여: through all ages gogeumeul tong-hayeo 고금을 통하여

throughout I PREP ...dongan ...동안 II ADV 1 cheoeumbuteo kkeutkkaji 처음부터 끝까지 2 docheoe 도처에

throw, to V deonjida 던지다

throw away, throw out, to V beorida 버리다: throw out trash sseuregireul beorida 쓰레기를 버리다

throw out, give up, to V naedeonjida 내던지다

thumb N eomji 엄지

thunder N cheondung 천둥

Thursday N mogyoil 목요일

ticket N 1 pyo 표: buy a ticket pyoreul sada 표를 사다 2 (for entertainment) ipjangkkwon 입장권

ticketing N maepyo 매표

tickle N ganjireom 간지럼: be ticklish ganjireomeul tada 간지럼을 타다

tide N josu 조수, milmulgwa sseolmul 밀물과 썰물

tidy up, straighten up, put in order, set right, to V jeongdonhada 정돈하다

tie, to V maeda 매다

tie, halve a match, to V bigida 비기다

tiger N horang.i 호랑이

tight (space) ADJ binteumeopda/bin-teumeomn eun 빈틈없다/빈틈없는: a tight space binteumeomneun gonggan 빈틈없는 공간

tightly, firmly ADV bassak 바싹

till I PREP ...kkaji 까지 II CONJ ...kkaji 까지

timber N mokjae 목재

time N sigan 시간: time flies sigani jal gada 시간이 잘 가다; timetable sigan-pyo 시간표

time, hour N si 시: 3 o'clock se si 세 시

timely ADJ matda 맞다, manneun 맞는: a timely measure ttae manneun jochi 때에 맞는 조치

times (multiplying) N ...bae ...배: five times more expensive daseot bae bis-sada 다섯 배 비싸다

tiny ADJ jageun 작은: There is one tiny problem jageun munjega hana itda 작은 문제가 하나 있다

tip N 1 (gratuity) tip 팁 2 (end, finish, edge) kkeut 끝

tire N taieo 타이어

tire, to V pirohaejida 피로해지다

tired, worn out ADJ pigonhada 피곤하다, pigonhan 피곤한: mentally tired jeongsinjeogeuro pigonhada 정신적으로 피곤하다

title N 1 (of book, film) jemok 제목: title of a movie yeonghwa jemok 영화 제목 2 (designation) chingho 칭호

to (a person) PREP ...kke ...께

to (destination) PREP ...e ,..에

to, at, for, by (a person) PREP ...hante ...한테: be angry at a friend chingu-hante hwareul naeda 친구한테 화를 내다; throw a stone at a dog gaehante doreul deonjida 개한테 돌을 던지다

to, toward PREP ...ege ...에게: to you neoege 너에게; to a friend chinguege 친구에게

to a certain extent, to some degree ADV jeongdo 정도: to some extent eoneu jeongdo 어느 정도

to one's heart's content ADV maeum-kkeot 마음껏: He shouted to his heart's content geuneun maeumkkeot sorireul jilleotda 그는 마음껏 소리를 질렀다

to some degree, enough, pretty ADV wenmankeum 웬만큼: enough of your jokes! nongdamdo wenmankeumhaera 농담도 웬만큼해라

to sum up, in sum ADV yokeondae 요컨대

tobacco N dambae 담배

today N oneul 오늘

toddling steps, with ADV ajangajang 아장아장

toe N balkkarak 발가락

toenail, claw, talon N baltop 발톱

T

together ADV hamkke 함께

toilet, restroom N hwajangsil 화장실

tolerate, to v yonginhada 용인하다, chamda 참다

toll N tonghaengnyo 통행료

toll bar N chadanbong 차단봉

tomato N tomato 토마토

tomorrow N nae.il 내일

tone N eojo 어조, maltu 말투: *Her tone of voice suddenly changed* geunyeoui eojoga gapjagi bakkwieotda 그녀의 어조가 갑자기 바뀌었다

tone-deaf ADJ eumchi 음치

tongue N hyeo 혀

tonight N oneulbam 오늘밤

tonsure N sakbal 삭발

too ADV 1 *(also)* ttohan 또한 2 *(so, overly)* neomu 너무

too much ADV neomu mani 너무 많이, murihan 무리한

tool, instrument N yeonjang 연장, dogu 도구

tooth, teeth N i 이: *brush one's teeth* ireul dakda 이를 닦다

toothbrush N chissol 칫솔: *tooth brushing* yangchijil 양치질

toothpaste N chiyak 치약

toothpick N issusigae 이쑤시개

top N 1 paengi 팽이 2 *(apex, summit)* kkokdacgi 꼭대기 3 *(upper end)* sangdan 상단

topic N juje 주제

torrential rain N pogu 폭우

toss, to v deonjida 던지다: *Toss your fishing line far out into the river* naksitjureul gangmul meolli deonjyeora 낚싯줄을 강물 멀리 던져라

total N hapgye 합계

touch, to v manjida 만지다

tough, coarse ADJ eokseda 억세다

tour N yeohaeng 여행, gwangwang 관광

tourism N gwangwangeop 관광업

tournament N toneomeonteu 토너먼트

tourist N gwan.gwanggaek 관광객

toward, to *(direction)* PREP ...(eu)ro …(으)로

towel N sugeon 수건

tower N tap 탑

town N si 시

toy N jangnankkam 장난감, wangu 완구

traces, signs, marks N jachwi 자취: *disappear without a trace* jachwireul gamchugo sarajida 자취를 감추고 사라지다

track N 1 gil 길 2 jaguk 자국

track, to v chujeokhada 추적하다

trade I N *(commerce)* muyeok 무역 **II** v *(exchange)* georaehada 거래하다

tradition N jeontong 전통: *This is a tradition from age to age* igeoseun daedaero naeryeooneun jeontongida 이것은 대대로 내려오는 전통이다

traditional, conventional, old-fashioned, old school ADJ jeontongjeokin 전통적인: *traditional values* jeontongjeogin gachigwan 전통적인 가치관

traffic N gyotong 교통

tragedy N bigeuk 비극

tragic ADJ bigeukjeogin 비극적인: *This tragic event killed many* geu bigeukjeogin sageoneuro inhae maneun ideuri jugeotda 그 비극적인 사건으로 인해 많은 이들이 죽었다

trail N jaguk 자국, jachwi 자취

trail, to v kkeulda 끌다

train I N gicha 기차, yeolcha 열차 **II** v kiuda 키우다: *train a hidden competent person* injaereul kiuda 인재를 키우다

trainer N hullyeonja 훈련자, teureineo 트레이너

training, drill N hullyeon 훈련

transaction N 1 georae 거래 2 cheori 처리

transfer *(college)* N pyeonip 편입

transfer, to v garatada 갈아타다: *transfer to subway train from a bus* beoseueseo jihacheollo garatada 버스에서 지하철로 갈아타다

transit, pass, to v danida 다니다: *The bus passes through this route* i noseoneuro beoseuga daninda 이 노선으로 버스가 다닌다

transition N ihaeng 이행

translate, to v beonyeokhada 번역하다

translation N beonnyeok 번역

transmit, spread, to v omgida 옮기다: *transmit illness (disease)* byeongeul omgida 병을 옮기다; *spread lice* ireul omgida 이를 옮기다

transplant, to v isikhada 이식하다:

T

kidney transplant sinjang isik 신장 이식

transport N susong 수송

transport, to V susonghada 수송하다

trap N deot 덫

trap, to V deocheul lota 덫을 놓다

trash N sseuregi 쓰레기

travel, to V yeohaenghada 여행하다

traveler N yeohaengja 여행자

tray N jaengban 쟁반

treasure N bomul 보물

treat, to V 1 *(behave towards)* dae.uhada 대우하다 2 *(something special)* daejeophada 대접하다 3 *(medical care, cure)* chiryohada 치료하다 4 *(deal with, handle)* daruda 다루다

treatise, thesis N nonmun 논문

treatment, cure, remedy *(medical)* N chiryo 치료

tree frog N cheonggaeguri 청개구리

tree, wood N namu 나무: *roadside tree* garosu 가로수

tremendous ADJ eomaeomahada 어마어마하다

trend N gyeonghyang 경향, yuhaeng 유행

trespass(ing), intrusion N nanip 난입

trial N jaepan 재판

triangle N samgakhyeong 삼각형

tribe N bujok 부족

trick N sogimsu 속임수, jangnan 장난

trim, groom, to V dadeumda 다듬다: *get a trim (haircut)* meorireul dadeumda 머리를 다듬다

trip, journey N yeohaeng 여행

triumph N seungni 승리

triumphant ADJ uigiyangyanghada 의기양양하다

trivial, minor ADJ sasohada 사소하다, sasohan 사소한

troops N gundae 군대

tropical ADJ yeoldaeui 열대의: *They grow well only in tropical regions* geugeotdeureun yeoldaeui jiyeogeseoman jal jaranda 그것들은 열대의 지역에서만 잘 자란다

trouble N malsseong 말썽: *trouble-maker* malsseongkkureogi 말썽꾸러기

troublesome, annoying, causing a headache ADJ golchi apeun 골치 아픈

truck N teureok 트럭

true ADJ sasil ida 사실이다, sasilui 사실의

true meaning N chamtteut 참뜻

trumpet, bugle N napal 나팔

trunk N 1 namu julgi 나무 줄기 2 yeohaengyong gabang 여행용 가방

trust N silloe 신뢰: *I don't want to flatter people to gain thier trust* naneun saramdeurui silloereul eotgi wihae geudeurege acheomhaneun geoseun wonchi anneunda 나는 사람들의 신뢰를 얻기 위해 그들에게 아첨하는 것은 원치 않는다

trust, to V silloehada 신뢰하다

try, to V haeboda 해보다: *try a job* ireul haeboda 일을 해보다

try on *(clothes)*, **to** V ibeo boda 입어 보다: *try on new clothes* saeoseul ibeoboda 새옷을 입어보다

tube N gwan 관, tyubeu 튜브

Tuesday N hwayoil 화요일

tumor N jongyang 종양: *The tumor was confirmed as being benign* geu jongyangeun yangseongeuro panmyeongdoeeotda 그 종양은 양성으로 판명되었다

tune N gokjo 곡조, seonnyul 선율

tune, to V joyulhada 조율하다

tunnel N teoneol 터널, gul 굴

turkey N chilmyeonjo 칠면조

turn around, to V dolda 돌다

turn away, look away, to V oemyeonhada 외면하다

turn off, to V jamgeuda 잠그다: *turn off the valve* baelbeureul jamgeuda 밸브를 잠그다

turn over, to V dwijipda 뒤집다, eopda 엎다

turn up, to V kiuda 키우다: *turn up the volume* bollyumeul kiuda 볼륨을 키우다

turtle N 1 *(land)* geobuk 거북 2 *(sea)* badageobuk 바다거북

tuxedo N teoksido 턱시도

TV, television N tibi 티비

twelve NUM 1 sibi 십이 2 yeolttul 열둘

twenty NUM 1 seumul 스물 2 isip 이십

twice ADV du beon 두 번: *The tide flows twice a day* josuneun harue du beon millyeoonda 조수는 하루에 두 번 밀려온다

twin N ssangdungi 쌍둥이

twinkle, sparkle, glitter, to v banjja-gida 반짝이다: *the stars are twinkling* byeoldeuri banjjagida 별들이 반짝이다

twisted, warped ADJ teureojida 틀어지다: *the board was warped in the sun* haetbiche panjaga teureojida 햇빛에 판자가 틀어지다

two NUM 1 dul 둘 2 i 이: *two plus two equals four* i deohagi ineun sa 이 더하기 이는 사; *two days* iteul 이틀

type, to v taipinghada 타이핑하다

type of industry N eopjong 업종: *What type of business are you in?* museun eopjonge jongsahasinayo? 무슨 업종에 종사하시나요?

typhoon N taepung 태풍

typical ADJ jeonhyeongjeogida/-jeogin 전형적이다/-적인

tyrannize, domineer, bully, to v hoengporeul burida 횡포를 부리다

tyranny N hoengpo 횡포

U

udon N udong 우동

ugly ADJ 1 (*unattractive*) motsaenggida 못생기다, motsaenggin 못생긴 2 (*homely, detestable*) mipda 밉다

uh INTERJ eo... 어...

ulterior motive N sasim 사심

ultimate ADJ choehuui 최후의

ultimately ADV gyeolguk 결국, machimnae 마침내: *They ultimately decided not to go* geudeureun gyeol-guk gaji ankiro gyeolsimhaetda 그들은 결국 가지 않기로 결심했다

umbrella N usan 우산

unable ADJ ...hal su eomneun ...할 수 없는: *He was unable to attend the meeting* geuneun geu moime cham-seokhal su eopseotda 그는 그 모임에 참석할 수 없었다

unanimous voice N igudongseong 이구동성

unavoidable ADJ eojjeolsueopda 어쩔수없다

unbalanced diet, deviated food habit N pyeonsik 편식

uncertain ADJ bulhwaksilhan 불확실한

uncertainty N bulhwaksilseong 불확실성

uncle N 1 (*husband of a maternal aunt*)

imobu 이모부 2 (*mister, male adult*) ajeossi 아저씨

uncomfortable ADJ bulpyeonhan 불편한: *I feel very uncomfortable with chopsticks* naneun jeotgarageul sseuneun geonni bulpyeonhada 나는 젓가락을 쓰는 것이 불편하다

under I PREP ...ui araee ...의 아래에 II ADV araee 아래에

underclassman N hageupsaeng 하급생

underdone, unripe, undercooked ADJ seorigeun 설익은

undergo, to v gyeokda 겪다: *He began to undergo a series of changes* geuneun yeonsokjeogin byeonhwareul gyeokgi sijakhaetda 그는 연속적인 변화를 겪기 시작했다

undergraduate N daehaksaeng 대학생

undershirt N meriyaseu 메리야스

undersized ADJ waesohada 왜소하다

understand, to v ihaehada 이해하다: *understand well* jal ihaehada 잘 이해하다; *misunderstand* jalmot ihaehada 잘못 이해하다

understanding I ADJ ihaesim 이해심: *He is very understanding* geuneun ihaesimi maneun saramida 그는 이해심이 많은 사람이다 II N (*consent*) yanghae 양해: *ask for understanding* yanghaereul guhada 양해를 구하다

undertaker N janguisa 장의사

underwear N sogot 속옷

undoubtedly, clearly ADV eomnyeonhi 엄연히

unemployment N sireop 실업, siljik sangtae 실직 상태

unexpected ADJ yegichi aneun 예기치 않은, yesang bakkui 예상 밖의: *We faced up to an unexpected difficulty* urineun yesang bakkui nangwane buditchyeotda 우리는 예상 밖의 난관에 부딪쳤다

unexpectedly ADV uioeui 의외의

unfair ADJ bulgongpyeonghan 불공평한

unfold, stretch, open, spread, to v pyeolchida 펼치다

unfortunate, out of luck ADJ uni eopda/eomneun 운이 없다/없는

unfortunately ADV bulhaenghagedo 불행하게도

U

unhappy ADJ bulhaenghada 불행하다, bulhaenghan 불행한: *be unhappy* bulhaenghada 불행하다; *an unhappy childhood* bulhaenghan eorin sijeol 불행한 어린 시절

unhesitating, being not hesitant ADJ seoseumeopda 서슴없다: *talk without hesitation* seoseumeopsi malhada 서슴없이 말하다

uniform N yunipom 유니폼, jebok 제복

uniformed ADJ jebok charimui 제복 차림의

uniformly, neatly ADV gajireonhi 가지런히: *neatly placed shoes* gajireonhi noyeoinneun sinbal 가지런히 놓여있는 신발

union N gyeolhap 결합, yeonhap 연합, dongmaeng 동맹

unique, extraordinary, uncommon ADJ namdareuda 남다르다: *unique (excellent) sense of fashion* paesyeongamgagi namdareuda 패션감각이 남다르다

unit, measure N danwi 단위

unite, to V gyeolhapada 결합하다, hapchida 합치다, tonghapada 통합하다

United Kingdom N daeyeongjeguk 대영제국

unity, union N dangyeol 단결

universal ADJ ilbanjeogin 일반적인, jeon segyejeogin 전 세계적인

universe, cosmos N uju 우주

university N daehak 대학

unknown ADJ allyeojiji aneun 알려지지 않은: *The cause of the fire is unknown* geu hwajaeui wonineun allyeojiji anatda 그 화재의 원인은 알려지지 않았다

unless CONJ ...i anin han ...이 아닌 한

unlike I ADJ gatji aneun 같지 않은 II PREP ...dapji anke ...답지 않게

unlikely ADV ...hal geot gatji aneun ...할 것 같지 않은, iseumjikhaji aneun 있음직하지 않은

unmanageable, too big to handle ADJ beogeopda 버겁다

unnecessary ADJ bulpiryohada 불필요하다, bulpiryohan 불필요한: *unnecessary expenses* bulpiryohan jichul 불필요한 지출

unripe, undercooked ADJ an ikda/igeun 안 익다/익은 *under(un)cooked* *meat* an igeun gogi 안 익은 고기; *unripe strawberries* an igeun ttalgi 안 익은 딸기

unrivaled, unequaled, matchless ADJ dokbojeogin 독보적인

unsparingly, generously ADV akkimeopsi 아낌없이

untie, unpack, undo, to V pureonota 풀어놓다

until PREP -(eu)l ttaekkaji -(으)ㄹ 때까지

until, by PREP ...kkaji ...까지

unused ADJ sayonghaji aneun 사용하지 않은

unusual ADJ teugihan 특이한, deumun 드문: *Harry Potter was a highly unusual boy in many ways* haeri poteoneun yeoreo myeoneseo maeu teugihan sonyeonieotda 해리 포터는 여러 면에서 매우 특이한 소년이었다

unusually, especially ADV yudalli 유달리

unyielding, unflinching ADJ dokhada 독하다

up, upward ADV ...wie ...위에

up until now ADV yeotae 여태

update, to V gaengsinhada 갱신하다, saeropge hada 새롭게 하다

update N gaengsin 갱신

upright, true ADJ bareuda 바르다

uproar, clamor N yadan 야단

uproarious, noisy, loud ADJ yoranhada 요란하다

upset ADJ 1 *(displeased)* eonjjanta 언짢다 2 *(unhappy)* gibuni sanghan 기분이 상한

upstairs N wicheung 위층

urban ADJ dosiui 도시의

urge, to V jaechokhada 재촉하다

urgent ADJ gin.geuphada 긴급하다, gin.geupan 긴급한

urinate, to V sobyeonboda 소변보다

use, to V sayonghada 사용하다

used to, accustomed to ADJ -neunde iksukhada -는데 익숙하다

used to do something V -gonhaetda -곤했다: *we used to sing* urineun noraereul bureugon haetda 우리는 노래를 부르곤 했다

useful ADJ sseulmo itda/inneun 쓸모 있다/있는

useless ADJ sseulmo eopda/eomneun 쓸모 없다/없는

user N sayongja 사용자

usual ADJ botongui 보통의

usually ADV botong 보통, neul 늘

uterus N jagung 자궁

utility N gongiksaeop 공익사업, yutilliti 유틸리티

utilize, to V hwaryonghada 활용하다

V

vacantly, blankly ADV udukeoni 우두 커니: *stare blankly at* udukeoni bara-boda 우두커니 바라보다

vacation *(school)* N banghak 방학

vaccination N yebang jeopjong 예방 접종

vaccine N baeksin 백신

vacuum cleaner N cheongsogi 청소기: *operate a vacuum cleaner* cheongso-gireul dollida 청소기를 돌리다

vagina N *(yeoja)* seonggi *(여자)* 성기

vague ADJ 1 *(non-specific)* mohohada 모호하다, mohohan 모호한 2 *(obscure)* magyeonhan 막연한

valid ADJ yuhyohada 유효하다, yuhyo-han 유효한

validity N jeongdanghan 정당함

valley N gyegok 계곡

valuable ADJ gwijunghan 귀중한, sojunghan 소중한: *It was a valuable experience for me* geugeoseun naege gwijunghan gyeongheomieotda 그것 은 나에게 귀중한 경험이었다

value I N *(worth)* gachi 가치 II V gwihage yeogida 귀하게 여기다

van N baen 밴, seunghapcha 승합차

vanish, to V 1 *(disappear)* sarajida 사라지다 2 *(vanish into thin air)* onde-gandeeeopda 온데간데없다

variable ADJ byeonhagi swiun 변하기 쉬운

various ADJ yeoreo gajiui 여러 가지의: *It can be interpreted in various ways* geugeoseun yeoreo gajiro purideol su itda 그것은 여러 가지로 풀이될 수 있다

vase N kkotbyeong 꽃병

vast ADJ geodaehan 거대한: *He once ruled over a vast empire* geuneun hanttae geodaehan jegugeul tongchi-haeseotda 그는 한때 거대한 제국을 통치했었다

vegetable diet N chaesik 채식

vegetables, greens N chaeso 채소

vegetarian N chaesikjuuija 채식주의자

vehicle N charyang 차량

vein, blood vessel N pitjul 핏줄

vendor N haengsangin 행상인

ventilation N hwangi 환기, tongpung 통풍

verbal ADJ marui 말의

verbal promise N eonnyak 언약

verdict N pyeonggyeol 평결

version N -pan −판, beojeon 버전

versus PREP ...dae ...대

vertical ADJ sujigui 수직의

very meaningful ADJ uimisimjang-hada 의미심장하다: *a serious mean-ingful look* uimisimjanghan pyojeong 의미심장한 표정

very, so, pretty, quite, extremely ADV aju 아주

vest N jokki 조끼

via ADV ...reul/eul geochyeoseo ...를/을 거쳐서: *return via Europe* yureobeul geochyeoseo doraoda 유럽을 거쳐서 돌아오다

victim N huisaengja 희생자

victory N useung 우승

video cassette N bidio (teipeu) 비디오 (테이프)

video recorder, VCR N bidio (rekodeu) 비디오 (레코드)

videotape, to V nokhwahada 녹화하다

Vietnam N beteunam 베트남

view N gwanjeom 관점, siya 시야

view, to V 1 baraboda 바라보다 2 gan-juhada 간주하다

vigor, vitality N hyeolgi 혈기: *be vig-orous, be passionate* hyeolgiwang-seonghada 혈기왕성하다

village, town N ma.eul 마을

villain N akdang 악당

vinegar N sikcho 식초

violate, to 법을 어기다 V eogida 어기다

violation N wiban 위반

violence N poak 포악

violent language, verbal abuse N pogeon 폭언: *use violent language* pogeoneul hada 폭언을 하다

violin N baiollin 바이올린: *play the violin* baiollineul kyeoda 바이올린을 켜다

virgin N cheonyeo 처녀

V

Virgin Mary, the N maria 마리아
virus N baireoseu 바이러스
virtual ADJ sasilsangui 사실상의
virtue N seon 선, deok 덕
visa N bija 비자
visible ADJ nune boineun 눈에 보이는
vision N 1 siryeok 시력 2 hwansang 환상
visit I N bangmun 방문 II v (to pay a visit) bangmunhada 방문하다
visitor N bangmungaek 방문객
visual ADJ sigagui 시각의
vitamin N bitamin 비타민
voice N 1 moksori 목소리: voice mail eumseong mesiji 음성 메시지 2 (tone) eonseong 언성: raise voices eonseong-eul nopida 언성을 높이다
volcano N hwasan 화산
volume N 1 yongnyang 용량 2 eumnyang 음량
voluntary N jabal(jeok) 자발(적)
volunteer, to v jajinhada 자진하다
vomit, to v tohada 토하다: vomit blood pireul tohada 피를 토하다
vote, to v tupyohada 투표하다
voter N tupyoja 투표자, yugwonja 유권자
vulnerable ADJ chwiyakhan 취약한, yeonnyakhan 연약한

W

wager, to make a v geolda 걸다
wages N jugeup 주급
wagon N hwamul gicha 화물 기차
waist N heori 허리
wait for, to v gidarida 기다리다
waiter, waitress, worker N jong.eob-won 종업원
wake, to v jami kkaeda 잠이 깨다
wake N cheoryaje 철야제
wake someone up, to v kkae.uda 깨우다
walk, to v geotda 걷다: walk along the street gireul geotda 길을 걷다
walk, to take a v sanchaekhada 산책하다
wall N byeok 벽
wallet N jigap 지갑
wander, to v doradanida 돌아다니다: Don't wander around late at night bam neutge doradaniji mara 밤 늦게 돌아다니지 마라
want, to v wonhada 원하다: want to be a doctor uisaga doegireul wonhada 의사가 되기를 원하다
war I N (battle) jeonjaeng 전쟁 II v (to make war) jeonjaenghada 전쟁하다
warehouse N changgo 창고
warm ADJ ttatteuthada 따뜻하다, ttatteutan 따뜻한
warm, calm, mild, quiet ADJ onhwahada 온화하다
warm (hot) water N onsu 온수
warmth N ttatteuteum 따뜻함, (heat) ongi 온기: lingering warmth namainneun ongi 남아있는 온기
warn, to v gyeonggohada 경고하다
warning N gyeonggo 경고
wash, to v hengguda 헹구다, ssitda 씻다
wash over, surge, to v millyeooda 밀려오다
wash the dishes, to v seolgeojihada 설거지하다
waste, to v nangbihada 낭비하다: It's just a waste of time and money sigangwa don nangbiil ppunida 시간과 돈 낭비일 뿐이다
wasteful ADJ hepeuda 헤프다: spend money wastefully sseumsseumiga hepeuda 씀씀이가 헤프다
watch I N (wristwatch) (sonmok)sigye (손목)시계 II v (show, movie) gug-yeonghada 구경하다
watch over, guard, to v gyeonghohada 경호하다
water N mul 물
water-resistant ADJ bangsu 방수
waterfall N pokpo 폭포
watermelon N subak 수박
wave, to v mulgyeolchida 물결치다
wavelength, impact N pajang 파장
waver, hesitate, to v eonggeojuchumhada 엉거주춤하다
wax N wakseu 왁스
way, method, manner N bangbeop 방법
way: by way of v ...eul/reul tonghayeo ...을/를 통하여
we, us PRON uri 우리: just us, between us, we alone urikkiri 우리끼리
weak ADJ 1 (poor hearing, eye-sight) eodupda 어둡다, eoduun 어두운: be

W

weak-sighted nuni eodupda 눈이 어둡다 2 *(feeble, bad at)* yakhada 약하다, yakan 약한: *have a weak heart* simjangi yakhada 심장이 약하다; *be weak at math* suhage yakhada 수학에 약하다

weakness N yakham 약함

wealth N bu 부: *a symbol of wealth* buui sangjing 부의 상징

wealth and poverty N binbu 빈부

weapon N mugi 무기

wear, put on *(clothes),* **to** V ipda 입다: *put on a jacket* jakeseul ipda 자켓을 입다

weary, fatigued ADJ pirohada 피로하다, pirohan 피로한

weather N nalssi 날씨

weave, to V (jingmureul) jjada (직물을) 짜다, *(plait)* yeokda 엮다

weaving N jjagi 짜기

web N geomijul 거미줄

website N wepsaiteu 웹사이트

wedding ceremony N gyeolhonsik 결혼식

Wednesday N suyoil 수요일

weeds N japcho 잡초

week N ju 주: *weekend* jumal 주말

weekly N jugan 주간

weigh out, to V daranaeda 달아내다

weight I N 1 *(body weight)* chejung 체중 2 *(weight of things)* muge 무게 II V mugereul dalda 무게를 달다

weight, to gain V chejung.i neulda 체중이 늘다

weight, to lose V chejung.i julda 체중이 줄다

welcome, to V hwanyeonghada 환영하다

welcome! PHR eoseo oseyo! 어서 오세요!

welfare N bokji 복지

well ADV jal 잘

well *(for water)* N umul 우물: *draw water from a well* umul mureul gitda 우물 물을 긷다

well done! good job! INTERJ jal haesseoyo! 잘 했어요!

well up, to V ureonaoda 우러나오다

well-behaved, *(character)* **with good moral** ADJ pumhaeng.i jota/jo.eun 품행이 좋다/좋은

well-being N geongang 건강,

haengbok 행복

well-cooked, well-done ADJ jal ikda/ igeun 잘 익다/익은

well-done, well-cooked, well-ripe ADJ jal igeun 잘 익은

well-known ADJ jal allyeojin 잘 알려 진: *Soybeans are well-known as nutritious food* kongeun yeongyangga inneun eumsigeuro jal allyeojyeo itda 콩은 영양가 있는 음식으로 잘 알려져 있다

well-mannered, courteous, polite ADJ yeuibareuda, yeuibareun 예의바 르다, 예의바른

west N seojjok 서쪽

westerner N seoyang saram 서양 사람

wet ADJ jeojeun 젖은: *wet towel* jeojeun sugeon 젖은 수건

wet, drenched, to get V jeotda 젖다

whale N gorae 고래

what PRON mueot 무엇

what? INTERJ mworagoyo? 뭐라고요?

what a pity!, that's a shame!, I'm sorry PHR andwaetda! 안됐다: *feel sorry for (about)* andwaetda 안됐다!

what for? PHR mwo hasigeyo? 뭐 하시게요?

what happened? what's going on? PHR museun irieyo? 무슨 일이에요?

what is called, so called ADV ireunba 이른바

what kind of?, which? PHR eotteon 어떤

what time? PHR myeot siyo? 몇 시요?

whatever PRON ...geoseun mueonnideunji ...것은 무엇이든지

wheat N mil 밀

wheel N bakwi 바퀴

wheelchair N hwilcheeo 휠체어

wheel-car, handcart N rieoka 리어카

when PRON eonje 언제

when, at the time ADV -(eu)l ttae -(으)ㄹ 때

whenever CONJ ...hal ttaeneun eonjena ...할 때는 언제나

where ADV eodie 어디에

where are you going to? PHR eodiro gaseyo? 어디로 가세요?

wherever CONJ ...haneun goseun eodirado ...하는 곳은 어디라도

whether CONJ ...inji eotteonji ...인지 어떤지

which CONJ eoneu 어느

which one? PHR eoneu geoyo? 어느 거요?

while *(period)* N -neun dong.an –는 동안

whisper, to V soksagida 속삭이다

white ADJ hayata 하얗다, hayan 하얀

who N nugu 누구: *Whom did you meet?* nugureul mannanna? 누구를 만났나?

who PRON nuga 누가: *Who is coming?* nuga oneunga? 누가 오는가?

whoever PRON nuguna 누구나

whole, complete ADJ wanjeonhada, wanjeonhan 완전하다, 완전한: *a complete sentence* wanjeonhan munjang 완전한 문장

whole body, the N jeonsin 전신

whole country, the N jeonguk 전국

whose PRON nuguui 누구의

why? PHR waeyo? 왜요?

wicked, evil, malicious ADJ saakhada 사악하다, saakan 사악한

wide, spacious, broad, big, large ADJ neopda 넓다, neolbeun 넓은

wide and flabby ADJ peongpeojim-hada 펑퍼짐하다

widely ADV neolge 넓게

widow N gwabu 과부

widower N horabi 홀아비

width, breadth N garo 가로

width, range N pok 폭: *1 meter in width* pogi il miteo 폭이 1 미터

wife N anae 아내

wig N gabal 가발

wild N yasaeng 야생

wilderness N hwangya 황야

wildlife sanctuary, reserve N bohoguyeok 보호구역

will, desire, drive N uiyok 의욕

will, dying wish N yueon 유언: *leave a will* yueoneul namgida 유언을 남기다

willing ADJ gikkeoi haneun 기꺼이 하는

wily, sly, sneaky ADJ eongkeumhada 엉큼하다

win, take possession of, to V chaji-hada 차지하다: *win (capture) a person's heart* maeumeul chajihada 마음을 차지하다

win a prize *(lottery)*, **to** V dangcheom-doeda 당첨되다

wind, breeze N baram 바람: *wind velocity* pungsok 풍속

window N 1 *(in house, building)* chang-mun 창문 2 *(counter for paying, buying tickets)* changgu 창구

wine N podoju 포도주

wing N nalgae 날개

winner N useungja 우승자

winter N gyeo.ul 겨울

wipe, to V dakda 닦다: *wipe the table* teibeureul dakda 테이블을 닦다; *wipe one's tears* nunmureul dakda 눈물을 닦다

wire N cheolssa 철사

wisdom N jihye 지혜

wisdom tooth N sarangni 사랑니

wise ADJ hyeonmyeonghada, hyeon-myeonghan 현명하다, 현명한

wish I N *(hope)* won 원: *as one wished* wondaero 원대로 II V yeomwonhada 염원하다

wish you the best PHR jal doegireul baranda 잘 되기를 바란다

wit, tact N jaechi 재치

with *(along)* PREP ...hago ...하고: *go on a trip with a friend* chinguhago yeo-haengeul gada 친구하고 여행을 갔다

with *(by means of)* PREP ...(eu)ro ...(으)로

with PREP irang 이랑: *go for a walk with uncle* samchonirang sanchaegeul hada 삼촌이랑 산책을 하다

with ease, easily ADV munanhi 무난히

withdrawal, pullout N cheolsu 철수

without ADV ...eopsi ...없이

without notice, without reason ADV dajjagojja 다짜고짜

witness I N mokgyeokja 목격자 II V mokgyeokhada 목격하다

wolf N neukdae 늑대

woman N yeoja 여자

woman's heart N yeosim 여심: *captivate women's hearts with songs* noraero yeosimeul sarojapda 노래로 여심을 사로잡다

won *(Korean monetary unit)* N won 원: *one hundred won* baegwon 100원

wonder, to V gunggeumhada 궁금하다: *I wonder why he is late* geuga wae neunneunji gunggeumhada 그가 왜 늦는지 궁금하다

wonderful, nice, cool ADJ meotjida 멋지다, meotjin 멋진

wood N namu 나무

wooden ADJ namuro doen 나무로 된

wool N ul 울, yangmo 양모

word N daneo 단어

work I N 1 *(piece of)* jakpum 작품 2 *(operation)* jageop 작업 II v 1 *(operate, run)* jakdonghada 작동하다 2 *(put in effort)* ilhada 일하다: *work hard* yeolsimhi ilhada 열심히 일하다

workplace N jikjang 직장

world N se.gye 세계

worldwide ADJ segyejeogin 세계적인: *He is a scholar of worldwide fame* geuneun segyejeogeuro yumyeonghan hakjaida 그는 세계적으로 유명한 학자이다

worn out *(clothes)* ADJ darabeorin 닳아버린

worry, to v geokjeonghada 걱정하다

worry, seethe, to v kkeurida 끓이다: *seethe with anger* hwaro sogeul kkeurida 화로 속을 끓이다

worse ADJ deo nappeuda/nappeun 더 나쁘다/나쁜

worship I N yebae 예배: *have a worship service* yebaereul deurida 예배를 드리다 II v sungbaehada 숭배하다

worst ADJ gajang nappeuda/nappeun 가장 나쁘다/나쁜

worth, to be ADJ gachi itda 가치 있다

wound, injury N sangcheo 상처

wrap N raep 랩: *wrap leftover food with plastic wrap* nameun eumsigeul laebe ssada 남은 음식을 랩에 싸다

wrath, rage N yeokjeong 역정

wrestling N reseulling 레슬링

wretched ADJ bichamhada 비참하다

wrist N sonmok 손목

write *(a letter)*, **compose** *(a poem)*, **note down, to** v sseuda 쓰다: *write a book* chaegeul sseuda 책을 쓰다

writer N jakga 작가

writhe, squirm, to v beoreujeokgeorida 버르적거리다

writing N sseugi 쓰기

written ADJ munjaro sseun 문자로 쓴

wrong, mistaken, false ADJ teullida 틀리다, teullin 틀린

wrong refereeing, bad call N osim 오심

wrongful deed N bihaeng 비행

Y

yard, garden N madang 마당

yawn N hapum 하품

year N yeon 년: *year 2012* icheon sibi nyeon 이천 십이 년; *year-end party* mangnyeonhwe 망년회; *years of experience* yeollyun 연륜

years, age N se 세: *a 15 year-old boy* sibose sonyeon 15세 소년

yell, to v sorichida 소리치다: *I yelled at him to stop* naneun geuege meomchurago sorichyeotda 나는 그에게 멈추라고 소리쳤다

yellow ADJ norata 노랗다, noran 노란: *yellow green* yeondusaek 연두색

yes INTERJ ne 네, ye 예

yesterday N eoje 어제

yet: not yet ADV ajik 아직: *haven't finished one's work yet* ajik ireul kkeunnaeji motaetda 아직 일을 끝내지 못했다

yield, to v 1 sanchulhada 산출하다 2 yangbohada 양보하다

yield N sanchul 산출

you N *(informal)* neo 너; *(informal, plural)* neohui(deul) 너희(들): *You are all in one team* neohuineun han timida 너희는 한 팀이다

young ADJ eorida 어리다, eorin 어린

younger brother *(or sister)* N dongsaeng 동생

younger sister N yeodongsaeng 여동생

youngest, the N mangnae 막내

youngster N jeolmeuni 젊은이

your PRON neoui 너의

yours PRON neoui geot 너의 것

yourself PRON jasin 자신: *Don't be too confident of yourself* jasineul leomu gwasinhaji mara 자신을 너무 과신하지 마라

youth 1 N *(young person)* jeolmeuni 젊은이, *(young people)* cheongnyeon 청년 2 *(juvenile)* yeonso 연소: *the youngest person* choeyeonsoja 최연소자

youth, youthfulness N jeolmeum 젊음

Z

zeal, enthusiasm N yeorui 열의
zealously ADV yeolsimhi 열심히
zero NUM 1 gong 공 2 yeong 영: *five to nothing* 5:0 o dae yeong 오 대 영
zone N jiyeok 지역

zoo N dongmurwon 동물원
zucchini, pumpkin, squash N (ae) hobak (애)호박